# A Guide to the Children Act 1989

# A Guide to the Children Act 1989

**Richard White,**
LLB, Solicitor

**Paul Carr,**
MA (Cantab), Barrister,

Clerk to the Justices,
South West Essex Magistrates' Courts

**Nigel Lowe,**
LLB, Barrister,

Reader in Law,
University of Bristol

*Consulting Editor*
**Professor Brenda Hoggett,**
QC, MA (Cantab),

Law Commissioner, Professor of Law at King's College, London

London
BUTTERWORTHS
1990

| | |
|---|---|
| United Kingdom | Butterworth & Co (Publishers) Ltd., 88 Kingsway, LONDON WC2B 6AB, and 4 Hill Street, EDINBURGH EH2 3JZ |
| Australia | Butterworths Pty Ltd, SYDNEY, MELBOURNE, BRISBANE, ADELAIDE, PERTH, CANBERRA and HOBART |
| Canada | Butterworths (Canada) Ltd, TORONTO and VANCOUVER |
| Ireland | Butterworth (Ireland) Ltd, DUBLIN |
| Malaysia | Malayan Law Journal Sdn Bhd, KUALA LUMPUR |
| New Zealand | Butterworths of New Zealand Ltd, WELLINGTON and AUCKLAND |
| Puerto Rico | Equity de Puerto Rico, Inc, HATO REY |
| Singapore | Malayan Law Journal Pte Ltd, SINGAPORE |
| USA | Butterworth Legal Publishers, ST PAUL, Minnesota; SEATTLE, Washington; BOSTON, Massachusetts; AUSTIN, Texas; Equity Publishing, ORFORD, New Hampshire; and D & S Publishers, CLEARWATER, Florida |



ISBN 0 406 50209 9

Printed and bound by
Mackays of Chatham PLC, Kent

# Preface

The Children Act 1989 received the Royal Assent on 16 November 1989. It will, when implemented, bring about the most fundamental change of child law this century. Much of it has been the subject of debate for six years, yet some of the most complex provisions only found final form shortly before their enactment and were, therefore, not adequately debated in Parliament.

At the time of going to press we believe that most of the Act is likely to be implemented in October 1991. Four provisions have been brought into force already. Rules of court in relation to the evidence of children and their upbringing are expected to resolve an urgent problem as to admissibility. The position of an unmarried father as regards his child in care has been improved. In paternity cases applicants have been made responsible for choosing a blood tester from an authorised list. With effect from 16 January 1990 funds can be made available for a child to be sent for treatment outside England and Wales, for example, at the Peto Institute in Hungary.

The remainder will come soon enough. There is much work still to be done on the rules and regulations, which will be so important to practice. However, we have endeavoured to produce the book as quickly as possible, because we believe it to be vital to have an early understanding of the principles of the legislation, so that the detail can be more easily placed in context as it is published over the next eighteen months.

The law is bound to reflect the complexity of the subject. It is impossible to put into the statute all the detail that one might wish to see in establishing principles of law for children. Nevertheless, we are concerned about the degree of power given to the Executive to amend statute and the volume of delegated legislation, both of which will control how practice develops.

We have had to write within constraints of time, space and ability to interpret amendments which have been tabled late in the day. We have attempted to examine all the important parts of the Act and to relate them to each other.

We owe a considerable debt of thanks to Butterworths, for their efficiency and patience and their determination to ensure that the book was published quickly. We thank Professor Brenda Hoggett, our consulting editor, who gave extensively of her wide experience and understanding of the principles underlying the legislation.

Legislation of this length inevitably generates its own complexity. The Children Act will be no exception. It would be wrong, however, to dwell on negatives, for the Act does much to improve child law and given a fair wind by Government, judiciary and practitioners will provide a sound basis for good practice for the 1990s and beyond.

December 1989 — Richard White, Paul Carr, Nigel Lowe

# Introduction

The Children Act has reached the statute book at last but it was a "damn close run thing". The first Bill to be introduced in the House of Lords in the 1988–89 session, it was one of the last to receive the Royal Assent. It might even have been lost: shortage of time to debate the large number of amendments put down (mainly by the Government) combined with a filibuster (on quite another matter) meant that the Commons Report Stage had to be guillotined — an unfortunate end for a Bill which had received so much support and attention from all sides up until then.

Indeed, that was one of the reasons why it took so long. The Bill was described by Sir Geoffrey Howe in moving the guillotine motion (HC Deb, 26 October 1989, Vol 158, col 1071) as 'the most comprehensive and far-reaching reform of this branch of the law ever introduced. It meets a long-felt need for a comprehensive and integrated statutory framework to ensure the welfare of children.' The Act does indeed cover virtually all the law relating to the care and upbringing of children and the social services to be provided for them. It will revolutionise the law to be applied by courts hearing all kinds of children cases, whether in divorce or other family proceedings, care proceedings, or wardship. It will create a whole new jurisdictional scheme to deal with children cases, under which, for the first time, all proceedings relating to the same child can be heard together in the same court, and the same rules of law will apply in all courts and all proceedings (apart from wardship, which will, however, be largely restricted to the private law field).

The Act is the product of a long and thorough consultation process, which continued during its passage through Parliament. (This was one of the reasons for the large number of late amendments, although others were simply catching up with the nuts and bolts of such a large enterprise, the consequentials, transitionals, repeals etc.) The process began with the *Review of Child Care Law*, an Interdepartmental Working Party set up (in response to a recommendation of the Second Report from the House of Commons Social Services Committee, 1983–84, on *Children in Care* HC 360–I) by the then DHSS and assisted by the Family Law team at the Law Commission. The review produced twelve informal consultation papers during 1984 and 1985 and a Report to Ministers in September 1985, which was published as a further Consultation Document. This was followed by the Government's White Paper on *The Law Relating to Child Care and Family Services* (Cm 62) in January 1987. These, of course, were concerned with the public law — the services to be provided for children and their families and the procedures to protect children where families fail.

Meanwhile, the Law Commission was reviewing the private law on the allocation of responsibility between parents and other individuals. The Family Law Reform Act 1987 (which followed two Law Commission Reports on *Illegitimacy*, No 118 in 1982, and No 157 in 1986) had removed most of the remaining differences between children whose parents were married to one another and those whose were not, and provided for the first time that unmarried parents might share full responsibility for their children. Against this background, the Commission published Working Papers on *Guardianship* (1985, No 91), *Custody* (1985, No 96), *Care, Supervision and Interim Orders in Custody Proceedings* (1987, No 100), and *Wards of Court* (1987, No 101). The first three of these resulted in the Commission's Report on *Guardianship and Custody* (Law Com No 172), published in July 1988.

Annexed to that Report was a Bill to give effect, not only to the Law Commission's recommendations, but also to the Government's proposals on care proceedings. The object was to show how an integrated scheme of court orders might look. That Bill was taken up by the Government and expanded to cover virtually all the civil law relating to children, apart from adoption (to which, however, some modifications are made) and education (although it does deal with children who are not being educated properly). By then, of course, much of the pressure to legislate was the result of the Report of the Inquiry by Lord Justice Butler-Sloss and her colleagues into Child Abuse in Cleveland (Cm 412, 1988). This, together with earlier reports into the deaths of Jasmine Beckford (1985), Heidi Koseda (1986), Tyra Henry (1987), Kimberley Carlile (1987) and more recently Doreen Aston (1989), has contributed much to a balanced view of the procedures needed to protect children, especially in the early stages when abuse is suspected.

It was, as the Lord Chancellor said in his Child & Co Lecture in April 1988, the coincidence of the two reviews (of Child Care Law and of Guardianship and Custody) with the Cleveland Report, which presented 'an historic opportunity to reform the English law into a single rationalised system as it applies to the care and upbringing of children'. It is impossible to exaggerate the effect which the Act will have upon the practice of all who are concerned with court decisions and social services for children. Inevitably, the field is too large to cover in detail in one short book but the authors have introduced readers to all the major features of the Act in the minimum of time and space. It is planned to bring almost all the Act into force at the same time, in Autumn 1991. There will be a lot of learning for all of us to do and it is never too soon to start!

Brenda Hoggett

# Contents

Chapter 1

# The welfare principle

**1.1** Section 1 sets out the general principles that are to be applied in court proceedings, namely:

(1) the child's welfare is paramount in deciding all questions about his upbringing and the administration of his property;
(2) regard is to be had to the general principle that delay in deciding any question with respect to the child's upbringing is likely to prejudice the child's welfare;
(3) in contested 'family proceedings' (defined by s 8 (3), see para 3.23) and all care or supervision proceedings, the courts should, when applying the welfare principle, pay particular regard to certain specific matters; and
(4) the court should not make an order unless to do so is considered better for the child than making no order.

**1.2** The general application of s 1 should be appreciated. The welfare principle, for instance, applies equally to care proceedings or emergency proceedings (under Parts IV and V, see Chapters 6 and 7)[1] as it does to disputes between parents. Similarly, the requirement for the court to make an order only if to do so is better for the child than making no order at all, applies throughout the 1989 Act (see para 1.20).

1 At any rate, once the 'threshold' provisions under s 28(2) have been satisfied.

## THE WELFARE PRINCIPLE

**1.3** Section 1(1) states:
'[w]hen a court determines any question with respect to:

(a) the upbringing of the child; or
(b) the administration of the child's property or the application of any income arising from it,

the child's welfare shall be the court's paramount consideration'.
Although modelled on s 1 of the Guardianship of Minors Act 1971, which it replaces, this principle is not an exact replica. It also differs from that recommended by the Law Commission.

### 1 'Paramount' not 'first and paramount'

**1.4** Unlike the 1971 Act, which directed the court to treat the child's welfare as its first and paramount consideration, s 1(1) of the 1989 Act, omitting the words 'first and', directs the court to treat the child's welfare as its paramount consideration. It is neither contemplated nor intended that this change will lead to a change of practice. Although in the past the word 'first' had, in the words of the Law Commission,[1] 'led some courts to balance other considerations *against* the child's welfare rather than to consider what light they shed upon it', that view has long ceased to to be the law. In *J v C* [1970] AC 688 and, more recently, *Re KD (A Minor)(Ward: Termination of Access)* [1988] AC 806, the House of Lords emphasised the paramountcy of the child's welfare. As Lord MacDermott said, the principle laid down by s 1 connotes:[2]

> 'a process whereby, when all the relevant facts, relationships, claims and wishes of parents, risks, choices and other circumstances are taken into account and weighed, the course to be followed will be that which is most in the interests of the child's welfare as that term has now to be understood. That is the first consideration because of its first importance and the paramount consideration because it rules upon or determines the course to be followed'.

In this sense, therefore, the 1989 Act's paramountcy formulation simply reflects the previous well established position.

1 *Report on Review of Child Law, Guardianship and Custody* (Law Com No 172, 1988) para 3.13, citing *Re L (Infants)* [1962] 1 WLR 886 and *Re F (An Infant)* [1969] 2 Ch 238, 241.
2 In *J v C* [1970] AC 688 at 710-711.

**1.5** The Law Commission had argued (Law Com No 172, para 3.13) that simply to omit the reference to 'first' did nothing to resolve the earlier confusion. With respect to the Commission, since that confusion had already been resolved by effectively making the word 'first' redundant at a time when it was included in the Act, its omission in the new s 1 surely does clarify the law. The Commission was also concerned that the paramountcy formulation carried the risk that litigants might still be tempted to introduce evidence that had no relevance to the child in the hope of persuading the court to balance one against the other. This seems an exaggerated fear since the paramountcy principle is well tested and in practice seems to produce the right balance, both in terms of the evidence submitted and the weight put on it.

**1.6** In choosing the paramountcy formulation, the Government rejected the Law Commission's recommendation, that in determining any question under the Act the welfare of *any child likely to be affected* shall be the court's only concern. A possible reservation about that recommendation is that the requirement to consider the welfare of *any child* could lead to wide and speculative enquiries which ultimately could blur the court's view and duty towards the welfare of the child before it. Under such a test, the court might have had to compromise between the interests of two or more children. Even under the paramountcy principle, however, in cases involving siblings the court cannot always, as it is theoretically bound to do, treat *each* child's welfare as its paramount consideration.[1]

1 See, for example, *Clarke-Hunt v Newcombe* (1983) 4 FLR 482.

## 2 When the principle applies

**1.7** The welfare principle laid down by s 1(1) has a wide, although not unlimited, application. The provision states that it applies whenever a court is called upon to determine any question about the child's upbringing (defined by s 105 (1) to include 'the care of the child but not his maintenance') or the administration of the child's property. However, if the case-law on the ambit of s 1 of the Guardianship of Minors Act 1971 is followed, the paramountcy principle will apply only where such questions are *directly* in issue. It has previously been held, for example, that the paramountcy principle did not apply to the question of whether to order a blood test to establish paternity, nor when deciding whether to prevent publication of a book alleged to be harmful to a ward of court, nor in determining whether to grant permission to use evidence admitted in wardship proceedings in subsequent criminal proceedings.[1] On the other hand, since the child's upbringing is directly in issue, s 1(1) clearly applies *whenever*[2] a court is considering, for example, whether to make a s 8 order.

1 See respectively, *S v McC, W v W* [1972] AC 24; *Re X (A Minor) (Wardship: Jurisdiction)* [1975] Fam 47, and *Re S (Minors) (Wardship: Police Investigation)* [1987] Fam 199. Note also *Richards v Richards* [1984] AC 174 — principle held not to apply to the granting of ouster orders, per Lord Hailsham LC at 203. For a detailed discussion of these and other decisions, see Lowe and White *Wards of Court* (2nd ed) paras 7-10 et seq. Note that the inapplicability of the welfare principle does not necessarily mean that the court has no powers, for it seems that the High Court, at least, has an inherent *protective* jurisdiction: see *S v McC* supra and Lowe and White, op cit, paras 7-17 et seq. Under this jurisdiction the child's welfare, although still important, is not the paramount consideration and must be weighed against any other competing interests: see, eg, *Re S* supra.

2 Ie, regardless of who the parties are or in which proceedings (eg, adoption or wardship) the issue is raised.

**1.8** Even if the child's upbringing etc is directly in issue, the paramountcy principle might not always apply. It clearly will not apply if it is expressly excluded by statute. Section 105(1), for example, excludes the principle from applications for maintenance under s 15 and Sch 1. Statute can also impliedly exclude the application of s 1(1). Hence, while the paramountcy principle applies in proceedings under Parts IV and V of the 1989 Act, it will only come into play provided the applicant can satisfy the court that the preconditions for a care order or for an emergency order have been made out.[1]

1 It is, however, arguable that, in interpreting the 'threshold' provisions, the courts should bear in mind the welfare principle and, in the case of ambiguities, should choose the interpretation that is most consistent with the child's welfare. See further paras 6.7.

**1.9** Other statutes may also override the paramountcy principle. Adoption applications, clearly, directly concern the child's upbringing but in deciding that question[1] welfare is only the first consideration because of the express provision under the Adoption Act 1976, s 6. The House of Lords has also held[2] that s 1 of the 1971 Act does not apply in proceedings under what is now the Matrimonial Homes Act 1983 and in effect that it has been superseded by the comprehensive legislation vesting in local authorities wide-ranging discretion for dealing with children in their care.[3]

1 *Aliter* if, in the adoption proceedings, the court is considering whether to make a residence or contact order etc under s 8 of the 1989 Act.
2 *Richards v Richards* [1984] AC 174.
3 *A v Liverpool CC* [1982] AC 363.

**1.10** Whether all the established case-law referred to above will be followed, is debatable. It is, at least, arguable that the new s 1(1) re-opens the issue. It seems, however, unlikely that the courts will change their minds on these questions. In particular, it seems highly improbable that, in reliance on the new s 1(1), the courts will change their policy and allow wardship generally to be used to question local authority decisions (discussed further para 10.20).

**1.11** Another problem regarding the application of s 1(1) is in respect of children who are sufficiently mature to make their own decisions. Despite the decision in *Gillick v West Norfolk and Wisbech Area Health Authority* [1986] AC 112, even if a court can be persuaded that the particular child is sufficiently mature to make the particular decision in question, it seems doubtful whether the court would follow the child's views if it thought that to do so would be prejudicial to his welfare.[1] Although such a view could be justified either by applying the paramountcy principle or by holding that, although s 1(1) did not apply, the High Court still has an inherent power to protect the child[2], the probability is that the court would simply dispose of the case by holding that the child was not mature enough to make the decision in question.

1 Two attempts were made to amend the Bill on precisely these terms, see HL Deb, 19 December 1988, Vol 502, col 1147 et seq and HC Deb, Standing Committee B, 9 May 1989, col 25 et seq.
2 See Lowe and White, op cit, 7.13.

## 3 Regard is to be had to the general principle that delay is likely to be prejudicial to a child's welfare

**1.12** Section 1(2) enjoins the court, in any proceedings in which any question with respect to a child's upbringing arises, 'to have regard to the general principle that any delay in determining the question is likely to prejudice the welfare of the child'. The principle applies to all proceedings concerning children (for example, in adoption or wardship proceedings) and not only those under the 1989 Act.

**1.13** The case for making some provision about the harmful effect of delay was cogently argued by the Law Commission. It pointed out (Law Com No 172, para 4.55) that 'prolonged litigation about their future is deeply damaging to children, not only because of the uncertainty it brings for them, but also because of the harm it does to the relationship between the parents and their capacity to co-operate with one another in the future'. The Commission also commented that in most cases it is to the advantage of one of the parties to delay proceedings as long as possible. The principal effect of s 1(2) is to place the onus upon the courts to ensure that all proceedings concerning children are conducted as expeditiously as possible. To this end, the courts are directed (ss 11(1) and 32(1)), in applications for both s 8 orders and orders under Part IV (and in the light of rules to be drafted), to draw up a timetable and to give appropriate directions for adhering to that timetable.

## 4 Applying the paramountcy principle — the introduction of a checklist of relevant factors

**1.14** As under the previous law 'welfare' is not defined.[1] A welcome innovation of the 1989 Act, however, is the introduction of a checklist of relevant factors (contained in s 1(3), to which the court is directed by s 1(4)) to pay particular regard when applying the paramountcy principle in *contested* s 8 order applications and in *all* applications relating to local authority care and supervision of children. Such a checklist had been recommended by the Law Commission (Law Com No 172, paras 3.17 et seq) as 'a means of providing greater consistency and clarity in the law' and 'as a major step towards a more systematic approach to decisions concerning children'.

1 But for a good explanation see *Walker v Walker and Harrison*, noted in [1981] NZ Recent Law 257 and cited by the Law Commission in its *Working Paper No 96* at para 6.10, where Hardie Boys J commented: "Welfare" is an all-encompassing word. It includes material welfare, both in the sense of adequacy of resources to provide a pleasant home and a comfortable standard of living and in the sense of adequacy of care to ensure that good health and due personal pride are maintained. However, while material considerations have their place they are secondary matters. More important are the stability and the security, the loving and understanding care and guidance, the warm and compassionate relationships, that are essential for the full development of the child's own character, personality and talents'.

**1.15** The checklist contained in s 1(3) is as follows:

'(a) the ascertainable wishes and feelings of the child concerned (considered in the light of his age and understanding);
(b) his physical, emotional and educational needs;
(c) the likely effect on him of any change in his circumstances;
(d) his age, sex, background and any characteristics of his which the court considers relevant;
(e) any harm which he has suffered or is at risk of suffering;
(f) how capable each of his parents, and any other person in relation to whom the court considers the question to be relevant, is of meeting his needs;
(g) the range of powers available to the court under this Act in the proceedings in question'.

This checklist is not exhaustive and indeed might properly be regarded as the minimum that will be considered by the court. Many, for example, might think that the parents' wishes and feelings should be considered. It always open to the court to specify other matters which it would like to see included in the welfare officer's report.[1]

1 See Law Com No 172, paras 3.18 and 3.21.

**1.16** The content of the checklist follows that recommended by the Law Commission, save for that under s 1(3)(g), the purpose of which is to emphasise the court's duty to consider not only whether the order being sought is the best for the child but also to consider the alternatives that the Act makes available. In an application for a care order, it is incumbent upon the court to consider not only whether or not to make the care order but whether, for example, a residence order under s 8 would better serve the child's interests.

**1.17** As a result of s 1(3)(a), the courts are directed for the first time in this context[1] to have regard to the child's own wishes. Although such views are normally taken into account, the statutory duty to do so is long overdue. The child's view, however, is not expressed to be determinative[2], although, clearly, the older the child, the more persuasive his views will be.

**1** Cf adoption, where it has long been a statutory requirement: Adoption Act 1976, s 6.
**2** See Lord Mackay LC's comments at HL Deb, 19 December 1988, Vol 502, col 1135. See also para 1.11 above for a discussion of the position where the child is thought mature enough to make his own decisions.

**1.18** Although under s 1(4) the courts are directed to have regard to the checklist only in contested s 8 applications and all care and supervision applications, there is nothing to prevent them from considering the factors in other applications and indeed in contested applications under ss 4 and 5 (discussed respectively at paras 2.20 and 2.35) it would seem prudent to do so. The reason for restricting the application of s 1(3) to *contested* s 8 cases is that in many family proceedings such as divorce there is often no choice as to where and with whom the child should live. If s 1(3) applied to all s 8 cases courts might feel compelled to investigate even these cases in depth.[1] Such an investigation would not only be a waste of resources but also, arguably, an unwarranted intrusion into family autonomy.

**1** See Law Com No 172, para 3.19.

**1.19** Although s 1(3) specifically directs *the court* to have regard to the checklist, it will clearly be useful to legal advisers and their clients both in preparing and in arguing their case. The Law Commission envisaged (ibid at 3.18) that the list would enable parties to prepare relevant evidence and by focusing clients' minds on the real issues, might help to promote settlements.

## ORDERS TO BE MADE ONLY WHERE THE COURT IS SATISFIED THAT MAKING THE ORDER IS BETTER THAN MAKING NO ORDER

**1.20** Section 1(5) lays down the general principle that whenever a court is considering whether to make one or more orders under the 1989 Act with respect to a child, it 'shall not make the order or any of the orders unless it considers that doing so would be better for the child than making no order at all'. This important provision effectively implements the Law

Commission's recommendation with regard to 'private law' proceedings and takes on board those of the Child Care Review and Government White Paper with respect to care proceedings.[1]

1 See, respectively, Law Com No 172, paras 3.2-3.4 and cl 1(1) of their draft Bill; the *Review of Child Care Law* (DHSS, 1985) paras 15.24-15.25 and *The Law on Child Care and Family Services* (Cm 62, 1987) para 59.

**1.21** In the private law context, the s 1(5) principle is new. It is expected, and was intended, to have greatest impact in divorce and separation proceedings. The Law Commission was concerned that under the pre-1989 Act law, many custody and access orders were merely 'part of the divorce package'. It accepted that while sometimes orders might bring stability and certainty even in uncontested cases, there was a risk that in other cases orders could polarise the parents' role and perhaps alienate the child from one or other of the parents. Section 1(5) is intended to focus the court's attention as to whether *any* order is necessary. This provision should be seen as part of the strategy, particularly in divorce cases, of 'lowering the stakes'.

**1.22** Section 1(5) is an important and welcome provision. It should, in practice, focus attention on those cases where there is a need for court intervention. It can also be seen as part of an underlying philosophy of the 1989 Act, namely, to respect the integrity and independence of the family save where court orders have some positive contribution to make towards the child's welfare.

Chapter 2

# Parental responsibility and guardianship

## INTRODUCTION

**2.1** In its Report on *Guardianship and Custody* (Law Com 1988, No 172, Part II), the Law Commission pointed out that the law had no inherent legal concept of parenthood but instead was still conceptually based upon guardianship. Even that concept had been inadequately developed, for while for practical purposes mothers and fathers had equal authority, in strict legal theory fathers remained, during their lifetime, the sole guardians of their legitimate children. The Commission regarded as unsatisfactory the position where parents who had effectively the same rights and authority were nevertheless sometimes guardians and sometimes not. Accordingly, it recommended that parenthood should become the primary concept, with that of 'guardian' being reserved for those formally appointed to take the place of parents upon their death.

**2.2** The Commission was also concerned that the law did not adequately recognise that parenthood is a matter of responsibility rather than of rights. As it pointed out, scattered throughout the statute book were such terms as 'parental rights and duties', or 'powers and duties' or the 'rights and authority' of a parent. Not only were these terms inconsistent with one another but they were also outdated and misleading for, as the House of Lords emphasised in *Gillick v West Norfolk and Wisbech Area Health Authority* [1986] AC 112, the parental power to control a child exists not for the benefit of the parent but for the benefit of the child. Accordingly, the Commission recommended the introduction of the concept of 'parental responsibility' to replace all the ambiguous and misleading terms referred to above. As it was put, although such a change 'would make little difference in substance . . . it would reflect the everyday reality of being a parent and emphasise the responsibility of all who are in that position'. Furthermore, employing the same concept to define the status of local authorities in relation to children compulsorily committed to their care would both simplify and clarify the law in that respect.

**2.3** The Government accepted the Law Commission's recommendations. As Lord Mackay LC said, when introducing the Bill for its second reading (HL Deb, 6 December 1988, Vol 502, col 490), the concept of 'parental responsibility':

> 'emphasises that the days when a child should be regarded as a possession of his parent — indeed when in the past they had a right to his services and to sue on their loss — are now buried forever. The overwhelming

purpose of parenthood is the responsibility for caring for and raising the child to be a properly developed adult both physically and morally'.

# PARENTAL RESPONSIBILITY

## 1 The meaning of 'parental responsibility'

**2.4** Section 3 defines and outlines the scope of the duties and authority comprised in 'parental responsibility'. Section 3(1) does so by reference to 'all the rights, duties, powers, responsibilities and authority which by law a parent has in relation to the child and his property'.[1] Section 3(2) and (3) make it clear that this includes the rights, powers and duties which a guardian of the child's estate (appointed before the 1989 Act came into force[2]) had, viz (see s 3(3)) the right 'to receive or recover in his own name, for the benefit of the child, property of whatever description and wherever situated which the child is entitled to receive or recover'.[3] Those with parental responsibility also have the right to consent to the child's marriage: Marriage Act 1949, s 3(1A) (added by Sch 12, para 5(2)). On the other hand, as s 3(4)(b) states, the concept of parental responsibility does not include rights of succession to the child's property. This implements the Law Commission's recommendation (Law Com No 172, para 8.6 and explained at para 2.7) and emphasises that the incidents of parenthood with which the parental responsibility concept is concerned are those which relate to the care and upbringing of a child until he grows up. While this must include some power to administer the child's property on his behalf it does not include the right of succession. The latter right is a feature of being related to the deceased in a particular way and operates irrespective of who has responsibility for his upbringing.

1 'Section 12 parents' (or 'co-parents') and local authorities do not acquire all aspects of parental responsibility, see respectively ss 12(3) and 33(6), discussed further at para 2.9. There are also further restrictions on those who acquire parental responsibility through an emergency protection order, see s 44(5), discussed at para 7.30.
2 It is intended to limit such appointments being made in the future: see s 5(11).
3 This implements the Law Commission's recommendation: Law Com No 172, para 8.5 and explained at para 2.8.

**2.5** Whether or not a person has parental responsibility does not affect any obligation that a person may have towards the child, for example, a statutory duty to maintain the child; nor does it affect the right of the child to succeed to that person's estate: s 3(4)(a). As the Law Commission commented (Law Com No 172, para 2.9), this provision should be seen as furthering the policy established by the Family Law Reform Act 1987 that children should have the same rights regardless of their parents' marital status.

**2.6** In defining parental responsibility by reference to parental rights and duties, the Act implements the strategy recommended by the Law Commission. The Commission did not consider it practicable to include a list of factors that are comprised in parental responsibility. It pointed out that such a list would have to change from time to time to meet differing needs and circumstances. Moreover, such a list would, in the light of the decision in *Gillick v West Norfolk and Wisbech Area Health Authority* [1986] AC 112, have to vary with the age and maturity of the child and the circumstances of each case. On balance, it is submitted that the Act has adopted the right strategy. In practice, the law has worked reasonably well without such a list and to produce one now might simply have caused unprofitable debate. The inestimable advantage of the scheme laid down by the 1989 Act is that it provides a single, modern and appropriate concept which is applied throughout the statute law affecting children.

## 2 Who has parental responsibility?

**2.7** The Law Commission did not propose any change in the basic rules for allocating parental responsibility. Adopting this strategy, s 2(1) and (2) respectively provide that where the father and mother of the child were married to each other at the time of the child's birth, they each have parental responsibility, but where they were not, only the mother has parental responsibility. The reference to a child whose parents were or were not married to each other at the time of his birth must, as s 2(3) emphasises, be interpreted in accordance with s 1 of the Family Law Reform Act 1987. Read with s 1(2)-(4) of the 1987 Act, s 2(1) refers to a child whose parents were married to each other at any time during the period beginning with insemination or (where there was no insemination) conception and ending with birth, including a child who (a) is treated as legitimate by virtue of the Legitimacy Act 1976, s 1; (b) is a legitimate person within the meaning of s 10 of the 1976 Act; (c) is an adopted child within the meaning of the Adoption Act 1976, Part IV; or (d) is otherwise treated in law as legitimate. Section 2(2) refers to children who are not covered by s 2(1).

Stated simply, s 2(1) and (2) provide that both the father and mother automatically have parental responsibility in respect of a 'legitimate child' but only the mother in respect of an 'illegitimate child'. The rule of law that a father is the natural guardian of his legitimate child is abolished: s 2(4). Schedule 14, para 6(1) makes it clear that each married parent continues to have parental responsibility notwithstanding that an order determining custody (including joint as well as sole custody), access or any other matter with respect to the child's education or upbringing has been made under the Domestic Proceedings and Magistrates' Courts Act 1978, the Children Act 1975, the Matrimonial Causes Act 1973, the Guardianship of Minors Acts 1971 and 1973, the Matrimonial Causes Act 1965 or the Matrimonial Proceedings (Magistrates' Courts) Act 1960.

**2.8** Reflecting the former law, s 2(2)(b) expressly provides that the 'unmarried' father shall not have parental responsibility unless he acquires it in accordance with the provisions of the 1989 Act. The Act itself provides a number of ways in which he can do this, namely, by obtaining a parental responsibility order under s 4, or by being granted a residence order upon which the court is obliged (by s 12(1)[1])to make a separate parental responsibility order under s 4. He can also acquire parental responsibility by means of a formal agreement with the mother (see s 4(1)(b)) and upon being appointed a guardian accordance with the terms set out in s 5.

1 If he already has a custody or care and control order made under any of the enactments mentioned in para 2.7 above, a s 4 order giving him parental responsibility for the child is *deemed* to have been made: Sch 14 paras 6(2) and (4).

**2.9** Apart from the parents referred to above, no-one else has parental responsibility automatically. However, other persons can subsequently acquire it. Any person who has been appointed a guardian under s 5 has parental responsibility for the child concerned: s 5(6). Similarly, any person (who is not a parent or guardian) in whose favour a residence order has been made, has responsibility while the order remains in force: s 12(2). Such persons also have parental responsibility as long as they have custody or care and control of the child by virtue of a court order made under any of the enactments mentioned in para 2.7 above: Sch 14, para 7. 'Section 12 parents' or 'co-parents' (as they may become known), however, do not thereby acquire the right to consent to, or refuse consent to, the making of an application to free a child for adoption, nor to agree or refuse to agree to the making of an adoption order nor the right to appoint a guardian: s 12(3). A local authority also has parental responsibility while a care order is in force (s 33(3)(a)) but, like 's 12 parents' they do not acquire the right to consent to a freeing order nor to agree to the making of an adoption order nor to appoint a guardian (s 33(6)(b)); nor is an authority entitled to cause the child to be brought up in any religious persuasion other than that in which he would have been brought up if the order had not been made: s 33(6)(a). Any person who has an emergency order in his favour has limited parental responsibility: s 44(4)(c) and (5) — discussed at para 7.30'.

## 3 Sharing parental responsibility for a child

**2.10** Although implicit in s 2(1), s 2(5) expressly provides that more than one person may have parental responsibility for the same child at the same time. Section 2(5) needs to be read in conjunction with s 2(6)-(8). Section 2(6) provides that a person with parental responsibility does not cease to have that responsibility solely because some other person subsequently acquires it. Section 2(7) states that, where more than one person has parental responsibility for a child, 'each of them may act alone and without the other (or others) in meeting that responsibility . . . [subject to] the operation of any enactment which requires the consent in a matter affecting the child'. Under s 2(8), a person with parental responsibility is not entitled to act in any way that would be incompatible with any order made in respect to the child under the 1989 Act nor, where relevant, any order made under enactments mentioned in para 2.7 above: Sch 14 para 6(1)-(3).

**2.11** The effects of s 2(5)-(8) are perhaps best approached by first considering the position of the married parents of a child. Under s 2(1) each parent has parental responsibility and by s 2(7) each may act independently and without the other, subject only to express statutory provisions to the contrary. This latter qualification preserves, for example, the embargo imposed by s 1 of the Child Abduction Act 1984, against one parent taking the child outside the United Kingdom without the other's consent and maintains the need to obtain each parent's agreement to an adoption order as laid down by s 16 of the Adoption Act 1976. This general ability to act independently resolves the uncertainty created by the inconsistent wording of the Guardianship Act 1973, s 1(1), which provided for equal and separately exercisable rights between the parents, and the Children Act 1975, s 85(3), which qualified that right if the other parent had signified his disapproval (both of these statutory provisions have been repealed). The absence of a legal duty upon parents to consult one another implements the Law Commission's view (Law Com No 172, para 2.7) that such a duty was both unworkable and undesirable. Where there is disagreement between the parents, the burden will be on the one seeking, for example, to prevent a step which the other is proposing, to take the issue to court. The current position should be seen as part of the general aim of encouraging both parents to feel concerned and responsible for the welfare of their children.

**2.12** Where the parents separate or divorce, each continues to have parental responsibility even if a residence order has been made in favour of one of them. As the Law Commission emphasised (ibid, para 4.6), a parent who does not have the child with him should still be regarded in law as a parent and should be treated as such by, for example, schools and, therefore be given information and an opportunity to take part in his child's education.[1] Where that parent has the child with him then, subject to not acting in a way that is incompatible with any court order, he will be able to exercise his responsibilities to the full. In other words, even where a residence order has been granted in one parent's favour, *each* will still be able to exercise their responsibilities without having to consult the other. This finally resolves doubts raised by *Dipper v Dipper* [1981] Fam 31 in which Cumming Bruce LJ suggested that there was a duty upon the custodial parent both to inform and consult with the non-custodial parent about long-term decisions with respect to the child. It also means that neither parent has the right of veto over the other's action. The Law Commission (ibid, para 2.11) illustrated the effect of these points with the following example: where a child has to live with one parent and go to a school nearby, it would be incompatible for the other parent to arrange for him to have his hair done in a way which will exclude him from the school. It would not, however, be incompatible for that parent to take him to a particular sporting occasion over the weekend, no matter how much the parent with whom the child lived might disapprove.

1 To this end it should be noted that the former definition of 'parent' in s 114(1) of the Education Act 1944, which referred, inter alia, to 'every person who has actual custody' has been repealed by Sch 15.

**2.13** Section 2(6) makes it clear that neither parent will lose parental responsibility solely because someone else has acquired it through a court order. This means, for example, that upon divorce a father does not lose parental responsibility even if a step-father also acquires it under a residence order made in his favour.[1] In other words, the mother, step-father and father will all share parental responsibility for the child and, subject to not acting in a way that is incompatible with a court order, all three will be able to exercise their responsibilities independently of the others.

1 Step-parents may acquire parental responsibility only through a residence order or upon being appointed a guardian. They do not acquire responsibility simply by marrying the child's parent.

**2.14** Another effect of s 2(6) is that parents do not lose parental responsibility when a local authority obtains a care order, nor where an emergency protection order is made. The effect of this change is discussed at para 6.23.

**2.15** Although s 2(6) states that parental responsibility is not lost *solely* because someone else acquires it, that provision should not be read as meaning that a court order can never end a parent's responsibility. An adoption order will clearly do so. As Lord Mackay LC said during the debates on the Bill (HL Deb, 19 December 1988, Vol 502, col 1175), the word 'solely' is used advisedly here. An adoption order deprives a parent of parental responsibility not *solely* because adoptive parents acquire it but because s 12(3) of the Adoption Act 1976 (as amended by Sch 10, para 3 of the 1989 Act) expressly extinguishes the previous parents' responsibility. Similarly, since ultimate responsibility for a ward of court rests with the court,[1] the warding of a child must operate at least to limit a parent's freedom to exercise parental responsibility. For this latter reason, s 2(8) should not be interpreted as meaning that in the absence of a court order[2] a parent may always exercise his responsibility without qualification.

1 See, eg *Re E (SA) (a minor) (wardship)* [1984] 1 All ER 289 at 290, per Lord Scarman.
2 A child becomes a ward of court immediately the originating summons is issued, ie, without the need for any court order.

## 4 Arrangements and agreements between parents and others

**2.16** Section 2(9) preserves the previous position that a person with parental responsibility may not surrender or transfer that responsibility to another person save by a court order. The former exception to this rule provided by s 3 of the Family Law Reform Act 1987 — namely, to permit, subject to the child's welfare, agreements between the parents — has been repealed. This implements the Law Commission's view (Law Com No 172, para 2.15) that as between married parents such a provision had outlived its usefulness, while as between unmarried parents a more formal method for making agreements to share parental responsibility was required. In this latter regard, provision has now been made under s 4(1)(b) for the making of 'parental responsibility agreements' (see para 2.25).

**2.17** Section 2(9), however, recognises for the first time the power of those with parental responsibility to delegate some or all of their responsibility to one or more persons acting on their behalf. Such delegation can be made to another person who already has parental responsibility (s 2(10)) or to those who have not, such as schools or holiday camps. The idea behind this provision is primarily to encourage parents (regardless of whether or not they are separated) to agree among themselves on what they believe to be the best arrangements for their children. Section 2(9) does not, however, make such arrangements legally binding. Consequently, they can be revoked or changed at will. Furthermore, as s 2(11) provides, delegation will not absolve a person with parental responsibility from any liability for failure on his part to discharge his responsibilities to the child.[1]

1 For example, not to neglect, abandon, expose or cause or procure a child under the age of 16 to be assaulted or ill-treated etc under ss 1 and 17 of the Children and Young Persons Act 1933.

### 5 The position of those caring for a child but who do not have parental responsibility

**2.18** Following the Law Commission's recommendation (Law Com No 172, para 8.12), s 3(5) usefully clarifies the legal position of those who are caring for a child but who do not have parental responsibility, by providing that they 'may (subject to the provisions of this Act) do what is reasonable in all the circumstances for the purpose of safeguarding or promoting the child's welfare'. This would entitle, for example, a carer to consent to the child's medical treatment in the event of an accident, though not major elective surgery.

## ACQUISITION OF PARENTAL RESPONSIBILITY BY UNMARRIED FATHERS

**2.19** As stated by s 2(2)(b), an unmarried father does not have parental responsibility for his child unless he acquires it in accordance with the provisions of the 1989 Act.[1] Apart from acquiring responsibility by being appointed a guardian,[2] the Act provides two means whereby he may obtain that responsibility, namely, by a court order or by formal agreement with the mother.

1 Of course a father may also obtain parental responsibility by marrying the mother. For the effect of subsequent marriage upon a parental responsibility order or agreement, see para 2.31.

2 Ie, upon appointment by the mother or by a court order under s 5, discussed below at para 2.34 et seq.

### 1 Parental responsibility orders

**2.20** Under s 4(1)(a) the court may, upon an application by an unmarried father, order that he shall have parental responsibility for the child. If there is a doubt about the applicant's paternity, and *a fortiori* if paternity is disputed, it will have to proved before the action may proceed.[1] An application may be made only in respect of a 'child', that is a person under the age of eighteen: s 105(1).

1 A similar requirement obtained in the case of an unmarried father's application for custody or access under the Guardianship of Minors Act 1971: see *Re O (a Minor: Access)* [1985] FLR 716 and *Re W (a Minor)* (1989) *Times* 21 November.

**2.21** In deciding whether to make a parental responsibility order, the court must, in line with the general principles laid down by the Act, treat the child's welfare as its paramount consideration,[1] and be satisfied that making the order 'would be better for the child than making no order at all'.[2] There is no enjoinder to have particular regard to the circumstances set out in s 1(3) (discussed at para 1.15) since, under s 1(4), a court is required to do so only when considering contested s 8 order applications or applications for orders made order under Part IV (see para 1.14). There is, however, nothing to prevent the court from considering the s 1(3) factors if it so chooses. Indeed, it might be thought that the court should at least take an older child's views into account in deciding whether to make a s 4 order.[3] The restriction under s 9(6) which prevents the court from making s 8 orders in respect of a child aged sixteen or over, save where the circumstances are 'exceptional', does not apply to s 4 orders.

1 Pursuant to s 1(1). It could be argued that s 1(1) does not apply on the basis that a parental responsibility order is not a question with respect to 'the upbringing of the child', or at least rate not directly so — see the discussion at para 1.7 — but the argument seems unlikely to succeed in this instance.
2 Pursuant to s 1(5). It could be argued that this provision does *not* apply since a parental responsibility order relates to the *parent* and not the child. Although this argument seems stronger than that in relation to the inapplicability of s 1(1), it is still likely to be rejected since, following the majority's reasoning in *Gillick v West Norfolk and Wisbech Area Health Authority* [1986] AC 112, it can reasonably be said that as parental responsibility exists for the benefit of the child, parental responsibility orders also relate to the child.
3 In the light of the *Gillick* decision, where a child is mature enough to make his own decisions, his own view might be considered decisive. In any event, since a child with sufficient understanding may, with leave, apply to have the order ended (s 4(3)(b) and (4) — discussed at para 2.32), it is logical to assume that such a child's view is relevant to the issue of whether or not to make the order in the first place.

**2.22** As well as applying for a parental responsibility order, the father may also seek, in s 4 proceedings,[1] a s 8 order, including, in particular, a residence or contact order (for details of which see paras 3-10 et seq). Indeed, even if he does not so apply, it is open to the court to make a s 8 order of its own motion: s 10(1)(b). The court may *not*, however, make a parental responsibility order of its own motion, save as an automatic consequence of making a residence order in favour of the father.

1 Pursuant to s 10(1)(a)(i) and 10(4)(a). Section 4 proceedings are classified as 'family proceedings' for the purposes of the 1989 Act under s 8(3) and (4), discussed at para 3.23.

**2.23** It is open to an unmarried father to seek, for example, a residence or contact order, without also applying for a parental responsibility order. He may do so by applying (as he is entitled to do under s 10(4)(a), discussed at para 3.40) for a s 8 order: s 10(2)(a). In such an application, however, although the court is bound (by s 12(1)) to make a parental responsibility order if it makes a residence order in the father's favour, it has no such power if it is only prepared to make a contact order in his favour. Since the father will be in a stronger legal position if he has a parental responsibility order[1] and a contact order in his favour than simply a contact order fathers seeking residence or contact orders who are in dispute with the mother should be advised to apply for a s 4 order as well as a s 8 order.

1 The effect of having parental responsibility is discussed at para 2.29, below.

## 2 When should a parental responsibility order be sought?

**2.24** Section 4 replaces the action provided for by the Family Law Reform Act 1987. As that provision was brought into force only in April 1989, it is still too early to say when in practice this provision will be used. However, when originally recommending the new order, the Law Commission[1] envisaged its use in three types of situation, namely: (1) where the mother and father are living together and agree to the order; (2) where the mother dies having appointed no guardian; and (3) where the father seeks full parental rights rather than legal custody. Now that provision is made for making a parental responsibility agreement (see below), s 4 *orders* seem unlikely to be sought in the first situation. With regard to the second situation, it might seem no less advantageous to apply to become a guardian under s 5, since a guardian also has parental responsibility.[2] However, it might nevertheless be in the unmarried father's interests to seek a s 4 order rather than an appointment as guardian if only because there are fewer opportunities for bringing the former to an end (cf s 4(3) with s 6(7), discussed respectively at paras 2.32 and 2.54). With regard to the third situation, as was discussed at para 2.23, the unmarried father would be well advised to seek a s 4 order as well as a residence or contact order. On occasion, however, s 4 might prove of use in other circumstances. For example, as *Re H and Another (Minors) (Adoption: putative father's rights)* [1989] 2 All ER 353 shows, an intended application under s 4 can be an effective counter to a local authority application to free the child for adoption.[3]

1 *Illegitimacy* (Law Com No 118, 1982) para 7.29.
2 See s 5(5). Guardianship is discussed in detail at paras 2.34 et seq.
3 Under the Adoption Act 1976, s 18(7) (as amended by the Children Act 1989, Sch 10, para 6(3)), before making an order freeing the child for adoption (on which see *Clarke Hall & Morrison on Children* (10th edn) **D** [21]-[27] and **D** [46]), the court must be satisfied either that the unmarried father has no intention of applying for a parental responsibility order or that, if he did make such an application, the application is likely to be refused. As was established by *Re H* supra, since such orders give the father only *locus standi*, they are not properly regarded as challenging the local authority discretion and are therefore not caught by the principle laid down in *A v Liverpool CC* [1982] AC 363, discussed in *Clarke Hall & Morrison* at **C** [110] et seq.

## 3 Parental responsibility agreements

**2.25** Pursuant to s 4(1)(b), an unmarried father and mother may by agreement provide for the father to have parental responsibility. Under s 4(2), however, such agreements will have effect only if they are made in the prescribed form and recorded in such manner as may be prescribed by regulations to be made by the Lord Chancellor under the powers vested in him by s 4(2).

**2.26** Although it was previously possible for an unmarried couple to make an agreement between themselves as to the exercise by either of them of any of the parental rights and duties during any period when they were not living together,[1] this is the first time that an agreement may be made conferring parental responsibility upon the father. Furthermore, it is the first time that such an agreement remains effective notwithstanding that the couple are still living together.

1 Under the Guardianship Act 1973, s 1(2), as substituted by the Family Law Reform Act 1987, s 3 — both repealed by Sch 15.

**2.27** This new power to make parental responsibility agreements implements the recommendation of the Law Commission (Law Com No 172, para. 2.18). As the Commission pointed out, although the father could apply for what was then a parental rights and duties order under s 4 of the Family Law Reform Act 1987, the need to resort to judicial proceedings to obtain parental responsibility 'unduly elaborate, expensive and unnecessary unless the child's mother object[ed]'. On the other hand, in recommending this new power, the Commission was also aware of the dangers of undue pressure being exerted upon mothers to make such agreements.[1] Accordingly, they recommended a relatively formal procedure whereby, in order to be binding, the agreement would have to be in prescribed form and checked by the county court. However, unlike clause 4(2) of the Law Commission's draft Bill, the formal requirement that the agreement be recorded in the county court is not included in the 1989 Act. It is, of course, still open to the Lord Chancellor to so provide in the Regulations.[2]

1 Indeed, it was because of the potential pressure, that the Law Commission did not originally recommend the power to make binding agreements — see *Illegitimacy* (Law Com No 118) para 4.39.
2 Query whether, given the deterrence of involving formal court proceedings, it would be preferable if the agreement in prescribed form had to be recorded by the Registrar of Births, Deaths and Marriages. Formal records could then be held by the Registrar-General.

**2.28** In response to concern[1] that unmarried mothers might be susceptible to undue pressure to make agreements, the Lord Chancellor accepted, during debate on the Bill, that the prescribed form should contain a clear explanation that signing it will have important legal consequences and that it should also contain a warning to the following effect: 'If you are in any doubt about your legal rights you should seek legal advice before signing this form'.[2]

1 Voiced particularly by Lord Banks — see HL Deb, 19 December 1988, Vol 502, cols 1180-82 and 6 February 1989, Vol 503, col 1319.
2 See HL Deb, 6 February 1989, Vol 503, col 1320. He also pointed out that there was a limit as to what could be included on the form and he seemed to draw the line at including a statement that the parties could subsequently apply to the court to end the agreement.

## 4 The effect of parental responsibility orders and agreements

**2.29** The effect of a court order or a properly recorded agreement is the same, namely, it confers parental responsibility upon the unmarried father. In most cases he will share responsibility jointly with the mother[1] or, if the mother is dead, with any formally appointed guardian. He could also share responsibility with some other person in whose favour a residence order has been made.[2]

1 It is for this reason that the power to make agreements under s 4(1)(b) is not inconsistent with the embargo under s 2(9) against surrendering or transferring parental responsibility, since the father does not gain responsibility at the expense of the mother.

2 Under s 12(2) a residence order confers parental responsibility upon 'non parents', though this is subject to s 12(3): see para 2.9.

**2.30** An unmarried father who has parental responsibility will be in the same legal position with regard to the child as if he had married the mother. He will have the right to consent or refuse consent, to the making of an application to free the child for adoption; the right to agree, or refuse to agree, to the making of an adoption order;[1] and the right to appoint a guardian upon his death.[2] On the other hand, granting parental responsibility to the unmarried father, does not alter the status of the child. Hence, the child will not take British citizenship through his father, nor will he be able to succeed to a title of honour through his parents.

1 Under the Adoption Act 1976, s 72(1) (as amended by the Children Act 1989, Sch 10, para 30(7)), such fathers are treated as 'parents'. Cf the position under the Family Law Reform Act 1987 where fathers with a s 4 order in their favour were nevertheless treated as 'guardians'.

2 S 5(3). Furthermore, the court will thereby be prevented from appointing a guardian upon the mother's death: see s 5(1)(a).

## 5 Ending parental responsibility orders or agreements

**2.31** Parental responsibility orders or agreements end automatically once the child attains his majority: s 91(7) and (8). It is submitted that both an order and an agreement are automatically overridden if the father subsequently marries the mother during the child's minority. This is because, by virtue of s 2(1), marriage confers parental responsibility upon the father which, unlike a court order or agreement, cannot subsequently be ended by a court order, save upon adoption.[1]

1 Furthermore, the court no longer has the power to declare a parent 'unfit to have custody': see para 3.69.

**2.32** Apart from cases where it is ended automatically, parental responsibility may be brought to an end only upon a court order to that effect. Such an order may be made only upon the application of any person who has parental responsibility for the child (this will include the father himself) or, with leave of the court, of the child himself (s 4(3)). In the latter case, the court may grant leave only if it is satisfied that the child has sufficient understanding to make the proposed application (s 4(4)). The court may not end a s 4 order while a residence order in favour of the unmarried father remains in force.[1]

1 S 11(4). Read literally, this would allow a court to end a s 4 *agreement* even though a residence order in favour of the father is still in force, but it seems inconceivable that a court would do so: see further para 2.33.

**2.33** In deciding whether to end a s 4 order or agreement, the court must regard the child's welfare as its paramount consideration and be satisfied that discharging the order is better than making no order at all: s 1(1) and (5). Nevertheless, it is submitted that the court should be slow to grant such an order particularly where the court made a s 4 order in the first place.[1] It should be borne in mind that parental responsibility vested in the married father may be ended only upon the child's adoption. It should not, for example, be thought that the ending of a residence order in the father's favour automatically means that parental responsibility should also come to an end. In any event, a separate order expressly ending the s 4 order will be required to end the father's parental responsibility.[2]

1 *Aliter*, perhaps following an agreement. For example, if it could be shown that the mother had been subjected to undue pressure to sign, that might provide a good reason to make an order under s 4(3).
2 A separate order will also be necessary where, by virtue of Sch 14, para 6(4), a s 4 order is deemed to have been made, ie, the ending of a custody or care and control order in the father's favour does not end his parental responsibility.

## GUARDIANSHIP

**2.34** Unlike the previous law, which was a complicated product of common law, equity and statute, the new law of guardianship is exclusively statutory and has, consequently, been simplified. Whereas before there were different types of guardians, namely: parental guardians and non-parental guardians; guardians of the estate and guardians of the person; and guardians appointed for a single purpose only,[1] under the 1989 Act this is no longer possible.[2] The concept of parental guardianship is abolished[3] and any person appointed a guardian under s 5 has parental responsibility.[4] Whereas previously the High Court, at least, possibly had an inherent power[5] as well as a statutory power to appoint guardians, now all the courts have the same powers,[6] namely, those derived from s 5. In making these changes, the Act implements the recommendations of the Law Commission (Law Com No 172, paras 2.22-2.32).

1 For a detailed discussion of the various types of guardian, see *Guardianship* (Law Com Working Paper No 91, 1985) pp 29-46.
2 Unless, pursuant to s 5(11), rules of court make provision permitting the High Court to exercise its inherent jurisdiction to appoint a guardian of the estate of any child. This provision is to preserve the possibility of the Official Solicitor being appointed in a few exceptional circumstances.
3 S 2(4) expressly abolishes the rule of law that a father is the natural guardian of his legitimate children, while s 3 of the Guardianship of Minors Act 1971,

which provided (in the case of legitimate children) that upon the death of one parent, the other became the guardian, has been repealed (see Sch 15).

**4** S 5(5). However, those appointed as guardians of the child's estate, or for one specific purpose (eg, to give or to withhold agreement to the child's marriage) before s 5 came into force, will be able to act only within the terms of their appointment: Sch 14, para 12.

**5** See *Re McGrath (Infants)* [1893] 1 Ch 143; *Re N (Infants)* [1967] Ch 512 and Guardianship of Minors Act 1971, s 17. But cf *Re C and another (minors) (wardship: adoption)* [1989] 1 All ER 395.

**6** Save to the limited extent that the High Court's inherent jurisdiction to appoint guardians of the estate is preserved under s 5(11).

## The court's power to appoint guardians

### *When may the power be exercised?*

**2.35** The court's power to appoint a guardian is now exclusively (s 5(13)) governed by s 5(1) and (2). Under s 5(1), the court (ie, the High Court, county court or magistrates' court (s 92(7)) may appoint an 'individual' to be a child's guardian if:

'(a) the child has no parent with parental responsibility for him; or
(b) a residence order has been made with respect to the child in favour of a parent or guardian of his who has died while the order was in force'.

Under s 5(2) the above powers may be exercised in any 'family proceedings' (defined by s 8(3): see para 3.23) either upon application or 'if the court considers that the order should be made even though no application has been made for it'.

**2.36** Applying s 6 (c) of the Interpretation Act 1978 (which states that, unless there is a contrary intention in the statute, the singular includes the plural), the court may appoint more than one person. On the other hand, by confining the power to appoint an 'individual', it is clear that the court cannot appoint a body such as a local authority to be a guardian.[1]

**1** This means, contrary to the recommendation made in the Government White Paper *The Law on Child Care and Family Services* (Cm 62 1987), that a local authority cannot apply to become a guardian of an orphan.

**2.37** The power under s 5(1)(a) is similar to that formerly provided by s 5 of the Guardianship of Minors Act 1971. Under this new provision, however, the court cannot make an appointment if the child has a *parent* with parental responsibility. It can, therefore, make an order even though the child has a guardian (other than the child's unmarried father, see below) or is the subject of a residence order in favour of a non-parent. It can also make an order if the child's unmarried father is still alive,[1] provided he has not obtained parental responsibility by agreement with the mother or under a court order (ie, under s 4) or as a result of being appointed the child's guardian.[2]

**1** As was the case under the previous law: see *Re N (Minors)* [1974] Fam 40.

**2** Under s 5(6) a guardian has parental responsibility.

**2.38** The court's power to appoint a guardian is narrower than that formerly provided by s 3 of the Guardianship of Minors Act 1971, since it no longer arises simply upon the death of one of the parents. This means that a case like *Re H (an Infant)* [1959] 3 All ER 746, in which a father opposed the dead mother's sister's application to become the child's guardian, can no longer arise. Instead, in such cases application must be made for a s 8 order (discussed at para 3.40). This narrower power brings our law into line with the recommendations of the Council of Europe.[1]

1 *Parental Responsibilities* Principle 9. Indeed, as the Law Commission pointed out (ibid, para 2.27), we were apparently the only member country of the Council of Europe that permitted guardianship to operate during the lifetime of a surviving parent.

### *Who may apply?*

**2.39** Like the previous law, the 1989 Act is silent as to who can apply to become a guardian. Presumably, any individual seeking to become a guardian, can apply. In addition, since the court's powers do not appear to be confined to appointing the applicant to be a guardian, it may be open to any other interested person, including the child himself, to apply under s 5 to seek the appointment of another individual to be a guardian.[1] Once proceedings have been set in motion, it is open (pursuant to s 10(1), discussed at para 3.40) to any interested person to seek leave of the court to intervene in the proceedings and to seek a s 8 order. Insofar as an application is made for the appointment of a guardian, there is no statutory requirement that leave of the court must first be obtained.

1 Such a possibility was canvassed by the Law Commission in their Working Paper No 91, para 3.49.

### *In respect of whom may applications be made?*

**2.40** It is clear that an application may be made only in respect of a 'child', that is, a person under the age of eighteen: s 105(1). There is no express embargo against making an appointment in respect of a married child, although it remains to be seen whether in practice the courts would be prepared to make an appointment in such a case.[1]

1 A similar problem obtained in respect of the former law, but the Law Commission (see Working Paper No 91, para 3.64) was inclined to leave the question open.

## The court's powers in guardianship applications

**2.41** In deciding whether to make an appointment, the court is enjoined to regard the child's welfare as the paramount consideration and to be satisfied that making an order is better than making no order at all (s 1(1) and (4)). It is not, however, obliged to have specific regard to the circumstances set out in s 1(3).[1] Furthermore, the restriction under s 9(6) on making s 8 orders in respect of a child aged sixteen or over (discussed at para 3.32) does not apply to the making of a guardianship order under s 5. To enable the court to decide what decision to make, it may, for the first time in guardianship applications, order a welfare report.[2]

1 This is because the enjoinder to do so under s 1(4) applies only when the court is considering whether to make a contested s 8 order or an order under Part IV of the Act. There is nothing to prevent the court considering such factors if it so chooses.
2 Pursuant to the powers under s 7, discussed at para 8.3. This new power implements one of the Law Commission's suggestions (Working Paper No 91, para 3.54) for improving the procedure and criteria for court appointments of guardians.

## Parental appointment of guardians

**2.42** While preserving a parent's right to appoint a guardian to replace him upon his death, the 1989 Act makes some important and welcome changes, namely, the introduction of a simpler method of making an appointment and the provision that unless the child is living under a residence order with the parent who dies, the appointment will not take effect until both parents are dead. In consequence of the latter change, the former rights[1] of the surviving parent to object to the appointment taking effect and of the guardian to apply to the court if he considers the surviving parent 'unfit to have legal control' have been removed.[2]

1 Conferred by s 4 of the Guardianship of Minors Act 1971. For a discussion of the defects of the former position, see Law Com No 172, para 2.26.
2 In practice little use seems to have been made of these actions. For an account of what action can be taken under the 1989 Act to resolve disputes in those cases where it is still possible for a guardian to take office during the lifetime of a parent, see para 2.47 below.

### *Making an appointment*

**2.43** As formerly, s 5(3) entitles any parent with parental responsibility[1] to appoint an individual to be the child's guardian in the event of his death. In addition, s 5(4) vests, for the first time, a similar right in any guardian.[2] A parent or guardian is entitled to appoint more than one person as a guardian,[3] nor is there anything to prevent an appointment being made by two or more persons jointly: s 5(10).

1 This will exclude the unmarried father unless he has parental responsibility as a result of a court order or an agreement with the mother, pursuant to s 4, discussed at paras 2.19 et seq.
2 Note the consequential amendment of s 1 of the Wills Act 1837 in Sch 15, para 1 of the 1989 Act.
3 This is implicit in s 5(6) and, as is discussed in para 2.36, the word 'individual' should be interpreted as including the plural.

**2.44** Whereas formerly the appointment had to be by deed or by will, under s 5(5), it is now sufficient that the appointment 'is made in writing, is dated and is signed by the person making it'. It is hoped that this simpler method of appointment will encourage parents to appoint guardians.[1] Section 5(5) does not preclude appointments being made in a will or deed, since clearly such means will satisfy the minimum requirements laid down by that section.[2]

1 See the Law Commission's comments at Law Com No 172, para 2.29.

2 See Lord Mackay LC's comments at HL Deb, 19 December 1988, Vol 502, col 1199.

### *Revoking an appointment*

**2.45** Section 6 now deals with the formerly complex question of revocation of appointments. The basic principle is set out in s 6(1), namely, that a later appointment revokes an earlier appointment (including one made in an unrevoked will or codicil) made by the same person in respect of the same child, unless it is clear that the purpose of the later appointment is to appoint an additional guardian.[1] It is also open to the person who made the appointment (including one made in an unrevoked will or codicil) expressly to revoke it in a signed written and dated instrument: s 6(2). Section 6(4) further provides that an appointment made in a will or codicil is revoked if the will or codicil is revoked. An appointment, *other* than one made by will or codicil, will also be revoked if the person making it destroys the document with the intention of revoking the appointment (s 6(3)).

1 This reverses the former position following s 20 of the Wills Act 1837 that an appointment under a will cannot be revoked by a subsequent appointment by deed and it ends the debate (on which, see Bromley and Lowe's *Family Law* (7th ed) p 531) as to whether an appointment by deed can be revoked by a later deed.

## When the appointment takes effect

**2.46** Formerly, an appointment took effect[1] immediately upon the death of the appointing parent. Under s 5(7), however, an appointment will take effect immediately upon the death of the appointing person only where: (a) following that death, the child has no parent with parental responsibility;[2] or (b) there was a sole[3] residence order in force in favour of the person making the appointment immediately before his death. In this latter instance, the surviving parent has no right to object to the appointment but he can apply to the court for an order ending the appointment: s 6(7) (see further para 2.47). Where the child does have a parent with parental responsibility, the appointment will take effect only upon the death of that person: s 5(8).

1 Subject to the surviving parent's right of objection under s 4 of the Guardianship of Minors Act 1971.
2 It *will*, therefore, take effect if the child's unmarried father is still alive, unless that person has obtained parental responsibility as a result of a court order or an agreement with the mother under s 4; (discussed at paras 2-19 et seq).
3 *Aliter*, if a residence order had also been made in favour of another, surviving parent: s 5(9).

**2.47** The rationale of delaying the operation of a guardianship appointment is to avoid unnecessary conflict between a surviving parent and a guardian appointed by the deceased parent. This is a welcome change for, as the Law Commission said (Law Com No 172, para 2.27), there seems little reason why the surviving parent should have to share parental responsibility with a guardian who almost invariably will not be sharing the household. On the other hand, different considerations apply where the parents have divorced or separated and in particular it seems right that if one parent has a residence order in his favour, that person ought to be able to provide for his child's future in the event of his death. In these circumstances, although the surviving parent may no longer object to the appointment, he may, under s 6(7), seek a court order to end the appointment. Other disputes can be resolved by either the parent or the guardian seeking a s 8 order.

## Disclaiming the appointment

**2.48** Section 6(5) provides, for the first time, a formal right to disclaim an appointment. This new right, which applies only to appointments made by a parent or guardian (ie, not to court appointments), must be exercised 'within a reasonable time of his first knowing that the appointment has taken effect'. Furthermore, it must be disclaimed by an instrument in writing, signed by the appointee, and recorded in accordance with any regulations that may be made by the Lord Chancellor: s 6(6).

**2.49** Welcome as this new power is, it does make it all the more important for parents to discuss their proposed appointment with the person concerned. It must be hoped that some official guidance will be published reminding parents of the desirability of prior consultation.

## Effect of being appointed a guardian

**2.50** A person appointed a guardian under s 5 (ie, whether by the court or by parental appointment) has parental responsibility for the child: s 5(6). For many purposes a guardian will be in the same legal position as a parent with parental responsibility. Indeed, for the first time, a guardian appointed under s 5 can himself appoint a guardian to take his place in the event of his death: s 5(4). Unlike a parent, however, a guardian is not a 'liable relative' under the Social Security Act 1986,[1] nor may he be subjected to the same orders for financial provision or property adjustment as a parent.[2] It remains the case that guardians have no rights of succession upon the child's death, nor can the child take British citizenship from his guardian.

1 S 26, as amended by the Family Law Reform Act 1987, s 2(1), (3).
2 Viz under the powers provided for by s 15 and Sch 1 of the 1989 Act, discussed in Chapter 4.

**2.51** A guardian is in a stronger legal position than a non-parent in whose favour a residence order has been made. Unlike the latter (see s 12(3)), a guardian has the right to consent or withhold consent to an application to free a child for adoption, to agree or withhold agreement to the child's adoption and to appoint a guardian.

## Termination of Guardianship

### *Death, majority or marriage of the child*

**2.52** The guardian's duties clearly cease if the child dies. They automatically determine when he attains the age of 18: s 91(7) and (8). Whether the guardian's powers cease upon the child's marriage is perhaps debatable for, while s 5 imposes no such express limitation, it may well be held that there is no scope for the operation of guardianship. In any event, it seems highly unlikely that a guardian would be permitted to interfere with the activities of a married child even if the guardianship continues.

### *Death of the guardian*

**2.53** Guardianship ends upon the death of a sole guardian unless, pursuant to the powers vested by s 5(4), the guardian has appointed another individual to be the child's guardian in his place. If a guardian dies leaving others in office, the survivors continue to be guardians.

### *Removal by the court*

**2.54** For the first time, county courts and magistrates' courts as well as the High Court can make an order bringing *any* appointment of guardian made under s 5 to an end. Such an order can be made at any time upon the application of: (1) any person who has parental responsibility; or (2) the child himself, with leave of the court; or (3) upon the court's own motion in any family proceedings, if the court considers that it should be brought to an end: s 6(7). In deciding whether to end the guardianship, the court must be guided by the welfare principle.[1] Unlike formerly, in reaching its decision the court is entitled to order a welfare report: s 7 (discussed in Chapter 8). If it decides to end the guardianship, the court may appoint another individual to take the former guardian's place. It is also open to the court to make a s 8 order.

1 Ie, pursuant to s 1(1). If the guardian expresses his unwillingness to continue, it is unlikely that the court will hold it to be in the child's interests for the appointment to continue. For cases where the court has forcibly removed a guardian in the past, see the cases cited by Bromley and Lowe's *Family Law* (7th ed) p 361.

Chapter 3

# The courts' powers in family proceedings

## INTRODUCTION AND BACKGROUND

**3.1** In this chapter consideration is first given to the courts' powers under Part II of the 1989 Act to make orders in what are termed 'family proceedings' and then to the impact of Part II and other amendments in the 1989 Act both on the jurisdictions dealing with inter-parental disputes over their children and those affecting third parties. Financial orders in favour of children are discussed in Chapter 4.

**3.2** Part II is based on the Law Commission's recommendations contained in its Report on *Guardianship and Custody* (Law Com No 172, 1988). The Commission commented (para 1.1) that while the main principles of the pre-1989 Act law were reasonably clear and well accepted, the details, particularly concerning custody, were complicated and confusing. Three major difficulties were identified (paras 4.2 et seq).

First, different courts had different powers. For example, while the divorce courts could allocate 'custody', 'care and control' and 'access' in any way they thought fit, other courts acting under the Guardianship of Minors Act 1971 or the Domestic Proceedings and Magistrates' Courts Act 1978 could only make 'legal custody' orders and 'access' orders. There were also wide variations in the different courts' powers to make orders in favour of third parties. Second, there was confusion, especially following the decision in *Dipper v Dipper* [1981] Fam 31, as to the precise effect of orders. It was not immediately obvious (especially to the parents concerned), for example, that a sole custody order did not put the custodial parent in sole control, nor that a joint custody order technically gave the parent without care and control a right of veto over the custodial parent's long-term plans for the child. Third, the law was applied inconsistently. For example, the Commission's supplemental study (conducted by Priest and Whybrow, *Supplement to Working Paper No 96)* found that in one busy court only 2 per cent of the custody orders made were joint custody orders but nearly 33.8 per cent in another court.

**3.3** Complexity and technicality were not, however, in the Commission's view, the only things wrong with the law relating to custody. The Commission was also concerned that the law made the stakes too high. As they pointed out (para 4.5) all the research evidence[1] shows that children who fare best after their parents' separation are those who are able to maintain a good relationship with both parents. While recognising the obvious limitation that law cannot make people co-operate, the Commission argued that at least it should not stand in their way. Hence, if the parties can co-operate with one another, the law should intervene as little as possible, but if they cannot, the law should at least try to 'lower the stakes' and avoid the impression that the 'loser loses all'.

1 Notably, that of J S Wallerstein and J B Kelly *Surviving the Breakup*. But see now Wallerstein and Blakeslee *Second Chances: Men, Women and Children A Decade After Divorce*.

**3.4** With the above considerations in mind, the Law Commission recommended, inter alia, that: (a) orders should be made only where the court believes it is the most effective way of safeguarding or promoting the child's welfare; and (b) the differing powers of the various courts under the different jurisdictions to make custody and access orders should be replaced by a new set of powers which are designed to be less emotive and more flexible and which are common to all courts. The first of these recommendations has been implemented by s 1(5) (discussed ante at para 1.20) and the second by Part II of the 1989 Act.

## THE COURTS' POWERS UNDER PART II

### 1 The general strategy

**3.5** The courts' previous statutory powers[1] to make custody and access orders have been removed: Sch 15. Instead, the courts are empowered to make a range of new orders, collectively known as 'section 8 orders', namely, 'residence orders', 'contact orders', 'prohibited steps orders' and 'specific issue orders'. While the first two roughly equate (although they are not the same) to custody and access orders, the other two orders are new. They are modelled on the wardship jurisdiction and implement the Law Commission's recommendation (Law Com No 172, para 1.4) to incorporate the most valuable features of the prerogative jurisdiction into the statutory jurisdiction. Overall, the section 8 powers are intended to concentrate both the court's and the parties' minds on the practical issues which generally arise with respect to children, rather than on the allocation of theoretical rights and duties.

1 Viz under the Matrimonial Causes Act 1973, s 42(1) and (2); the Domestic Proceedings and Magistrates' Courts Act 1978, s 8(2) and 14; the Guardianship of Minors Act 1971, ss 9, 10, 11 and 14A; the Children Act 1975, ss 33(1) and 34(1); and the Adoption Act 1976, s 25.

**3.6** As well as providing a new range of powers, Part II also provides a clear plan governing who can apply for an order. The basic scheme (under s 10) is that some people, for example, parents or guardians, are entitled to apply for s 8 order, while others, for example, relatives, will be able to seek the court's leave either to intervene in existing 'family proceedings' or to initiate their own proceedings to seek a s 8 order.

**3.7** Another important change under the 1989 Act is the removal of the court's power in matrimonial and other private law proceedings concerning children to make committal to care or supervision orders. Instead under s 37 (see post para 7.4) the courts are merely empowered to invite the local authority to investigate the circumstances and to decide whether to apply for a care or supervision order. However in place of these former powers is a new power under s 16 to make 'family assistance' orders, the object of which is to provide short-term help to the family.

## 2 Section 8 orders

### *The powers*

**3.8** The expression 'a section 8 order' means any of the orders mentioned in s 8(1) and any order varying or discharging such an order (s 8(2)). Section 8(1) states that in the 1989 Act:

> ''a contact order' means an order requiring the person with whom the child lives, or is to live, to allow the child to visit or stay with the person named in the order, or for that person and the child otherwise to have contact with each other;
> 'a prohibited steps order' means an order that no step which could be taken by a parent in meeting his parental responsibility for a child, and which is of a kind specified in the order, shall be taken by any person without the consent of the court;
> 'a residence order' means an order settling the arrangements to be made as to the person with whom the child is to live; and
> 'a specific issue order' means an order giving directions for the purpose of determining a specific question which has arisen, or which may arise, in connection with any aspect of parental responsibility for a child'.

**3.9** In making any of the above orders the court has further supplemental powers (designed to ensure maximum flexibility) under s 11(7) to: (a) include directions as to how the order is to be carried out; (b) impose conditions to be complied with by any person in whose favour the order has been made or any parent or any non-parent who has parental responsibility, or any parent with whom the child is living; (c) specify the period for which the order or any provision in it is to have effect; and (d) make such incidental, supplemental or consequential provision as the court thinks fit.

### *Residence orders*

**3.10** Insofar as they determine where the child is to live, residence orders are similar to the custody orders which they replace. There are, however, two important differences. First, based on the fundamental principle (see Law Com No 172, para 4.16) that changes in the child's residence should interfere as little as possible in his relationship with both parents, *each* parent retains full parental responsibility and with it the power to act independently unless this is incompatible with the court's order, regardless of who has a residence order (see the discussion at para 2.12). Second, it is intended that the new order should be flexible enough to accommodate a wider range of situations than previously.

**3.11** Although under s 8(1) residence orders are said to settle the arrangements to be made as to *the person* with whom the child is to live, because of the general presumption under the Interpretation Act 1978, s 6(c) that words appearing in a statute in the singular include the plural, residence orders may be made in favour of more than one person.[1] This means that residence orders can be made in favour of two[2] people, for example, parent and step-parent. Furthermore, more than one residence order may be made in respect of one child. For example, as s 11(4) makes clear (see para 3.14), orders may be made in favour of each parent. Indeed, there seems no reason why residence orders may not be made in favour of *each* parent *and* their respective new partners.

1 As was pointed out in this context by Lord Mackay LC during the debates on the Bill (HL Deb, 19 December 1988, Vol 502, col 1219).
2 In theory, there is nothing to stop the court from making an order in favour of more than two people, although in practice it is rarely likely to do so.

**3.12** In theory, residence orders may be made to accommodate shared care arrangements between the parents. Indeed it is expected that the position established by *Riley v Riley* [1986] 2 FLR 429 that shared care and control *cannot* be granted, will be reversed. In that case, the Court of Appeal commented that a divorce court order approving an arrangement by which a child was to spend alternate weeks with each of her parents, should never have been made in the first place, even though the arrangement had been working well for three years prior to the original order. However, as the Law Commission observed (Law Com No 172, para 4.12), it is not the intention of these provisions that children *have* to spend their time more or less equally between their parents. The argument that a child needs a single settled home will be a strong one in most cases.

**3.13** A more common 'sharing' arrangement is one where the child will spend more time with one parent than the other. The Law Commission instanced the arrangements where the child spends term-time with one parent and holidays with the other, or two out of the three holidays from boarding school with one and the third with the other parent. In the Commission's view, these arrangements are more realistically reflected by an order that the child live with both parents. What about the even more common arrangement whereby the child spends weekdays with one parent and the weekends with the other? It will be equally open to the court to sanction this arrangement by granting each parent a residence order rather than by making a residence order in favour of one parent and a contact order in favour of the other. Indeed, if it can be shown that the former will thereby reduce hostility between the parents, it would seem to be in the interests of the child's welfare to make that type of order.

**3.14** Where a residence order is made in favour of two parents who do not live together, then, under s 11(4), the order may specify the periods during which the child is to live in the different households concerned. Such directions may be general rather than specific and in some cases may not be needed at all. Since a residence order only settles the arrangements as to where the child is to live, any other conditions that are needed must be specified separately by the court acting under the powers vested by s 11(7).

**3.15** Under s 11(5), where as a result of a residence order 'the child lives, or is to live, with one of two parents who each have parental responsibility for him', that order will cease to have effect if the parents live together for a continuous period of more than six months. Although such a provision is not novel, it is to be noted that, unlike the previous law (see Law Com No 172, para 4.13), orders will lapse in *all* such cases.

### *Contact orders*

**3.16** As the Law Commission pointed out (Law Com No 172, para 4.17), where the child is to spend much more time with one parent than the other, the more realistic order will be for the child to live with one and to 'visit' the other parent. In its final version, however, s 8(1) defined contact order as allowing the child to visit or 'stay with' the person named in the order.[1] Orders may be made for contact with *any* person. They are not restricted to contact with parents, nor is there anything to prevent the court from making more than one contact order in respect of a child.

1 This amendment was made at the Committee stage of the House of Lords: see HL Deb, 19 December 1988, Vol 502, cols 1217-1218.

**3.17** Although contact orders are similar to access orders, which they replace, the form of the order is different in that rather than provide for the parent to have access to the child,[1] it provides for the child to visit or stay with the person named in the order. It should also be appreciated that while the child is with the parent, that parent may exercise all his parental responsibility subject to not doing anything incompatible with a court order (see the discussion at para 2.12). Contact orders are also wider than access orders in that in cases where physical contact is not thought appropriate, the court may nevertheless order that the child should have some other form of contact, for example, by telephone or letter.

1 Although it is understood that in some parts of the country it is the practice of the courts to order that the child should have access to the parent etc.

**3.18** As with access orders, it is contemplated that the usual order will be for reasonable contact (encompassing both physical and other forms of contact). Where appropriate, however, the court, by virtue of s 11(7), may attach conditions. As with residence orders, contact orders automatically cease if the parents subsequently live in the same household for a continuous period of more than six months: s 11(6).

### *Prohibited Steps and Specific Issues Orders*

**3.19** These two new orders, which are modelled on the wardship jurisdiction, are intended to broaden all the court's powers when dealing with children. The idea of the prohibited steps order is to enable the court to place a *specific* embargo upon the exercise of parental responsibility. The Law Commission (Law Com No 172, para 4.20) instanced the embargo that the child should not be removed from the United Kingdom, which they said might be useful in cases where no residence order has been made so that the automatic restrictions against removal under s 13 (discussed at para 3.46) do not operate. A prohibited steps order may be made against anyone. It could, for example, be used to restrain persons from associating with the child. An important proviso, however, is that the only 'steps' that may be prohibited are those 'which could be taken by the parent in meeting his parental responsibility'. The court may not, therefore, make a prohibited steps order restricting publicity about the child, since that has nothing to do with parental responsibility.

**3.20** Specific issue orders are intended (see Law Com No 172, para 4.18) to enable either parent or, with leave, other persons, to bring a specific question relating to the child before the court. Orders may be made either in conjunction with residence or contact order or on their own. Disputes as to the child's education or medical treatment are examples of the type of issues that could be resolved with such an order. The Law Commission contemplated that the court could, in resolving the dispute, attach a condition to a residence or contact order that certain decisions may not be taken without informing the other parent or giving the other the opportunity to object.

**3.21** Neither a prohibited steps nor a specific issue order should be made (a) with a view to achieving a result which could be achieved by a residence or contact order, or (b) in any way which is denied to the High Court (by s 100(2)) in the exercise of its inherent jurisdiction: s 9(5). The former embargo is to guard against the slight risk, particularly in uncontested cases, that the orders might be used to achieve the same practical results as residence or contact orders but without the same legal effects (see Law Com No 172, para 4.19 and also para 3.39 below). The latter embargo has a general limiting effect but, inter alia, scotches the possible argument that such orders could be used in some circumstances to challenge local authority decisions.

### *When the court has power to make section 8 orders*

**3.22** Under s 10(1), the court is empowered to make a section 8 order in 'any family proceedings in which a question arises with respect to the welfare of any child'.

#### 'FAMILY PROCEEDINGS'

**3.23** The term 'family proceedings' is defined by s 8(3) as meaning any proceedings 'under the inherent jurisdiction of the High Court in relation to children' or under the enactments listed in s 8(4). With regard to the former, which principally, though not exclusively,[1] refers to wardship proceedings, it is expressly added that the term does not refer to applications for leave by local authorities to invoke the High Court's inherent jurisdiction.

1 See Lord Mackay LC's observation (at (1989) 139 NLJ 505 at 507) that 'wardship is only one use of the High Court's inherent *parens patriae* jurisdiction . . . it is open to the High Court to make orders under its inherent jurisdiction in respect of children otherwise than through wardship'. See further para 10.4.

**3.24** The enactments listed in s 8(4) are as follows: Parts I, II and IV of the 1989 Act; the Matrimonial Causes Act 1973, the Domestic Violence and Matrimonial Proceedings Act 1976; the Adoption Act 1976; the Domestic Proceedings and Magistrates' Courts Act 1978; the Matrimonial Homes Act 1983, ss 1 and 9 and the Matrimonial and Family Proceedings Act 1984, Part III.

**3.25** The introduction of the term 'family proceedings' is intended to rationalise, harmonise and, in some cases, expand the court's powers. As the Law Commission pointed out (Law Com No 172, para 4.34), under the former law the court's powers to make orders over children were 'strangely limited'. For example, whereas domestic courts could, under the 1978 Act, make orders about the children regardless of whether the application for financial relief was successful, divorce courts could make such orders in financial provision cases only if an order for financial relief was actually made. In other proceedings, namely, variation of maintenance agreements or financial relief after a foreign divorce, the court had no powers over the children at all. Similarly, the court had no powers over the children in domestic violence cases, yet, as the Commission pointed out, the needs of the children are frequently an important factor in determining the relief sought. Indeed, it seemed to the Commission 'highly artificial' for the court to be able to exclude one person from the matrimonial home, at least in part for the children's sake, yet not to be able to order that the child should live with the parent remaining in the home.

**3.26** Under the 1989 Act, all such restrictions have been removed and in each of the proceedings mentioned in para 3.24 above, the court may make s 8 orders. However, as the Law Commission pointed out, unlike divorce or financial applications in the magistrates' court, in domestic violence proceedings the court is not obliged to consider the children, and indeed in many cases the matter will be too urgent for it to do so.

**3.27** The Commission also saw the need for expanding the court's powers in certain proceedings involving children,[1] on the broad principle that by extending the range of options the court will be able best to meet the children's needs. This is particularly so with regard to adoption, the implications of which are discussed in Chapter 11. A similar strategy lies behind the inclusion of proceedings under Part IV of the 1989 Act (under which applications may be made for care and supervision orders — see Chapter 6). Although the power to make s 8 orders is restricted where the child is in local authority care (see para 3.39 below), it is nevertheless open to the court to grant a residence order instead of a care order or to make a s 8 order upon an application to discharge a care or supervision order.

1 It will be noted, for example, that the courts may, in applications under s 4 or 5 of the 1989 Act, make s 8 orders.

**3.28** The inclusion of wardship proceedings under 'family proceedings' furthers the policy of reducing the need to resort to the jurisdiction, the strategy being (see Law Com No 172, para 4.35) that if the outcome is likely to be the same as in other proceedings there will be less incentive to use it. Furthermore, where an application is made the expectation is that, where appropriate, the court will make a s 8 order and discharge the wardship.

'ANY CHILD'

**3.29** Section 10(1) empowers a court in family proceedings to make a s 8 order in respect of *any* child (ie, a person under the age of eighteen: s 105(1)). In other words, the court's powers are not limited to 'children of the family' nor to the biological children of the parties. On the other hand, the power is restricted in the case of children who have reached the age of sixteen (see para 3.32 below).

### *Section 8 orders may be made upon application or by the court acting on its own motion*

**3.30** Section 8 orders may be made either upon application or upon the court's own motion: s 10(1)(a) and (b). The Law Commission commented (Law Com No 172, para 4.38) that it nevertheless expected that orders would normally be made upon application.

### *Restrictions on making s 8 orders*

**3.31** The general enjoinder under s 1(5) (discussed at paras 1.20 et seq) that an order should not be made unless the court considers it is better for the child than making no order is expected to lead, particularly in the divorce context, to fewer orders being made. It may well be that in absence of dispute no orders will be made unless they can be specifically justified.

### *Children aged sixteen or over*

**3.32** Implementing the Law Commission's recommendation (see above para 3.25) and effectively confirming the former practice with respect to custody orders, s 9(7) and (6) respectively provide that a s 8 order (other than a variation or discharge) should not be made in respect of a child who has attained the age of sixteen, nor should any order be expressed to have effect beyond a child's sixteenth birthday, unless the court is satisfied that the 'circumstances of the case are exceptional'. Orders not expressed to extend beyond the child's sixteenth birthday automatically end when he reaches sixteen: s 91(10). Where a direction is made, the order will cease to have effect when the child reaches the age of eighteen: s 91(11).

### *Children in local authority care*

**3.33** Section 9(1) prevents the court from making a s 8 order, other than a residence order, with respect to a child who is in the care (ie, by virtue of a care order: see s 105(1)) of a local authority.

**3.34** The above embargo is based on the well-established principle, endorsed both by the *Review of Child Care Law* (DHSS, 1985, paras 8.2-8.10) and the Law Commission (Law Com No 172, para 4.52), that in general the court's 'private law' powers should not be used to interfere with local authorities' exercise of their statutory parental responsibilities. The unavailablity of s 8 contact orders in respect of a child in care does not, however, mean that there is no statutory redress. On the contrary, s 34 (discussed at paras 6.56 et seq) provides a separate regime for making contact orders for a child in care.

**3.35** One effect of the embargo is that local authorities themselves will not be able to seek a prohibited steps or specific issue order in relation to a child in their care (*aliter* where the child is being accommodated — see para 3.39 below). If therefore they require the court's assistance (although the general expectation is that they will make their own decisions) in that regard they must instead seek the court's leave to invoke the High Court's inherent jurisdiction (discussed in Chapter 10).

**3.36** Residence orders are different from the other s 8 orders, since their whole purpose is to determine where the child is to live. Hence, such orders may be made even though the child is in care. Obviously, if the court thinks the child ought to be living with someone else (who will also have parental responsibility), it is inconsistent with the continuation of the care order. The Law Commission (Law Com No 172, para 4.53) thought that in principle, just as care orders may supersede whatever previous arrangements for the child's upbringing have been made, so should residence orders. Accordingly, s 91(1) provides that the making of a residence order discharges any existing care order.

**3.37** Applications for residence orders in respect of a child in care operate, therefore, as applications to discharge care orders. For some, ie, those with parental responsibility, this remedy will be an alternative to seeking a discharge under s 39 (see paras 6.46 et seq), although (as the Law Commission pointed out) where the parents are living together a residence order would not be necessary, but would be useful in cases where they are divorced or separated. For others, for example, fathers who do not have parental responsibility and relatives, an application for a residence order is the only means open to them to seek a discharge of a care order. This new scheme under the 1989 Act reverses *M v H* [1988] 3 All ER 5, in which the House of Lords held that while there is jurisdiction for unmarried fathers to apply for custody under the Guardianship of Minors Act 1971 they should nevertheless decline to exercise it.

**3.38** The embargo under s 9(1) applies only where the child is subject to a care order. It does not apply where the child is being 'accommodated' (see post para 5.20) by a local authority. Furthermore, even if the child is initially the subject of a care order, once a residence order has been made, since that discharges the care order, *any* other s 8 order can *then* be made — at least in favour of an individual (the position with regard to local authorities is more complicated see: para 3.39 below).

### *Restrictions in the case of local authorities*

**3.39** Section 9(2) prevents local authorities from applying for and the courts from granting them a residence or contact order. The embargo is intended to prevent local authorities from obtaining parental responsibility other than by a care order under s 31. If local authorities wish to restrict contact to a child accommodated by them, they must seek a care order and have the matter dealt with in those proceedings.[1] On the other, hand authorities may seek leave to obtain a prohibited steps or specific issue order in respect of a child accommodated by them, though this provision may not be used a disguised route to seeking a residence or contact order: s 9(5) (discussed above at para 3.21).

1 Individuals are *not* so prohibited.

## 3 Who may apply for s 8 orders?

**3.40** Section 10 (which governs both initiating and intervening in proceedings) provides a detailed plan as to who may apply for a s 8 order.

The scheme is as follows:

(a) Parents (including unmarried fathers), guardians and those with a residence order in their favour are entitled to apply for *any* s 8 order (s 10(4)).

(b) Parties to a marriage (whether or not subsisting) in relation to whom the child is a 'child of the family';[1] persons with whom the child has lived for a period of at least three years;[2] and those having the consent: (i) of each of the persons in whose favour a residence order is in force; (ii) if the child is in local authority care under a care order, of the local authority; or (iii) in any other case, each of those who have parental responsibility for the child, are entitled to apply for a residence or contact order: s 10(5).

(c) Those not otherwise included in (a) or (b) above will nevertheless be entitled to apply for a variation or discharge of a s 8 order if, either the order in question was made on his application or, in the case of a contact order, he is named in that order: s 10(6). Furthermore, s 10(7) reserves the power of rules of court to prescribe additional categories of people who may make applications without prior court leave.

(d) Any one else may apply for leave of the court to apply for *any* s 8 order: s 10(1)(a)(ii).

(e) *But*, in the case of any person 'who is, or was at any time during the last six months, a local authority foster parent' then, unless he is a relative of the child, or the child has been living with him for at least three years[3] preceding the application, he must have the consent of the local authority to apply for the court's leave: s 9(3).

1 'Child of the family' is defined by s 105(1) as a child of both the married parties and 'any other child, not being a child who is placed with those parties as foster parents by a local authority or voluntary organisation, who has been treated by both of those parties as a child of their family'.

2 This period need not be continuous but must not have begun more than five years before, or ended more than three months before the making of the application: s 10(10).

3 This period need not be continuous but must not have begun more than five years before, or ended more than three months before the making of the application: s 9(4).

**3.41** Provisions (a)-(d), but not (e) (see para 3.79 post) implement the Law Commission's recommendations (Law Com No 172, paras 8.54-8.58), and bring much needed rationalisation, particularly with regard to third parties (discussed at para 3.73). The child himself can seek leave to apply for a s 8 order, although under s 10(8) the court may grant leave only if it is satisfied that the child has sufficient understanding to make the proposed application.

## 4 Drawing up timetables

**3.42** Pursuant to the general principle that delay is likely to be prejudicial to a child's welfare (s 1(2), discussed ante, para 1.12), the court is directed by s 10(1) that in any proceedings in which any question of making a s 8 order, or any other question with respect to such an order, arises, and in the light of any rules made under s 10(2), to draw up a timetable with a view to determining that question without delay and to give directions for adhering to that timetable. As the Law Commission commented (Law Com No 172, para 4.57), placing the onus upon the courts rather than leaving such matters to the parties approach is something of a novelty within the English legal system. Hence, the need to make legislative provision for it. In the absence of rules further details obviously cannot be given, although as Lord Mackay LC pointed out during the passage of the Bill, in drawing up a timetable the courts will obviously have to be realistic and will have to take account of all the circumstances; otherwise it will not be adhered to.[1]

1 HL Deb, 6 February 1989, Vol 503, col 1347. Note also the attempt by Lord Elwyn Jones at HL Deb, 20 December 1988, Vol 502, col 1253, to add a clause stating that the court had power to commit for contempt anyone not adhering to the timetable. This was rejected, inter alia, because the courts have that power anyway and there was no desire to give prominence to powers of punishment.

## 5 Effect of residence orders

### *Parental responsibility*

**3.43** As has already been discussed (see ante paras 2.8-2.9), residence orders confer parental responsibility on those who would not otherwise have that responsibility: s 12.

### *Change of child's surname*

**3.44** Under s 13(1)(a), it is an automatic condition of *all*[1] residence orders[2] that no person may cause the child to be known by a new surname without either the written consent of every person who has parental responsibility or leave of the court. This implements the Law Commission's recommendation, following their comment (Law Com No 172, para 4.14) that a child's surname is an important symbol of his identity and relationship with his parents and that while it may be in his interests for it to be changed, it was not a matter on which a parent with whom the child lives should be able to take unilateral action.

1 Formerly, this rule was only expressly written into divorce court custody orders, under r 92(8) of the Matrimonial Causes Rules 1977.
2 For a similar rule where the child is subject to a care order, see s 33(7) and (8), discussed post at para 6.25.

**3.45** Although it is not a statutory requirement to have the child's consent to the change of his surname,[1] as Lord Mackay LC pointed out during the debates on the Bill,[2] if the child (if he has sufficient understanding: see s 10(8)) objects to the change of name, he may seek a prohibited steps or specific issue order to prevent the change.

1 Two attempts were made to amend s 13 so as to require the child's consent: see HL Deb, 20 December 1988, Vol 502, col 1262, per Lord Meston and HL Deb, 6 February 1989, Vol 503, col 1347 per Lord Elwyn Jones.
2 HL Deb, 20 December 1988, Vol 502, col 1264.

### *Removal of child from the jurisdiction*

**3.46** Under s 13(1)(b), where a residence order is in force, no person may remove the child from the United Kingdom without either the written consent of every person who has parental responsibility or leave of the court. However, s 13(1)(b) does not prevent a person in whose favour a residence order has been made from removing the child for a period of less than one month: s 13(2). Under s 13(3), the court may grant leave either generally or for specified purposes.

**3.47** Although divorce court custody orders have long since contained automatic restrictions against unilateral removal from the jurisdiction (under r 94(2) of the Matrimonial Causes Rules 1977), this is the first time that an automatic embargo operates against *all* orders. Unlike the former law, however, the automatic embargo prevents removal from the United Kingdom (ie, England and Wales, Scotland and Northern Ireland) rather than from England and Wales. The freedom to remove a child for a temporary period of less than one month is new.[1]

1 To accommodate this change, the Child Abduction Act 1984 has been amended (by Sch 12, para 37) so such temporary removals no longer constitute an offence.

**3.48** These provisions implement the Law Commission's recommendations (Law Com No 172, para 4.15) and are intended to provide simple and clear rules which can be remembered and observed. Permitting unrestricted temporary removals is intended to allow a person in whose favour a residence order has been made to make arrangements for holidays without having to seek the permission of the non 'residential' parent(s), and without even having to give notice. Furthermore, there appears to be no limit on the number of temporary removals permitted. Concern about both these points was expressed during the debates on the Bill,[1] but no amendments were agreed to. However, as Lord Mackay LC pointed out,[2] parents who are concerned about this issue, are entitled to go to court to seek a prohibited steps order to curtail the right or to ask for a restriction of the rights to be added to the order, pursuant to the courts' powers to add conditions under s 11(7).

1 Notably by Lord Meston — see HL Deb, 20 December 1988, Vol 502, col 1267 and 6 February 1989, Vol 503, col 1356 — and by Lord Elwyn Jones at ibid, col 1353.
2 HL Deb, 6 February 1989, Vol 503, col 1354.

## 6 Enforcing residence orders

**3.49** Section 14 provides that where a residence order is in force and 'any other person (including one in whose favour the order is also in force) is in breach of the arrangements settled by that order', the person named in the order may, as soon as a copy of the residence order has been served on the other person, enforce the order under the Magistrates' Courts Act 1980, s 63(3).

**3.50** The effect of this provision is to give a person with the benefit of a residence order (but not, it seems, any other s 8 order) a means of enforcing it in the magistrates' court. Breaches of any s 8 orders made in the higher courts can be treated as contempt of court.

## 7 Family assistance orders

**3.51** Section 16 empowers the court to make a 'family assistance order'. Such an order will require either a probation officer to be made available or the local authority to make an officer of the authority available to 'advise, assist and (where appropriate) befriend any person named in the order': s 16(1) (but note s 16(7), see para 3.56). Those who may be named in the order are: any parent (which includes the unmarried father) or guardian, any person with whom the child is living or in whose favour a contact order is in force[1] with respect to the child, and the child himself: s 16(2).

1 Note that the contact order must still be in force. In the original Bill it would have been possible to have named a person in whose favour a contact order *had been made* but this was amended to the present form: see HL Deb, 16 March 1989, Vol 505, col 346.

**3.52** Although in one sense s 16 replaces the former power to make supervision orders in private law proceedings,[1] a family assistance order is better regarded as a new type of order. According to the Law Commission (Law Com No 172, para 5.12), on whose recommendation s 16 is based, the drawback of the former law was that it failed to reflect the different purposes for which supervision orders were made, namely, those in favour of local authorities where the main concern was child protection, and those in favour of a welfare or probation officer which were aimed at giving short-term help to the family. Family assistance orders simply have the latter function. The Commission considered (Law Com No 172, para 5.19) that the purpose of such orders 'would be to formalise the involvement of a welfare officer for a short period in helping the family to overcome the problems and conflicts associated with their separation or divorce'. Section 16, however, has a wider ambit than originally envisaged since orders can be made in proceedings under Part IV of the 1989 Act.[2] In that context it may be thought that such orders are more likely to made where a care or supervision order has been refused or where a care order has been discharged, that is, in cases where the local authority is not or no longer formally involved with the family. Although an assistance order might be useful in cases where the local authority decides to place the child 'at home on trial' (ie, where the child is still subject to a care order) it seems unlikely that an application may be made *solely* for that purpose (see para 3.55).

1 Eg in matrimonial proceedings under the Matrimonial Causes Act 1973, s 44(1) — see *Clarke Hall & Morrison on Children* (10th ed) at **C** [29]; in proceedings under the Guardianship Acts 1971 and 1973 — see s 2(2)(a) of the 1973 Act discussed in *Clarke Hall & Morrison* at **C** [43]; in proceedings under the Domestic Proceedings and Magistrates' Courts Act 1978 — see s 9, discussed in *Clarke Hall & Morrison* at **C** [55]; in wardship proceedings under the Family Law Reform Act 1969 s 7(4) (discussed in *Clarke Hall & Morrison* at **C** [100]) and in adoption proceeedings under the Adoption Act 1976, s 26 (discussed in *Clarke Hall & Morrison* at **D** [44]). For the power to make supervision orders under the Children Act 1989, see s 35 discussed at paras 6.28 et seq.

2 Ie, they can be made in *any* 'family proceedings', which includes Part IV of the 1989 Act: s 8(4)(a), discussed at paras 3.25-3.26.

**3.53** Family assistance orders may be made whether or not any other order has been made: s 16(1). On the other hand, before such orders may be made, the court must be satisfied that 'the circumstances of the case are exceptional': s 16(3)(a). Precisely what is meant by 'exceptional circumstances' in this context will have to be determined by the courts. In general, however, it seems clear that the order should not be made as a matter of routine. On the other hand, given the nature of the new power, it is submitted that it should not be so restricted as the former power to make supervision orders. For this reason it is submitted that decisions under the former powers to make supervision orders in matrimonial or other private law proceedings do not provide much guidance as to when family assistance orders should be made.[1]

1 A possible exception is *Re C (Minors) (Wardship: Jurisdiction)* [1978] Fam 105, where the court was concerned to provide an experienced person to whom the custodial parties could turn to for advice.

**3.54** As well as having to be satisfied that the circumstances are exceptional, the court must also be satisfied that the consent of every person named in the order, other than the child, has been obtained: s 16(3)(b). There is, therefore, no formal requirement that the child himself consents, nor is there a statutory requirement to ascertain the child's own wishes and feelings about such an order since the enjoinder to do so under s 1(4) does not apply to making s 16 orders (see paras 1.14 et seq). Nevertheless, there is nothing to prevent the court from discovering the child's views and, indeed, in the light of *Gillick v West Norfolk and Wisbech Area Health Authority* [1986] AC 112, the court may take the view that the child's own wishes (at least where the child is mature enough to make his own decisions) ought to be taken into account.

**3.55** Unlike s 8 orders, there is no statutory right for parties to apply for a family assistance order. Instead the power may be exercised only by the court acting upon its own motion. Of course, there is nothing to stop parties requesting the court to make such an order during the course of family proceedings. However, the lack of the right to apply for such an order would seem to prevent parties from applying to court *solely* for a family assistance order, for example, after a residence, contact or care order has been made.

**3.56** A family assistance order may not be made requiring a local authority to make one of its officers available unless either the authority agrees or the child concerned lives or will live in its area: s 16(7).

Where an order requires a probation officer to be made available, that officer must be selected in accordance with arrangements made by the probation committee for the area in which the child lives or will live: s 16(8). If the selected probation officer is unable to carry out his duties, another probation officer must be selected in the same manner: s 16(9).

**3.57** Despite the above provisions, s 16 gives little guidance as to which officer should be appointed. In 'private law proceedings' (ie, those not involving a local authority), the most appropriate appointee, as the Law Commission pointed out (Law Com No 172, para 5.19), will usually be the welfare officer who had compiled the welfare report for the court. In the context of care proceedings, the obvious candidate for appointment is the social worker attached to the particular case. It is not possible to appoint a guardian ad litem (even where that person has made a report to the court) since such a person will be neither a probation officer nor an officer of the local authority and will therefore be outside the terms of s 16(1)(a) and (b). In all cases, as the Law Commission pointed out (ibid para 5.20), it is important for the court making the order to make it plain at the outset why family assistance is needed and what it is hoped it will achieve. This in turn will clarify the role that the officer is to play in any particular case.

**3.58** Under s 16(4), a family assistance order may direct the person named in the order or such of the persons so named as may be specified 'to take such steps as may be so specified with a view to enabling the officer to be kept informed of the address of any person named in the order and to be allowed to visit such person'.

**3.59** A family assistance order is intended to be only a short-term remedy. Hence, s 16(5) provides that unless a shorter period is specified the order will have effect only for six months from the day on which it is made. However, there would seem to be nothing to prevent a second order being made, for example, in an application to vary a s 8 order (see Law Com No 172, para 5.20).

**3.60** Provided a s 8 order is also in force, while a family assistance order is in force the officer is empowered to refer to the court the question of whether a s 8 order should be varied or discharged: s 16(6).

## IMPACT OF PART II AND OTHER AMENDMENTS ON THE JURISDICTIONS DEALING WITH DISPUTES BETWEEN PARENTS AND OTHER INDIVIDUALS

### 1 The statutory scheme

#### *Applications under MCA 1973 and DPMCA 1978*

**3.61** As under the former law, the divorce courts still have power to make orders relating to children in proceedings under the Matrimonial Causes Act 1973, as do the magistrates in applications for financial relief[1] under the Domestic Proceedings and Magistrates' Courts Act 1978. However, the court's powers, under each of these jurisdictions, are controlled by Part II of the 1989 Act. The 1989 Act also makes various other changes which are considered below (at paras 3.63 et seq).

1 Note that magistrates now also have jurisdiction to make s 8 orders etc upon an application for a personal safety and/or exclusion orders under ss 16-18 of the 1978 Act.

### *Free standing applications*

**3.62** The 1989 Act makes important changes to the statutory jurisdictions under which 'free-standing' applications (ie, those applications solely concerning the child and not related to other proceedings, such as divorce or maintenance) may be made. Following the repeal (see Sch 15) of the Guardianship of Minors Acts 1971 and 1973 and the Children Act 1975 (in particular, Part II, which governed custodianship), the sole *statutory* jurisdiction[1] under which free-standing applications may now be made is provided for by s 10(2) of the 1989 Act. In line with the policy throughout the 1989 Act, the High court, county court and magistrates' courts have concurrent jurisdiction to hear applications under this provision, although the Lord Chancellor is empowered under Sch 11 to specify that proceedings must be commenced in a specified class of court (see para 9.7 below). The courts' powers are controlled by Part II of the 1989 Act.

1 This statutory provision, however, is without prejudice to an individual's continued ability to invoke the court's wardship jurisdiction: see further Chapter 10.

## 2 Amendments to existing legislation

### *The Matrimonial Causes Act 1973*

THE COURT'S POWERS

**3.63** The court's powers under ss 42-44 of the 1973 Act to make custody, care and control, access, committal to care and supervision orders have been repealed (by Sch 15) and are replaced by those under Part II of the 1989 Act. Orders[1] made before implementation of the 1989 Act remain in effect but will cease to do so if a residence or care order is made subsequently: Sch 14, para 11.

1 Apart from declarations of unfitness, see para 3.69 below.

THE NEW S 41

**3.64** Apart from the change in the court's powers, the most important change is that relating to s 41 of the 1973 Act. Under the former law no decree of divorce or nullity could be made absolute until the court had declared that it was satisfied that the arrangements for the welfare of any child of the family were 'satisfactory' or 'the best that can be devised in the circumstances' or that 'it is impractical for the party or parties appearing before the court to make any such arrangements'. The original aims of this provision and the accompanying 's 41 hearing' were to ensure that divorcing parents made the best possible arrangements for their children and to identify cases of particular concern where protective measures might be necessary. The Law Commission felt (Law Com No 172, para 3.6) that the procedure was not truly successful in achieving either objective. They therefore recommended (ibid para 3.9) that the former duty be replaced with a more modest one to *consider* the arrangements proposed for the children in order to decide what order, if any, to make. This recommendation is now embodied in the new s 41(1) (as rewritten by Sch 12, para 31) under which the court must consider:

'(a) whether there are any children of the family[1] to whom this section applies; and

(b) where there are any such children, whether (in the light of the arrangements which have been, or are proposed to be, made for their upbringing and welfare) it should exercise any of its powers under the Children Act 1989 with respect to any of them'.

**1** For the amended definition of 'child of the family' under s 52(1), see para 3.68 below.

**3.65** The Law Commission recognised that there would still be exceptional circumstances, for example, where the parties are refusing to consider how best to meet their parental responsibilities in the changed circumstances, where the court should delay the granting of a decree absolute. Reflecting this view, the new s 41(2) provides:

> 'Where, in any case to which this section applies, it appears to the court that —
> (a) the circumstances of the case require it, or are likely to require it, to exercise any of its powers under the Act of 1989 with respect to any such child;
> (b) it is not in a position to exercise that power or (as the case may be) those powers without giving further consideration to the case; *and* [emphasis added]
> (c) there are exceptional circumstances which make it desirable in the interests of the child that the court should give a direction under this section,
>
> it may direct that the decree of divorce or nullity is not to be made absolute, or that the decree of judicial separation is not to be granted, until the court orders otherwise'.

**3.66** In line with the court's powers to make s 8 orders, the duty under s 41 applies only to those children under the age of sixteen, save where the court expressly directs otherwise: s 41(3) as amended.

**3.67** The overall effect of this amendment to the 1973 Act is to abolish 'satisfaction hearings' in most cases. The Law Commission anticipated, however, that accompanying this change would be procedural reform along the lines recommended by the 'Booth Committee' (*Report of the Matrimonial Causes Procedure Committee* 1985 paras 4.33-4.35), namely, that the respondent would be encouraged to join with the petitioner's statement or file his own and would be required to file a statement if he wished to dispute residence. It was also anticipated that the inquiries would be undertaken by a registrar at an earlier stage than the s 41 hearing before the judge. Whether these recommendations will also be acted upon remains to be seen.

OTHER AMENDMENTS

**3.68** The definition of 'child of the family' under s 52(1) of the 1973 Act (which is relevant to the exercise of powers under s 41) has been amended by Sch 12, para 33 in line with that under s 105(1) of the 1989 Act (see ante para 3.40, n1).

**3.69** Following the Law Commission's recommendation (Law Com No 172, paras 7.2-7.4) the power to declare a party to a marriage unfit to have custody under s 42(3) of the 1973 Act is repealed: Sch 12, para 32. Furthermore, any such declaration made under the 1973 Act ceases to have effect, upon the coming into force of Parts I and II of the 1989 Act: Sch 14, para 3.

**3.70** The provisions under s 10(1) (see para 3.40 ante) governing who can intervene in family proceedings replace those formerly provided for under the Matrimonial Causes Rules 1977, r 92(3).

### *The Domestic Proceedings and Magistrates' Courts Act 1978*

**3.71** Like the divorce courts, magistrates' powers under the 1978 Act to make orders are now governed by Part II of the 1989 Act. Section 8 of the 1978 Act has been amended (by Sch 13, para 36) to read:

> 'Where an application is made by a party to a marriage for an order under section 2, 6 or 7 of this Act, then, if there is a child of the family[1] who is under the age of eighteen, the court shall not dismiss or make a final order on the application until it has decided whether to exercise any of its powers under the Children Act 1989 with respect to the child'.

The powers to make to make supervision and committal to care orders under ss 9 and 10 of the 1978 Act have been repealed by Sch 15. Orders made before implementation of the 1989 Act remain in effect but will cease to do so if a residence or care order is made subsequently: Sch 14, para 11.

1 The definition of 'child of the family' under s 88(1) of the 1978 Act has been slightly amended by Sch 13, para 43 to bring it into line with that under s 105(1) of the 1989 Act (see above para 3.40, n1).

**3.72** The provisions under s 10(1) (see ante para 3.40) governing who can intervene in family proceedings mean that for the first time third parties have a right to intervene in proceedings under the 1978 Act.

## 3 The position of non-parents when seeking section 8 orders

**3.73** As the Law Commission recommended (Law Com No 172, paras 4.40 et seq), the 1989 Act replaces the former confusing array of statutory provisions, including custodianship, with a simple and rational system under which non-parents can apply for s 8 orders. The basic scheme is that any person with whom the child has lived for three years[1] is *entitled* to apply for a residence or contact order (s 10(5)(b)) either by intervening in existing family proceedings (s 10(1)(a)) or by bringing his own proceedings (s 10(2)(a)). Any other non-parent (who does not have the requisite consents as set out by s 10(5)(c) — see ante para 3.40 — or who otherwise does not have a residence order in his favour) may seek the court's leave to apply for a s 8 order either in existing family proceedings (s 10(1)(a)(ii)) or upon the applicant's own application (s 10(2)(b)).

1 This period need not be continuous but must not have begun more than five years before, or ended more than three months before the making of the application: s 10(10).

**3.74** The overall result of the scheme is that any person[1] with a genuine interest in a child's welfare may make an application to the court about his upbringing. In this respect the position is now similar to that obtaining in wardship. However, unlike the latter jurisdiction, specific guidance is given to the court when considering whether to grant leave. This is provided by s 10(9), which directs the court to consider:

'(a) the nature of the proposed application for the s 8 order;
(b) the applicant's connection with the child;
(c) any risk there might be of that proposed application disrupting the child's life to such an extent that he would be harmed by it; and
(d) where the child is being looked after by a local authority —
 (i) the authority's plans for the child's future; and
 (ii) the wishes and feelings of the child's parents'.

**1** Including any body, authority or organisation professionally concerned with children: see Law Com No 172, para 4.41, although note the restrictions on local authorities adverted to ante at para 3.33.

**3.75** The requirement of leave is intended, as the Law Commission said (Law Com No 172, para 4.41), to act as a filter to protect the child and his family against unwarranted interference in their comfort and security, while ensuring that the child's interests are properly respected.[1] It is anticipated that the more tenuous the applicant's connection with the child, the harder it will be to obtain leave.

**1** As Lord Mackay LC eloquently put it (see HL Deb, 20 December 1988, Vol 502, col 1227): 'There is clearly a danger both in limiting and expanding the categories of persons who may apply for orders in respect of children. On the one hand, a too wide and uncontrolled gateway can expose children and families to the stress and harm of unwarranted interference and the harassment of actual or threatened proceedings. If too narrow or over-controlled the gateway may prevent applications which would benefit or safeguard a child from harm'.

**3.76** This above mentioned scheme applies to all 'family proceedings' (defined by s 8(3) and (4): see ante para 3.23). This means that for the first time non-parents may intervene, either as of right or upon leave, to seek s 8 orders in adoption proceedings, care or supervision proceedings,[1] domestic violence proceedings, proceedings for financial relief under the Domestic Proceedings and Magistrates' Courts Act 1978 or under Part III of the Matrimonial and Family Proceedings Act 1984, as well as proceedings under Part I of the 1989 Act. In many of these cases it is also the first time that the court may make orders in favour of third parties.

**1** Note that certain grandparents formerly had a right to seek leave to become a party in care or supervision proceeedings under the Children and Young Persons Act 1969: see para 3.77 below.

## 4 Impact of changes upon grandparents and other relatives

**3.77** As a result of the above mentioned changes, grandparents (unless the child has lived with them for three years) are no longer *entitled* to apply for a contact order as they formerly could to seek access in certain circumstances under the Domestic Proceedings and Magistrates' Courts Act 1978 and the Guardianship of Minors Act 1971.

**3.78** The position of grandparents attracted considerable debate and a number of attempts were made to give them an entitlement to apply for a residence order or a contact order, or, most extremely, a right to access. The Government response to each of these attempts was that the legislation struck the right balance. In many cases, for example, where the parents are divorcing, it is anticipated that grandparents will readily obtain leave. As the Law Commission put it (Law Com No 172, para 4.41), the requirement of leave will 'scarcely be a hurdle at all to close relatives such as grandparents . . . who wish to care for or visit the child'. On the other hand, as Lord Mackay LC commented:[1]

> '[t]here is often a close bond . . . between a grandparent and a grandchild . . . and in such cases leave, if needed, will no doubt be granted. Indeed, in many cases it will be a formality; but we would be naive if we did not accept that not all interest shown by a grandparent in a child's life is necessarily benign, even if well intentioned. Arguably, at least until we have some experience of wider rights of application, the law should provide some protection to children and their parents against unwarranted applications by grandparents when they occur'.

However, as the Lord Chancellor also pointed out, there is power under s 10(7) to add to the category of persons who may apply for orders as of right. If, therefore, it became apparent that the leave requirement was an unnecessary impediment in the case of grandparents, it could be dropped.

1 HL Deb 6 February 1989 Vol 503 col 1342.

## 5 Impact of changes upon local authority foster parents

**3.79** As we have seen (ante at para 3.40), under s 9(3) unless the applicant is a relative or someone with whom the child has had his home for three years then, if he is or was at any time during the previous six months a local authority foster parent, he may not apply for leave of the court to apply for a s 8 order in respect of that child without the consent of the local authority.

**3.80** The purpose of this restriction[1] is to prevent premature applications unduly interfering with local authority plans for the child and so undermine their efforts to bring stability to the child's life. It is also intended to guard against the risk of deterring parents from voluntarily using the fostering services provided by local authorities which, it is argued, could easily happen if the restrictions were relaxed. The same arguments were used to justify the not dissimilar time period in relation to custodianship applications.

1 See HL Deb, 19 December 1988, Vol 502, cols 1221-1222, per Lord Mackay LC.

**3.81** Without wishing to gainsay the importance of these objectives, many might agree with Lord Meston's observation[1] that having to obtain local authority consent and leave of the court is one hurdle too many. In any event the time restriction lies at odds with that in adoption where foster parents can obtain an order after providing a home for the child for twelve months.[2]

**1** HL Deb, 19 December 1988, Vol 502, col 1221.

**2** In this respect it seems a pity that Lord Meston's move (see HL Deb, 19 December 1988, Vol 502, col 1222) to have the three-year period in s 9(3) reduced to twelve months, did not attract support.

Chapter 4

# Financial provision for children

## INTRODUCTION

**4.1** The power to make financial provision for the benefit of children is contained in s 15 and Sch 1. Implementing the recommendations of the Law Commission (Law Com No 172, paras 4.59-4.79) both to simplify and rationalise the law, Sch 1 provides a single set of provisions to replace those under the Family Law Reform Act 1987, the Children Act 1975 and the Guardianship of Minors Acts 1971 and 1973. Schedule 1, however, is without prejudice to the court's powers to grant financial relief in matrimonial proceedings under the Matrimonial Causes Act 1973 or the Domestic Proceedings and Magistrates' Courts Act 1978.[1] In proceedings under the 1973 and 1978 Acts, unlike those under the 1989 Act, the court has power to make financial orders for adults as well as for the children. Consideration was given to replacing all provisions dealing with financial provision for children with a single set of provisions but the Law Commission felt (ibid, para 4.59) that the task would be too complicated and, in any event, where the court has power to make orders for the benefit of an adult it is more convenient for all the orders to be made in the same proceedings. Accordingly, the powers under the 1973 and 1978 Acts have been left intact.

1 The power to make financial provision for wards of court under s 6 of the Family Law Reform Act 1969 has also been left in place.

**4.2** The general scheme is that where proceedings concern the child alone, individuals seeking financial provision for children from either or both parents must (save where an application is made in respect of wards of court) seek redress under the 1989 Act. If the issue of financial provision for children of the family arises in matrimonial proceedings, the court is free, as before, to make orders under the powers vested in it by the 1973 or 1978 Acts.[1]

1 It is to be noted that, pursuant to s 10(2) (discussed ante at para 3.62) third parties may seek leave to apply for a s 8 order in matrimonial proceedings, and, if successful, may then seek financial relief in those proceedings.

## ORDERS FOR FINANCIAL RELIEF AGAINST PARENTS

### 1 When orders may be made

**4.3** The court may make financial provision for children upon the application of parents (including unmarried fathers), guardians[1] and any person in whose favour a residence order is in force:[2] Sch 1, para 1. In addition, the court is entitled to make an order upon making, varying or discharging a residence order even though no application for financial relief has been made: Sch 1, para 6. Furthermore, in such cases, if a financial relief order has previously been made under any enactment other than the 1989 Act,[3] the court is empowered to revoke or vary it, or to substitute the applicant for the person to whom sums are otherwise payable: Sch 1, para 8.

1 As the Law Commission pointed out (Law Com No 172, para 4.61), as a result of s 5 (discussed above at paras 2.34 et seq) guardians will rarely take office during the lifetime of the surviving spouse and so will rarely be able to apply for a Sch 1 order.
2 This right replaces the former right of the custodian (ie, the person in whose favour a custodianship order had been made) to apply for financial relief under the Children Act 1975. However, this new provision will mean that for the first time such persons may apply for capital provision: see Law Com, ibid, para 4.62.
3 Eg the Domestic Proceedings and Magistrates' Courts Act 1978, the Matrimonial Causes Act 1973 or, in wardship proceedings, under the Family Law Reform Act 1969: see Law Com, ibid, paras 4.68-4.69.

## 2 The court's powers

**4.4** The High Court, county court and magistrates' courts all have jurisdiction to make Sch 1 orders but, as under the Guardianship of Minors Act 1971, magistrates' powers are more restricted than those of the two higher courts.

**4.5** All courts may order the making of unsecured periodical payments either to the applicant for the benefit of the child or to the child himself, for such term as may be specified in the order: Sch 1, para 1(1)(a), (b) and (2)(a) (but see para 4.15 below). Similarly, they can order lump-sum payments (Sch 1, para 1(1)(a), (b) and (2)(c)), although in the case of magistrates' orders there is prescribed maximum limit of £1000 'or such larger amount as the Secretary of State shall fix': Sch 1, para 5(2). Lump-sum orders may provide for payment to be made by instalments: Sch 1, para 5(5).

**4.6** The High Court and county court may additionally order the making of secured periodical payments, settlements of property and property transfers: Sch 1, paras 1(1)(a) and respectively (2)(b), (d) and (e). Where any of these latter orders are made the court may direct that the matter be referred to one of the court's conveyancing counsel to settle a proper instrument to be executed by all necessary parties: Sch 1, para 13. Orders for periodical payments or lump sums may be made, notwithstanding that the child is living outside England and Wales, provided it is sought against a parent living in England and Wales: Sch 1, para 14.

**4.7** All orders may be made either in favour of the applicant for the benefit of the child or to the child himself.[1] However, in the light of the Finance Act 1988, there are no longer any fiscal advantages in making payments direct to the child, although there may be in making payments to the payer's spouse in favour of the child, provided that spouse abstains from remarriage.

1 An unsuccessful attempt was made by Lord Meston (see HL Deb, 20 December 1988, Vol 502, cols 1269-70) to empower the courts to order payment to be made 'to such other person as the court may direct for the benefit of the child'.

**4.8** There is power to make interim orders. Under Sch 1, para 9(1), the court may order either or both parents to make such periodical payments as the court thinks fit, and to give any other direction. No order may take effect earlier than the date of application and shall cease to have effect either upon the final disposal of the application or, if earlier, upon the date specified by the court: Sch 1, para 9(2) and (3). These simple provisions replace the more complex ones under the Guardianship Act 1973. There is, for example, no longer a prohibition (as there was under the Guardianship Act 1973, s 5E) against making a second interim periodical payments order.

## 3 Against whom may orders be made?

**4.9** Orders may be made against either or both parents of the child. 'Parents' includes the unmarried father[1] and also 'any party to a marriage (whether or not subsisting) in relation to whom the child is a 'child of the family'.[2]

1 By reason of s 1(1) of the Family Law Reform Act 1987, s 1(1). See also Sch 1, para 16(2).
2 Sch 1, para 16(2). See also para 4.13 below. 'Child of the family' is defined by s 105(1).

**4.10** With regard to unmarried fathers, these provisions are a virtual re-enactment of those under the Guardianship of Minors Act 1971, as amended by the Family Law Reform Act 1987, which in turn replaced affiliation proceedings. On the other hand, the power to order spouses of a 'child of the family' to make financial provision is new and implements the recommendation of the Law Commission (Law Com No 172, para 4.63). As the Commission pointed out, such persons could already be ordered to make payments in proceedings under the Matrimonial Causes Act 1973, the Domestic Proceedings and Magistrates' Courts Act 1978 or the Children Act 1975, and there seemed no logical reason not to make them similarly liable where proceedings have been brought under the 1989 Act. Although this theoretically means that applications may be made against step-parents, the Commission envisaged that applications will more likely be made *by* step-parents. As was noted (at p 39, n 172), the criteria for making an order against a person who is not the biological parent of the child includes the liability of any other person to maintain the child (see Sch 1, para 4(2), discussed at para 4.13 below), whereas the criteria for making orders against a parent do not. No orders may be made against a guardian. This is line with the general policy of not making such persons liable to make financial provision or property transfers in the same way as a parent (see Law Com, ibid, para 2.25).

## 4 Guidelines on making orders for financial relief

**4.11** In deciding whether to exercise its powers and, if so, in what manner the court, is directed by Sch 1, para 4(1) to have regard to all the circumstances including:

'(a) the income, earning capacity, property and other financial resources which [any parent, the applicant and any other person in whose favour the court proposes to make the order][1] has or is likely to have in the foreseeable future;
(b) the financial needs, obligations and responsibilities which [any parent, the applicant and any other person in whose favour the court proposes to make the order][1] has or is likely to have in the foreseeable future;
(c) the financial needs of the child;
(d) the income, earning capacity (if any), property and other financial resources of the child;
(e) any physical or mental disability of the child;
(f) the manner in which the child was being, or was expected to be, educated or trained.'

1 The subsection actually refers to each person mentioned in para 4(3) but the reference should clearly be to para 4(4).

**4.12** These guidelines mean that for the first time in this context the court is directed to have regard to the manner in which the child was being or was expected to be educated. The court is similarly directed under the Matrimonial Causes Act 1973 and the Domestic Proceedings and Magistrates' Courts Act 1978 (see respectively ss 25(3)(e) and 3(3)(e)).

**4.13** Where an order against a spouse of a 'child of the family' is contemplated, the court is directed by Sch 1, para 4(2) to have regard to:

'(a) whether that person had assumed responsibility for the maintenance of the child and, if so, the extent to which and basis on which he assumed that responsibility and the length of the period during which he met that responsibility;
(b) whether he did so knowing that the child was not his child;
(c) the liability of any other person to maintain the child.'

This is in line with the position under the Matrimonial Causes Act 1973 and the Domestic Proceedings and Magistrates' Courts Act 1978. If the court makes an order against a person who is not the father of the child, it must record in the order that the order is made on that basis: Sch 1, para 4(3).

**4.14** With regard to the making of lump-sum orders, Sch 1, para 5 states that, inter alia, they may be made to enable the applicant to meet any liabilities or expenses incurred in connection with the birth of the child or in maintaining the child or those reasonably incurred before the making of the order.

## 5 Duration of orders

**4.15** A periodical payments order (whether secured or unsecured) may not begin earlier than the date of the making of the application (Sch 1, para 3(1)), nor may it in the first instance extend beyond the child's seventeenth birthday (although the court may prescribe a shorter period) unless the court thinks it right to specify a later date: ibid, para 3(1)(a). In the latter event, the order may not extend beyond the child's eighteenth birthday unless it appears to the court that the child is or would be (if an order were made) receiving instruction at an educational establishment or undergoing training for a trade, profession or vocation, whether or not while in gainful employment, or there are special circumstances justifying the making of an order: ibid, para 3(1)(b) and (2). Where an order ceases at the child's sixteenth birthday, the child himself can apply to revive the order. Such revived orders may extend beyond the child's eighteenth birthday only if the criteria set out above are satisfied: ibid, para 6(5) and (6).

**4.16** All periodical payment orders cease to have effect if the child's parents live together for more than six months. Unsecured periodical payment orders cease to have effect upon the death of the payer: respectively Sch 1, para 3(4) and (3).

## 6 Variation of orders

**4.17** All periodical payment orders (whether secured or unsecured) may subsequently be varied or discharged upon the application of any person by or to whom payments are required to be made (Sch 1, para 1(4)), or by the child himself, if he has reached the age of sixteen: Sch 1, para 6(4). Secured periodical payment orders may be varied or discharged notwithstanding the death of the payer: ibid, para 6(8).[1] However, court permission will be required if the application is made more than six months after the date on which representation in regard to the estate of the deceased parent was first taken out: Sch 1, para 7(2). Where a lump sum order is payable by instalments, application may be made to vary the number or amount of the instalments or the date on which they were due: ibid, para 5(6).

1 In such cases, application may be made by the personal representatives of the deceased parent's estate: ibid, para 7(1).

**4.18** Upon a variation application, the court may temporarily suspend periodical payments orders and, subsequently, revive them: Sch 1, para 6(2). The court is also entitled, provided the child has not yet reached the age of eighteen, to make further orders for both periodical payments *and* lump sums: ibid, para 1(5)(a). It is not allowed, however, to make more than one property settlement or property transfer order against the same person in respect of the same child: Sch 1 para 1(5)(b).

## 7 Enforcement

**4.19** Any person obliged to make payments under a magistrates' court order is under an obligation to give notice of any change of address to any person specified in the order: Sch 1, para 12(1). Failure to do so is an offence: ibid, para 12(2). Magistrates' court orders for the payment of money are enforceable as magistrates' maintenance orders within the meaning of the Magistrates' Courts Act 1980, s 150(1): Sch 1, para 12(3).

## 8 The possible impact of these provisions

**4.20** Although Sch 1 tidies up the law, with a few exceptions the courts' powers to make financial orders (cf the power to make s 8 orders: see para

4.21 below) are essentially the same as before. However, the higher courts' powers to make financial orders for 'illegitimate children' and (outside the divorce context) to make capital provision for 'legitimate children', were only recently introduced by the Family Law Reform Act 1987 (implemented in April 1989). It is, therefore, too early to say what the courts' practice will be. In particular, it remains to be seen what use, if any, will be made of the power to make capital provision especially with regard to 'illegitimate children'. Although the Law Commission (Law Com No 118, para 6.6) did not envisage frequent use being made of the power to make property transfer orders,[1] it has been suggested[2] that in cases of lengthy cohabitation between the parents the courts might well accept the need to preserve the parties' home as a home for the children. Hence, even if the court might not be disposed to make an outright transfer for the child's benefit, it might be disposed to make a limited transfer at least until the child has grown up.

1 Relying upon the practice of the divorce courts to lean against making such orders, see, eg, *Chamberlain v Chamberlain* [1974] 1 All ER 33, at 38, per Scarman LJ.
2 See, eg, Bromley and Lowe's *Family Law* (7th ed) p 643.

**4.21** One potentially important change under the 1989 Act is that since an application for financial relief would appear to rank as 'family proceedings',[1] the court is empowered, under s 10(1)(b), to make any s 8 order upon its own motion. This means that, unlike under the Guardianship of Minors Act 1971 where the court had no power to make custody orders, under the 1989 Act an unmarried mother, for example, wishing to obtain financial relief from the father, cannot be sure, upon such an application, that the court might not see fit to make a s 8 order or even invite the local authority to investigate the circumstances of the case under its s 37 powers. Whether such a possibility will deter potential applicants (particularly unmarried mothers) remains to be seen.

1 'Family proceedings' are defined by s 8(4) as including applications made under Part II of the 1989 Act. Presumably, applications for financial relief are made made under s 15 (which is within Part II) with powers provided for under Sch 1.

## ORDERS FOR FINANCIAL RELIEF FOR PERSONS OVER 18

**4.22** Schedule 1, para 2 preserves the independent right, first introduced by the Family Law Reform Act 1987, of a person who has attained eighteen to apply for an order requiring either or both of his parents to make periodical and/or lump-sum payments to him. Unlike previously, applications may be made in the magistrates' court as well as the county court or the High Court. Before any order may be made, the court must be satisfied that the applicant is or will be (or would be if an order was made) receiving instruction at an educational institution or undergoing training for a trade, profession or vocation, or that there are other exceptional circumstances justifying an order: ibid, para 2(1). An order may not be made if, immediately before the applicant was sixteen, a periodical payments order (as defined by para 2(6)) was in force (ibid, para 2(3)), nor may an order be made if the applicant's parents are living together in the same household: ibid, para 2(4). In deciding what order to make, the court is to have regard to the same circumstances as it should have in the case of other applications for financial orders under the Children Act 1989: ibid, para 4 (for details see para 4.11 above). Both the child and the parent (or parents) ordered to pay may subsequently seek a variation or discharge of a periodical payments order: ibid, para 2(5). There is no power to vary a lump sum payments order save, where the sum has been ordered to be paid in instalments, to vary the number or amount or date of those instalments: ibid, para 6(6).

## ALTERATION OF MAINTENANCE AGREEMENTS

**4.23** The powers to alter maintenance agreements made between mothers and fathers (regardless of whether they are married to each other) in favour of their child(ren), first introduced by ss 15 and 16 of the Family Law Reform Act 1987, are now contained in Sch 1, paras 10 and 11.[1] As before, only written agreements making provision for the making or securing of payments or the disposition or use of any property, for the maintenance or education of the child, may be altered: ibid, para 10(1). Applications may be made by either parent, but in the case of an agreement designed to continue after the death of one of the parents, application may be made either by the surviving parent or the personal representative: ibid, para 11(1). An application may not be made, save with leave of the High Court or county court, after the end of a period of six months from the day on which representation in regard to the estate of the deceased is first taken out: ibid, para 11(3). A claim may be overtaken by proceedings under the Inheritance (Provision for Family and Dependants) Act 1975.

1 Applications to vary maintenance agreements made between spouses, including those making provision for their children, may still be made under s 35 of the Matrimonial Causes Act 1973.

**4.24** Application may be made to the High Court, county court or magistrates' court, but the latter court has power only where both parties are resident in England and Wales and at least one of them is resident in the relevant commission area: Sch 1, para 10(6). The High Court and county court have jurisdiction provided each party is either domiciled or resident in England and Wales: ibid, para 10(2). Magistrates only have the power to increase, reduce or terminate periodical payments (ie, they have no power to alter arrangements made in connection with property): ibid, para 10(6)(a) and (b).

**4.25** Under Sch 1, para 10(3) the court may exercise its powers only if it is satisfied either:

'(a) that, by reason of a change in the circumstances in the light of which any financial arrangements contained in the agreement were made (including a change foreseen by the parties when making the agreement), the agreement should be altered so as to make different financial arrangements; or

(b) that the agreement does not contain proper financial arrangements with respect to the child'.

Provided it is so satisfied, the court may vary or revoke any financial arrangements as may appear just. Any altered periodical payment provision should not in the first instance extend beyond the child's seventeenth birthday, save in the circumstances outlined in Sch 1, para 3(1) and (2) (discussed at para 4.15 above): ibid, para 10(5). As before, these powers are retrospective and apply to agreements made before or after the commencement of the provision: ibid, para 10(1).

Chapter 5

# Local authority services

## INTRODUCTION

**5.1** Part III of the 1989 Act contains provisions on the services that a local authority must or may provide for children and their families. It takes the place of s 1 and and Part III of the Child Care Act 1980 and parts of the National Assistance Act 1948 and the National Health Service Act 1977, so that services for children in need and disabled children are brought under one statute. However, there are many important differences. The new provisions are developed from the *Review of Child Care Law* published in September 1985, although the White Paper on the *Law on Child Care and Family Services* (Cm 62, 1987) subsequently introduced further important changes. The provisions are intended to enable authorities to support family life, although they may in certain circumstances charge for the service. The scheme of Part III is to impose a general duty in relation to the welfare of children, specific duties and powers in relation to day care and accommodation of children and further specific duties and powers contained in Sch 2 aimed at facilitating the general duty.

## GENERAL DUTY TO CHILDREN IN NEED

**5.2** Every authority has a general duty to safeguard and promote the welfare of children in their area who are in need and, so far as is consistent with that duty, to promote the upbringing of such children by their families by providing a range and level of services appropriate to those children's needs: s 17(1). The provisions of s 1 of the Child Care Act 1980 to diminish the need to receive children into care or bring them before the courts were thought to be unnecessarily negative (see *Review of Child Care Law*, para 5.10). The new provisions have the same underlying principle but represent a more positive approach through the general duty and several specific provisions in Sch 2. It is noteworthy that the word 'general' has been added to the duty and it appears that this is intended to avoid the effect of *Attorney-General (ex rel Tilley) v London Borough of Wandsworth* [1981] 1 All ER 1162, where the Court of Appeal held that the welfare duty applied to individual children.

**5.3** Authorities are required to facilitate the provision of Part III services by others, in particular voluntary organisations, and may make such arrangements as they see fit for others to provide such services (for example day care or fostering services).

**5.4** Services provided under Part III may include giving assistance in kind or in exceptional circumstances in cash, unconditionally or conditionally as to repayment: s 17(6) and (7). This removes the doubt which existed in s 1 of the 1980 Act as to whether loans could be given. Authorities are required to have regard to the means of the child and each of his parents, although no person is liable for repayment at any time when he is in receipt of income support or family credit: s 17(8) and (9). This would suggest that an authority must consider individual means before giving assistance or cash and must not have a blanket policy in relation to any group, and that authorities could impose a condition as to repayment when a person became able to pay. An authority may also contribute to the cost of looking after a child who is living with a person under a residence order, such as a relative or foster parent, except where that person is a parent or step-parent: Sch 1, para 15. This replaces the provision in s 34(6) of the Children Act 1975 in relation to custodians.

## Definitions in section 17

### *'In need'*

**5.5** Various terms are defined for the purpose of s 17. A child, ie, a person under eighteen (s 105(1)), is in need if he is unlikely to achieve or maintain, or to have the opportunity of achieving or maintaining, a reasonable standard of health or development without the provision for him of services by a local authority under Part III, or his health or development is likely to be significantly impaired or further impaired, without the provision for him of such services, or he is disabled: s 17(10).

### *'Disabled'*

**5.6** A child is disabled if he is blind, deaf or dumb or suffers from mental disorder of any kind or is substantially and permanently handicapped by illness, injury or congenital deformity or such other disability as may be prescribed: s 17(11). This is the same definition as in s 29(1) of the National Assistance Act 1948 in respect of adults. Since disabled children are children in need, they will be able to benefit from the same services as are available for other children in need. This implements the Government intention referred to in the White Paper in 1987 to incorporate local authority responsibilities for children in a single piece of legislation, so that the National Assistance Act 1948 and the National Health Service Act 1977 will largely cease to apply to children under eighteen. An authority has the same responsibilities for all children and should not discriminate between neglected and disabled children.

### *'Health' and 'development'*

**5.7** Health' means physical or mental health and 'development' means physical, intellectual, emotional, social or behavioural development — the same definitions as are provided in s 31(9) on care proceedings: s 17(11).

### *'Family'*

**5.8** 'Family' includes any person who has parental responsibility for the child and any other person with whom he has been living and thus is not limited to relatives: s 17(10). A local authority service may be provided for a family if provided with a view to safeguarding or promoting the child's welfare: s 17(3).

## SPECIFIC POWERS AND DUTIES

**5.9** In pursuance of the general duty, authorities have specific duties and powers which are set out in Sch 2, Part I: s 17(2). These may be amended or added to by the Secretary of State (s 17(4)), a device said to be used to ensure that the Government can keep up with local authority practice. As the provisions exist at present, they leave wide discretion to the local authority, since duties are expressed in terms of 'taking reasonable steps' or providing 'as they consider appropriate'. There are only two absolute duties: to publish information about services provided, and to open and maintain a register of disabled children.

### 1 Identification of children in need

**5.10** By Sch 2, para 1, every local authority must take reasonable steps to identify the extent to which there are children in need in their area. They are required to publish information about the services they provide under the general duty, day care services under s 18 (see para 5.19), accommodation for children under s 20 (see para 5.20) and the availability of advice and assistance for certain children under s 24 (see para 5.38). Where they consider it appropriate, they must publish information about similar services provided by others. They must also take such steps as are reasonably practicable to ensure that those who might benefit from the services receive the information relevant to them: Sch 2, para 1.

### 2 Provisions for disabled children

**5.11** Every local authority must open and maintain a register of disabled children in their area, which may be kept by means of a computer: Sch 2, para 2. It would seem that this should be a voluntary register, in the sense that a child would be registered only with the agreement of a parent. Although s 2 of the Chronically Sick and Disabled Persons Act 1970 contains provision for a register, it does not seem to have been much used. Given the concern about local authority registers, there may be some resistance to such a register, especially in relation to, for example, mentally disordered children. This concern could be exacerbated if separate registers are maintained by social services departments, health authorities and education departments. In this respect there would seem to be a good case for a common register and a clear indication of the purpose to which it would be put.

**5.12** Authorities are required to provide services for disabled children which are designed to minimise the effects of their disabilities and to give them the opportunity to lead lives that are as normal as possible: Sch 2, para 5. Assessment of needs for the purpose of the Children Act 1989 may be undertaken at the same time as an assessment under the Chronically Sick and Disabled Persons Act 1970, the Education Act 1981, the Disabled Persons (Services, Consultation and Representation) Act 1986 or any other enactment: Sch 2, para 3.

## 3 Promoting the upbringing of children by their families

**5.13** In order to discharge the general duty to promote the upbringing of children by their families, local authorities are given a number of duties in relation to what might broadly be described as family support mechanisms. They should make provision for advice, guidance, counselling and home help. This would include family aids or perhaps therapists who might advise on improving family dynamics. Occupational, social, cultural or recreational activities or assistance with holidays may be provided: Sch 2, para 8. If the child is neither living with his family (as defined by s 17(10)), nor being looked after (as defined by s 22(1)), by the local authority, such steps as are reasonably practicable should be taken to enable the child to live with his family or to promote contact between him and his family, if it is necessary, in the authority's opinion, to do so in order to safeguard or promote his welfare: Sch 2, para 10.

**5.14** Every authority shall provide such family centres as they consider appropriate in relation to children within their area: Sch 2, para 9. Although many authorities have provided a wide range of family centres, as an important part of their service to children in need, they have not previously been under any duty to make such a provision. This is the first statutory reference to 'family centre', which is described as a centre at which a child, his parents, a person with parental responsibility for him or any other person looking after him may attend for: (a) occupational, cultural, social or recreational activities or; (b) advice, guidance or counselling; and, in case (b), may be accommodated at the same time.

## 4 Prevention of abuse and neglect

**5.15** Every authority shall take reasonable steps through the provision of Part III services to prevent children in their area suffering ill-treatment or neglect. There is a duty to inform another authority if a child who the authority believe is likely to suffer harm, lives or proposes to live in the area of that authority: Sch 2, para 4. There is a connected duty to take reasonable steps, through the provision of Part III services, to reduce the need to bring proceedings for care or supervision orders, family or other proceedings which might lead to placement in care, High Court proceedings under the inherent jurisdiction or criminal proceedings in respect of children. Authorities should also encourage children not to commit criminal offences and avoid the need for placing them in secure accommodation: Sch 2, para 6. This paragraph would appear to be a general encouragement to local authorities to offer services to families which may be breaking up, so as to try to avoid the worst effects of marital disharmony.

## 5 Provision of accommodation to third party to protect children

**5.16** Where it appears to an authority that a child is suffering or is likely to suffer ill-treatment at the hands of another person living at the same premises and that other person proposes to move from those premises, the authority may assist that other person to obtain alternative accommodation, including assistance in kind: Sch 2, para 5. The provisions in s 17(7)-(9) on conditions as to repayment apply: Sch 2, para 5(3) (see para 5.4).

**5.17** This provision is a response to concern expressed in the Cleveland Report[1] that children, who were allegedly sexually abused, were removed from the family home, when it might have been in their interests for the alleged abuser to have left, if he could have been provided with alternative accommodation. It is something of a compromise. It is intended to allow local authorities to assist those who are willing to leave voluntarily but it stops short of giving the court the power to order removal of a person from a child's household.

1 *Report of the Enquiry into Child Abuse in Cleveland 1987* (Cm 412, 1988).

## 6 Duty to consider racial groups

**5.18** In making any arrangements either for the provision of day care under s 18 or designed to encourage persons to act as local authority foster parents under s 23(3), the authority shall have regard to the different racial groups to which children in need in their area belong: Sch 2, para 11. This provision was introduced late in the passage of the Bill through Parliament, shortly after the decision in *Re P (a Minor)* (1989) *Times* 24 August. The case exposed the difficulties arising where black children, placed with white foster parents because of the shortage of same-race foster parents, were subsequently moved to same-race adopters. The provision gives weight to the importance of early attachment to appropriate parenting figures.

## 7 Day care

**5.19** Every local authority is required to provide such day care as is appropriate for children in need within their area who are under five and not yet attending school: s 18(1).[1] Day care is defined as any form of care or supervised activity provided for children during the day, whether or not on a regular basis: s 18(4). The authority may provide day care for such children even though they are not in need: s 18(2). They may also provide facilities including training, advice, guidance and counselling for those caring for children in day care or who accompany children in day care. An authority is required to provide for children in need who are attending school, such care or supervised activities, ie, supervised by a responsible person, as is appropriate outside school hours or during school holidays and may make such provision for children who are not in need: s 18(5) and (6). Additionally, authorities are required to review in accordance with s 19 their provision under s18 and the provision of child minding services and private day care facilities in their area for children under the age of eight.[2]

1 Note the requirement to have regard to the need for different racial groups in the provision of day care: Sch 2, para 11, discussed at para 5.18 in relation to the provision of foster parents.
2 See also the duties under Part X of the Act, discussed in Chapter 15.

## ACCOMMODATING CHILDREN

### 1 Introduction

**5.20** The provisions for accommodation of children reflect one of the most important changes of philosophy in the Act. The concept of voluntary care under the Child Care Act 1980 is abolished and effectively replaced with the concept of accommodation. It is intended that this should be provided as a service which the parents of all children who satisfy the conditions may use or decline or terminate as they wish. The child is not in care, although the authority has certain duties in respect of the child. There is no provision corresponding to the assumption of parental rights under s 3 of the 1980 Act, but the authority may seek a care order from the court under s 31, if appropriate, as the only way in which a child can be in care.

### 2 Duty to accommodate

**5.21** Local authorities must provide accommodation for a child in need who requires it as a result of there being no person with parental responsibility for him, or because he is lost or abandoned, or because the person who has been caring for him is prevented (whether or not permanently and for whatever reason) from providing suitable accommodation or care: s 20(1). This duty replaces s 2 of the Child Care Act 1980 but, with the addition of the words 'for whatever reason', the new provision clarifies that accommodation may be provided because of the disability of the child as well as that of the parent. Otherwise the circumstances in which the duty to accommodate arises are similar to those under the old provision. Accommodation becomes one of the range of services which a local authority has a responsibility to provide.

**5.22** The 1989 Act does not follow the recommendations on accommodation of the *Review of Child Care Law*, which proposed a distinction between short-term respite care and longer-term shared care. The Government's view in the White Paper on the *Law on Child Care and Family Services* was that such a distinction would be unhelpful (Cm 62, para 26). Paragraph 21 indicates the philosophy underlying the new provisions:

> '. . . . a service by the local authority to enable a child who is not under a care order to be cared for away from home should be seen in a wider context and as part of the range of services a local authority can offer to parents and families in need of help with the care of their children. Such a service should, in appropriate circumstances, be seen as a positive response to the needs of families and not as a mark of

failure either on the part of the family or those professionals and others working to support them. An essential characteristic of this service should be its voluntary character, that is it should be based clearly on continuing parental agreement and operate as far as possible on a basis of partnership and co-operation between the local authority and parents.'

## 3 Criteria for accommodating children

**5.23** Whether the criteria for accommodating children should be the same as they were previously for reception into care is debatable. If there is no person with parental responsibility, it is to be hoped that accommodation would only be a short-term solution. The authority cannot obtain parental responsibility without a care order but, for a young child, someone should be exercising parental responsibility. Thus the authority should try to find a guardian or person who would seek a residence order for the child.

**5.24** Clearly, if the child is temporarily lost, he needs to be looked after, and his parent will resume care as soon as he is found. 'Abandoned' is a more problematic concept. It was not defined in previous child-care legislation, but has been held to mean 'leaving the child to its fate'.[1] It seems unlikely that such a child should in the future be accommodated for more than the shortest period, in view of the expected partnership for such an arrangement and because such a case would clearly come within the new grounds for care proceedings (see para 6.4).

1 See discussion in *Clarke Hall and Morrison* (10th ed) at **A** [137] and [156].

**5.25** Where a person is prevented from providing a child with suitable accommodation or care, whether a partnership arrangement or care proceedings is more appropriate must depend on the circumstances. If the child is suffering significant harm, the authority will want to consider carefully whether the welfare of the child requires a care order rather than an agreement for accommodation. The local authority discretion, however, clearly remains wide.

**5.26** Local authorities have a duty to accommodate a child in need in their area who has reached the age of sixteen and whose welfare the authority consider is likely to be seriously prejudiced if they do not provide accommodation. The authority also has a discretion to provide accommodation for any child in their area (not necessarily one in need) if they consider that to do so will safeguard and promote the child's welfare, and may accommodate a person between 16 and 21-years-old in a community home which takes children over sixteen, if they consider that to do so would safeguard and promote the child's welfare. With the increasing number of homeless young persons and the reluctance of housing authorities to provide accommodation for itinerant young people, it remains to be seen whether these provisions will encourage or force authorities to reach agreement between housing and social services departments, so that destitute sixteen and seventeen-year-olds are provided with accommodation.

**5.27** Authorities must provide for the reception and accommodation of children removed or kept away from home under Part V of the Act (see Chapter 7): s 21. The duty to accommodate also arises where:

(a) a child has been removed into police protection and the authority is requested to provide accommodation under s 46(3)(f) (see para 7.39);
(b) an arrested juvenile has been kept in police detention and arrangements are made for him to be accommodated under s 38(6) of the Police and Criminal Evidence Act 1984, as amended by Sch 13, para 53;
(c) a child is neither released on bail nor certified by the court to be of unruly character, and the court remands the child to local authority accommodation under s 23(1) of the Children and Young Persons Act 1969, as substituted by Sch 12, para 26;
(d) a young offender is the subject of a supervision order imposing a residence requirement under s 12AA of the 1969 Act, as inserted by Sch 12, para 23 (see para 6.33);
(e) a child is in the care of a local authority: s 23(1).

## 4 Limits on providing accommodation

**5.28** The provision of accommodation for a child is (subject to para 5.27) a voluntary arrangement with the parent. Further, the authority must, as far as is reasonably practicable and consistent with the child's welfare, ascertain the child's wishes regarding the provision of accommodation and give due consideration to them having regard to his age and understanding: s 20(6).

**5.29** In view of the voluntary nature of the service, the authority may not provide accommodation if any person with parental responsibility for the child, who is willing and able to provide or arrange accommodation, objects to the authority so doing: s 20(7). Furthermore, any person who has parental responsibility may remove the child at any time: s 20(8). These provisions do not apply where a child of sixteen or over agrees to being provided with accommodation. The provisions mean that if one parent places the child in accommodation the other parent can remove him. This is limited insofar as, if a person with a residence order, or a person who has care of the child pursuant to an order under the High Court's inherent jurisdiction — or all of them if there are more than one (s 20(10)) — agrees to the child being accommodated, another person with parental responsibility may not object or remove the child. Orders made under pre-1989 Act legislation also protect the person in whose favour they are made by virtue of Sch 14, para 8(4).

**5.30** Given the encouragement to make no order for the child, this would appear to leave some children vulnerable to the whims of parents, who might seek to exercise their rights of removal to play out a dispute with the other parent. Local authorities will have to ensure that they involve all those with parental responsibility in the initial negotiations and written agreements on the provision of accommodation, and consider carefully whether accommodation is in the child's interests, given the nature of the agreement which may be reached. It may be necessary to suggest to some parents that they seek a residence order, even though the child is being accommodated, to ensure that the other parent does not arbitrarily remove the child. Although s 9(5) does not allow the court to make a specific issue or prohibited steps order requiring an authority to provide accommodation against the wishes of a parent, it would appear to be possible to make such an order preventing removal from accommodation by one parent against the wishes of the other. It might, however, be more satisfactory to make a residence order under s 8 in such circumstances, with a direction pursuant to s 11(7) that the child reside with a particular person.

## 5 Restricting removal from accommodation

**5.31** There is no requirement, as was contained in s 13(2) of the Child Care Act 1980, that the parent has to give notice of intention to remove the child from accommodation after a specified period. This issue was hotly debated at various stages of the Bill's passage through Parliament.[1] There was cross-party support for a short period of notice: 'it allows the child to prepare himself for his return home and protects the parents from the consequences of any rash decision or behaviour on their part'.[2] The Government's view was that a notice period 'would blur the distinction between compulsory and voluntary'.[3] It was determined that nothing would undermine the view of accommodation of children as a service to families.

1 See, eg, HC Deb, 18 May 1989, Standing Committee B, cols 137.154.
2 Ibid at col 142, per R Sims.
3 Ibid at col 149, per D Mellor.

## 6 Planning for accommodated children

**5.32** Substantial numbers of children are currently in voluntary care. They will be treated as accommodated on implementation of the Act by virtue of Sch 14, para 20. One intention of the Act is that, where appropriate, the kind of children previously in voluntary care should be accommodated and that the kind previously the subject of care proceedings should also be considered for accommodation. These arrangements should be by agreement with parents and, where it is in the interests of the child, may operate on a long-term basis. For this purpose there will be a requirement to enter into written agreements (see para 5.39), which will state the services which the parents can expect to be provided. In the majority of cases where authorities are dealing with responsible parents, these provisions, although time-consuming, should not be difficult to implement.

**5.33** During the 1980s there has been a move towards obtaining compulsory orders as an initial response to poor parenting of the child, rather than seeking to work with parents, partly because of the difficulties of obtaining care orders in relation to children who were in voluntary care. Fundamental to the new philosophy, therefore, is the way in which the provisions will operate in relation to children who are initially accommodated, but whose parents become unwilling to make plans for their long-term future, are inconsistent in their attitude towards them, or seek to undermine their placement or to remove them without notice or proper planning. (See paras 6.13 et seq for further discussion of this problem.)

The 1980s has also seen a move towards fostering children in care, as it has been thought that it is better, especially for young children, to continue to experience family life, or to have a beneficial experience, if there are shortcomings in their own home. The parents of accommodated children will have the right to be consulted about where their child should live (s 22(4), discussed at para 5.43) and will have to be counselled carefully on the benefits of family life, if they are to accept it as a service.

**5.34** Authorities must develop co-operative strategies with parents to resolve these problems. The Act provides for what can be broadly described as 'doing what is reasonable' or working with parents by agreement. If no agreement can be reached, the authority will have to consider seeking compulsory powers under an emergency protection order or care proceedings (discussed in Chapters 6 and 7). The authority will have to consider the duties in s 22 set out at para 5.42.

### *Doing what is reasonable*

**5.35** Section 3(5) provides that a person who does not have parental responsibility but has care of a child may (subject to other provisions of the Act) do what is reasonable in all the circumstances of the case for the purpose of safeguarding or promoting the child's welfare. 'A person' would include a local authority or a foster parent. The primary purpose of the provision is to enable a carer to make routine decisions, such as medical consents, in the interests of the child which are not likely to be controversial. If there was a choice or it was known that the parent might object, then an application for a specific issue order under s 8 should be considered.

**5.36** In debate in the House of Commons the Minister said that the provision would allow the authority to refuse to hand over the child to an inebriated parent'.[1] Those working with children may have to take a robust view of s 3(5) and retain the care of the child for a time, but this is not without difficulty.

**1** HC Deb, 18 May 1989, Standing Committee B, col 148, per D Mellor.

**5.37** Section 3(5) is expressed to be subject to the provisions of the Act and s 20(8) states that a person with parental responsibility may remove 'at any time'. Foster parents doing what they regard as safeguarding the child's welfare, especially where they have developed a close and caring relationship with the child, will not necessarily be seen to be doing what is reasonable in the eyes of the parent, or even objectively. Local authorities will have to distinguish carefully and advise foster parents on the action to be taken, depending on whether they are dealing with sensible parents with whom reasonable arrangements have been made, or with those who are unpredictable and inconsistent and run the risk of proceedings being taken in respect of their children.

**5.38** A further difficulty arises in relation to what a local authority may regard as reasonable. Theoretically, it would be possible to argue that detention of the child indefinitely was reasonable to safeguard his welfare. It is submitted that detention for a period longer than overnight, or as long as it takes to interview the relevant parties, would be contrary to the philosophy of the Act. Any longer period should be authorised by a court.

### *Agreements with parents*

**5.39** It is central to the philosophy of the Act that an authority should seek to reach agreement with the parent or other person with parental responsibility on such matters as the purpose of accommodating the child and the period for which it might be provided, schooling and contact with the child. Negotiating such agreements will require considerable skill and time: 'The Government want a memorandum evidencing agreements in every case. We should prefer such a memorandum to be drawn up before a child was received, where possible'.[1] It is doubtful whether such an agreement could be of more than persuasive effect. It would not be binding on the parent who may still exercise his right of removal under s 20, but its breach might provide evidence for an application for an emergency protection order or care proceedings. Clearly, if the authority were seeking to foster an accommodated child, this would be part of the agreement, and if a parent refused to agree to fostering or expressed a wish for a child to be moved, the authority would have to consider whether to offer accommodation or whether the care criteria could apply. An authority will wish to ensure that they can abide by any agreement reached, since they will obviously be exposed to criticism if they do not.

1 HC Deb, 18 May 1989, Standing Committee B, Col 151, per D Mellor.

## Accommodation and housing provision

### *Homeless families*

**5.40** It is not intended that the accommodation provisions should be used to look after children where their parents are homeless. Although there may be circumstances where that would be necessary in an emergency, the Government's view is that the principal responsibility for accommodating homeless families lies with the housing authority under the Housing Acts.[1]

1 See HC Deb, 18 May 1989, Standing Committee B, col 138.

### *Homeless adolescents*

**5.41** Provisions for the accommodation of 16 to 21 year olds are less clear. Local authorities may accommodate them in a community home: s 20(5). They are required to provide accommodation for sixteen and seventeen year olds in need if they consider their welfare is likely to be seriously prejudiced if children are not provided with accommodation: s 20(3). There is a discretion in relation to 18 to 21 year olds: s 20(4). The introduction of these duties and powers are of major importance in promoting the welfare of adolescents but several problems remain. An increasing number of young persons are suffering from the low level of housing and social security benefits and have difficulty in obtaining accommodation. In certain parts of the country facilities available are inadequate and housing authorities are reluctant to accommodate this age group. These provisions impose a new and stricter duty on local authorities, which is assigned to the social services committee by Sch 13, para 26. While authorities may call upon the housing authority under s 27 to assist in the exercise of this function, they may also need to use community homes as temporary accommodation.

## LOCAL AUTHORITY DUTIES FOR CHILDREN 'LOOKED AFTER' BY THEM

**5.42** The phrase 'looked after' is important. It refers to children who are in the care of the local authority or who are provided with accommodation, (defined as accommodation for a continuous period of more than 24 hours (s 22(2)) pursuant to any of the functions of a social services committee. In relation to such a child, the authority has a number of primary duties:

(a) to safeguard and promote his welfare and to make such use of services available for children cared for by their own parents as appears to the authority reasonable in the case of a particular child: s 22(3);
(b) to ascertain as far as practicable the wishes and feelings of the child, his parents, any other person who has parental responsibility and any other person the authority consider to be relevant, before making any decision with respect to a child they look after or propose to look after: s 22(4);
(c) to give due consideration, having regard to his age and understanding, to such wishes and feelings of the child as the authority have been able to ascertain and to his religious persuasion, racial origin and cultural and linguistic background and to such wishes and feelings of any person as mentioned above: s 22(5);
(d) to advise, assist and befriend him with a view to promoting his welfare when he ceases to be looked after by the authority: s 24(1);
(e) to provide advice and assistance to qualifying persons between 16 and 21 years old in accordance with s 24.

Paragraphs (a), (b) and (c) replace the duty owed to a child in care in s 18 of the Child Care Act 1980. They differ in that there is no specific requirement to promote and safeguard the child's welfare 'throughout his childhood'. However, 'welfare' must require consideration of the child's short- and long-term needs. The authority may exercise its powers in a way which is inconsistent with these duties for the purpose of protecting members of the public from serious injury and the Secretary of State may give directions to an authority in this respect: s 22(6)-(8).

**5.43** Where an authority is 'looking after' a child, they must provide him with accommodation while he is in their care and must maintain him: s 23(1). In carrying out this duty the authority may place the child with a family, a relative of his or any other suitable person[1], maintain him in a home[2] or make such other arrangements as seem appropriate to the authority: s 23(2). If it is proposed to place him in an establishment providing education for children, the authority must as far as reasonably practicable consult the education authority, before doing so: s 28. In relation to a child statemented under the Education Act 1981, the authority is that which maintains the statement. In relation to a disabled child, accommodation should not be unsuitable to his particular needs (s 23(8)), an odd double negative, which appears to limit the extent to which accommodation has to be suitable.

1 Known as a local authority foster parent, unless the child falls within s 21(4): see paras 5.46-5.50.
2 See Chapter 13 for discussion about children's homes.

## 1 Duty in respect of rehabilitation

**5.44** Unless to do so would not be reasonably practicable or consistent with the child's welfare, s 23(6) requires the authority to make arrangements to enable him to live with what may broadly be described as his family, that is a person falling within s 23(4) or a relative, friend or other person connected with him, but if the child is in care he may be placed with a person falling within s 23(4) only under strictly controlled conditions.[1] As far as is reasonably practicable and consistent with the welfare of the child, the authority must secure that the accommodation is near his home and that siblings are accommodated together: s 23(7).

1 See para 5.48.

**5.45** The principle that authorities should consider the family for rehabilitation was not provided for specifically in the original Bill. The change, it has been suggested, is the result of 'sustained pressure on the Government . . . throughout the Bill's progress through Parliament',[1] although in fact the inclusion of s 23(6) is clearly in line with the philosophy of the Act. It is a most important principle and it is surprising that it is necessary to analyse subsections and Schedules to elucidate it. It can be argued that s 17(1)(b), which imposes the general duty to promote the upbringing of children by their families, is sufficient emphasis on rehabilitation, but this does not apply specifically to children looked after by an authority. Previous provisions under s 2(3) of the 1980 Act and s 27 of the 1969 Act have required the authority respectively to try to secure the child's return home or to consider the discharge of a care order. Section 23(6) is unequivocal that a child should be returned to live with his family unless that is not practicable or consistent with his welfare. The duties in Sch 2, paras 8 and 10 (discussed at para 5.13) may be used to further the duty in s 23(6). The *Code of Practice on Access to Children in Care* (HMSO, 1983) would also still appear to be relevant here.

1 See M Ryan (solicitor, Family Rights Group) 'The Children Bill 1988 — the philosophy and the reality' *Child Care Law Journal* Vol 1, No 4, p 104.

## 2 Placement of children 'looked after'

**5.46** Numerous provisions regulate the placement of a child whom an authority are looking after, dependent upon whether or not the child is in care, and with whom he is placed.

## *Placement with own family*

**5.47** If a child is accommodated, he may simply be returned to his own family, and the authority then has no any further legal responsibility (other than the general duty under s 17). As under the voluntary provisions of the Child Care Act 1980, if the child is placed with a relative (as defined by s 105(1)) or friend, he could be discharged from accommodation at the request of the person with parental responsibility (subject to s 20(9), discussed at para 5.30)) or be placed with a relative under regulations made under s 23(2) and Sch 2, para 11 based on the Boarding-Out of Children (Foster Placement) Regulations 1988.[1] If he is in care, he could be placed with a relative under those regulations or be placed under regulations discussed in the next paragraph.

1 See *Clarke Hall and Morrison* (10th ed) **A** [1160].

**5.48** Section 23(4) and (5) also provide that a child subject to a care order may only be placed with a parent, another person who has parental responsibility for him or a person who had a residence order in respect of the child immediately before the care order was made, in accordance with regulations made under s 23(5) and Sch 2, para 13, which are based on the Accommodation of Children (Charge and Control) Regulations 1988.[1] These may include requirements as to who must be consulted and notified about the decision, the supervision and medical examination of the child and the circumstances in which he may be removed. The 1988 Regulations differ from the s 23 provision in that the latter apply to a narrower range of people, not including relatives unless they have parental responsibility. Other relatives would come within the boarding-out provisions, where it should be noted the effect of the current regulations are limited in emergencies[2].

1 See *Clarke Hall and Morrison* (10th ed) **A** [1132].
2 Ibid, **A** [1168].

**5.49** The provisions under s 23 significantly inhibit local authority discretion to place a child subject to a care order at home. They came about as a result of provisions in the Children and Young Persons (Amendment) Act 1986 following the Report into the death of Jasmine Beckford.[1] The Regulations have proved to operate quite restrictively and may require amendment when they are introduced for the purpose of the 1989 Act.[2]

1 1985, commissioned by the London Borough of Brent and the Brent Area Health Authority.
2 See *R v Newham London Borough Council* (1989) *Times* December 12.

## *Local authority foster parents*

**5.50** A local authority foster parent is any person with whom a child whom an authority are looking after is placed under s 21(2)(a). Regulations referred to in para 5.47 will apply and the authority may make arrangements as to payment and other terms. There is no specific reference to regulating the position on trans-racial foster placements, but since the authority are required (by Sch 2, para 11, discussed at para 5.18) to have regard to the different racial groups when encouraging persons to act as local authority foster parents, a detailed provision may be expected in the regulations.

### *Secure accommodation*

**5.51** If an authority wish to use secure accommodation, they must obtain the authority of the court (no longer only the juvenile court) under s 25, which updates s 21A of the Child Care Act 1980 with one important amendment. Formerly, the court had to be satisfied that, in addition to having a history or likelihood of absconding, it was likely that the child's physical, mental or moral welfare would be at risk. The latter part of the new test is that the child is likely to suffer significant harm (as defined by s 31(9): see para 6.11). Alternatively, it must be shown that if the child is kept in any other description of accommodation, he is likely to injure himself or other persons.

A court order under s 25 only authorises the child to be kept in secure accommodation, although s 25(8) preserves the power of the court to give directions. If the child is accommodated (and not in care), s 25(9) specifically preserves the right of the parent under s 20(8) to remove him.

Regulations may be made under s 25(2), which will replace the Secure Accommodation (No 2) Regulations 1983. Although the regulations may provide that the application may be made only by a local authority, the Lord Chancellor has indicated that the opportunity will be taken to include within their scope children who are accommodated by a health authority, local education authority, or in a residential home, nursing home or mental nursing home.[1]

**1** HL Deb, 8 November 1989, Vol 512, col 851.

## CONTROLS ON THE LOCAL AUTHORITY

## 1 Case reviews and complaints procedures

**5.52** Regulations will be made under s 26 to require the review of the case of each child being looked after by a local authority. They will provide in detail for the manner, content and frequency of reviews, and who is to be consulted beforehand and notified of the result afterwards. An authority must establish and publicise their procedure for considering any representations, including complaints, made by the following:

(a) a child whom they are looking after or who is not being looked after but is in need. This is intended to ensure that children are consulted on decisions taken about them, but will also establish the system of complaints procedures for children which some authorities already have for children they are looking after. It could also assist a child who believes he should be accommodated where the authority are refusing to offer the service;
(b) a parent or other person with parental responsibility;
(c) any local authority foster parent; or
(d) such other person as the authority consider has a sufficient interest in the child's welfare to warrant representations being considered by them.

**5.53** The s 26 provision is most important. Although it is developed from the review system, it is of far wider application than the case review.

Complainants will be able to use the procedure for a wide range of issues but, given the limited opportunity for intervention by the courts,[1] it must and will be scrutinised for its effectiveness in controlling poor local authority practice. The essential elements are:

(a) It is available to a wide range of people: s 26(3). In addition to the child, as discussed above, parents or other persons with parental responsibility or other members of the family, who cannot achieve their objectives by applying for discharge of a care order or an application for contact with the child, will be able to have their complaint heard. Foster parents, who are currently excluded from right of complaint, will be able to question why a child is being moved away from them or why they are being denied an enhanced fostering allowance.
Other interested people will be able to use the procedure. While the authority may decide who it considers has a sufficient interest in the child's welfare, it would be difficult to deny that professionals in other agencies providing a service to the child would qualify.

(b) There must be an independent element: s 26(4). The procedure must ensure that at least one person who is not a member or officer of the authority takes part in the consideration of the complaint and any discussions held by the authority about the action to be taken in relation to the child in the light of the complaint.

(c) The authority must have due regard to the findings of those considering the representation and must notify the child, the person making the representation and other affected persons of their reasons for their decision and of any action taken or to be taken: s 26(7). Thus, although the decision about the child remains with the authority, if they ignore findings or fail to give any or any satisfactory reasons, they may be subject to judicial review.

(d) Regulations will be made on the procedure to be followed and as to how the authority should monitor their arrangements: s 26(5) and (6).

Both Government and local authorities should be keen to ensure that these arrangements work effectively. Otherwise, the courts will be faced with dissatisfied complainants attempting to use care and contact proceedings as an opportunity to air grievances, thus slowing the pace of those proceedings. It may also be expected that the High Court will expand the use of judicial review, if it perceives when dealing with care and contact, that authorities are not acting in the interests of children and that complaints procedures are ineffective.

1 In the Joseph Jackson Memorial Lecture, (1989) 139 NLJ 505, the Lord Chancellor said: 'We have not thought it appropriate or practicable for the responsibility for a child in the care of a public authority which is statutorily charged with looking after him to be subject to the detailed directions of another public authority, namely the courts'.

## 2 Default powers of the Secretary of State

**5.54** Section 84, which was added to the Act in Committee in the House of Commons without debate, enables the Secretary of State to declare a local authority in default, where he is satisfied that they have without reasonable cause, failed to comply with a duty under the Act. He may then give the necessary directions to the authority to ensure that they comply with the duty within a specified period. He may enforce a direction by application to the High Court for judicial review under RSC Ord 53.

The section appears to afford persons aggrieved by a local authority decision (or lack of it) scope for making a complaint to the Secretary of State. It is similar to the default power given to the Secretary of State for Social Services by s 36 of the National Assistance Act 1948 'on representations made to him or otherwise'. Furthermore, s 99(1) of the Education Act 1944 (default powers of the Secretary of State for Education and Science) permits default powers to be taken 'upon complaint by any person interested or otherwise'. These words are not in the 1989 Act, but it would appear that there is no restriction on the material, or its source, from which the Secretary of State may draw his conclusions.

## 3 Judicial review

**5.55** The complaints and default provisions are a significant improvement to the statutory procedures available to control local authority decisions in the child-care field. It remains to be seen what effect they will have on the willingness of the courts to use judicial review for this purpose. Generally, courts expect alternative remedies to be used first, although they may intervene if the statutory procedure is ineffective or inappropriate, particularly where the local authority has clearly acted in breach of their legal powers or duties. Although the courts have shown some recent willingness to develop judicial review in relation to child care, this has been for the lack of any satisfactory alternative.[1] The future of judicial review in this field may depend on whether authorities operate satisfactory complaints procedures.

1 See, eg, *R v Hertfordshire CC ex p B*; *R v Bedfordshire CC ex p C* [1987] 1 FLR 239; *R v North Yorkshire CC ex p M* [1989] FLR 82 and *R v Norfolk CC ex p M* [1989] 2 All ER 359. The circumstances of each case could lead to a complaint under the procedure in s 26 of the 1989 Act.

## 4 Inquiries and inspection

**5.56** Sections 81 and 82 give the Secretary of State powers of inspection of premises used for accommodating children and of inquiry in relation to local authorities and other organisations concerned with the welfare of children. Inquiries may be held privately: s 81(2) and (3).

## 5 Research and returns of information

**5.57** Section 83 re-enacts ss 70, 77 and 79 of the Child Care Act 1980, with amendments to enable the Secretary of State and local authorities to conduct or assist others in conducting research into their functions under the 1989 Act, the Children and Young Persons Acts 1933 and 1969, adoption and s 116 of the Mental Health Act 1983 (relating to children looked after by an authority).

## 6 Financial support from the Secretary of State

**5.58** Section 82 largely re-enacts ss 78 and 80-82 of the Child Care Act 1980. It defines 'child care training' and empowers the Secretary of State to contribute to 'approved child care training'. This means training undergone by any person with a view to, or in the course of employment for the purpose of, specified local authority or voluntary organisation functions. The Secretary of State may also, with the consent of the Treasury, make grants to local authorities for the provision of secure accommodation and to voluntary organisations for the establishment, maintenance or improvement of certain voluntary homes.

# CONTRIBUTIONS TO MAINTENANCE OF CHILDREN BEING 'LOOKED AFTER'

**5.59** Where a local authority are looking after a child they must consider whether it is reasonable to recover contributions towards the child's maintenance from a parent if the child is under sixteen, or from the child if he is over sixteen: Sch 2, para 21. No person is liable while in receipt of income support or family credit and liability does not arise during an interim care order or the period of any provision under Part V of the Act.[1]

**1** Or certain criminal provisions: see Sch 2, Part III, para 20(7).

**5.60** Contributions may be recovered only after service of a contribution notice or, if that is not agreed, on the making of a contribution order by the court. The notice may not specify a weekly sum greater than that which the authority would normally be prepared to pay if they had placed a similar child with local authority foster parents and it must be reasonably practicable for the contributor to pay, having regard to his means. A contribution order may not specify a sum greater than that in the contribution notice: Sch 2, paras 22 and 23. Whereas previously the authority was allowed to make a reasonable charge, under the 1989 Act they must consider what it is reasonably practicable for the contributor to pay, having regard to his means and he has a right to be heard on the amount to be paid.

Chapter 6

# Care and supervision

## INTRODUCTION

**6.1** This chapter considers the public law orders available to the court in relation to the care and supervision of children, including contact with the child in care. The law supersedes the civil parts of the Children and Young Persons Act 1969. The structure is based on the recommendations of the *Review of Child Care Law* (DHSS, 1985). The precise wording of the criteria for care proceedings has seen various forms in the *Review*, in the White Paper on the *Law on Child Care and Family Services* (Cm 62, 1987) and in both Houses of Parliament, and only reached its final form shortly before the Act received Royal Assent.

**6.2** Important features to remember are:

(a) A care or supervision order may only be considered in respect of a child if the criteria set out in para 6.4 are established. The criteria focus on significant harm to the child, or the likelihood of it, and replace the numerous grounds of the Children and Young Persons Act 1969 and other legislation under which a child could be committed to care. The power to make care and supervision orders under other legislation or proceedings is abolished.

(b) The principle contained in s 1 that the welfare of the child is paramount, applies to care proceedings. So also do the requirements to have regard to the principle that delay is likely to prejudice the welfare of the child, that the court must have regard to the checklist contained in s 1(3) and that the court shall not make an order unless to do so would be better for the child than making no order (see generally Chapter 1).

(c) Magistrates' courts and, for the first time, county courts and the High Court have jurisdiction to make care or supervision orders. Rules of Court will provide for proceedings to be commenced at a particular level, which in the case of care proceedings is expected to be at the magistrates' court. The court will decide which level of court should hear the application, although this decision may be subject to appeal. Rules will establish criteria for deciding the venue for a case. These are likely to include complexity and length of the case, the nature of evidence, including whether there are to be experts, the availability of court time for deciding which level of court will hear the case and geographical considerations (see generally Chapter 9).

(d) The court may not make a care or supervision order of its own motion, except on an interim basis under s 38(3) (see paras 6.34 et seq). It may direct a local authority to investigate a case and report to the court: s 37(1) (see para 7.4).

(e) An application for care or supervision may be made in any existing family proceedings, as defined by s 8(3), or as a separate application: s 31(4).

(f) An application for care or supervision may only be made by a local authority or authorised person (see below). The police or education authority may no longer apply, although an education authority may seek an education supervision order (see para 12.7).

(g) A child may enter care only by order of the court. The concept of voluntary care is ended and thus there is no question of assumption of parental rights and duties as existed under the Child Care Act 1980.

(h) The power of a court to make a care order in respect of a child who has committed an offence is abolished. Under the Children and Young Persons Act 1969 a care order could be made in criminal proceedings under s 7(7) or in care proceedings under s 1(2). It is consistent with current philosophy that a child should not enter care only because he has committed an offence. The power was limited by s 23 of the Criminal Justice Act 1982 and is abolished by s 90(2) of the 1989 Act.

(i) The court may not give directions to the local authority in relation to a child in care, save during an interim care order (see para 6.34) or because of transitional arrangements (see para 6.26).

(j) The court can attach directions to a supervision order in relation to both a child and 'a responsible person' (see para 6.28).

(k) In care proceedings the court will be able to make s 8 orders, so that, most importantly, if the court considers that a child should live with a relative, it will be able to make a residence order. It may not make any other s 8 order if the child is in the care of the authority: s 9(1) (see Chapter 3).

(l) There is a presumption that the child in care has a right of reasonable contact with a parent and other specified people: s 34. If dissatisfied with contact, they may apply to the court for contact and a wider group may seek the leave of the court to apply. Linked with this provision is the requirement that local authorities must indicate to the court their plans for contact on an application for a care order, so that the court will be able to control the child's future (see paras 6.52 et seq).

(m) The court may order the child concerned to attend such stage or stages of the proceedings as may be specified: s 95(1). Thus, it is not necessary for the child to attend court unless there is a specific purpose — a reversal of the presumption, which has existed in proceedings under the 1969 Act, that the child should attend.

## CARE PROCEEDINGS

## 1 Applicants

**6.3** Application to the court may be made only by a local authority or an authorised person, which is defined by s 31(9) as the NSPCC or any other person authorised by the Secretary of State, of which there are none as yet. Thus applications may no longer be made by the police and an education authority is limited to making an application for an education supervision order under s 36 (see para 12.7). Where an authorised person proposes to make an application, he must, if it is reasonably practicable to do so and before making the application, consult the authority where the child is ordinarily resident: s 31(6). An application by an authorised person will not be entertained by the court in respect of a child who is the subject of outstanding care proceedings or subject to a care or supervision order, including an order under the Children and Young Persons Act 1969, s 7(7)(b) or a supervision requirement under the Social Work (Scotland) Act 1968: s 31(7).

## 2 Criteria for the court

**6.4** Section 31 empowers the court to make a care order or a supervision order, in respect of a child under seventeen (or sixteen if married), only if it is satisfied that (s 31(2)):

(a) the child concerned is suffering significant harm, or is likely to suffer significant harm; and

(b) the harm or likelihood of harm is attributable to —

  (i) the care given to the child, or likely to be given to him if the order were not made, not being what it would be reasonable to expect a parent to give to him; or

  (ii) the child's being beyond parental control.

Additionally, the court must apply the principle contained in s 1, that the welfare of the child is the paramount consideration (s 1(1)), have regard to the checklist in s 1(3) and not make an order unless it considers that doing so would be better for the child than making no order at all: s 1(5) (see Chapter 1). Before making a care order, the court must also consider the arrangements which the authority have made, or propose to make, for affording any person contact with a child and invite the parties to the proceedings to comment on the arrangements: s 34(11).

## 3 Threshold criteria

**6.5** The conditions in s 31(2)(a) and (b) have been the subject of much debate over the precise wording, since proposals were made in the *Review of Child Care Law* (paras 15.12-15.27). The *Review* set out the basic elements of the criteria:

(a) that there should be harm or likely harm to the child;

(b) the criteria should reflect the care which would be reasonable for the particular child;

(c) it should be necessary to show some substantial deficit;

(d) the source of the harm should be the absence of a reasonable degree of parental care.

The White Paper on the *Law on Child Care and Family Services* (Cm 62, 1987) accepted these proposals. During the progress of the Bill through Parliament, the conditions were expressed in different ways, but the final wording reflects the recommendations of the *Review*. The difficulty of finding an agreed form of words raises concerns about the extent to which the meaning of the criteria will be argued in the courts.

**6.6** The conditions in s 31(2)(a) and (b) have come to be known as the 'threshold criteria', because they are not in themselves grounds or reasons for making a care or supervision order. As the Lord Chancellor has said:

> 'Those conditions are the minimum circumstances which the Government considers should always be found to exist before it can ever be justified for a court even to begin to contemplate whether the State should be enabled to intervene compulsorily in family life'.[1]

**1** Lord Mackay LC *Joseph Jackson Memorial Lecture* (1989) 139 NLJ 505 at 506

**6.7** Statutory criteria require precise analysis, but the President of the Family Division has expressed the view that the courts should be slow to place technical interpretations on the provisions, which might prevent courts considering whether an order is in the interests of a child.[1] However, the Lord Chancellor[2] has said:

> 'Wherever rules of law apply there will always be borderline cases where it may be difficult both as a matter of law and on the merits to say whether a case falls or indeed should fall within or without a rule. The only means of avoiding borderline cases is to avoid rules and to operate a discretion . . . once the court become involved in intervention from outside the family, and especially where State intervention is proposed, I do not believe that a broad discretion without defined minimum criteria, whatever its guiding principle, can be justified . . . Unless there is evidence that a child is being, or is likely to be, positively harmed because of a failure in the family, the State, whether in the guise of a local authority or a court, should not interfere.'

**1** Seminar on the Children Act 1989, London, 6 July 1989.
**2** *Joseph Jackson Memorial Lecture* supra.

**6.8** If only certain factors causing harm satisfy the criteria, there will be cases which fall outside them, where the child will be harmed. The question then arises as to whether the prescribed factors are sufficient. The criteria reflect the recommendation of the *Review of Child Care Law* and the White Paper that those factors must relate to the absence of a reasonable degree of parental care. However, there could be other, as yet uncontemplated, circumstances where it would be appropriate for local authorities to assume parental responsibility for children who have been or may be harmed. For the last twenty years wardship has filled the gaps in statutory provisions, but in the future that will not be available.[1]

**1** See Chapter 10.

## 4 Analysis of the criteria

### *'The child concerned is suffering or is likely to suffer'*

**6.9** The original draft of the Bill had the words 'has suffered' instead of 'is suffering'. The amendment was introduced at the Commons Committee stage on the basis that the test should be one of present, not past, harm.[1] Thus historical evidence, while it may be relevant to the future likelihood of harm, will not be sufficient to satisfy the criteria. The continuous tense anticipates an existing condition, but this would not rule out proceedings where the local authority had taken action to prevent harm continuing and the hearing took place later.[2] It may limit proceedings in respect of an isolated incident, unless there is also a likelihood of future harm.

**1** See HC Deb, 23 May 1989, Standing Committee B, col 221.
**2** *M v Westminster CC* [1985] FLR 325 has continuing relevance on this issue. It was held that the present continuous tense did not restrict the court to considering whether the conditions existed at the time of the hearing (which was unlikely since the child would have been removed from harm), but was descriptive of the category into which the child had to fall.

**6.10** The introduction of the likelihood of suffering is an important element in the criteria. Previous experience and case-law demonstrated the shortcomings of the grounds under the Children and Young Persons Act 1969, which allowed for anticipated harm only in limited circumstances and caused local authorities to resort to wardship. It also discouraged local authorities from receiving children into care on a voluntary basis because it was not possible to satisfy the grounds on the basis of what might happen if the child left care.[2] The test is sufficient even though the child has never been cared for by the parent or the harm has arisen during pregnancy as occurred in *Re D (a Minor)* [1987] AC 317.

**1** See *Clarke Hall and Morrison* (10th ed) **B** [655]
**2** See the example of *Essex CC v TLR and KBR* (1978) 9 Fam Law 15.

## *'Significant harm'*

**6.11** 'Significant' is referred to in the Oxford Dictionary as 'noteworthy, of considerable amount or effect or importance' and conveys that the harm should be sufficient to justify public intervention. Section 31(9) provides a number of definitions. 'Harm' means ill-treatment or impairment of health or development. 'Ill-treatment' includes sexual abuse, so that statutory recognition is given to the view that sexual abuse is by definition ill-treatment, although that may still leave open the question as to what sexual activity is abusive. 'Ill-treatment' also includes other forms of abuse which are not physical, so that there need not be a demonstrable physical injury or danger to health and emotional abuse would be sufficient. 'Development' is defined as physical, intellectual, emotional, social or behavioural development and 'health' as physical or mental health. This endorses the principle contained in *F v Suffolk CC* (1981) 2 FLR 208 that development extends to mental and emotional development.

**6.12** Section 31(10) provides that 'where the question of whether harm suffered by a child is significant turns on the child's health or development, his health or development shall be compared with what could reasonably be expected of a similar child'. Comparison with the health or development of a hypothetical similar child should help the court decide whether the particular child has the standard of health or development that he should have and, if not, whether the harm he is suffering is significant.

### *'Attributable to'*

**6.13** By these words the harm is linked to the care given by the parent. This raises the question of what is meant by the term 'care', especially where the child is being accommodated by the local authority and the parent wishes to remove him. If the term 'care' is limited to the day to day care given to a child by the person with whom he is living, then many cases in which local authorities might at present wish to assume parental responsibility for a child in voluntary care will not be covered. If, on the other hand, the term is capable of encompassing how the parent has been behaving towards the child while he is in local authority accommodation, then the criteria may be satisfied in some cases, although not in others.

Thus, for example, the child may be likely to suffer harm simply because he is moved from the foster parents to whom he has become attached, even though his parent is now able to look after him properly. If the reason for this is that the parent has not been visiting or keeping in touch in the way that a reasonable parent would, then under the wider interpretation of 'care' the threshold criteria would be satisfied. If, however, the parent has shown all the care and concern that a reasonable parent would show to a child living away from home for a time, then even under the wider interpretation the criteria would not be satisfied. In such cases the court may wish to consider whether it would be preferable to make a residence order in favour of the foster parents. On such an application, the threshold criteria will not have to be satisfied. Similarly, the child may be suffering in his local authority placement because of his parent's disruptive, inconsistent or uncaring behaviour and will continue to do so, even though the parent has no intention of removing him, unless the authority is able to assume parental responsibility for him. Once again, under the wider interpretation of 'care', the threshold criteria could be satisfied but not under the narrower.

It is unfortunate that the Act contains no definition of 'care', given that it tends to be used to connote actual care at present. It is to be hoped that the courts will interpret it to include emotional care, concern, love and attention, as well as purely physical care so that some of these problems may be resolved.

### *'The care given to the child, or likely to be given to him if the order were not made, not being what it would be reasonable to expect a parent to give to him'*

**6.14** This wording was introduced at Report stage in the House of Commons to replace the clause 'the standard of care given to the child, or likely to be given to the child if the order were not made, being below that which it would be reasonable to expect the parent of such a child to give to him'. The main effect lies in the replacement of the words 'the parent of such a child' by 'a parent'. The change was not debated because of shortage of time at the Report stage, but the Lord Chancellor told the House of Lords[1] that the resulting condition 'seems to centre more on the needs of the child whose case is before the court rather than on some hypothetical child and the hypothesis is transferred to the parent'. Certainly the provision has the advantage of being simpler. The test is an objective standard of what the reasonable parent would provide for the child in question, so that the court is not required to make allowances for irresponsible parents. This seems preferable to the previous option which appeared to require the court to consider what the parent in question should provide for that type of child. That raised the spectre of odious comparisons between children of different backgrounds. While the new criteria will require the child's circumstances to be put in context, they do not invite unnecessary comparisons.

1 HL Deb, 8 November 1989, Vol 512, col 756.

### *'Beyond parental control'*

**6.15** This criterion is the one relic of the old law,[1] although it is now dependent upon harm to the child. Under the old law it was possible for a parent to require a local authority to take proceedings on this ground in certain circumstances. The Government was not prepared to accept that parents should have any right to compel a local authority to take proceedings in spite of cross-bench support for such a course.[2]

1 Children and Young Persons Act 1963, s 3: *Clarke Hall and Morrison* (10th ed) **B** [561].
2 HC Deb, 23 May 1989, Standing Committee B, cols 218–222.

## 5 Application of the criteria

**6.16** Case examples are helpful in considering how the provisions will work in practice.

*Child A: a baby with brittle bones* The child is suffering significant harm, because he is getting fractures. If the parents are providing care which is reasonable, given the condition of that particular child, condition (b) is not satisfied. If they are not providing care which is reasonable for that particular child, taking into account his vulnerability, condition (b) applies whether their actions are deliberate or because of parental incompetence. Even if conditions (a) and (b) are satisfied, is it in the interests of the child for there to be an order?

*Child B: an adolescent who has been sexually abused* It is clearly harm in view of the definition of ill-treatment, but is all sexual abuse 'significant'? If it is significant, is the harm attributable to the parents' care not being reasonable? If it is attributable to the parents' care, can the position be improved by means other than an order, for example, by the abusing parent leaving the home? In any event, is it better to make an order than not make an order?

*Child C: a five-year-old where the house is filthy and the parents drink excessively* The child attends school irregularly and has frequent colds and chest infections. Is the harm significant? Is the child likely to suffer significant harm? If so, in what way is it attributable to the care given by the parents? Can the parents be helped to provide better for him? Would a short period in accommodation improve matters? In any event, what would care achieve?

*Child D: a two-year-old who has been living with foster parents for one year while accommodated by the local authority, during a period of post natal depression suffered by his mother following the birth of a second child* The mother who has just started living with a new boyfriend about whom nothing is known has requested that her child be returned to her within 24 hours. She signed an agreement when the child was first accommodated stating that she would give the authority a week's notice during the first six months and a month's notice thereafter, if she wished to remove him. She has never visited as regularly as advised, but her psychiatrist says she is now fully recovered from her depression. Is the child likely to suffer significant harm if he returns to her? How would such a test be proved? What is the relevance of the possible unknown male carer?

*Child E: a ten-year-old who has been living with foster parents for two and a half years while accommodated by the local authority* The mother has had a long-term drinking problem, which has recently been resolved. She has asked for the girl to be returned to her. The girl does not wish to return. What harm is she likely to suffer? Does the care likely to be given to her have to be consistent and throughout her childhood? Should the foster parents apply for a residence order? Will they get leave of the local authority?

## 6 Commentary

**6.17** Consideration of these cases suggests that reasonable solutions may be found for children A, B, and C through care proceedings and E through a residence order. The case of child D presents the most serious problem when considering the criteria from the child's viewpoint. A similar case was put during debate in the House of Commons Committee on an amendment that there should be added to condition (b) that the harm could be attributable to 'the removal of the child from the particular family with whom he is now living':[1] '. . . when a child is well attached to the substitute parents, a change of circumstances in the real parent's life — an improvement in health or a remarriage — might make successful parenting of subsequent children possible. In such circumstances it may be difficult to demonstrate that the natural parent's standard of care will be inadequate'. The amendment was not accepted on the basis that 'to suggest that, even when parents could care for the child satisfactorily, the child should nevertheless remain with the foster parents might run contrary to the spirit of the Bill and the important principle of trying to keep families united'.[2]

**1** HC Deb, 23 May 1989, Standing Committee B, col 223, per David Hinchcliffe.
**2** Ibid, col 224, per David Mellor.

**6.18** In spite of lobbying from a number of influential organisations, the Government has stuck to its desire to give first priority to keeping families united rather than framing provisions in terms of promoting the welfare of children. Thus, as discussed in para 6.13, there may be circumstances in which the parent can give care which is objectively reasonable, but which would still cause the child significant harm because of the breaking of the attachment with established carers. Interpretation of the word 'care' (see para 6.13) will be crucial to the operation of the criteria. In any event, there will be an onus on authorities to work actively with parents (see para 5.39) to resolve such problems, failing which they will want to consider whether the care criteria may apply. The only other provision which might allow a court to review the arrangements for the child would be for the foster parents to apply for a residence or adoption order, neither of which might be immediately desirable in the interests of the child.

**6.19** Although the framework of the Act is intended to encourage the use of the service provisions considered in Chapter 5 rather than court proceedings, where local authorities have the opportunity of obtaining a court order for the care of the child and believe that long-term work is likely to be necessary, they should think carefully before deciding to accommodate as the alternative. It may be more difficult to satisfy the minimum criteria for a care order once the occasion which led to the child being accommodated has passed. Even if the application was unsuccessful, the court would be obliged to give reasons for its decision and this would establish a yardstick for future work.

## 7 Outcome of proceedings

**6.20** The court has various options in relation to care proceedings. It may make no order[1]. Whereas a care or supervision order can only be made if the threshold criteria are satisfied, the court may make other orders whether or not the criteria are satisfied. It may decide to make a s 8 order. This would allow the court to make a residence order in favour of a relative in care proceedings. If care proceedings were taken in respect of an accommodated child, it would be possible for the court to make a residence order in favour of a foster parent. It may not make a residence order in favour of the local authority, nor make any other s 8 order if the child is in care.

1 For the position pending appeal if the court dismisses an application see para 9.20.

## 8 Duration of a care order

**6.21** A care order lasts until the child is eighteen, unless it is brought to an end by a residence order (s 91(1)) or by its discharge under s 39. The making of an adoption order extinguishes any order under the 1989 Act: Adoption Act 1976, s 12(3), as amended by Sch 10, para 3(3).

## 9 The effect of a care order

**6.22** The making of a care order discharges any s 8 order, so that no parent could continue to have a residence order. It discharges a supervision order and a school attendance order and brings wardship to an end: s 91.

**6.23** Section 33 sets out further effects of a care order, but this must be read in conjunction with s 2. By s 33(1), the local authority is required to receive the child and keep him in their care while the order is in force (ibid) and has parental responsibility (s 33(3)), but the parent does not cease to have parental responsibility solely because some other person acquires it (s 2(6)), nor is a person with parental responsibility entitled to act in a way which would be incompatible with any order made under the Act:

s 2(8) (see Chapter 2). Lest this might leave room for doubt, s 33(3)(b) provides that the authority has the power to determine the extent to which a parent or guardian may meet his parental responsibility insofar as it is necessary to do so to safeguard or promote the child's welfare. A parent or guardian is still entitled to do what is reasonable in all the circumstances of the case for the purpose of safeguarding or promoting the child's welfare (s 33(5)) and retains any right, duty, power, responsibility or authority in relation to the child and his property under any other enactment: s 33(9). These would include the right to consent to the child's marriage, rights under the Education Act 1981 in relation to the child's special educational needs, financial responsibility for the child and some responsibility for his acts if he is in the parent's charge and control.

**6.24** The parental responsibility acquired by a local authority has some specific limitations. They are not allowed to cause the child to be brought up in any religious persuasion other than that in which he would have been brought up if no order had been made. They do not have the right to consent, or refuse to consent, to the making of an application for a freeing for adoption order or to agree, or refuse to agree, to an adoption order or a proposed foreign adoption order. An authority may not appoint a guardian: s 33(6).

**6.25** While a care order is in force no person may cause the child to be known by a new surname without the written consent of every person with parental responsibility or by the leave of the court: s 33(7). The same consents are required before a child may be removed from the United Kingdom except where removal is by the care authority for less than a month or the authority is arranging for a child to live outside England and Wales: s 33(7) and (8). In the latter case, the approval of the court is required under the system set out in Sch 2, para 19. The previous scheme under the Child Care Act 1980, s 24 required the consent of the Secretary of State.

## 10 Transitional provisions on care orders

**6.26** What might broadly be described as compulsory care provisions under the legislation predating the Children Act 1989, operate by virtue of Sch 14, para 15 as care orders under the 1989 Act, including those provisions where the child was deemed by a court order to be in care under s 2 of the 1980 Act. This covers the following: the Children and Young Persons Act 1969, ss 1, 15, 25, 26; the Army Act 1955, the Air Force Act 1955 and the Naval Discipline Act 1957; the Child Care Act 1980, where there was a resolution in force under s 3 or 65; the Matrimonial Proceedings (Magistrates' Courts) Act 1960, s 2(1)(e); the Family Reform Act 1969, s 7(2) (but committal to care under the inherent jurisdiction of the High Court is not included); the Matrimonial Causes Act 1973, s 43(1); the Guardianship Act 1973, s 2(2)(b); the Domestic Proceedings and Magistrates' Courts Act 1978, s 10; the Children Act 1975, s 36; and the Adoption Act 1976, s 26.

**6.27** Where a court had previously given directions as to the exercise by the authority of any powers in respect of a child in care, they will continue to be effective until varied or discharged. This applies to the Guardianship Act 1973, s 4(4)(a) and the Matrimonial Causes Act 1973, s 43(5)(a). There is no reference to wardship and it would appear that an authority will have to return to the court for directions as to the relationship between directions previously given and the care order effective in the light of the previous paragraph.[1]

**1** see also para 10.10 as to whether wardship is terminated by s 91(4) where a child becomes subject to a care order under the 1989 Act by virtue of the transitional provisions.

# SUPERVISION

## 1 Introduction

**6.28** As with care orders, supervision orders may be made by the court only if the criteria set out in s 31 and the principles in s 1 are satisfied. A supervision order is an order putting the child under the supervision of a designated local authority or a probation officer. There is a new power to make an interim supervision order under s 38 (discussed at paras 6.35-6.42). There is a new power to make an education supervision order (discussed at para 12.7). New powers are provided for in Sch 3 to include requirements in relation to 'a responsible person', who it is hoped will be encouraged to play a positive role in making supervision orders work. Supervision by a local authority will be subject to regulations under Sch 3, para 11. Many of the provisions are already contained in the Children and Young Persons Act 1969, but in future that Act will apply only in criminal proceedings.

**6.29** The supervisor has the duty to advise, assist and befriend the child and take such steps as are reasonably necessary to give effect to the order: s 35. If the order is not wholly complied with or the supervisor considers the order may no longer be necessary, he should consider applying to the court for variation or discharge.

## 2 Duration of supervision order

**6.30** A supervision order lasts for one year subject to discharge under s 91 and extension by the court for up to a total of three years: Sch 3, para 6.

## 3 Directions attached to supervision order

**6.31** A supervision order may contain a direction that the supervised child must comply with directions given by the supervisor. They may be effective for up to 90 days and may require that the child lives at a specified place, presents himself at specified places on specified days and participates in specified activities, but it is a matter for the supervisor to decide whether to exercise the power to give directions and to decide their form. This provision emphasises that 'intermediate treatment'[1] is available for children who are not offenders. It does not empower the supervisor to give directions as to medical or psychiatric examination or treatment, which have to be dealt with by direction of the court (see below). A supervision order may also include a requirement, with the consent of a responsible person,[2] that he takes all reasonable steps to ensure that the child complies with directions given by the supervisor and directions to submit to medical or psychiatric examination or treatment and that he himself takes part in specified activities.

**1** The term is not used in the Act. See *Clarke Hall and Morrison* (10th ed) **B** [94].
**2** Ie, any person who has parental responsibility for the child and any other person with whom the child is living: Sch 3, para 1.

### *Directions on psychiatric and medical examinations and treatment*

**6.32** A supervision order may require the child to submit to a medical or psychiatric examination or treatment, provided the child consents, if he has sufficient understanding to make an informed decision: Sch 3, paras 4 and 5. The provisions require that the order should contain directions as to a specified medical practitioner who is to carry out the examination or treatment and whether the child is to attend as a resident or non-resident patient.

Insofar as the provisions deal with treatment, they re-enact s 12B of the Children and Young Persons Act 1969,[1] with two additions. The requirement as to the consent of the child is new and satisfactory arrangements must have been made for the treatment. Second, if the specified medical practitioner is unwilling to continue to treat or direct the treatment or is of the opinion that there should be changes to the arrangements, he must make a written report to the supervisor, who must refer the report to the court. The court may then cancel the order or vary the requirement.

**1** See *Clarke Hall and Morrison* (10th ed) **B** [722.4].

## 4 Juvenile offenders and removal from home requirements

**6.33** In respect of juvenile offenders, a new s 12AA is added to the Children and Young Persons Act 1969, which enables a court, in addition to other requirements under ss 12-12C, to require a young offender to live, for up to six months, in local authority accommodation: Sch 12, para 23. As the Lord Chancellor explained,[1] it was thought appropriate to give the court power to attach a 'removal from home' requirement to a supervision order, in respect of persistent offenders over the age of ten, although he said that such orders should be used sparingly. The order is intended to provide a short period during which the authority can work with the problems of the child and his family in the hope that the home circumstances contributing to the offending behaviour can be improved.

The conditions set out in s 12AA(6) for attaching the requirement are:

(a) a supervision order with a condition of residence or 'specified activities' has previously been made with respect to the child;
(b) the child is found guilty of an offence committed while the order was in force;

(c) the offence is punishable in the case of an adult with imprisonment and in the opinion of the court is serious;
(d) the court is satisfied that the behaviour which constituted the offence was due, to a significant extent, to the circumstances in which the child was living (unless the previous supervision order contained a residence requirement).

The court may not impose the requirement without first consulting the local authority. It must consider a social enquiry report and ensure that the child has had an opportunity to be legally represented.

**1** HL Deb, 16 February 1989, Vol 504, col 375.

### 5 Transitional arrangements for supervision orders

**6.34** After the commencement of Part IV of the Act, existing supervision orders made under the Children and Young Persons Act 1969 shall be deemed to have been made under s 31 and any requirements imposed shall continue. If the order was in force more than six months, it ceases six months after commencement unless extended by the court or it ceases earlier. If the order was in force less than six months, it will take effect as described in para 6.26, unless the court orders an extension. Orders made under other legislation are not deemed to be made under the Act but continue for a year, unless they cease to have effect earlier: Sch 14, paras 25 and 26. The court has no power to order an extension in relation to such orders.

## INTERIM MEASURES

**6.35** Following the issue of proceedings under s 31, there will usually be a period of time while parties prepare their case and the guardian ad litem prepares a report before the court is able to make a final decision about what order, if any, to make. Under the Children and Young Persons Act 1969 the juvenile court could make an interim order under s 2(10) after the commencement of care proceedings or under s 28(6) during the period of a place of safety order. Neither provision specified the grounds on which the court should decide whether or not to make an order. No other order was available to the court, apart from a simple adjournment.

**6.36** In contrast under the 1989 Act, once care proceedings have been started, the court has the option of making:

(a) a residence order under s 8 for a limited period;
(b) an interim care order; or
(c) an interim supervision order.

**6.37** The ability to make an interim order under s 8 is consistent with the policy of giving the court power to make a similar order as a final disposal in care proceedings. Section 11(3) makes it clear that s 8 orders can be made even though the court is not yet in a position finally to dispose of the proceedings. Section 11(7) (discussed more fully at paras 3.9 et seq) provides, inter alia, for an order to be made for a specified period and it may impose conditions. Thus, the court could make a residence order until the next hearing in favour of a relative and to control the child's contact with a parent for the time being, through a contact order or a prohibited steps order. The court would not have power to make a contact order in favour of a local authority because of the restriction contained in s 9(2). If the court makes a residence order on an application for a care or supervision order, it must make an interim supervision order unless satisfied that the child's welfare will be satisfactorily safeguarded without it: s 38(3).

**6.38** Where, on an application for a care or supervision order, the proceedings are adjourned or where the court in any proceedings gives a direction under s 37(1) for an authority to investigate the child's circumstances, the court may make an interim care or supervision order. It may not make the order unless satisfied that there are reasonable grounds for believing that the circumstances with respect to the child are as set out in s 31(2). The threshold criteria (discussed at para 6.3) for care proceedings are applied, but the court has only to be satisfied that there are reasonable grounds for believing they exist, rather than be satisfied as to their existence. The court must also apply the overriding principles in s 1 that the welfare of the child is paramount and that no order should be made unless it is better for the child than making no order.

## 1 Directions on interim applications

**6.39** Where the court makes an interim care or supervision order it may give such directions as it considers appropriate with regard to medical or psychiatric examination or other assessment of the child and may direct that no examination or assessment is to take place at all or unless the court directs. A direction may be given or varied at any time during the period of an interim order. During the period of an interim supervision order the court may not impose directions as to medical examination or treatment of a child in accordance with Sch 3, paras 4 and 5 (see paras 6.27 and 6.28).

**6.40** If the child is of sufficient understanding to make an informed decision, he may refuse to submit to an examination or assessment (see para 7.18).

**6.41** The power to make directions will enable the court to control the investigation of suspected abuse or neglect in the same way as with emergency protection orders (see paras 7.23-7.36). The court could direct a joint medical assessment or prevent a particular type of assessment. This provision has clearly been made with a view to interviews of children alleged to have been sexually abused. Thus, evidence of the desirability or otherwise of such an interview will have to be produced at an early stage of proceedings (see also para 7.36).

**6.42** Authorities will have to distinguish between circumstances where they apply for an interim supervision order and those where they apply for a child assessment order (see paras 7.8-7.22). If the authority believes that an order of some kind is likely to be necessary, even though the child does not need to be removed, an interim supervision order is to be preferred.

On the other hand, if the authority considers that it is only necessary to persuade a parent to agree to an assessment, the child assessment order should be sufficient.

## 2 Timetable for proceedings

**6.43** Section 32 requires a court hearing an application under Part IV to draw up a timetable with a view to disposing of the application without delay and to give such directions as it considers appropriate for the purpose of ensuring, so far as is reasonably practicable, that the timetable is adhered to.[1] This is an extension of the duty of the court in s 1(2) to have regard to the general principle that any delay in determining the question is likely to prejudice the welfare of the child (see paras 1.12 and 1.13). Rules of court will provide further requirements, in particular specifying periods within which certain steps must be taken. Courts and practitioners will want to be confident that a timetable acts as an encouragement to bring the matter before the court expeditiously, while not discouraging sensible negotiation.

1 Concern has been expressed about the length of time it takes for care proceedings to reach final hearing: Murch and Mills *The length of care proceedings* (Bristol University, 1988).

## 3 Duration of interim orders

**6.44** An interim care or supervision order may be made for such period as the court orders but may not last longer than eight weeks in the case of an initial order or 'the relevant period' in the case of a second or subsequent order. The relevant period is four weeks, or eight weeks from the date of the first order if that is longer. Thus, if the first order was made for two weeks, the second order could be made for six weeks. If the first two orders were made respectively for one week and two weeks, the third order could be made for five weeks. When deciding the period, the court must consider whether a party who was or might have been opposing the order was in a position to argue the case in full: s 38(10).

**6.45** If the court orders an investigation by a local authority under s 37(1), a care or supervision order may be made for no longer than the period within which the authority must report to the court. The maximum period is eight weeks: s 37(4). The authority may decide within that period to commence and obtain an order in separate proceedings.

# DISCHARGE OF ORDERS

**6.46** Section 39 provides for the discharge and variation of supervision and care orders. The Children and Young Persons Act 1969 provided for variation and discharge under s 15 in relation to supervision and s 21 in relation to care. The provisions were unsatisfactory in two important respects. First, a care order could be made on an application to vary a supervision order without further proof of the grounds for care proceedings; and, second, the grounds for discharging either order were unclear. The sections required the court to consider only whether it was appropriate to discharge the order. It was not established that a specific welfare test under s 1 of the Guardianship of Minors Act 1971 applied. The welfare criterion which appeared to apply was the general provision under s 44 of the Children and Young Persons Act 1933 to have regard to the welfare of the child. The new provisions are a significant improvement.

**6.47** Application for discharge of a care order may be made by any person who has parental responsibility for the child, the child himself or the local authority: s 39(1). No application may be made without the leave of the court within six months of the disposal of a previous application: s 91(15). The court may substitute a supervision order on such an application. It needs to consider only the welfare principle under s 1. The Act does not implement the intention expressed in the White Paper, that the court should satisfy itself that control would be provided for the child if needed. If it wishes to make a supervision order, the court does not need to be satisfied as to the criteria under s 31(2): s 39(5).

**6.48** Application for discharge or variation of a supervision order may be made by any person who has parental responsibilty for the child, the child himself or the supervisor: s 39(2). This includes variation of a requirement imposed under the order in accordance with Sch 3 (see para 6.27) and in such a case a person on whom the requirement is imposed may also apply for its variation. No application may be made without the leave of the court within six months of the disposal of a previous application: s 91(15).

**6.49** If the authority is seeking a care order in substitution for a supervision order, there is no similar provision to that under s 39(5) discussed above at para 6.47. Thus, the authority must satisfy the criteria under s 31(2).

**6.50** A third party, including an unmarried father (see Chapter 2), who wished a care or supervision order to be discharged, could seek a residence order under s 8. By virtue of s 91(1), the making of such an order would discharge the care order.

**6.51** The Act has not followed one important recommendation of the *Review of Child Care Law* (para 20.26), namely giving the court power to postpone the discharge of a care order to allow for a gradual return of the child to his family. It seems probable that rehabilitation may be controlled under the parental contact provisions. The High Court and county court at present commonly exercise their discretion to control how their orders are to be carried out. The magistrates' court might also consider the seldom used powers in s 63(1) of the Magistrates' Courts Act 1980 to the same effect.

## CONTACT WITH CHILDREN IN CARE

### 1 Introduction

**6.52** A child in care under the Children and Young Persons Act 1969 has access to his family only at the discretion of the care authority. A court is involved with the decision only if it had power to give directions on committal to care, as in wardship, custody proceedings in the High Court or following divorce, or if the authority sought to terminate access.[1] The House of Lords held in *A v Liverpool CC* [1982] AC 363 that the High Court could not interfere with the exercise of the authority's discretion.

1 See *Clarke Hall and Morrison* (10th ed) **A** [206].

**6.53** During the early 1980s authorities used these powers to carry out a policy of achieving stability for children in care, by terminating access and placing children for adoption. The difficulty was that parents and other interested parties had no opportunity of challenging the authority's plans. The insertion in 1983 of provisions in the Child Care Act 1980 to require notice of termination of access and an appeal against that notice to the court, provided only a partial remedy, because the rights did not arise until access was terminated.

**6.54** The *Review of Child Care Law* recognised (p 146) that 'on the one hand, questions about a child's day-to-day contacts and the circumstances in which they occur are quite plainly a matter of management. On the other hand, lack of access can, over a period, have vital consequences for the rights of parents and children'. Although the House of Commons Committee on Social Services, which reported in 1984 (HC 360-I), was concerned that local authority power may have been eroded too far, the *Review* considered that 'if questions of access are, so far as practicable, decided in accordance with the general law, much of the concern expressed to us about the subsequent relationship between parents and their children in compulsory care will cease to apply'.

**6.55** The new provisions follow this principle but are separate from the contact provisions regulating visiting or staying in the private law (see Chapter 3). If the child is in care, no court may make a s 8 contact order: s 9(1). If there is a contact order under s 8 in existence, it is discharged on the making of a care order: s 91(2).

**6.56** Section 34(1) requires the local authority to allow the child reasonable contact with his parents or guardian, a person in whose favour there was a residence order immediately before the making of the care order or a person who had the care of the child by virtue of an order under the inherent jurisdiction of the High Court. Regulations will be made as to the notification to be given by an authority of any variation or suspension of arrangements. Although there is no specific provision, all parties should expect to reach a written agreement on the terms for contact and other arrangements while the child is in care, in line with the provisions in relation to accommodated children (see para 5.35).

**6.57** A person referred to in the preceding paragraph may apply to the court as of right for an order under s 34 with regard to the contact they are to be allowed with the child. This is not specifically defined as a contact order. Indeed, it differs from the order under s 8, which is an order requiring the person with whom the child lives to allow contact (see para 3.16), whereas under s 34 the order is described in terms of the contact which is to be allowed between the child and the applicant. However, the same interpretation as in s 8 may be placed on the concept of contact, which includes visiting, staying or other contact, for example, by letter or telephone.

**6.58** Applications may also be made by any person who has obtained the leave of the court: s 34(3)(b). This will enable relatives to seek contact and in most cases they are likely to be granted leave to apply. In some circumstances former foster parents may wish to seek contact.

**6.59** Applications may be made by the local authority (s 34(2)), so that if it is thought that a particular person is likely to cause trouble for the child or the authority understand, that he does not wish to have contact with the person, it may make the application and seek a defined contact order.

**6.60** A child in care has a right to make an application that he is not to be allowed contact with a named person: s 34(2). It may be that in most cases it would be desirable for the authority to take the proceedings if so requested by the child but, if the authority are obstructive or delaying, the child may wish to take the initiative.

**6.61** On the making of a care order or later, the court may make such order as it considers appropriate as to the contact to be allowed: s 34(1) and (2). The welfare of the child is the paramount consideration and the other s 1 principles of considering the checklist and making no order unless making an order is better, apply. Such conditions as the court considers appropriate may be attached: s 34(7). This may include restriction of contact to specific periods or places. It seems probable that the court would make a detailed order, since arrangements would not have been successfully negotiated. The court may make a contact order of its own volition, whether or not an application has been made: s 34(5). This provision is particularly important since the court is required to consider the arrangements which the authority has made or proposes to make for affording any person contact with the child and invite the parties to the proceedings to comment on the arrangements: s 34(11).

**6.62** These provisions give the court wide power to control the future direction of a case. The court will have to look at the question of contact afresh and not necessarily be limited by what the local authority regards as reasonable, although the arrangements for contract which an authority may in practice make will have to be taken into account. An authority seeking a care order or opposing discharge of an order will be obliged to consider carefully the arrangements, arguments and evidence in relation to contact with the child in respect of any connected person. Those arrangements must be discussed with the child if old enough and with those connected with the child. Regulations will be made about the circumstances in which terms of an order may be varied by agreement and notifications to be made of any agreed variations.

**6.63** The court has power, by virtue of s 10(1), where a child is in care, to make an order about contact under s 34 in any family proceedings (as defined by s 8(4): see paras 3.22-3.28), which concern the same child. This includes domestic violence, divorce and adoption cases. Authorities will have to be on the alert constantly for questions about contact with the whole range of people who might be interested in the child, in case there are other proceedings in which the child may be involved.

**6.64** The court may vary or discharge an order on the application of the authority, the child or the person named in the order: s 34(9). Although the Act is not specific on the point, the making of a residence order under s 8 must discharge a s 34 order since it is dependent upon the existence of the care order which is itself discharged by virtue of s 91(1). The court should make an appropriate contact order under s 8.

## 2 Refusal of contact

**6.65** The authority or the child may apply for an order authorising the authority to refuse to allow contact between the child and any named person: s 34(4). The child's welfare is the paramount consideration: s 1. As a matter of urgency an authority may refuse to allow contact for up to seven days, if they are satisfied that it is necessary to do so in order to safeguard or promote the child's welfare: s 34(6). Regulations will be made concerning steps to be taken by an authority exercising this power.

## 3 Termination of contact and adoption

**6.66** Since any order under the section may, by s 34(9), be varied at any time, the refusal of contact by the court will not bring about a final termination of contact, as is possible under Part IA of the Child Care Act 1980.[1] In wardship proceedings where the court has taken the view that the future interest of the child lies in adoption, the practice has developed of ordering that there be no order for access or that it be in the discretion of the authority. Section 91(17) provides that where an applicant has been refused an order under s 34, he may not make another such application within six months without the leave of the court. That effectively reverses the position under the 1980 Act. However, there is a further provision under s 91(14) which empowers the court to order that no application for an order under the Act may be made by a named person without the leave of the court. It remains to be seen whether the courts will permit this provision to be used as an effective first step towards adoption or whether they will require authorities to deal with adoption only by way of proceedings under the Adoption Act 1976.

1 In *T v West Glamorgan CC* (1989) *Times* 16 October, the President held that a finding by the court that a notice of termination of access should be upheld, prevented a parent from seeking a further notice, so that the parent was thereafter dependent for access upon the decision of the local authority.

## 4 Code of Practice on Access to Children in Care

**6.67** There is no provision, as in the Child Care Act 1980, for the Secretary of State to publish a Code of Practice on Access to Children in Care (HMSO, 1983). Although many of the principles of the Code are applied in s 34 and in other places in the Act, there is no guidance about the circumstances in which it might be considered reasonable to refuse or restrict contact. The regulations authorised by s 34 do not provide for such guidance. The Code would appear to have some continuing relevance unless further guidance is given.

## 5 Transitional provisions

**6.68** On implementation of the 1989 Act, an order in force under s 12C of the Child Care Act 1980 will have effect as an order under s 34. Thus, a parent who has an access order under the 1980 Act continues with the same rights under s 34 and could apply to vary the order. An authority could apply to vary or seek an order refusing contact: Sch 14, para 18. There is no provision for dealing with cases where a parent has been served with notice[1] of termination before the Act and the parent has taken no action in response to the notice. It would appear that the parent would be entitled to reasonable contact on implementation of the Act and that the authority would be obliged to refuse contact as a matter of urgency and seek an order from the court confirming that decision.

1 If proceedings are pending under s 12C then under Sch 14, para 1, the 1989 Act will not apply.

**6.69** The unmarried father is given a right of access to his child in care pending full implementation of the Act. He may seek access and if the authority does not wish to grant it it must serve a notice of termination under s 12A of the Child Care Act 1980. The procedures by which a parent can appeal to the juvenile court then apply: Sch 12, para 35. The provision came into force on 16 November 1989: s 108(1).

Chapter 7

# Protection of children

## INTRODUCTION

**7.1** This chapter examines the new procedures provided for the protection of children. Duties to investigate are laid on the local authority and applications may be made to the court for a child assessment order, an emergency protection order or a recovery order. Additionally, a child may be taken into police protection and a warrant may be obtained to search specified premises for a child.

## 1 Definition of 'significant harm'

**7.2** Running throughout this chapter in relation to all the orders is the concept of 'significant harm'. It is also used in the provisions on care proceedings (see Chapter 6), where 'harm' is defined in s 31(9) as ill-treatment or the impairment of health or development. For the purposes of that section, 'health' and 'development' are further defined (see para 6.10). The definition of 'harm' in s 31 is also applied to the Act generally by s 105, but the definitions of 'health' and 'development' are not. However, it is reasonable to assume that the same definitions should be applied.

## 2 Duties to investigate

**7.3** A local authority has duties under a number of provisions to investigate the child's circumstances. The previous duty to investigate was contained in s 2(1) of the Children and Young Persons Act 1969, which required an authority to cause enquiries to be made if they received information suggesting that there were grounds for bringing care proceedings, unless they were satisfied that such enquiries were unnecessary. The *Review of Child Care Law* thought that this was too narrow and that an authority should investigate whenever it suspected that a child was suffering harm or was likely to do so. The Act gives effect to this wider remit, and requires an authority to make such enquiries as they consider necessary to enable them to decide what action to take: s 47(2).

### *Court-directed investigation*

**7.4** In any family proceedings where it appears to the court that it might be appropriate for a care or supervision order to be made with respect to a child, the court may direct an authority to investigate the child's circumstances (s 37(1)) and may make an interim care or supervision order pending the investigation: s 38(1). When undertaking the investigation, the authority are required to consider whether to apply for a care or supervision order or to provide services or assistance for the child or his family or whether to take any other action with respect to the child: s 37(2).

### *Investigation after notification by education authority*

**7.5** If a child persistently fails to comply with a direction given in an education supervision order, the education authority must notify the appropriate local social services authority, which are then required to investigate the child's circumstances: Sch 3, para 17.

### *Investigation of information given to the local authority*

**7.6** Where an authority

(a) have obtained an emergency protection order; or
(b) are informed that a child who lives or is found in their area is the subject of an emergency protection order or is in police protection; or
(c) have reasonable cause to suspect that a child who lives or is found in their area is suffering or is likely to suffer significant harm,

they must make, or cause to be made, for example by another authority or the NSPCC, such enquiries as they consider necessary to enable them to consider what action they should take: s 47(1) and (2). It is clear that even if enquiries are made through a second agency, the responsibility to make a decision about the child rests with any authority receiving information. This should avoid the problem which was identified in the *Doreen Aston Report*[1], where adjacent local authorities felt that it was the other's responsibility to investigate and take a decision on the case.

1 *Report to the Area Review Committee for Lambeth, Lewisham and Southwark London Boroughs* (1989).

**7.7** The aim of an enquiry is to establish whether an authority should apply to the court or exercise any of its powers under the Act, including whether an offer of accommodation should be made for the child and whether the police should be asked to make an application for an emergency protection order under s 44(7): s 47(3). The authority should try to ensure that the child is seen unless they are satisfied they already have enough information to decide what action to take: s 47(3). If necessary they should consult any education authority, any housing authority, any health authority and any other local authority, who are obliged to assist unless it would be unreasonable for them to do so: s 47(5) and (9)-(11). If the authority are refused access to the child or denied information as to his whereabouts, the authority should apply for an emergency protection order, a child assessment order, a care order or a supervision order unless satisfied that his welfare can be safeguarded without such an order: s 47(6). If at the end of their enquiries they decide not to make an application for a court order, they must consider whether to review the case and, if so, fix a date for the review: s 47(7).

# CHILD ASSESSMENT ORDERS

## 1 Introduction

**7.8** This is a new type of order, broadly in line with a proposal made in *A Child in Mind*.[1] It was introduced at a late stage of the Bill's passage through Parliament, in response to a demand for a power to be able to see, examine and assess a child, where there is concern as to his welfare, in the face of lack of co-operation from those responsible for the child. The Government appears to have been uncertain whether such an order was necessary, in addition to the emergency protection order, but eventually decided to include the provision:

> 'There are other circumstances in which there might be serious cause for concern about the welfare of a child. There may be a repeated failure to produce a child and perhaps it cannot be asserted that the matter is quite so urgent that there is an immediate need to intervene to take the child away — it is at the heart of our concerns that the emergency protection order is used only in those very serious circumstances, so the issue is whether there should be a lesser order requiring the production of a child and one which allows for the assessment of the child to take place.'[2]

1 *The Report of an Inquiry into the Death of Kimberley Carlile* (1987).
2 HC Deb, 23 October 1989, Vol 158, cols 593 and 607, per D Mellor.

**7.9** The order has been referred to as 'a multi-disciplinary assessment in non-emergency situations'[1] and there is a clear expectation that it will comprise at least a medical and social work assessment. However, since the order shall not have effect for a period exceeding seven days (s 43(5)), it seems likely that it will be primarily a medical assessment, as a social work assessment normally takes rather longer. This period appears to have been a compromise, reduced from the 28 days originally proposed to a period shorter than the emergency protection order.

1 HC Deb, 23 October 1989, Vol 158, col 596.

**7.10** The order is distinct from the proposal for a child production notice, which was considered as an alternative. That would have required a parent to produce a child before a doctor or health visitor and refusal would have been the basis for an emergency protection order. The Government rejected the notice on the grounds that it would allow an authority to take control of the situation by administrative action rather than by court order, and that production might mean no more than showing that the child was alive without any examination or assessment of his health or development.

## Application and criteria for child assessment order

**7.11** The court may make a child assessment order under s 43 on the application of a local authority or authorised person[1], if it is satisfied that

(a) the applicant has reasonable cause to suspect that a child is suffering, or is likely to suffer significant harm;

(b) an assessment of the state of the child's health or development, or of the way in which he has been treated, is required to enable the applicant to determine whether or not the child is suffering, or is likely to suffer, significant harm; and

(c) it is unlikely that such an assessment will be made, or be satisfactory, in the absence of a child assessment order.

It must again be remembered that the overriding provisions in s 1 apply — the welfare of the child is paramount and the order should not be made unless doing so would be better than making no order.

1 Ie for the time being, the NSPCC, but not any person as with the emergency protection order: see para 7.25.

## 3 Purpose of child assessment order

**7.12** A child assessment order is an inter partes application, and is not intended to be used in an emergency nor as a substitute for an emergency protection order. The child assessment order is appropriate where attempts to achieve an assessment have been frustrated, whereas the emergency protection order suggests a more immediate risk to the child, either because the applicant has information to satisfy the court that there is reasonable cause to believe that the child is likely to suffer significant harm or because access is urgently required to carry out enquiries and is being refused.

**7.13** The order may be of most use where parents are ignorant or resistant to thinking about the possible harm to their child because of the state of his health or development. No order would be required where one parent consents to the assessment, since s 2(7) empowers one parent to act alone. The threat of the order may be sufficient in many cases to persuade the parents to agree to an assessment. The order is not available once a care order is made, when by s 33, the authority may exercise parental responsibility, nor where an emergency protection order is made, when by s 44 the authority has limited responsibility subject to the court's direction. It could be used in conjunction with, or as an alternative to, an interim supervision order (see s 35), where supervision is thought desirable over a longer period than the seven day period of an assessment under s 43. There appears to be no reason why an order should not be made in respect of an accommodated child.

## 4 Treating as emergency protection order

**7.14** The court may treat the application as an application for an emergency protection order, and if it is satisfied that there are grounds for making an emergency protection order and that it ought to do so, it shall do so: s 43(3) and (4). This provision reflects concern that social workers might be tempted to apply for the less serious order, when in reality the welfare of the child requires his removal.

## 5 Procedure

**7.15** The applicant must take such steps as are reasonably practical to ensure that notice of the application is given to the child and his parents, any other person who has parental responsibility for him, any other person with whom the child is living, and any person in whose favour there is a contact order or who is allowed to have contact by virtue of an order under s 34: s 43(11). Court rules may provide for the circumstances in which the order may be varied or discharged: s 43(12). The court may appoint a guardian ad litem to act on the child's behalf: s 40(6)(f). It is expected that an appointment will usually be made to help the court decide at a full hearing whether an assessment order is needed[1].

1 HC Deb, 23 October 1989, Vol 158, col 594.

## 6 Directions

**7.16** The court may make directions on any matter relating to the assessment: s 43(6). These may include directions as to the kind of assessment which is to take place and with what aim, by whom and where it will be carried out, and whether it will be subject to conditions, such as that the assessment should be a joint one involving experts appointed by the child's parents or the guardian ad litem as well as by the local authority.

## 7 Effect

**7.17** Any person who is in a position to produce the child is under a duty to produce him to the person named in the order and to comply with such directions relating to the assessment of the child as may be specified in the order: s 43(6). The order authorises any person carrying out the assessment, or any part of it, to do so in accordance with the order: s 43(7). The child may be kept away from home in accordance with directions specified in the order only if it is necessary for the purposes of the assessment and for such period or periods as specified in the order: s 43(9). It may be that the period away from home will not need to be more than one night. If the child is to be away from home, the order shall contain such directions as the court thinks fit as to the contact the child is to be allowed to have with other persons: s 43(10).

## 8 Child's refusal to be examined

**7.18** Even when the court makes a child assessment order, if the child is of sufficient understanding to make an informed decision, he may refuse to submit to a medical or psychiatric examination or other assessment: s 43(8). The court may no more overrule the child than may a parent. A doctor who is asked to carry out the examination will have to form his own opinion as to whether the child consents, although, since the application will be made inter partes and the child represented by a guardian ad litem, there may have been an opportunity to assess the willingness of the child to agree. This provision, introduced at a late stage of the Bill's passage through Parliament, may raise some interesting dilemmas. In *Gillick v West Norfolk and Wisbech Area Health Authority* [1986] AC 112, it was suggested that a child might be able to make an informed decision on an issue like contraception in early teenage years. It may be thought possible to have an informed view about whether to be examined or assessed at a rather earlier age, but it would be unclear whether that view might have been formed as a result of coercion of the child. Nonetheless it would not appear to be desirable to require a medical examination to be carried out on an unwilling child and most doctors would refuse to do so.

## 9 Practice

**7.19** 'Assessment' must be given a wide interpretation. It is not limited to a medical assessment. It is likely, however, that a medical assessment will form a vital, and probably the principal, part of the overall assessment in most cases, given the short period of seven days available for the assessment under an order. Arrangements will have to be planned carefully before the court application, since the directions that the court may make, especially under s 43(6)(b) and (9), suggest that a detailed assessment programme worked out by those who are to undertake the assessment, should be presented to the court. Nonetheless it must be accepted that it may not be possible within seven days to do more than an initial assessment and obtain an indication of whether further work is necessary. If it appears that the parents remain unco-operative, then it is probable that an interim care or supervision order with conditions should be sought.

**7.20** Whether or not to apply for a child assessment order must largely depend on the evidence available to the applicant and the attitude of the parents or other person with parental responsibility. If there is evidence of significant harm attributable to the care being given to the child and the authority considers that a care or supervision order would be in the interests of the child, those proceedings should be commenced and, if necessary, directions about further examinations obtained from the court should be attached to an interim supervision order or interim care order. On the other hand, if the authority has some indication of harm to the child but is doubtful as to the proper course of action and believe, that the child may be able to stay at home or be accommodated, an application for a child assessment order may be preferable.

**7.21** The Government clearly intends that orders will rarely be necessary and that the mere threat of an application will be sufficient to persuade most parents to agree to an assessment. To that end it has been indicated that Rules of Court will require the applicant to explain to the court what steps have been taken to secure an assessment of the child.[1] Thus, orders will be made only in respect of children whose parents are the most obstinate. It must be questionable whether an order will make them co-operative, since there are no enforcement provisions and no power to require the parents to participate in the assessment.

1 HC Deb, 23 October 1989, Vol 158, col 594.

**7.22** The shortage of medical facilities for thorough assessments raises questions about whether doctors will be pressed to give priority to those cases where an order is made, and whether this might encourage an applicant to obtain an order to 'jump the queue' of assessments undertaken with parental co-operation. Clear arrangements will need to be made about responsibility for financing a medical assessment, so that disputes over payment do not cause delays.

# EMERGENCY PROTECTION ORDERS

## 1 Introduction

**7.23** Section 43 empowers the court to make an emergency protection order, which is an order, initially limited to eight days, to ensure the safety of a child where he is otherwise likely to suffer significant harm. It replaces the place of safety order, which was available in a number of circumstances but was mainly used under s 28 of the Children and Young Persons Act 1969. It was the subject of much criticism because of its routine use as a method of starting care proceedings and setting children on the path into care. Research[1] showed that in many cases place of safety orders did not subsequently lead to compulsory care. The *Review of Child Care Law* (Ch 13) recommended major changes. In the *Cleveland Report* further criticisms were made, especially in relation to the ex parte nature of the application and the fact that the order could be made for a period of up to 28 days without a parental right of appeal.

1 See especially Packman et al *Who needs care?* (Blackwell, 1986) and Millham et al *Children Lost in Care* (Gower, 1985)

**7.24** The essentials of the new provisions are:

(a) the court has to be satisfied that the child is likely to suffer significant harm or cannot be seen in circumstances where the child might be suffering significant harm;
(b) duration is limited to eight days with a possible extension of seven days;
(c) certain persons may be able to apply to discharge the order between 72 hours and eight days;
(d) the person obtaining the order has limited parental responsibility;
(e) the court may make directions as to contact with the child and/or medical or psychiatric examination or assessment;
(f) as under the 1969 Act, there will be provision, by order of the Lord Chancellor under Sch 11, para 3(1), for a single justice to make an emergency protection order (and see s 93(2)(i));
(g) application is still likely to be made in the absence of any interested party. Although an application could be made on notice, it would place in doubt the need for an emergency order;
(h) the application must name the child and, where it does not, must describe him as clearly as possible: s 44(14).

## 2 Grounds for an emergency protection order

**7.25** The court may make an emergency protection order under s 44(1)(a) on the application of any person if it is satisfied that there is reasonable cause to believe that the child is likely to suffer significant harm if the child:

(a) is not removed to accommodation provided by or on behalf of the applicant; or
(b) does not remain in the place where he is being accommodated.

This condition requires a number of points to be emphasised.

(1) Any person can apply. This would usually be a local authority or an authorised person (ie, at the time of writing the NSPCC), but it would be open to other people such as a police officer or hospital worker to apply. A parent or relative in a family dispute could use the provision, but in practice they are not likely to do so because the application would bring in the local authority because of their duty under s 47(1) to investigate an emergency protection order. It seems unlikely that the provision will be used other than by local authorities, authorised persons or other corporate representatives.
(2) Significant harm must be likely. Evidence of harm which was occurring at the time of the application or has occurred in the past is not sufficient unless it indicates that harm is more likely than not to occur in the future. This gives effect to the recommendations of the *Review of Child Care Law* (paras 13.8-13.10) that the order should concentrate on apprehended harm. Unlike the place of safety order,[1] the order could be made even though no harm had yet occurred.
(3) The court has to be satisfied that there is reasonable cause to believe that the child is likely to suffer significant harm, rather than, as under the 1969 Act, being satisfied that the applicant had reasonable cause to believe that the condition was satisfied.
(4) The court may take account of any statement contained in any report made to the court in the course of, or in connection with, the hearing or any evidence given during the hearing, which is in the opinion of the court relevant to the application: s 45(7). This enables the court to give proper weight to hearsay, opinions, health visiting or social work records and medical reports.
(5) The court will wish to know what it is that makes it necessary to remove the child as a matter of urgency. Why take the risk of separating the child from the carer immediately? If removal is necessary can it not be done with the co-operation of the parents and the child provided with accommodation? Why can the decision not wait until the parents have had an opportunity to put their case at an interim hearing or until all the relevant evidence is available and an independent report from a guardian ad litem at a full hearing?

**1** With certain very limited exceptions: see s 28(1) of the 1969 Act.

**7.26** A local authority may also apply for an order under s 44(1)(b) where they are making enquiries under s 47(1)(b),[1] ie, because they have reasonable cause to suspect that a child is suffering, or is likely to suffer, significant harm, and those enquiries are being frustrated by access to the child being unreasonably refused to a person authorised to seek access and they have reasonable cause to believe that access to the child is required as a matter of urgency. An authorised person (the NSPCC) may apply for an order under s 44(1)(c) in the same circumstances, save that they must additionally satisfy the court as to their reasonable cause for suspicion, whereas it would appear that the existence of a local authority enquiry would be sufficient.

An important part of the test will obviously be whether the refusal to allow the child to be seen is unreasonable. The Lord Chancellor suggested that it might be seen as unreasonable 'if it were not accompanied by co-operation in some form, such as taking the child to the GP, sufficient to allay fears about the child's welfare'. He also indicated that rules of court would require 'the applicant to explain what steps he had taken to communicate with the person having care of the child and to warn that emergency protection order proceedings could result'.[2]

**1** See paras 7.6 and 7.7
**2** HL Deb, 8 November 1989, Vol 512, col 783.

**7.27** The conditions concerning frustrated access were introduced during the Committee stage in the House of Commons, but attracted little discussion when emergency protection orders were debated.[1] The proposal was withdrawn for further consideration and re-introduced at the Report stage. It was not discussed further in the House of Commons because of the introduction of the guillotine during the final debate. The Lord Chancellor later[2] indicated that the grounds were being introduced because it was felt there was a chance that the first condition might not suffice, if there was a lack of firm information to show that the child was likely to suffer significant harm if not removed. Such circumstances were shown to exist in the Reports on the deaths of Kimberley Carlile[3] and Doreen Aston[4]. In both cases, parents obstructed the social worker's access to a child, who, it was thought, might be in danger. The powers contained in the new condition could have enabled them to gain sight of the child and remove if necessary.

The following points should be noted on the conditions:

(1) Condition (b) applies only to a local authority, but it does not specify that the authority must be making the enquiries.
(2) A person authorised to seek access is defined (s 44(2)(b)) as an officer of the local authority or a person authorised by the authority to act on their behalf in connection with the enquiries, but such a person may be asked to produce a duly authenticated document as evidence that he is authorised: s 44(3).
(3) The circumstances of the use of these conditions must be distinguished from the child assessment order. They are for use in an emergency, where enquiries cannot be completed because the child cannot be seen, but there is enough cause to suspect the child is suffering or is likely to suffer significant harm, whereas the child assessment order applies where there is a need for further investigation of the child's health and development but he is thought to be safe from immediate danger.
(4) Conditions (b) and (c) should be considered in conjunction with s 48(1), which empowers the court to include a provision in an emergency protection order requiring a person to disclose information as to the child's whereabouts, and s 48(3) by which it may authorise entry of premises to search for a child (see para 7.42).

(5) As the Lord Chancellor said (see para 7.26), the court will need to know what efforts have been made to see the child and what responses have been made by the child's carers. Where a call is made when the child is asleep, it may be reasonable for a parent to refuse to disturb the child and to offer to take the child to a local clinic later in the day or the following morning. Such an offer may not be a reasonable refusal of access where the risk to the child is believed to be immediate or where previous arrangements have been broken.

1 HC Deb, 25 May 1989, Standing Committee B, cols 311.321.
2 HL Deb, 8 November 1989, Vol 512, col 783.
3 *A Child in Mind* (1987).
4 *Report to the Area Review Committee of Lambeth, Lewisham and Southwark London Boroughs* (1989) see Ch 7, para 29.

**7.28** Even if the above conditions apply the court will not automatically make an emergency protection order. It must still consider the welfare principle and the presumption of no order: s 1(1) and (5) (see Chapter 1). In most cases the application will be made without the parents being present. In some circumstances, to put the parents on notice of the application might place the child in greater danger. Since only one side of the case will be heard, the court will want to examine the information it is given carefully, especially where the application is based on the likelihood of future harm or inability to see the child. There has been a tendency to regard the place of safety order as a routine way of starting care proceedings. Emergency protection orders are not intended to be so used.

## 3 Effect of emergency protection order

**7.29** An emergency protection order operates as a direction to any person who is in a position to do so to comply with any request to produce the child to the applicant and authorises removal to or prevention of removal from accommodation provided by or on behalf of the applicant: s 44(4). This would include, for example, a hospital. The court may authorise an applicant to enter specified premises and search for a child and may include another child in the order if is believed there might be another child on the premises: s 48(3) and (4). If the applicant is then refused entry, the court may issue a warrant authorising a constable to assist in the execution of the order using reasonable force if necessary: s 48(9).

**7.30** An emergency protection order gives the applicant parental responsibility for the child, but this is limited insofar as the applicant shall exercise the power to remove or prevent removal only in order to safeguard and promote the welfare of the child. Thus, if an applicant gains access and finds that the child is not harmed or likely to be harmed, he may not remove: s 44(5). Indeed, if during the period of the order, a return home to a parent or other connected person appears to be safe, then the applicant is required to carry that out: s 44(10); however, he may exercise the powers of removal again while the order remains in force if a change in circumstances makes it necessary: s 44(12).

Parental responsibility is to be exercised only as far as is reasonably required to safeguard or promote the welfare of the child, having regard in particular to the duration of the order: s 44(5). Thus, it would not be appropriate to make any changes in the child's life, which would have a long-lasting effect. Regulations under this section may set out further requirements: s 44(5).

## 4 Duration of emergency protection order

**7.31** The order may be granted for up to eight days,[1] though the court may order one extension for up to seven days if it has reasonable cause to believe that the child is likely to suffer significant harm if the order is not extended: s 45(1), (4)-(6). If there has been a genuine emergency and the authority believe care proceedings should follow, it should normally be possible to proceed to the extent of satisfying the court as to the grounds for an interim order within the first period. That has been the practice in many parts of the country for some years. If an extension is sought, the court will clearly want to be satisfied as to the reasons for the delay. However, since a first interim care order may be made for up to eight weeks, opposition to the initial order may occur more frequently and more vigorously so that close attention will have to be paid to whether the parties are ready for an interim application or whether an extension of the emergency order would be preferable.

**1** With extensions for public holidays: see s 45(2).

**7.32** There is no appeal against the making or refusal to make an emergency protection order: s 45(10). An application to discharge the order may only be heard between 72 hours and eight days after it was made by the child, a parent, any other person with parental responsibility or any person with whom he was living immediately before the making of the order, except where that person was present at or given notice of the hearing: s 45(8)-(11). Local authorities which are unsuccessful in their application will have to consider whether to start care proceedings and seek an interim order.

## 5 Contact during emergency protection order

**7.33** The applicant must allow the child reasonable contact, during the period of an order, subject to the directions of the court, with his parents, any other person with parental responsibility, any person with whom he was living immediately before the order, any person in whose favour there is a contact order in relation to him and any person acting on behalf of those persons: s 44(13). A local authority might indicate their intention to deny contact with a person or persons or may decide before or after the order that it wishes to allow only supervised contact.

**7.34** The court may (not must), on making the order, and at any time while it is in force, give such directions as it considers appropriate in relation to contact between the child and any named person: s 44(6). The court may give directions as to contact which is or is not to be allowed between the child and any named person and may impose conditions: s 44(6) and (8). The higher courts have experience of giving directions as to contact with children in care in wardship and custody proceedings, but the magistrates' court has little experience of that type of case. It is to be hoped that magistrates' courts will follow the normal court practice of leaving contact to the discretion of the local authority or ordering that there be reasonable contact to be negotiated between the parties, subject to the option of a restored hearing before the court. Examples of cases where local authorities will want to consider seeking directions to control contact are where they are dealing with families who they believe may be particularly troublesome, or where there are allegations of sexual abuse, or where there is a need to differentiate in the arrangements between parents. On the other hand, if the parents fear that the authority may prove obstructive, they might wish to obtain a direction.

## 6 Medical or psychiatric examination or assessment

**7.35** The parental responsibility acquired on the making of an emergency protection order would extend to decisions about medical or psychiatric examination or any assessment that the child should undergo, unless the court gives a direction. It is to be expected that medical evidence will be an important part of any future care proceedings, if they are to take place, so that early decisions or directions about examinations are crucial.

**7.36** The court may give directions as to a medical or psychiatric examination or other assessment of the child, and it is specifically provided that the court may direct that there is to be no examination or no examination unless the court directs otherwise: s 44(6) and (8)). It is difficult to see how this will work in practice. The court will be able to ensure that the child is not subjected to excessive examination. It may be possible to have examinations undertaken by doctors agreed between the parties or arranged by the guardian ad litem. This will depend on the type of case and how important it is for an early examination to be made. If parents are made aware of a direction for a medical examination and wish to oppose it, they will be unable to do so before 72 hours. It may be anticipated that the local authority will wish to carry out the examination before that time, so as to acquire evidence, if possible, to support their case against discharge of the emergency order or for a care order.

If it were feasible in resource terms, the authority might well wish to request a direction from the court under s 45(12) that, when executing the order, the social worker be accompanied by a medical practitioner, nurse or health visitor. This would provide the earliest possible opportunity for supporting medical evidence. If the court wishes to err on the cautious side it might wait to see if an application for discharge of the order is made, so that it can have the benefit of the view of a guardian ad litem: s 41(6)(g).

**7.37** The child may refuse to submit to an examination or other assessment if he is of sufficient understanding to make an informed decision, even though the court has ordered it: s 44(7). This provision is the same as in s 43(8) (see para 7.18).

**7.38** From a practical point of view, the provisions on discharge of emergency protection orders present potentially the most problematic area for practitioners in child protection. It seems likely that this provision will be used to challenge decisions made as to contact and possibly as to medical examinations or assessments. All parties will therefore have to act very quickly to assemble arguments and evidence as to those issues. Rules of court made under s 52 will prescribe the form in which any application is to be made or direction given, and under s 93(2)(a), may provide for the procedure to be followed, including the manner in which any application is to be made. It is to be hoped they will also give guidance on what the courts should expect in support of an application for an emergency protection order or on an application for its discharge. That part of the process is so fundamental to the safety of the child that it must not be left to the idiosyncrasies of individual courts.

## 7 Police protection

**7.39** A constable has powers to take a child, if he can get his hands on the body, 'into police protection' for up to 72 hours, if he has reasonable cause to believe that a child would be likely to suffer significant harm if he did not remove the child to suitable accommodation or take steps to prevent removal from a hospital or other place where the child is being accommodated: s 46(1). This section is the successor to s 28(2) of the 1969 Act, which has been most frequently used by the police to hold children such as runaways or glue sniffers or whose parents have abandoned them. It may also be used by a police officer who attends a domestic dispute and finds the parents drunk or the child living in unhygienic conditions. The police have existing powers to enter and search premises without a warrant for the purpose of saving life or limb under s 17(1)(e) of the Police and Criminal Evidence Act 1984, but this provision appears to be rarely used and is limited to cases of dire emergency.

**7.40** Section 46 requires a constable taking a child into police protection to inform, as soon as is reasonably practicable, relevant local authorities, the child, his parents and other specified persons about the steps that have been taken in relation to the child. He must secure that the case is inquired into by a designated officer and that the child is moved into local authority accommodation or to a refuge in accordance with s 51.

**7.41** The designated officer, on completing his enquiries, must release the child, unless he considers that there is still reasonable cause for believing that the child would still be likely to suffer significant harm if released. The local authority will have been informed of removal, so that they have a duty to conduct an investigation in accordance with s 47, which might lead to an application for an emergency protection order by the authority. The authority also have to consider whether to ask the police to apply for an order: s 41(3)(c). The designated officer may, in any event, apply on behalf of the local authority for such an order whether or not the authority are aware of the application: s 46(7) and (8). The period of the order then runs from the beginning of the time when the child was taken into police protection: s 45(3). In neither situation do the police have parental responsibility. The designated police officer must allow such contact between the child and his parents or other persons specified in s 46(10) as in his opinion is reasonable and in the child's interests.

## 8 Discovery of children

**7.42** The whereabouts of a child who may be in need of emergency protection are not always known. Section 48 gives powers to the court to include provision in an emergency protection order, if it appears to the court that information as to the child's whereabouts is available to a person, requiring that person to disclose, if asked to do so by the applicant, any information he may have: s 48(1). The order may also authorise an applicant to enter premises specified by an order and search for the child with respect to whom the order was made: s 48(3). It is an offence to obstruct the exercise of this power: s 48(7). Although this authorises entry to premises, if that is necessary to carry out the order, it may be used only where there is co-operation.

## 9 Warrant to enter and search

**7.43** If a person has been prevented from exercising powers under an emergency protection order, by being refused entry to premises or access to the child, or it appears to the court that he is likely to be prevented from doing so, a warrant may be issued authorising a constable to assist the entry and search, using reasonable force if necessary: s 48(9). As with s 45(12) (see para 7.36) the court may direct that the constable be accompanied by a registered medical practitioner, nurse or health visitor: s 48(11). This provision supersedes s 40 of the Children and Young Persons Act 1933, by which a warrant could be issued on reasonable suspicion that a child was being assaulted, ill-treated or neglected in a manner likely to cause him unnecessary suffering or injury to health.

**7.44** The new provision will require evidence of a failure to execute the emergency protection order or an indication of why it might not be executed. The warrant under s 40 of the 1933 Act had no such limitation, but that provision required suspicion of a criminal offence in relation to the child. Linking the need for a warrant with the need for an emergency protection order within one system is appropriate and will simplify the process. Its effectiveness could be impaired if courts interpret too rigidly the requirement that execution of the emergency protection order is likely to be obstructed. They may have to give weight to the history of a family, if it has proved obstructive in the past.

## 10 Discovering other children

**7.45** If the applicant believes there may be another child on the premises to be searched who ought also to be the subject of an emergency protection order, he may seek an order authorising a search for him: s 48(4). If such an order is made and the child is found on the premises, and the applicant is satisfied that the grounds for making an emergency protection order exist, the order under s 48(4) has effect as if it were an emergency protection order: s 48(5). If an order is made under s 48(4), the applicant must inform the court of its effect: s 48(6).

**7.46** This provision is intended to cover the situation where an applicant believes that there may be more than one child in the family or on premises, who is likely to suffer significant harm. Although in many cases the applicant will be aware of the existence of other children, and should, if there are grounds, seek an individual emergency protection order for each child, the new provision is of importance in two situations. First, the applicant may not be able to identify the specific child or children (as required by s 44(14)), but may want to check on the well-being of children in the same circumstances as the child in respect of whom the order is made. Second, if the police were, for example, to discover a sex ring, they might not know the number or identity of children involved. The provision does not resolve the problem where, in the course of a search, the applicant discovers another child not previously known.

## CHILDREN ABDUCTED FROM CARE OR PROTECTION

**7.47** A court may make a recovery order in respect of a child who is in care, or is the subject of an emergency protection order or in police protection, if there is reason to believe that he has been unlawfully taken away from the 'responsible person'[1], has run away or is staying away from the responsible person or is missing. The order operates as a direction to produce the child or disclose his whereabouts and authorises a constable to enter named premises and search for the child using reasonable force if necessary. Subject to s 51, s 49 provides for offences where a child is unlawfully removed or kept away, or induced, assisted or incited to run away or stay away from the responsible person.

**1** As defined in s 49(2), any person who has care of the child by virtue of a care order, emergency protection order or under s 46 following police removal.

## REFUGES

**7.48** The Secretary of State may issue a certificate for providing a refuge for children with respect to a voluntary home, a registered children's home or a foster parent: s 51. While the certificate is in force, they are exempt from offences under s 49 above, s 2 of the Child Abduction Act 1984[1], s 32(3) of the Children and Young Persons Act 1969[2] or s 71 of the Social Work (Scotland) Act 1968 (harbouring).

**1** See *Clarke Hall and Morrison* (10th ed) **C** [952].
**2** Ibid, **B** [810].

Chapter 8

# Welfare reports, guardians ad litem and evidence

## WELFARE REPORTS

**8.1** The court's powers to order welfare reports and the form and contents of such reports are governed by s 7, the provisions of which are based on the Law Commission's recommendations contained in their report on *Guardianship and Custody* (Law Com No 172, paras 6.14-6.21).

**8.2** Section 7(1) empowers a court, when considering any question with respect to a child under the 1989 Act, to ask either a probation officer or a local authority to report to the court 'on such matters relating to the welfare of that child as are required to be dealt with in the report'.

**8.3** This provision makes a number of changes to the previous law, namely:

(1) the power arises in relation to *any* issue raised under the 1989 Act;

(2) the varying criteria (see Law Com No 172, para 6.16) that formerly existed for ordering reports are replaced by a single criterion applicable in all cases; and

(3) in all cases the court may ask either a probation officer or a local authority to prepare a report.

**8.4** The power to ask for a report in relation to any issue arising under the 1989 Act ends the former, anomalous position whereby in some proceedings, namely, those concerned with the appointment or removal of guardians and the application by unmarried fathers for a parental rights and duties order, there was no power to order welfare reports. Additionally, for the first time welfare reports may be ordered in any case where the court is considering whether to make a care or supervision order. In most such cases, a guardian ad litem will have been appointed (see para 8.12), but while in general, as the Law Commission observed (ibid, para 6.21), such persons are better qualified to make independent assessments in care cases, to save time and resources it might be necessary for the court welfare officer to do so. Indeed, in some cases such an officer may have already done so, for example, in family proceedings where the court decides after hearing the evidence that it should exercise its powers under s 37 (discussed at para 7.4) and invite the local authority to investigate the case with a view to it applying for a care or supervision order. It is worth stressing, however, that the functions of a 'welfare reporter' and a guardian ad litem are different. The former is appointed to report to the court about the child's and family's background, whereas the latter's function is to look after the interests of the child and to try to see the matter from the child's point of view. As Lord Mackay LC put it during the debate on the Bill,[1] a guardian ad litem is more in the nature of a party representing the child than of a reporting person. Hence the appointment of one does not ipso facto preclude the appointment of the other, although given the scarcity of resources, the court should consider carefully what would be gained by appointing both.

1 HL Deb, 19 December 1988, Vol 502, Col 1209.

**8.5** The power in any proceedings to ask either a probation officer or a local authority to report to the court is an important change. For the first time divorce courts will be able to ask a local authority to report rather than a divorce court welfare officer. This change brings those courts' powers into line with the other courts. However, the ending of the welfare officers' monopoly in the divorce courts is not intended to result in local authorities being asked to report as a matter of routine, but only in those cases where there is an obvious connection (see Law Com No 172, para 6.17).

**8.6** Under s 7(5), it is the duty of the local authority or probation officer to comply with any court request for a welfare report. However, where the court decides to ask the local authority to report, it can ask them to arrange for it to be done either by one of their officers or 'such other person (other than a probation officer) as the authority consider appropriate': s 7(1)(b). The ability to arrange for the report to be done by someone other than one of its own officers is the only change from the Law Commission's recommendations. It was made, following representations made by Lord Mottistone on behalf of the NSPCC.[1] It is intended to accommodate the situation where, as a result of close interdisciplinary co-operation in a local area, the NSPCC, for example, acting on behalf of the local authority, is seen to be the key worker for a particular child.

1 See HL Deb, 19 December 1988, Vol 502, col 1205. The amendment was actually added at the subsequent Report stage: see HL Deb, 6 February 1989, Vol 503, cols 1329-1330.

## 1 When reports should be ordered

**8.7** The court is not bound to order welfare reports in every case. Indeed, as the Law Commission said (Law Com No 172, para 6.15), the court has to be moderate when exercising its powers. Welfare officers' time is limited (as is that of those working for local authorities) and must be targeted on cases where it will be most valuable. It must also be acknowledged that reports can be a source of delay and, mindful of the court's general duty under s 1(2) (see para 1.12) to be aware of the likelihood of delay prejudicing the child's welfare, the court might have to balance the advantages to be gained from a report against the disadvantage of the time it takes to obtain it. Further, in deciding whether to call for a report, the court must also have regard to its duty under s 1(5) (see para 1.20) to make orders only where to do so is better for the child than making no order.

## 2 The form and content of reports

**8.8** The court may specify what matters should be reported upon in any particular case. Section 7(2) empowers the Lord Chancellor to make regulations specifying matters which, unless the court orders otherwise, must be dealt with in the report; this implements the Law Commission's recommendations (Law Com No 172, para 8.94) and is aimed at promoting consistent practice. This power may be particularly useful where non-parents apply for a residence order: unlike under former custodianship provisions, detailed reports from local authorities will not be required in every case. Some guidance for courts and welfare officers may therefore be helpful.

**8.9** A report may be made in writing or orally as the court requires: s 7(3). This provision, which implements the Law Commission's recommendation (para 8.93), is intended to maintain maximum flexibility, although it is not envisaged that it will change the normal practice of requiring written reports. Such reports could, however, be supplemented at the hearing.

**8.10** The 1989 Act makes no express provision for the disclosure of reports to the parties, nor for the opportunity to put questions to the officer. It is expected that these matters will be dealt with in the rules.

## 3 Welfare reports and hearsay

**8.11** Following the Law Commission's recommendation (ibid, para 8.93), s 7(4) states that, regardless of any rule of law which would otherwise prevent it from doing so, the court may take into account any statement contained in, or evidence given in respect of matters referred to, the report. In effect, this provides statutory authority[1] that statements in a report may not be ruled inadmissible because of the hearsay rule. Given that this has been the accepted position in all the courts, it is unlikely to change practice.[2] Hence, regard should still be had to *Thompson v Thompson* [1986] 1 FLR 212 (where second-hand evidence is relied upon, this should be made explicit in the report as should the source of information and the reporter's reasons, if he has any, for agreeing with such an opinion).

1 Cf the Lord Chancellor's powers under s 96 to make rules restricting the application of the hearsay rule with regard to statements made by children (see para 8.28).

2 The Law Commission (para 6.18) also hoped that the provision would emphasise that reports are for the court and not evidence presented by one or other of the parties to the case.

# GUARDIANS AD LITEM

**8.12** The court is required to appoint a guardian ad litem to represent the child in specified proceedings unless satisfied that it is not necessary to do so in order to safeguard his interests: s 41. The specified proceedings are set out in s 41(6). They are:

(a) applications for the making, variation or discharge of a care or supervision order and related appeals;

(b) where a direction for the local authority to investigate has been given and the court has made, or is considering making, an interim care order;

(c) where the court is considering making a residence order with respect to a child who is the subject of a care order and related appeals;
(d) applications in respect of contact between a child in care and any person and related appeals;
(e) applications for a child assessment order or other proceedings under Part V of the Act, which would include an application to discharge an emergency protection order and related appeals.

Further proceedings may be specified by rules of court, but note that s 41 does not include education supervision orders or orders under Part II.

**8.13** The new provision places more emphasis on the appointment of a guardian ad litem than do the provisions under ss 32A, 32B of the Children and Young Persons Act 1969. There the court was obliged to appoint a guardian in unopposed applications to discharge orders, unless satisfied that it was not necessary for safeguarding the child's interests, but in initial applications the court had more discretion. As a result, the frequency of appointment of guardians varied from court to court. The Government considers that guardians should in future be appointed in over 90% of cases.[1]

1 HC Deb, 23 May 1989, Standing Committee B, col 255.

## 1 Appointment of guardian ad litem

**8.14** The guardian ad litem will be appointed in accordance with rules of court and will be under a duty to safeguard the interests of the child in the manner prescribed by rules of court. It is intended that guardians will be appointed at an early stage of proceedings, so that they should be able to advise the court about discharge of an emergency protection order, the making or extension of an interim care or supervision order and directions which may be attached to interim orders as to contact or medical examination or assessment. The guardian will have an important role in advising the court as to the timetable to be established, including the time required for the guardian to investigate and prepare a report for the final hearing of the matter, without delay prejudicial to the child's interests. Rules of court will provide for the assistance which a guardian may be required to give the court and the consideration to be given in certain types of proceedings as to whether to apply to vary or discharge an order: s 41(10).

## 2 Instruction of child's solicitor

**8.15** It is expected that the guardian will normally instruct a solicitor to act for the child in accordance with rules of court. If the guardian does not do so, the court may appoint a solicitor if there is no guardian or if the child has sufficient understanding to instruct a solicitor and wishes to do so or if it appears to the court that it is in the child's interests for him to be represented by a solicitor. There was debate in the Commons as to whether it was desirable to provide on the face of the Act for representation of the child by a solicitor. The Government view was that the rules were the proper place for such a matter[1]. It is intended that the rules will require the guardian to instruct a solicitor unless the court otherwise directs.

1 HC Deb, 23 May 1989, Standing Committee B, cols 259 and 260.

## 3 Panels of guardians ad litem

**8.16** The Secretary of State will make regulations providing for the establishment of panels of guardians ad litem. They may provide, inter alia, for joint management of panels and it is intended that area panels will be established which will give guardians more independence from a particular authority.[1]

1 HC Deb, 23 May 1989, Standing Committee B, col 271.

**8.17** Section 41(7) provides that the establishment of panels will not prejudice the appointment of the Official Solicitor. It is intended that the Official Solicitor will continue to act in many proceedings in the High Court and that some members of his staff will join panels of guardians. The individual will have to instruct a solicitor but presumably has the advantage of being able to instruct the Official Solicitor. However, these plans are not without difficulty. How would the case be conducted if there was a disagreement between the guardian and the Official Solicitor? If the Official Solicitor is only to act in the High Court how will cases be allocated given that even the most complex care cases will be commenced in the magistrates' court? One solution would be for guidance to allocating clerks to provide that cases involving complex legal questions or extensive investigation to be referred to the High Court before a guardian is appointed. Inevitably, there will be cases which appear less complex initially but become more so. The court will then have to consider whether to continue with the appointed guardian or ask the Official Solicitor to take over the case.

## 4 Guardian's right to inspect

**8.18** Under s 42 a guardian ad litem has a right at all reasonable times to examine and take copies of any records of or held by a local authority compiled in connection with the making or proposed making by any person of any application under the Act with respect to the child he represents and any other records of or held by an authority in relation to the child and compiled in connection with any function of the social services committee under the Local Authority Social Services Act 1970. This provision reflects current practice in that local authorities usually allow a guardian ad litem to inspect their records. It leaves no discretion to the authority to withhold information from the guardian. The provision would appear to be wide enough to include case conference minutes and files compiled with a view to adoption. The provision is limited to the local authority so that other organisations have no duty of disclosure. It may be questioned whether the NSPCC should be under a similar duty of disclosure, at least when they initiate care proceedings.

## 5 Evidence and report of the guardian ad litem

**8.19** Where copies are taken from local authority records by a guardian ad litem, the rules of hearsay do not apply to them. Further, if a guardian chooses to refer to them in any report to the court or in any evidence he gives in the proceedings, the local authority may not object, for example on grounds of privilege or public interest immunity: s 42(2) and (3).

## EVIDENCE

**8.20** The presentation of information to the court in cases concerning children may present difficulties. Often the child is the best source of information but it may not be appropriate or possible for him to give evidence. Information given by a parent or friend of the family may later be withheld. Professional witnesses may be unavailable, especially if, as is often necessary in child-care cases, evidence is needed of events over a number of years.

**8.21** With these considerations in mind, historically the courts have adopted a flexible approach to the admissibility of hearsay evidence. The problem has, however, come to a head where it is said that a child has made allegations of sexual abuse to a third party. The courts have had to consider the ability of the child to give evidence and, in circumstances where the child does not, the relevance of the information (including any interview of the child by a professional worker), whether it is strictly admissible if referred to by a third party and the weight to be given to it.

**8.22** Specific exceptions to the rules of evidence exist where information is provided in a welfare report (para 8.11) or by a guardian ad litem (para 8.19) or for the purposes of obtaining an emergency protection order (para 7.23). Where evidence is given by others, the rules of evidence have to be considered.

**8.23** The position in wardship has been well established since Lord Devlin in *Re K (Infants)* [1965] AC 201 at 242 said: 'A judge in chambers is quite capable of giving hearsay no more than its proper weight. An inflexible rule against hearsay is quite unsuited to the exercise of a parental and administrative decision.' This view has been confirmed by the Court of Appeal recently in *Re W (Minors)* (1989) *Times* 10 November.

**8.24** It may be alleged by a parent that a child has told her of sexual abuse by the other spouse. The allegation is then introduced as evidence in custody or access proceedings. This was the position in *Re H (A Minor)*; *Re K (Minors) (Child abuse: evidence)* [1989] 2 FLR 313. The Court of Appeal held that in the county court such evidence was inadmissible. The Civil Evidence Act 1968 applied, which meant that there were only three ways in which hearsay evidence could be admitted: under the provisions of the 1968 Act, under other statutory provisions (of which there was none relevant here) or by agreement. The practice had developed in many children's cases of admitting hearsay evidence by tacit agreement, but if objection was taken, the 1968 Act had to be studied.

**8.25** Section 2(1) of the 1968 Act provides:

> 'In any civil proceedings a statement made whether orally or in a document or otherwise, by any person, whether called as a witness in those proceedings or not, shall, subject to this section and to rules of court, be admissible as evidence of any fact stated therein of which direct oral evidence by him would be admissible.'

Direct oral evidence may be given only on oath. A child who is too young to give sworn evidence may not give direct oral evidence. Hearsay evidence of older children who could be sworn is admissible subject to compliance with the 1968 Act and rules of court. These require notice to be given and enable a party to give a counter-notice to require the relevant person to be called as a witness unless he is dead, beyond the seas, unfit by reason of bodily or mental condition to attend as a witness, cannot with reasonable diligence be identified or found, or cannot be reasonably expected to have any recollection of matters relevant to the accuracy or otherwise of the statement.

**8.26** In *Bradford City Metropolitan Council v K (Minors)* (1989) *Times* 18 August, a similar problem was considered in relation to care proceedings under the 1969 Act. The court held that evidence of what the child had said to a foster parent or teacher was not admissible as to the facts alleged, although on general principles it was admissible as to the state of mind of the child.

**8.27** The overall effect of these cases has naturally been to encourage applicants to use wardship proceedings where the rules of evidence are relaxed. This is not consistent with the policy of the 1989 Act, which makes substantial changes to the principles set out above.

**8.28** Section 96(1) and (2) provide that a child may give unsworn evidence in civil proceedings, provided he understands that it is his duty to speak the truth and he has sufficient understanding to justify his evidence being heard. This has long been possible in criminal proceedings: s 38 of the Children and Young Persons Act 1933. Further, since the child may give direct oral evidence without being on oath, his statement may be put in evidence under the Civil Evidence Act 1968. Nevertheless some children are too young to give evidence, sworn or unsworn, in which case their evidence will not be admissible even under the 1968 Act.

**8.29** Section 96(3)-(5) make provision for the Lord Chancellor by order to abrogate the hearsay rule in relation to civil proceedings (either in general or in particular types of case) and evidence in connection with the upbringing, maintenance or welfare of a child. The order may provide for the admissibility of statements made orally or in a prescribed form or which are recorded by any prescribed method of recording — clearly, video is in mind here. Different provisions may be made for different purposes and for different courts. Although these provisions were brought into force on Royal Assent on 16 November 1989 (s 108(2)), at the time of writing the necessary orders had not been made.

**8.30** At first sight, it could be argued that the welfare of the child would require video-recording to be used as the preferred method of putting the child's account of events before the court. However, it is necessary to consider whether first-hand evidence from the child rather than a video will be more compelling. It would be possible to provide for a form of interview to be conducted by a person with particular expertise and training in the interviewing of children for the purpose of establishing an early record of the child's story in a form which is acceptable to the court.

**8.31** Although the recent problems on hearsay evidence have related to the admissibility of children's evidence, there remains the question of admitting hearsay evidence where other persons are not able or are unwilling to give evidence. Section 96(4)(b) is general in its terms and would allow any hearsay evidence in connection with the upbringing, maintenance or welfare of the child. The difficulty of hearing admissions or retracted allegations, considered in some old cases like *Humberside CC v DPR* [1977] 3 All ER 964, could be solved by rules of court. The Government has announced (LCD Press Release 22 November 1989) that the whole issue of the admissibility of hearsay evidence in civil proceedings has been referred to the Law Commission.

## Self-incrimination

**8.32** In proceedings for an order under Part IV or V, no person shall be excused from giving evidence on any matter or answering any question put to him in the course of giving evidence on the ground that doing so might incriminate him or his spouse: s 98(1). A statement or admission made in such proceedings shall not be admissible in evidence against the person making it or his spouse in proceedings for an offence other than perjury: s 96(2).

This is beneficial in care proceedings, where it has often been argued that parents may not reasonably be expected to give evidence which might prejudice a subsequent criminal trial.[1] Parents will no longer be able to say they cannot answer and care proceedings need not be delayed pending a criminal trial.

1 See also *Home Office Circular* 84/1982.

## Paternity tests

**8.33** Section 89, which came into force on 16 November 1989 (s 108(2)) amends the Family Law Reform Act 1969 by adding two new provisions: s 20(1A) and (1B). Under s 20(1A), where a person applies under s 20 for a direction for tests so as to establish paternity in respect of a child under the age of 18, the applicant must nominate the person whom he wishes to carry out the tests. Under s 20(1B), the court must either make the direction specifying that the nominated person carry out the tests or decline to make the direction at all.

**8.34** The reason for this change lies in the rapidly developing nature of the paternity-testing business. With the advent of DNA testing, testers are now offering different tests at different prices. These measures enable applicants, who in any event have to pay for the tests, to choose the tester. The matter, however, is not entirely left in the hands of the applicant since, by giving a right of veto, s 20(1B) does preserve some court control. The chosen tester must also be on the Home Secretary's approved list: *Home Office Circular* 91/1989.

Chapter 9

# Courts, jurisdiction and legal aid

## INTRODUCTION

**9.1** Although the 1989 Act is primarily aimed at reforming the substantive law dealing with children and not at reforming generally court structure,[1] nevertheless it does make important jurisdictional and procedural changes. The most important of these changes are:

(a) the creation of concurrent jurisdiction in all proceedings under the 1989 Act;
(b) the introduction of 'start' rules under which the Lord Chancellor is empowered to regulate the commencement of proceedings;
(c) the introduction of 'transfer' rules under which the Lord Chancellor is empowered to make provision for the vertical and lateral transfer of proceedings or parts of proceedings either between tiers of courts or between courts within the same tier;
(d) the removal of the juvenile court's jurisdiction to hear care proceedings and the introduction in those proceedings of a right of appeal to the High Court; and
(e) the creation of a family proceedings court at the magistrates' level, staffed by a Family Court Panel.

1 This was one of the Government responses when resisting attempts to introduce into the Bill a provision for a Family Court: see, for example, the Solicitor-General's comments at HC Deb, Standing Committee B, 8 June 1989, col 459.

**9.2** The objectives of the changes are said to be[1]:

(1) to create a flexible system under which cases may, according to their complexity, be heard at the appropriate level of court;
(2) to enable all proceedings affecting the child to be heard in the same court at the same time; and
(3) to ensure that cases are heard by magistrates and judges who are experienced in, and who have made a special study of, family work.[2]

1 See Lord Mackay LC's comments at HL Deb, 6 December 1988, Vol 502, col 494.
2 There is to be a training programme for judges, registrars and magistrates beginning sometime in 1990. It is expected that 50 circuit judges will be selected for special training: *The Times* 17 November 1989.

**9.3** These changes follow and in some cases considerably build upon, suggestions made by the *Review of Child Care Law* (DHSS, 1985, Chs 22 and 23) and the Lord Chancellor's discussion document *Improvements in* *the Arrangements for Care Proceedings* (1988). Although a number of provisions was added at the final Report Stage of the Bill, many further points remain to be worked out (particularly with regard to the 'start' and 'transfer' provisions). To assist in this crucial a task the Lord Chancellor, together with the President of the Family Division, has appointed Her Honour Judge Bracewell to be responsible to the President for advising on the judicial administration necessary to ensure the best possible transition to the new procedures.[1]

1 See Lord Mackay's comments in his *Joseph Jackson Memorial Lecture* (1989) 139 NLJ 505 at 507.

## CONCURRENT JURISDICTION AND CONSOLIDATION OF PROCEEDINGS

**9.4** Concurrent jurisdiction among the three tiers of courts to hear all children's proceedings under the 1989 Act is created under s 92(7), which provides that for the purposes of the Act '"the court" means the High Court, a county court or a magistrates' court'. There are, however, some exceptions. For example, Sch 1, para 1 preserves the embargo against magistrates making secured periodical payments and property transfer orders in applications for financial provision for children (Chapter 4). Section 92(4) also bars magistrates from entertaining any application or making any order involving the administration or application of (a) any property belonging to or held in trust for the child, or (b) any income of such property.

**9.5** While some provision for concurrent jurisdiction has been made in the past (for example, under the Guardianship of Minors Acts 1971 and 1973 and the Children Act 1975, Part II), the new provisions are more extensive including, for the first time, concurrent jurisdiction in respect of care proceedings. However, while the High Court and county court may make statutory care or supervision orders, rules will provide that proceedings must commence in the magistrates' court: see para 9.7.

**9.6** It is also intended[1] that all proceedings involving the same child and family, wherever they are started, can be brought together and heard as a single proceeding. Substantively, consolidation is facilitated by s 10(1) (see para 3.22), which empowers *any* court in *any* family proceedings to make s 8 orders and, by s 37 (see para 7.4), under which the court may direct a local authority to investigate the child's circumstances with a view to them applying for a care order. It is expected that such local authority applications will be heard by the court which directed the investigation. Further, local authorities will, with leave, be able to apply to intervene in any existing family proceedings: s 10(1)(a)(ii). In this way, all courts in family proceedings will (subject to the exceptions referred to at para 9.4) have the same powers. Under Sch 11, paras 1(3) and 2, the Lord Chancellor is empowered to make orders for the consolidation of family proceedings in the event of proceedings under the 1989 Act, the Adoption Act 1976 or the inherent jurisdiction of the High Court having already been commenced.

1 See, eg, the Solicitor-General's comments at HC Deb, Standing Committee B, 8 June 1989, col 457.

## THE 'START' AND 'TRANSFER' PROVISIONS

**9.7** Central to the objective of speedy and efficient case management by the courts are the new 'start' and 'transfer' provisions. Under Sch 11, para 1(1) and (2), the Lord Chancellor is empowered to make orders regulating the level of court or the description of court within a tier in which proceedings under the 1989 Act or the Adoption Act 1976 may be started. Under Sch 11, para 2, the Lord Chancellor is empowered to order that in specified circumstances the whole or part of specified proceedings may be transferred to another court (whether or not at the same level). The order may provide for the transfer of proceedings at any stage.

**9.8** Although these provisions give the Lord Chancellor wide powers, it is expected that, with regard to the start provisions he will exercise them only in a minority of cases. As Lord Mackay said in his *Joseph Jackson Memorial Lecture* ((1989) 139 NLJ at 506), the vast majority of proceedings under the 1989 Act will be self-allocating in that by far the largest number of orders will continue to be made in the course of divorce or other matrimonial proceedings. There is no intention to make specific allocation in such cases.

**9.9** The Lord Chancellor has, however, announced (HL Deb, 6 December 1988, Vol 502, col 494) that he intends to require care cases to start in the magistrates' court. This is because he considers (see (1989) 139 NLJ 507) that the majority of such cases can be dealt with competently at that level, 'especially once the jurisdiction has been consolidated with the magistrates' jurisdiction in other family matters and the other improvements in magistrates' training and their court procedures have been implemented'. However, as the Lord Chancellor has explained, once a care case has been started in the magistrates' court, provision will be made to enable a clerk or the magistrates (under Sch 11, para 3(1)(b) the power is exercisable by a single magistrate) to order the case to be transferred up. Such a decision is to be governed by criteria prescribed by the Lord Chancellor, which will no doubt include matters such as the forensic or legal complexity of the case.[1] A particular problem, which will require careful scrutiny, is the 'straightforward' care case where the contact issues are complex. If a magistrates' court or clerk refuses to transfer a case, it is intended that an aggrieved party be able to apply direct to a county court for a transfer. Any decision will be based on the prescribed criteria. Once transferred, the case will be allocated either within a county court or the High Court. There is no intention to provide for a further transfer procedure to determine whether a case deserves a High Court hearing.

1 For other suggested criteria see Hall and Martin 'The Children Bill in context' (1989) Journal of Child Law, Vol 1 pp 98, 99-100.

**9.10** While these transfer provisions will provide essential flexibility, for the system to work, applicants will need to provide the court with sufficient information on which sensible decisions can be reached. Further, as Lord Mackay said (ibid), there will need to be effective administrative machinery and close co-operation between the magistrates' and county courts. In particular, there needs to be flexibility to ensure that cases initially heard at one level are subsequently heard at the appropriate level if the case changes in complexity.

## OTHER JURISDICTIONAL CHANGES

### The family proceedings court

**9.11** The magistrates' domestic court is renamed the 'family proceedings court' and the domestic court panel, the 'family panel': s 92(1). This is not intended to be simply a matter of nomenclature, but more an expression of the specific nature of such courts. They will be staffed by members of the panel consisting of magistrates whose training and expertise qualify them for such jurisdiction.[1] In other words, current members of the domestic panels (or juvenile court panels) will not automatically become members of the family panel.

1 See the Solicitor-General's comments at HC Deb, Standing Committee B, 8 June 1989, col 458.

**9.12** It is expected that in October 1990 'shadow' panels will be appointed and their members will be expected to undertake a minimum of eighteen hours of specific training for the new court.

**9.13** Under the general rule-making powers under s 93, provision may be made governing rules of procedure and evidence in the magistrates' courts. It may reasonably be anticipated, following the recommendations of the *Review of Child Care Law* (Ch 16), which were accepted in outline in the White Paper (Cm 62, 1987, paras 54-58) that quite far-reaching changes will be made. For example, provision may be expected to be made for the advance disclosure of evidence, the greater use of affidavits and for magistrates to give reasons for their decisions.

### Principal registry to be treated as county court

**9.14** In line with s 42 of the Matrimonial and Family Proceedings Act 1984, s 92(9) empowers the Lord Chancellor to make provision for the principal registry of the Family Division to be treated as if it were a county court for such purposes of the 1989 Act as may be specified.

## APPEALS

### 1 Appeals from the magistrates' courts

**9.15** The general rule, provided by s 94(1), is that an appeal lies to the High Court against both the making and the refusal to make any order (but see para 9.16) under the 1989 Act. Based on the recommendations first made by the *Review of Child Care Law* (Ch 22) and foreshadowed in the White Paper (para 66), s 94(1) makes three important changes in respect of care proceedings, namely:

(1) appeals lie to the High Court, not the Crown Court;
(2) appeals lie against the refusal as well as the making of a care or supervision order; and
(3) local authorities, like any other party, will have full rights of appeal.[1]

The switch of forum of appeal from the Crown Court to the High Court is part of the general strategy to emphasise the civil nature of applications for care or supervision orders. Unlike the former right of appeal, appeals to the High Court are not by way of rehearing.[2]

1 See the comments of the Solicitor-General at HC Deb, 23 October 1989, Vol 158, col 590.
2 This was one of the reasons why the *Review of Child Care Law* (paras 22.10-11) concluded that the appropriate forum for appeal was a 'finely balanced' issue.

**9.16** The exceptions to the general right of appeal are that no appeal lies:

(1) against a decision to decline jurisdiction because a case is considered more conveniently dealt with by another court: s 94(2)[1];
(2) the making or refusal of an interim periodical payments order under Sch 1: s 94(3);
(3) outside the circumstances to be laid down by the Lord Chancellor in connection with the transfer or proposed transfer of proceedings under Sch 11, para 2: s 94(10) and (11); or
(4) against the making or refusal to make an emergency protection order or against any direction given in connection with such an order: s 45(10).

With regard to this last point it was felt[2] that a formal appeals procedure, with the added delay that would be involved, was inappropriate, given the short duration and emergency nature of the order.

1 This is similar to the embargo under s 27 of the Domestic Proceedings and Magistrates' Courts Act 1978, which it replaces.
2 See the Solicitor-General's comments at HC Deb, 23 October 1989, Vol 158, col 591.

**9.17** Upon an appeal, the High Court may make such orders as may be necessary to give effect to its determination of the appeal and such incidental and consequential orders as appear just: s 94(5) and (6). Where the appeal relates to the making of a periodical payments order, the High Court may order[1] that its determination of the appeal shall have effect from such date, consistent with rules of court, as it thinks fit to specify: s 94(6) and (7). If it reduces the payments or discharges the order, it may order the payee to return the sums paid as it thinks fit, and may order the remittance of part or the whole of any arrears: s 94(8). Any order made on appeal, other than that directing the application to be reheard by the magistrates, for the purposes of enforcement[2] and any power to vary, revive or discharge the order, shall be treated as if it were an order of the original magistrates' court and not the High Court: s 94(9).

1 As it could under the Domestic Proceedings and Magistrates' Courts Act 1978, s 29.
2 Ie, s 63(3) of the Magistrates' Courts Act 1980 applies. See, eg, *B (BPM) v B (MM)* [1969] P 103.

## 2 Appeals from county courts and the High Court

**9.18** The 1989 Act has not changed the route of appeal from decisions of the county court or the High Court. In each case, an appeal will lie to the Court of Appeal.[1] Leave to appeal is not required[2] where residence, education or welfare of the minor is concerned, nor where the applicant has been refused *all*[3] contact[4] with the minor. Whether leave will be required to appeal against the making or the refusal to make a care or supervision order is perhaps a moot point, but since such decisions concern the child's welfare, it may be thought that they come within the above exception.

1 County Courts Act 1984, s 77(1) and the Supreme Court Act 1981, s 16.
2 Supreme Court Act 1981, s 18(1)(h)(i) and (ii), as amended by Sch 13, para 45(1) of the 1989 Act.
3 But leave will be required where contact has been *restricted*: see *Re H (Minors) (Access: appeals)* [1989] 2 FLR 174.
4 The change from 'access' to 'contact' in s 18(1)(h)(ii) means, contrary to the decision in *Allette v Allette* [1986] 2 FLR 427, that the granting of non-physical contact (eg by letter or telephone) will count as a restriction so that leave will be required.

## 3 The position pending appeal

**9.19** Under the general powers to impose directions and conditions under s 11(7), any court can postpone the operation of any s 8 order pending an appeal or make any other interim arrangement. It is anticipated that, as formerly,[1] stays will not normally be granted for more than fourteen days.

1 See *Hereford and Worcester CC v EH* [1985] FLR 975 at 977, per Wood J.

**9.20** Implementing the proposals outlined in the White Paper (paras 67-68), under s 40(1) and (2) the court may, if it dismisses an application for a care order *and* at the time of dismissal the child is the subject of an interim care or supervision order, make either a care or supervision order, as the case may be, for a limited duration pending an appeal. Similarly, upon granting a discharge, the court may order either that its decision is not to have effect or that the care or supervision order is to continue, pending the appeal: s 40(3).

**9.21** In each case these orders may have effect only for the 'appeal period', that is, either between the lodging of an appeal and the determination of it, or the time during which an appeal may be made: s 40(4) and (6).

# PRIVACY OF PROCEEDINGS

**9.22** One of the consequences of repealing the Guardianship of Minors Act 1971 and of removing the juvenile court's jurisdiction to hear care proceedings, is that the rules governing when magistrates may sit in private and what matters may be reported have had to be rewritten. Opportunity has thus been taken to replace the former 'hotch-potch' of protection with coherent and consistent provisions. On the other hand, apart from making consequential changes, the 1989 Act has not altered the position for proceedings in the higher courts.

## 1 The Power to Sit in Private

### *The magistrates' court*

**9.23** Under s 97(1), rules may be made under s 144 of the Magistrates' Courts Act 1980 enabling magistrates to sit in private when considering whether to exercise any of their powers under the 1989 Act. If the rules follow r 6 of the Magistrates' Courts (Guardianship of Minors) Rules 1974-80 (which they will replace) they will provide that the court shall hear an application in private where it considers it expedient in the interests of the child concerned. One effect of this rule-making power is that for the first time magistrates will be able to sit in private when hearing care proceedings.

### *The higher courts*

**9.24** The 1989 Act makes no specific amendment to the powers of the higher courts to sit in private, but it is expected that the current practice of the High Court normally to dispose of applications in chambers under RSC Ord 90, r 7, and that of the county court to hear cases in chambers unless it otherwise directs under the CCR 1981, Ord 47, r 6, will apply when hearing applications under the 1989 Act.[1]

1 This means that the Press may now be excluded: cf Children and Young Persons Act 1933, s 47(2).

## 2 Publicity

### *Magistrates' hearings*

**9.25** Under s 97(2), it is an offence, punishable on summary conviction by a fine not exceeding level 4 on the standard scale (s 97(6)), to publish[1] any material intended or likely to identify any child involved in the proceedings or that child's address or school. It is a defence if the accused can prove that he did not know and had no reason to suspect that the published material was intended, or likely, to identify the child: s 97(3). The court or Secretary of State may, if satisfied that the child's welfare requires it, lift the restriction: s 97(4). This power, which is modelled on that under the Children and Young Persons Act 1933, s 49, is to allow for the rare case where it is in the child's best interests for the facts to be fully published rather than to have rumour and speculation flourish (see the Solicitor-General's comments at HC Deb, 23 October 1989, Vol 158, col 633).

1 Under s 97(5) 'publish' includes radio and television broadcasts or to cause to be published, and 'material' includes any picture or representation.

**9.26** In addition to the above-mentioned restrictions, s 97(8) expressly preserves the operation of s 71 of the Magistrates' Courts Act 1980. Under this provision, newspapers or periodicals (but not television or radio) may publish only the grounds of the application, submissions on points of law and the court decision, including any observation made by the court in giving it.

**9.27** Both the above-mentioned provisions operate in any event, but further restrictions will apply if the court sits in private (see para 9.28).

### *Proceedings in the higher courts*

**9.28** The automatic reporting restrictions imposed by s 97(2) do not apply to cases heard in the higher courts. Instead, regard must be had to s 12 of the Administration of Justice Act 1960, which applies whenever a court sits in private. As amended by Sch 13, para 14 of the 1989 Act, s 12 prohibits publication of information relating to proceedings before *any* court in cases where the proceedings:

'(i) relate to the exercise of the inherent jurisdiction of the High Court with respect to minors;
(ii) are brought under the Children Act 1989; or
(iii) otherwise relate wholly or mainly to the maintenance or upbringing of any minor'.

**9.29** It is now established that s 12 affords only limited protection against publicity in that it does not prevent publication of the names and addresses or photograph of the child nor of details about the order.[1] What is restricted, however, is publication of the contents of any reports (eg, of the Official Solicitor, welfare officer or guardian ad litem) made in connection with the hearing, and of proofs of witnesses and submissions made during proceedings. It remains open to the High Court to impose specific restrictions under its inherent jurisdiction.[2] The county court would appear to have no such inherent powers nor, for the reasons discussed at para 3.19, may a restriction be imposed by a prohibited steps order under s 8. Given this limited protection, it seems unfortunate that s 97(2) is not expressed to apply to all cases under the 1989 Act.

1 See, eg, *Re L (a Minor) (Wardship: freedom of publication)* [1988] 1 All ER 418 and *Re W (Minors) (Wardship: contempt)* [1989] Fam Law 19.
2 See, eg, *Re X (a Minor) (Wardship: injunction)* [1984] 1 WLR 1421; *Re C (a Minor) (Wardship: medical treatment)(No 2)* [1989] 2 All ER 791; and *Re M and N (Minors)* (1989) 139 NLJ 1154.

## LEGAL AID

**9.30** The 1989 Act makes a number of important changes to the provision of legal aid. For example, Sch 12, para 45 amends para 2 of Part I of Sch 2 of the Legal Aid Act 1988 so as to provide that civil legal aid is available for all civil proceedings (which includes care proceedings) in the magistrates' courts. Section 99 amends the Legal Aid Act 1988 so that where a child is brought before the court on an application under s 25 to place him in secure accommodation, he must be granted legal aid if he wishes it without any merits test, nor, as formerly, a means test.

**9.31** Section 99(5) also makes general provision for the Lord Chancellor to make such further amendments to the Legal Aid Act 1988 as he considers necessary or expedient in consequence of any provision of the 1989 Act. In this regard, the Government has announced[1] that, to ensure that the Legal Aid Board may grant aid quickly, it intends to waive the merits test for those who are automatically parties in care proceedings and to grant legal aid in advance of the means test. Further, it intends to waive the means test entirely for children who are the subject of a care application.

**1** See the Solicitor-General's statement at HC Deb, 23 October 1989, Vol 158, col 520.

Chapter 10

# Wardship and the inherent jurisdiction

## INTRODUCTION

**10.1** Although the impact of the 1989 Act upon wardship is considerable, the jurisdiction is not in itself abolished. Echoing the earlier comments of the Law Commission (Law Com No 172, para 1.4), Lord Mackay LC said, when introducing the Bill (HL Deb, 6 December 1988, Vol 502, col 493), that subject to one important exception, it was not sought to reform wardship as such, although 'many of the reforms both in the private and public statute law should substantially reduce the need to invoke the High Court's inherent jurisdiction'.

**10.2** The one exception, which had not been specifically recommended either by the Law Commission or by the *Review of Child Care Law*, is that the High Court's inherent jurisdiction may not be used to make an order for the care, supervision or accommodation of children by local authorities.[1] The rationale behind this embargo is that the 'threshold provisions' under s 31 (see para 6.5), which had been carefully designed as the minimum circumstances justifying State intervention, must always be satisfied before either a care or supervision order may be made. This in turn is based on the philosophy, in Lord Mackay's words,[2] that 'the integrity and independence of the family is the basic building block of a free and democratic society and the need to defend it should be clearly perceivable in the law. Accordingly, unless there is evidence that a child is being or is likely to be positively harmed because of a failure in the family, the state, whether in the guise of a local authority or a court, should not interfere'.

1 As Lord Mackay LC explained in his *Joseph Jackson Memorial Lecture* (1989) 139 NLJ 505 at 507, the Government's decision to restrict its use was taken late in the day.
2 *Joseph Jackson Memorial Lecture* p 508. See also his comments when introducing the Bill HL Deb, 6 December 1988, Vol 502, col 493.

**10.3** Although the wardship jurisdiction in particular and the wider inherent jurisdiction in general can no longer operate as a fail-safe jurisdiction to commit children into local authority care when the statutory criteria cannot be satisfied, it has not lost its 'safety net' role altogether, even in the local authority context. In appropriate cases (see para 10.13) local authorities may still invoke the inherent jurisdiction to resolve specific questions provided that there is no alternative statutory procedure and there is an apparent likelihood of substantial harm to the child.

**10.4** With regard to the latter point, it was first contemplated that local authorities would still look to the *wardship* jurisdiction to resolve specific questions concerning children in their care. However, it became apparent that during the progress of the Bill the Government's thinking changed. This was most clearly signposted by Lord Mackay LC in his *Joseph Jackson Memorial Lecture* ((1989) 139 NLJ 505 at 507) when he commented: 'in the Government's view wardship is only one use of the High Court's inherent *parens patriae* jurisdiction. We believe therefore, that it is open to the High Court to make orders under its inherent jurisdiction in respect of children other than through wardship'. Accordingly, where a local authority wishes to obtain a High Court order in respect of a child already in care (see paras 10.13 et seq), they may seek to invoke that court's inherent powers rather than to ward the child.

**10.5** Although there is little doubt that the High Court does have a general inherent power to protect children outside wardship,[1] it has so far been little developed. Although proceedings under the inherent jurisdiction are prima facie assigned to the Family Division of the High Court,[2] as yet no procedure has been specified. It is suggested that application be by originating summons and headed 'In the Matter of the Inherent Jurisdiction'.

1 See, for example, *S v McC, W v W* [1972] AC 24, per Lord McDermott; and *Richards v Richards* [1984] AC 174, per Lord Scarman. See also Bradney 'The Judge as Parens Patriae' [1988] Fam Law 137, at 142, who argues that wardship is just a means of access to the *parens patriae* jurisdiction.
2 Supreme Court Act 1981, Sch 1, para 3 (b)(i), as amended by Sch 13, para 45(3) of the 1989 Act.

**10.6** Unlike wardship, the exercise of the inherent jurisdiction will not place the child under the ultimate responsibility of the court. This means that at no point will the child be subject to the rule obtaining in wardship that all important steps in the child's life have to be sanctioned by the court. As Lord Mackay LC has said (*Joseph Jackson Memorial Lecture*, ibid at 508) under the new scheme obtaining under the 1989 Act it was not thought 'appropriate or practicable for the responsibility for a child in the care of a public authority which is statutorily charged with looking after him to be subject to the detailed directions of another public authority, namely the courts'.

## RESTRICTIONS ON THE HIGH COURT'S POWER UNDER WARDSHIP AND THE INHERENT JURISDICTION

### 1 No power to commit into care or supervision of a local authority

**10.7** The statutory power to commit a ward of court into the care or supervision of a local authority under s 7 of the Family Law Reform Act 1969 has been repealed: s 100(1). Similarly, the High Court's inherent jurisdiction both to require a child to be placed in the care, or to be put under the supervision of a local authority, and to require a child to be accommodated by or on behalf of a local authority, has been expressly curtailed: s 100(2). Like any other court in family proceedings, in cases where it appears that a care or supervision order may be appropriate, all the High Court may do is direct a local authority to investigate the child's circumstances with a view to the authority making an application: s 37 (see para 7.4), and then make a care order if the local authority do apply.

**10.8** As a result of these provisions, there can now be no question of the High Court making a care or supervision order, save upon the criteria laid down by the 1989 Act. An immediate consequence is that there is no power to commit seventeen-year-olds, or married sixteen-year-olds, into care because the power to make care orders under s 31 is so expressly confined: s 31(3). Although the power to make a care order under the Children and Young Persons Act 1969 was similarly fettered, the High Court had nevertheless felt able to make committal to care orders under their wardship jurisdiction: see, eg, *Re SW (a Minor) (Wardship: jurisdiction)* [1986] 1 FLR 24.[1]

1 For differing views on the desirability of this change cf Lowe at (1989) 139 NLJ 87 with Eekelaar and Dingwall at (1989) 139 NLJ 217.

**10.9** Section 100(2)(c) states that the High Court may not exercise its inherent jurisdiction so as to 'make a child who is the subject of a care order a ward of court'. Further, the new s 41(2A) of the Supreme Court Act 1981 (added by Sch 13, para 45(2)) makes it clear that a child in care does not become a ward upon the making of a wardship application. The incompatibility of wardship and local authority care is further emphasised by s 91(4), which states that the making of a care order with respect to a ward brings that wardship to an end. These provisions, however, do *not* prevent the High Court from exercising its *inherent* jurisdiction to decide a specific question in relation to a child in local authority care - see para 10.16.

## 2 The transitional arrangements with regard to wards of court already placed in the care or supervision of local authorities

**10.10** Under Sch 14, para 15(1)(e) and (2), on the day that Part IV of the 1989 Act comes into force, orders made under the Family Law Reform Act 1969, s 7(2) (but not, it seems, those made under the High Court's inherent powers) committing wards of court into local authority care are deemed to be care orders as defined by the 1989 Act. The effect of this is not beyond dispute. If the deeming provision triggers s 91(4), under which the making of a care order automatically brings wardship to an end in respect of that child, then, upon implementation of Part IV, all wards committed to care under the 1969 Act cease to be wards. Although this would seem to be the intention of the legislation, it could nevertheless be argued that s 91(4) is not brought into operation since the court has not, after implementation, made a care order[1]. Given the number of wards in local authority care and the fact that unless they are dewarded they remain subject to the court's overall control, this point is important. Until it is clarified, local authorities might be wise to assume that the wardship continues and to seek a specific order ending it. Another uncertainty, even if the wardship is brought to an end, is the effect which court directions about a ward have. Unlike those made under the Guardianship Act 1973 and the

Matrimonial Causes Act 1973 (see Sch 14, para 16(5)), the 1989 Act makes no provision for the continuing effect of directions made in wardship proceedings. Consideration may need to be given for making further modifications to Sch 14 under the powers conferred by s 108(8)(a) to cover this point.

1 It could also be argued that existing wardships are "pending proceedings" so that, pursuant to Sch 14 para 1(1), they are unaffected by the 1989 Act.

**10.11** With regard to supervision orders in respect of wards of court made under s 7(4) of the Family Law Reform Act 1969, Sch 14, para 26 provides that the order shall continue in force for one year after implementation of Part IV unless (a) the court directs that it shall cease to have effect earlier than that, or (b) it would have ceased to have effect earlier than that, had the Act not been passed. Unlike care orders, there is no question but that the wardship continues, until the court orders otherwise.

### 3 Further restrictions

**10.12** Section 100(2)(d) prevents the High Court from exercising its inherent jurisdiction 'for the purpose of conferring on any local authority power to determine any question which has arisen, or which may arise, in connection with any aspect of parental responsibility for a child'.The none too clear result of this provision would appear to be that while the High Court may make orders under its inherent jurisdiction in respect of a child, in doing so, it may not confer any aspect of parental responsibility upon a local authority that that authority does not already have. If the child is in care, then the local authority will already have parental responsibility and so the determination of a particular question by the Court, for example, the sanctioning of specific medical treatment of the child, will leave the authority free to arrange for it to be carried out. If the local authority do not have parental responsibility for the child, the High Court may not under its inherent jurisdiction make orders which in any way confer parental responsibility upon the authority. Hence, for example, while the Court could sanction a named couple to look after the child (although it would probably do this by means of a residence order under s 8) it could not authorise a local authority to place the child nor, *a fortiori,* to place the child 'with a view to adoption'.

## RESTRICTIONS ON LOCAL AUTHORITIES' USE OF THE INHERENT JURISDICTION

### 1 The need to obtain leave

**10.13** Although local authorities can no longer look to the inherent jurisdiction as a means of putting them in charge of the child's living arrangements, they can nevertheless seek to use it to resolve specific questions about the child's future. Indeed, because of the embargos in s 9(1) and (2) (see paras 3.33 et seq), they must do so if the child is in their care. Nevertheless, this avenue is fettered because under s 100(3) local authorities must first obtain the court's leave to apply for any exercise of the High Court's inherent jurisdiction.

## 2 Criteria for granting leave

**10.14** Before granting leave, the court must first be satisfied that the result sought to be achieved cannot be achieved under any statutory jurisdiction: s 100(4)(a). This bar will operate even where the statutory remedy is contingent upon the local authority having first to obtain leave before being able to seek an order: s 100(5)(b). This restriction will make it particularly difficult for an authority to obtain leave for the exercise of the inherent jurisdiction in respect of a child not in their care, since in those circumstances they could seek to obtain a prohibited steps or specific issue order under s 8. One example, however, is where it is sought to restrain publicity about a child, since (see para 3.19) that seems to fall outside the scope of s 8.

**10.15** Even if there is no alternative remedy, before being able to grant leave, the court must be satisfied that 'there is reasonable cause to believe that if the court's inherent jurisdiction is not exercised with respect to the child he is likely to suffer significant harm': s 100(4)(b). Although this provision is in line with the need to establish at least a likelihood of significant harm before the court is entitled to intervene to make a care or supervision order, whether it was necessary to make the ground for leave quite so narrow may be questioned. As others have pointed out,[1] since the local authority's objective cannot be the acquisition of parental responsibility, a less stringent test, such as the court having to be satisfied that the exercise of its inherent jurisdiction is necessary to secure the child's welfare, would not have upset the general philosophy and might have better served children's interests.

1 Eekelaar and Dingwall at (1989) 139 NLJ 218.

## 3 Circumstances when the leave criteria might be satisfied

**10.16** It is not anticipated that local authorities will often be justified in having recourse to the inherent jurisdiction. The expectation is that, since they have parental responsibility, local authorities should make decisions themselves. Nevertheless, there will be occasions when recourse to the High Court will be appropriate. Lord Mackay LC instanced ((1989) 139 NLJ at 507) the exercise of the inherent power to sanction or forbid an abortion being carried out on a child in care, where there are no other statutory means of seeking a court order and the decision, if wrong, is clearly likely to cause significant harm. Even in this example it might be thought necessary to have recourse to the court only in the event of a dispute or, possibly, where there is some doubt about whether the proper process has been carried out. Another example is sterilisation. Indeed if Lord Templeman's lone dictum in *Re B (A Minor) (Wardship: Sterilisation)* [1988] AC 199, 205 is followed, local authorities *must* seek leave of the High Court (see also *Practice Note (official solicitor: sterilisation)* (1989) 139 NLJ 1380).

**10.17** Another issue where High Court help might be justified is whether a mentally or physically handicapped child should have a life-saving or life-prolonging operation. While such an issue is obviously crucial to the child concerned, it must not be assumed that leave will always be given. For example, if, as in a case like *Re C (a Minor) (Wardship: medical treatment)* [1989] 2 All ER 782, a baby is terminally ill and the medical team considers that the goal should be to ease the baby's suffering rather than to achieve a short prolongation of life, then even if the local authority disagree, it is not all certain that they would satisfy the criterion set out in s 100(4)(b).[1] In practice, the argument of substance may well take place on the application for leave.

1 *Aliter* if, as in *Re B (a Minor) (Wardship: medical treatment)* [1981] 1 WLR 1421, the baby's life can be saved by a reasonably straightforward operation, but possibly not if the continued life could be shown to be so demonstratively awful as to justify allowing the child to die.

**10.18** The above medical problems are extreme examples of situations when High Court intervention might be justified, but circumstances do not always have to be so extraordinary. For example, if a local authority wish to obtain injunctions, to prevent a violent father from discovering his child's whereabouts (as in *Re JT (a Minor) (Wardship: committal to care)* [1986] 2 FLR 107) or from molesting his child (as in *Re B (a Minor) (Wardship: child in care)* [1975] Fam 26), or to restrain harmful publicity about the child (as in *Re L (a Minor) (Wardship: freedom of speech)* [1988] 1 All ER 418), then the inherent jurisdiction is the only means of obtaining the remedy and it should not be too difficult to satisfy the leave criteria.

## 4 Commentary

**10.19** As the Lord Chancellor himself said, the restrictions upon the use of wardship are among the more controversial provisions of the Act. Some of the concern about the removal of the local authorities' ability to use the jurisdiction in order to have children committed into their care will be dispelled if the High Court continues to hear the difficult cases under its new care jurisdiction. To many, however, it still seems premature to remove the inherent power to commit children into local authority care without first waiting see how well the 'threshold' provisions work in practice. In his *Joseph Jackson Memorial Lecture* ((1989) 139 NLJ at 507) Lord Mackay acknowledged that there will be 'difficult borderline cases where at present wardship, which can be invoked simply on the basis of the child's best interests, would offer a remedy'. Notwithstanding this, he was resolute in defence of the new restrictions, arguing that where a court becomes involved in intervention from outside the family, and especially where State intervention is proposed, a broad discretion without defined criteria, whatever its guiding principle, cannot be justified.

# THE USE OF WARDSHIP AND THE INHERENT JURISDICTION AGAINST LOCAL AUTHORITIES

**10.20** The 1989 Act operates only to restrict access to wardship (and the inherent jurisdiction) by local authorities; it does not directly affect individuals' right to invoke the jurisdiction. By the same token, and despite the recommendations in the *Cleveland Report*[1] that the position be reconsidered, the 1989 Act does nothing to abrogate the principle laid down by *A v Liverpool CC* [1982] AC 363 and *Re W (a Minor) (Wardship: jurisdiction)* [1985] AC 791 that wardship may not be used as a means of challenging or reviewing local authority action in respect of children in their care. In general, therefore, recourse must be had either to the local authority complaints procedure (see Chapter 5) or to judicial review.

1 *Report of the Inquiry into Child Abuse in Cleveland* (Cm 412, 1988).

**10.21** The suggestion made by Ewbank J in *R v North Yorkshire CC, ex p M (No 3)* [1989] 2 FLR 82, that in exceptional cases, upon a successful application for judicial review, the court had power to make a child a ward of court, cannot in the light of s 100(2)(c) now be followed if the child is in care. Further, the practice of allowing local authorities to waive jurisdiction and permit wardship to be invoked even though the child is in care similarly cannot continue in view of s 100(2)(c). In each of these cases, however, it would still seem open to the court to exercise its inherent powers insofar as they are not restricted by s 100(2).

## IMPACT OF THE 1989 ACT ON THE USE OF WARDSHIP OUTSIDE THE LOCAL AUTHORITY CONTEXT

**10.22** Although the 1989 Act does not directly affect the use of wardship by individuals, the expectation and indeed the object (see para 10.1), is that the number of applications outside the local authority context (currently about 40 per cent of all wardships)[1] will also decline. Since wider powers under s 8 are available in all family proceedings, there will simply be less need to invoke the more expensive and often slow High Court jurisdiction. Grandparents and other relatives, for example, (who initiate about 13 per cent of all wardships) will be much better advised to seek, albeit with leave, s 8 orders in the lower courts.

1 According to the 1988 Judicial Statistics (Cm 745), Table 5.4, 1436 out of a total of 3704 originating summons were made by individuals.

**10.23** The one remaining advantage of wardship is its immediacy: as soon as the originating summons is issued, the child becomes a ward and no important step may then be taken with regard to that child's life without prior court sanction. Therefore, wardship is still often invoked with regard to threatened abduction particularly, where an international element is involved. But even in this context, if it is invoked with the sole aim of preventing the child's removal from the jurisdiction, it seems questionable to use wardship, since under the Child Abduction Act 1984 it is a crime wrongfully to take a child outside the United Kingdom and a court order is not a necessary requisite (although it will remain a useful device for convincing the police to intervene) to obtain police help to obtain an All Ports Warning.[1]

1 See generally *Clarke Hall and Morrison* (10th Ed) **C** [134].

Chapter 11

# Changes to adoption law

## INTRODUCTION

11.1 The Act makes a number of changes to adoption law, the most substantial and obvious being the amendments and repeals to the Adoption Act 1976 contained in Schs 10 and 15. There are, however, other parts of the 1989 Act that affect adoption, for example, the abolition of custodianship (see para 11.22) and the designation of adoption proceedings as 'family proceedings' (see paras 11.20 and 11.21).

**11.2** Although many of the changes resulting from the Sch 10 amendments are consequential upon the changes of concepts, terminology and philosophy introduced by the 1989 Act, there are a number of unrelated substantive changes. These are not based on any specific report but were apparently[1] introduced to meet the needs of particular groups, advantage being taken of the legislative opportunity to make some helpful but piecemeal changes pending a full-scale review of adoption law expected in the near future.

1 As explained by David Mellor when introducing the new Schedule: HC Deb, Standing Committee B, June 6 1989, col 380.

## THE CHANGES

### 1 The consequential amendments

**11.3** A key change in the 1989 Act is the introduction of the concept of 'parental responsibility' to replace the notion of 'parental rights and duties'. For example, s 12 of the Adoption Act 1976 ('the 1976 Act') has been amended[1] inter alia, to provide that an 'adoption order is an order giving parental responsibility for a child to the adopters' and that the making of an adoption order operates to extinguish 'the parental responsibility which any person has for the child before the making of an order'. The new s 12(3)(aa) also states that an adoption order extinguishes any order made under the Children Act 1989 (see para 11.22). The expression 'parental responsibility' has been added to the definition section (s 72) and is defined as having the same meaning as in the Children Act 1989: Sch 10, para 30(7).

1 Sch 10, para 3. For other changes of this nature, see Sch 10, paras 5(2), 6(2), 8(1) and (2), 9 and 11, respectively amending ss 16(2)(c), 18(5), 20(1)-(3) and 25(1) of the 1976 Act.

**11.4** Similarly, in general the words 'custody' or 'actual custody' have been replaced by the word 'home'.[1] In this latter respect, the new s 72(1A) of the 1976 Act (added by Sch 10, para 30(9)) provides that:

> 'in determining with what person, or where, a child has his home, any absence of the child at a hospital or boarding school and any other temporary absence shall be disregarded'.

Under this provision the direction to the court is mandatory, whereas under s 87(3) of the Children Act 1975 (which is repealed) the definition applied 'unless the context otherwise requires'.

1 See the amendments to ss 27(1) and (2), 28(1) and (2), 29(1) and (2), 31(1)-(3) and 35(1) and (2) of the 1976 Act made respectively by Sch 10, paras 12, 15, 16 , 17 and 19.

**11.5** In line with the changes introduced by the 1989 Act, references in the 1976 Act (as amended) to a child 'in care' of a local authority[1] mean in care as a result of a care order, and those to being 'looked after' by a local authority[2] include those being 'accommodated'[3] by them: s 72(1B), introduced by Sch 10, para 30(9). Section 2 of the 1976 Act, which refers to local authorities' social services functions, has been amended to be in line with new functions as defined by the 1989 Act.[4]

1 As, for example, in the new ss 18(2A) (discussed further below at para 11.13) and 27(2A) of the 1976 Act, respectively added by Sch 10, paras 6 and 13.
2 As, for example, in s 31(1) and (2) of the 1976 Act as amended by Sch 10, para 17.
3 The meaning of 'accommodated' is discussed at paras 5.20 et seq.
4 See the amendments to s 2 made by Sch 10, para 1. For a discussion of the new social services functions see Chapter 5.

## 2 Harmonising adoption law within the United Kingdom

**11.6** Some of the amendments are aimed at harmonising UK adoption law and in particular because of the introduction of new adoption provisions in Northern Ireland under the Adoption (Northern Ireland) Order 1987, which came into force on 1 October 1989.[1] References to the Scottish legislation, currently the Adoption (Scotland) Act 1978, have also been incorporated in the changes to the 1976 Act.

1 Pursuant to the Adoption (1987 Order) (Commencement) Order (Northern Ireland) 1989.

**11.7** The object of these changes is to enable adoption agencies throughout the UK to work in co-operation for the benefit of children who need to move from one part of the country to another.[1] Hence, for example, an adoption society approved in Scotland or Northern Ireland can act as an adoption society in England and Wales provided that it considers it to be in the interests of the child concerned.[2] An adoption order may be made in England and Wales following a freeing order made in Scotland or Northern Ireland.[3] An authorised court in England and Wales may order the return of a child following his wrongful removal (or make an order restraining such a removal) pending an adoption application in Scotland or Northern

Ireland.[4] A child will be considered a 'protected child' in England and Wales if he is so considered in Scotland or Northern Ireland.[5] There are reciprocal provisions in Scotland and Northern Ireland, although they are not an exact mirror because the new concepts introduced by the 1989 Act do not apply to Scotland and Northern Ireland.[6]

1 HC Deb, Standing Committee B, 1989 June 6, col 380, per David Mellor.
2 S 11(2) of the 1976 Act, as amended by Sch 10, para 2.
3 S 16(1)(a) of the 1976 Act, as amended by Sch 10, para 5.
4 S 29(1) and (2) of the 1976 Act, as amended by Sch 10, para 15.
5 S 32(2) of the 1976 Act, as amended by Sch 10, para 18. For other amendments involving references to Scotland and Northern Ireland, see ss 54(1)(d), 55(1), 56(1), 59, 60, 62(5) and 72(1) of the 1976 Act, as amended by Sch 10, paras 20(1), 22, 23(2), 26, 27, 28 and 30 respectively.
6 For the provisions of the 1989 Act that do apply to Scotland and Northern Ireland, see s 91(9) and (10).

## 3 The substantive changes

### *Changes in the legal requirements to be applicants*

**11.8** The new s 14(1B) (added by Sch 10, para 4) provides that an adoption order may be made upon the application of a married couple where one spouse is the father or mother of the child and aged at least eighteen, and the other spouse is at least 21. The previous law prevented *anyone* under the age of 21 from applying to adopt.[1]

1 Although in some ways this represents a partial return to the law under the Adoption Act 1958 which differentiated between parents, relatives and others. Under that law, mothers or fathers of any age could apply to adopt: Adoption Act 1958, s 2(1).

**11.9** The amended s 14 removes the previous disapproval of step-parent adoptions, through the repeal of ss 14(3) and 15(4) of the 1976 Act (contained in Sch 15), which formerly required the courts to dismiss an application involving a step-parent if it considered it better dealt with by a custody order in divorce proceedings. These provisions were introduced following the Houghton Committee's recommendations[1] and were originally intended (and so interpreted by the courts[2]) to discourage such applications. However, judicial attitudes changed, since it was established[3] that, before the adoption application should be dismissed, it had to be shown that the custody option was better. Since ss 14(3) and 15(4) ceased to operate as deterrents, their repeal should not make much difference in practice. However, since the courts are entitled to make a s 8 order, such as a residence or contact order, upon an adoption application (see para 11.20) some courts might consider it their duty to consider the appropriateness of those orders before granting an adoption order.

1 (Cmnd 5107, 1972) paras 103-110. See also Bromley and Lowe's *Family Law* (7th ed) pp 388-390.
2 See, eg, *Re S (Infants) (Adoption by parent)* [1977] Fam 173, [1977] 3 All ER 671, CA.
3 *Re D (Minors) (Adoption by step-parent)* (1981) 2 FLR 102, CA.

### *Changes with regard to serving notice on local authorities in the case of non agency placements*

**11.10** The requirement under s 22(1) of the 1976 Act that in the case of non-agency placements (classically, where the applicant(s) is a relative or foster parent), the applicant must give written notice to the relevant local authority of his intention to apply for adoption, has been amended by Sch 10, para 10(1). The court may not make an adoption order unless the applicant has given the requisite notice within the two-year period preceding the making of the application. The new requirement is intended to bring the requirement into line with the new provision (viz the new s 31(4), discussed at para 11.11) as to when a child ceases to be 'protected'.

### *Amendments to the provisions dealing with a 'protected child'*

#### WHEN 'PROTECTION' CEASES

**11.11** Schedule 10, para 18(4) substitutes a new s 32(4) into the 1976 Act setting out when a 'protected child' ceases to be 'protected'. Apart from providing, inter alia, that protection ceases upon the making of a residence order, a care order or supervision order under the 1989 Act or upon the appointment of a guardian under the 1989 Act (the new s 32(4)(d) and (e)), the key change is under the new s 32(4)(c), namely, that protection ceases if no application being made for an order within two years of notice of the intention to do so has been served on the local authority. This is a useful change which will end the theoretical possibility of some children being perpetually 'protected'.

#### ALTERATION OF LOCAL AUTHORITIES' POWER TO REMOVE 'PROTECTED CHILDREN' FROM UNSUITABLE SURROUNDINGS

**11.12** With the repeal of s 34 of the 1976 Act (by Sch 15), local authorities no longer have the power to apply for the removal of a 'protected child' to a place of safety. Instead, authorities will have to apply for an emergency order under Part V of the 1989 Act (see Chapter 7). This change is in line with the general scheme of the 1989 Act to have one set of criteria to justify an emergency order.

### *Amendments to the Freeing Provisions*

**11.13** Schedule 10 makes a number of amendments to the provisions dealing with the process known as 'freeing the child for adoption'. One of the more important is that effected by the new s 18(2A) of the 1976 Act (added by Sch 10, para 6(1))[1]. Unless a parent or guardian agrees, a local authority may not apply to free a child for adoption where that child is being 'accommodated' by them. This change is in line with the general philosophy of the 1989 Act that 'accommodation', being a voluntary service provided by local authorities, is not to be undermined by the possibility of the parents being unable to remove their children, save where an authority can satisfy the 'threshold' requirements to obtain a care order under s 31 (see Chapter 6). This means that in cases where a local authority wish to apply to 'free' a child accommodated by them and are unable to obtain the agreement thereto of a parent of the child, they must first obtain a care order. While this necessity might seem logical within the context of the overall philosophy of the 1989 Act, the introduction of a further stage in the legal process could be potentially damaging to the child (not least because of the inevitable delay thereby caused), not necessarily helpful to the birth parents and potentially wasteful of court time.

**1** S 18(2A) needs to be read together with the new s 72(1B), added by Sch 10, para 30(9), referred to at para 11.5.

**11.14** Useful tidying-up amendments make it clear that:

(a) as with a full adoption order, a freeing order may not be made in relation to a child who is or has been married but an order may be made notwithstanding that the child has previously been adopted;[1]

(b) a freeing order does not end any duty to make payments in respect of the child's maintenance or upbringing arising by virtue of an agreement that constitutes a trust or which expressly provides that the duty is not extinguished by the making of an adoption order.[2]

**1** Ie, s 12(5) and (7) of the 1976 Act apply: s 18(8) of the 1976 Act, as substituted by Sch 10, para 6(3).
**2** Ie, s 12(4) applies: s 18(5) of the 1976 Act, as amended by Sch 10, para 6(2).

**11.15** Section 18(7) of the 1976 Act has been amended by Sch 10, para 6(3) to provide that, in the case of a father who has no parental responsibility, the court may not make a freeing order unless satisfied either that he has no intention of applying for a parental responsibility order under s 4 (see para 2.20) or a residence order under s 8 of the 1989 Act, or that, if he did make such an application, 'it would be likely to be refused'. As this amendment is merely consequential it would seem that, relying on *Re H (Adoption: putative father's rights)* [1989] 2 All ER 353, CA, the unmarried father would be better advised to plead an intention to apply for a s 4 order rather than a residence order.

**11.16** The 1989 Act makes a number of changes with regard to the effect of a revocation of a freeing order. Section 20(3) of the 1976 Act, as rewritten by Sch 10, para 8(2), now makes it clear that a revocation order operates: (a) to extinguish the parental responsibility given to the adoption agency by the freeing order; and (b) to give that responsibility to the mother and, 'where the child's father and mother were married to each other at the time of his birth', to the father. Presumably, this latter phrase is intended to be construed in line with s 1 of the Family Law Reform Act 1987 so as to include, for example, the father who has married the mother after the child's birth. This interpretation was expressly provided for by the former s 18(8) of the 1976 Act (added by the Family Law Reform Act 1987, Sch 2, para 67) but that provision has now been substituted by another (see Sch 10, para 6(3), discussed at para 11.15). Section 1 of the 1987 Act itself provides that in all subsequent legislation expressions such as 'fathers and mother being married to each at the time of the child's birth' are, unless there is a contrary intention, to be construed in line with the meaning ascribed by that section. However, it may be argued that such an interpretation does not apply to later amendments of pre-1987 legislation.

**11.17** The new s 20(3)(c) of the 1976 Act states that a revocation order revives any parental responsibility agreement or order and the appointment of a guardian, previously extinguished by the making of a freeing order. On the other hand, the new s 20(3A) provides that a revocation order does *not* revive any order (save those made under s 4 or 5) made under the 1989 Act (eg, s 8 and care orders) that has been extinguished by the freeing order nor — *reversing the former position* — does it revive a duty to make payments for the child arising from a court order or agreement that has been extinguished by a freeing order. The new s 20(3A)(b) makes it clear that a revocation order does not affect any person's parental responsibility insofar as it relates to the period between the making and the revocation of a freeing order.

**11.18** Section 21 of the 1976 Act, as substituted by Sch 10, para 9, provides that where the court varies a freeing order so as to give parental responsibility to another adoption agency, that new agency will be deemed to have had the duties imposed under s 19 of the 1976 Act, ie, to make progress reports to the former parents[1] from the date of the original freeing order.

1 For the significance of such duties, see, eg, *R v Derbyshire CC, ex p T* (1989) *Times* 17 August, CA.

### *Amendments to the court's powers*

**11.19** With the repeal of s 26 of the 1976 Act (by Sch 15), the court hearing an adoption application no longer has the power to commit the child into local authority care if it refuses to make the adoption order. Instead, as in other 'family proceedings', the court may, if it thinks it appropriate, direct the local authority to investigate the child's circumstances with a view to the authority deciding whether or not to bring care proceedings: s 37. This change is in line with the general strategy of the 1989 Act that children should be committed into local authority care only if the threshold criteria laid down by s 31 have been satisfied.

**11.20** With the repeal of s 37 of the Children Act 1975 (Sch 15) and the consequential amendments of ss 14(1) and 15(1) of the 1976 Act (Sch 10, para 4 and Sch 15), the courts are no longer required to consider whether custodianship (which in any event is abolished) is a better alternative to adoption. In practice, the custodianship alternative was rarely used, not least because of the requirement that the parent(s)' agreement to the *adoption* had to have either been given or dispensed with,[1] before the alternative option could be considered. By themselves, therefore, these changes seem unlikely to have any great impact upon practice. However, because adoption proceedings are designated as 'family proceedings' (s 8(4)(d): see para 3.23) the courts are empowered, either upon application, or upon their own motion, to make a s 8 order (s 10(1)(b)). Whether the courts will regard it as their *duty* to consider in every case whether the making of a residence order is better for the child than the making of an adoption order remains to be seen, but it is at least arguable that they should, given that it is their statutory duty in this regard to treat the child's welfare as their paramount consideration. It has also to be said that, since the s 8 alternative is much more straightforward than the rather contorted provisions of s 37 of the 1975 Act, it is more likely to be used.

1 See *Re M (a Minor) (Custodianship: jurisdiction)* [1987] 2 All ER 88, CA.

**11.21** Another consequence of the designation of adoption proceedings as 'family proceedings' is that, for the first time, third parties will have the right at least to apply for leave to seek a s 8 order in the adoption proceedings (s 10(2)(b)). This in turn may be expected to lead to more requests, particularly, it is suspected, by grandparents, for both residence and contact orders. The ensuing position (assuming leave has been given) may be complex. For example, a child in local authority care (under a care order) may have been placed with foster parents and have maintained regular and beneficial contact with his grandparents. If the foster parents subsequently apply to adopt the child but the court rejects their application, it could still grant, under s 8 of the 1989 Act, a residence order in favour of the grandparents and in that event the care order will, pursuant to s 91(1), automatically be discharged. However, if a residence order is also refused or not even sought, then, because of the embargo contained in s 9(1) (see para 3.33), the court could not grant a contact order (nor could it make a prohibited steps or specific issue order). On the other hand, if the adoption were granted, the court would be empowered under s 12(6) of the 1976 Act to make a condition as to contact.[1] To overcome this possible gap, the grandparents would have to be advised to couple their application in the adoption proceedings with an application to seek leave to obtain a contact order under s 34.

1 See *Re C (Minor) (Access Conditions)* [1989] AC 1, HL.

**11.22** Another problem is whether a court is entitled to make both an adoption order (or freeing order) *and* a s 8 order. The new s 12(3)(aa) of the 1976 Act, added by Sch 10, para 3(3), which provides that an adoption order extinguishes *any* order under the Children Act 1989, could be interpreted as preventing a court from making both an adoption order and a s 8 order. Another interpretation, however, is that s 12(3)(aa) operates only to extinguish any *previous* s 8 order, so that there is nothing to stop a court first making an adoption order and then adding a s 8 order. Applying a similar interpretation with regard to freeing orders means that, for the first time, a court can make both a freeing order and a contact order.

### *The creation of an Adoption Contact Register*

**11.23** One of the innovations of the 1989 Act's amendments to adoption law is the creation of an Adoption Contact Register. This is provided for by the new s 51A of the 1976 Act, added by Sch 10, para 21. Under the new scheme the Registrar General is required to maintain a register comprising adopted persons and relatives (defined by s 51A (13)(a) as 'any person (other than an adoptive relative) who is related to the adopted person by blood (including half blood) or marriage'). The Registrar has, subject to certain conditions,[1] a duty to register applicants (who in each case must have attained the age of 18) in the relevant register and to transmit to an adopted person on the Register the name and address (which need only be a contact address: s 51A (13)(a)) of any relative in respect of whom there is an entry on the Register.

1 Viz on payment of any prescribed fee, that the applicant is eighteen or over;

that the Registrar General has either a record of the applicant's birth or sufficient information to obtain a certified copy of the record of the birth, and, in the case of relative applicants, he is satisfied that the applicant is a relative: s 51A (3)-(6).

**11.24** In general the creation of a statutory register is welcome and puts on a more satisfactory formal basis a former informal practice of the Registrar General to respond to requests to make contact. This is potentially an important development, enabling birth mothers for the first time to try to contact their adopted children, while leaving it to the child to decide. However, as some have pointed out,[1] given the sensitive nature of contact in such circumstances, it might have been thought that (as with disclosure of birth records under s 51), counselling should be available. The point has also been made that for some, rather than contact, the exchange of limited information, for example, medical information, would be welcome.

1 See, eg, Richard White at (1989) 139 NLJ 1003.

### *Amending the access to birth records provisions*

**11.25** As a result of the new s 51(6A) and (6B) of the 1976 Act (added by Sch 10, para 20(3)),[1] an adopted person living outside the United Kingdom who wishes to seek access to his birth records is now able to obtain counselling overseas.

1 For the other amendments to s 51, see Sch 10, paras 20(1) and (2).

### *Permitted allowances*

**11.26** Under the new s 57A(1) (added by Sch 10, para 25), the Secretary of State may make regulations enabling adoption agencies to pay allowances to 'persons who have adopted, or intend to adopt, children in pursuance of arrangements made by the agencies'. These regulations will replace the former system (introduced by s 56(4)-(7) of the 1976 Act) by which agencies had to submit to the Secretary of State for his approval their own individual schemes for allowances. Although introduced as an experiment, more or less all statutory agencies (and many voluntary ones as well) now have approved schemes. The new system of controlling schemes by registration seems a rational and welcome development.

Chapter 12

# Education

**12.1** Educational provision is affected by the Children Act in three areas: the relationship of local authorities and local education authorities; securing the attendance of children at school; and the safeguarding of the welfare of children in independent schools.

## CO-OPERATION BETWEEN LOCAL AUTHORITIES AND LOCAL EDUCATION AUTHORITIES

**12.2** A local authority may request the assistance of other authorities referred to in s 27(3), and in particular a local education authority, in the exercise of their functions under Part III of the Act (local authority support for children and families). It is the duty of the authority whose help is requested to comply with the request if this is compatible with their duties and would not unduly prejudice the discharge of their functions (s 27(2)). A particular obligation is imposed on a local education authority to comply with a request from a local authority for assistance in carrying out their functions under Part X of the Act (child minding and day care) (Sch 9, para 8).

A reciprocal duty is imposed on a local authority to assist with the provision of services for a child with special educational needs within their area (s 27(4)). 'Special educational needs' is defined by section 1 of the Education Act 1981 as a 'learning difficulty which calls for special educational provision to be made . . .'.[1] From 16 January 1990, s 3A of the Education Act 1981 (inserted by Sch 12, para 36 of the 1989 Act) enables a local authority to make payments for 'children with special needs' to attend an establishment outside England and Wales. This is primarily designed to meet expenses of children attending the Peto Institute in Hungary.

1 See further Education Act 1981, s 1: *Clarke Hall and Morrison* (10th ed) **F** [777].

**12.3** Where a local authority are themselves looking after a child and propose to accommodate him in an establishment where education is provided, they must normally consult the local education authority before doing so, inform them of the arrangements made for the child's accommodation and inform the local education authority when the child ceases to be accommodated by them (s 28(1)-(3)).[1]

1 For other duties imposed on local social services authorities in respect of children, see Part III (local authority support for children and families — Chapter 5), in particular : s 18(5) (care or supervised activities outside school hours or during school holidays); s 24(2) (a) and (8) (assistance in connection with education or training). Note s 24(12) (duty to notify when child ceases to be accommodated

by a local education authority after the age of sixteen years); and see paras 12.5 et seq on supervision orders.

**12.4** The local social services authority for the area where the child is ordinarily resident must be informed where accommodation is provided or is intended to be provided for a child by a health authority or local education authority or in a residential care, nursing or mental nursing home for a consecutive period of at least three months. The local authority may then take steps to ensure that the child's welfare is being adequately safeguarded or protected (ss 85–86).

## SCHOOL ATTENDANCE

### 1 Education supervision orders

**12.5** There is a new power for a court to make an education supervision order where a child is of compulsory school age and is not receiving efficient full-time education suitable to his age, ability and aptitude and any special educational needs he may have (s 36(1), (3) and (4)). Under the Children and Young Persons Act 1969, s 1(2) (e),[1] this was a ground for placing a child in compulsory care. However, the *Review of Child Care Law* (para 15.20) felt that the use of a care order might be an inappropriate response to some cases of a child's failure to attend school.

1 Repealed by the 1989 Act, Sch 15.

**12.6** Compulsory care may now be only ordered on the application of a local authority or 'authorised person' where the criteria in s 31(2) are met. These criteria are that the child is suffering or is likely to suffer significant harm which is attributable to a lack of reasonable parental care. The lack of intellectual development of a child at school may be a 'parenting problem' or it may be a 'school problem'. For example, where parents have done everything possible to persuade the child to go to school and made every provision for the child but once at school the child does not wish to stay there, it was felt wrong that a care order could be made under s 1(2) (e) of the 1969 Act. Under the new criteria for making a care order in s 31(2), it would not be appropriate to make a care order in these circumstances. A local education authority may not apply under s 31 but where a purely educational ground is the basis for local authority intervention, they may apply for an education supervision order under s 36.

However, this is not to exclude the possibility that a persistent failure to attend school might satisfy the criteria for social services intervention by way of care proceedings. Persistent absence from school attributable to poor parenting might cause the child to suffer 'significant harm' within the meaning of s 31(2), since 'harm' is defined to include the impairment of development, ie, physical, intellectual, emotional, social or behavioural development (s 31(9)).

**12.7** A local education authority may apply to the court for an 'education supervision order' on the ground that the child concerned is of compulsory school age and is not being properly educated, ie, he is not receiving efficient, full-time education suitable to his age, ability and aptitude and any special educational needs he may have (s 36(3) (4)). This ground is deemed to be satisfied where a school attendance order in force under s 37 of the Education Act 1944 is not complied with, or he is a registered pupil at a school and is not attending regularly within the meaning of s 39 of the Education Act 1944 (s 36(5)).

**12.8** Before instituting proceedings, the local education authority must consult with the social services committee of the appropriate local authority — generally, the authority for the area in which the child lives (s 36(8) and (9)). After such consultation, the local authority may decide to provide support for the child and his family under Part III of the Act (see Chapter 5) or to apply for the compulsory admission of the child to care or for an ordinary supervision order under Part IV (see Chapter 6). An education supervision order may not be made where a child is in care (s 36(6)) and where an education supervision order is in force any school attendance order under s 37 of the Education Act 1944 ceases to have effect and s 37 (school attendance orders), s 76 of that Act (pupils to be educated in accordance with the wishes of their parents) and ss 6 and 7 of the Education Act 1980 (parental preference and appeals against admission decisions) do not apply. An education supervision order may run concurrently with a supervision order made in criminal proceedings, but a supervision order made in criminal proceedings may not include an education requirement under s 12C of the Children and Young Persons Act 1969 while an education supervision order is in force and, if such a condition is already in existence, it ceases to have effect (Sch 3, para 13).

**12.9** An education supervision order lasts for up to one year initially but may be extended on application by the local education authority on further occasions for up to three years at a time. It may not last longer than the child's ceasing to be of compulsory school age or a care order being made in respect of him (Sch 3, para 15).

**12.10** Where an education supervision order is in force, it is the duty of the supervisor to advise, assist and befriend and give directions to the child and his parents in such a way as to secure that he is properly educated. 'Parent' has the same meaning as in the Education Act 1944 (Sch 3, para 21), where parent is defined so as to include any person who is not a parent of a child but has parental responsibility for him or has care of him (Education Act 1944, s 114(1D), as inserted by Sch 13, para 10).

**12.11** Before giving any directions, the supervisor shall, as far as practicable, ascertain the wishes and feelings of the child and his parents and in particular their wishes as to the place at which the child should be educated (Sch 3, para 12(2)), and he should give due consideration to these wishes and feelings when settling the terms of any directions (Sch 3, para 12(3)). The child may be required to inform the supervisor of any change of address and to allow him to visit him at the place where he is living. A parent must, if asked, inform the supervisor of the child's address (if known to him) and, if the child is living with him, allow the supervisor reasonable contact with the child (Sch 3, para 16).

## 2 Failure to comply with directions

**12.12** Where directions under an education supervision order have not been complied with, the supervisor must consider what further steps he should take under the Act (Sch 3, para 12(1)(b)). These include making new directions (ibid, para 12(4)); applying for a discharge of the order (ibid, para 17) or referring the matter to the relevant social services authority (ibid, para 19). Any failure to comply with a direction shall be disregarded where compliance would not have been reasonably practicable without failing to comply with a direction under a concurrent supervision order made under Part IV of the Act or in criminal proceedings (Sch 3, para 14).

Although parents have always been liable to prosecution under the Education Acts (see para 12.14), a new and complementary provision of the 1989 Act is that the parent of a child who persistently fails to comply with a direction under an education supervision order may be prosecuted. The offence is punishable on summary conviction by a fine not exceeding £400 unless he has a defence under Sch 3, para 18(2) (reasonable steps to ensure compliance; direction unreasonable; compliance with a conflicting requirement in another supervision order).

The local education authority must notify the appropriate local authority of the child's failure to comply and the local authority will then investigate the child's circumstances with a view to considering the necessity for them to use their powers under Parts III and IV of the Act (Sch 3, para 19).

**12.13** An education supervision order may be discharged on the application of the child, his parent or the local education authority and, if the order is discharged, the court may direct the local authority to investigate the circumstances of the child (Sch 3, para 17).

## 3 Proceedings under s 40 of the Education Act 1944

**12.14** A parent who fails to comply with a school attendance order in respect of his child under s 37 of the Education Act 1944 or the parent of a child who fails to attend regularly at the school at which he is a registered pupil, commits an offence (Education Act 1944, ss 37(5) and 39(1)). Proceedings may be brought only by a local education authority but, before instituting proceedings, the authority must consider whether it would be appropriate instead, or in addition, to apply for an education supervision order (ibid, s 40(2)(2A), as substituted by the Children Act 1989, Sch 13, para 8).

On conviction of an offence under s 37(5) or 39(1), the maximum penalty is now a fine of £400 (the power to imprison is repealed by the 1989 Act, Sch 15). Where a person is *convicted* of an offence under s 37(5), or *charged* (but not yet convicted) under s 39(1), the court may direct the local education authority to apply for an education supervision order (Education Act 1944, s 40(3), as amended). This replaces provisions relating to directions in respect of care proceedings. The local education authority need not comply with the direction where, having consulted the social services authority (who may decide to use their powers under Part III (local authority support for children and families: see Chapter 5) or Part IV (care and supervision: see Chapter 6)), they decide that the child's welfare will be satisfactorily safeguarded although no education supervision order is made. The court must be informed of the reasons for not applying for an order and the information must be given within eight weeks unless the court has directed otherwise (Education Act 1944, s 40(3A)-(3B), as inserted by the 1989 Act, Sch 13).

## WELFARE OF CHILDREN IN INDEPENDENT SCHOOLS

**12.15** While the Bill was being debated in Parliament, media attention had been focussed on cases of the abuse of children accommodated in private schools. Part X of the Act (child minding and day care) does not apply to a child looked after in a school (other than a nursery school)[1] where the provision is made by a person carrying on the establishment in question or an employee authorised to make that provision as part of the establishment's activities (Sch 9, para 3).

A school carried on by a voluntary organisation is not a voluntary home because of s 60(3)(b), but the voluntary organisation has a duty to safeguard and promote the welfare of the children accommodated there (s 61(1)).

**1** '"school" means an institution for providing primary or secondary education': Education Act 1944, s 114(1), as applied by s 105(1) of the 1989 Act.

**12.16** An independent[1] school which provides accommodation for not more than 50 children other than a school approved by the Secretary of State under s 11(3)(a) of the Education Act 1981 for special educational provision (a 'special school') will be a 'children's home' and will therefore be controlled by Part VIII of the Act (registered children's homes) and in particular the person carrying on the home has the duty to safeguard and promote the children's welfare (s 64(1)).

**1** '"Independent school" means any school at which full-time education is provided for five or more pupils of compulsory school age . . . not being a school maintained by a local education authority, a grant-maintained school or a special school not maintained by a local education authority': Education Act 1944 s 114(1) as applied by s 105(1) of the 1989 Act.

**12.17** The provisions referred to in para 12.16 formerly only applied where a child in care was accommodated in the school concerned but now there is no such requirement. Further protection for children in independent schools[1] is afforded by wholly new provisions in s 87, which have far-reaching effects. The proprietor[2] of any independent school (or any person who is not the proprietor of such a school but is responsible for conducting it) which provides accommodation for a child now has a duty to safeguard and promote the child's welfare (s 87(1)). The duty under this section does not apply where the school is a children's home or a residential care home (s 87(2)). The local authority in whose area the school is must take reasonably practicable steps to enable them to determine whether the child's welfare is adequately safeguarded and promoted while at the school (s 87(3)). If the authority are of the opinion that there is a failure to comply with the duty, they must notify the Secretary of State, who may choose to exercise his powers under Part III (ss 70-75) of the Education Act 1944, which includes the power for the Secretary of State to strike the school off the register of independent schools and disqualify a person from being the proprietor of, or a teacher at, an independent school.

A person authorised by a social services authority may enter any independent school so as to enable the authority to discharge their welfare duty. He may carry out such inspection of premises, children and records as is prescribed by regulations (s 87(5)-(8)). Public schools will therefore be subject to inspection by social services authorities. A person who intentionally obstructs a person in the exercise of these powers commits a summary offence punishable by a fine of up to £400 (s 87(9)). The Secretary of State has similar powers of entry and inspection of any independent school providing accommodation for a child (s 80(1)).

1 For 'independent school' see n 1 to para 12.16.
2 'Proprietor' in relation to any school, means the person or body of persons responsible for the management of the school: Education Act 1944, s 114(1), as applied by s 87(10) of the 1989 Act.

**12.18** Independent schools do not normally come within the scope of the private fostering provisions of Part IX (see s 66(3) and Sch 8, para 2(1)). Nevertheless, the 1989 Act continues the controls relating to fostering in s 17 of the Foster Children Act 1980, which apply to pupils under sixteen at a school not maintained by a local education authority, who live at the school during school holidays for a period of more than two weeks (Sch 8, para 9). Such children are treated as private foster children while living at the school except that requirements may not be imposed under Sch 8, para 6. Not less than two weeks' notice of the estimated number of children involved must be given to the local authority by the person who proposes to care for and accommodate the children, unless he has been exempted from this requirement (ibid, para 9(3)). The death of any child concerned must be notified to the local authority and each parent within 48 hours (ibid, para 9(6)). Notice must also be given to the local authority where any child ceases to be a child treated as a private foster child by these provisions (ibid, para 9(7)).

Chapter 13

# Community homes and voluntary organisations

## INTRODUCTION

**13.1** Parts VI-X of the 1989 Act contain provisions regulating accommodation and care for children: community homes (Part VI, ss 53-58 and Sch 4); voluntary homes and voluntary organisations (Part VII, ss 59-62 and Sch 5); registered children's homes (Part VIII, ss 63-65 and Schs 6 and 7); private arrangements for fostering children (Part IX, ss 66-70 and Sch 8); and child minding and day care for young children (Part X, ss 71-79 and Sch 9). The provision of day care for children under five and not yet at school and local authority fostering is discussed above under Part III (ss 17-30 and Sch 2) (local authority support for children and families). In relation to Parts VI-X of the 1989 Act to a large extent consolidates pre-existing statutory provisions which are noted more particularly below. However, in the White Paper, on the *Law on Child Care and Family Services* (Cm 62, 1987) the Government set out its intention 'to rationalise and improve the regulation of private day care and holiday facilities; and also . . . to simplify the private foster care law and provide clarification of the boundaries between the two areas'. Consequently, important amendments are introduced by the Act.

## COMMUNITY HOMES (Part VI, ss 53-58 and Sch 4)

**13.2** Every local authority has a duty to make such arrangements as they consider appropriate for securing that community homes are available for the care and accommodation of children looked after by them and for purposes connected with the welfare of children, whether or not looked after by them (s 53(1)).[1] A community home may be provided, managed, equipped and maintained by a local authority or it may be provided by a voluntary organisation, in which case, if the management, equipment and maintenance of the home is the responsibility of the local authority, it is designated a 'controlled community home' (s 53(4)) or where the responsibility for management remains that of the voluntary organisation, it is designated an 'assisted community home' (s 53(5)).

1 See, eg, the local authority duty to provide accommodation under s 20 above.

**13.3** Part VI of the 1989 Act replaces, with amendments, the Child Care Act 1980, Part IV, ss 31-44. In particular, the arrangements between a voluntary organisation and a local authority in respect of a controlled or assisted community home are set out in Sch 4, together with regulation-making powers for the placing of children in community homes, the conduct of such homes and securing the welfare of children in such homes. For the role of the Secretary of State, see paras 13.11 et seq.

**13.4** Section 58 fills a lacuna in the former s 44 of the Child Care Act 1980 identified in the White Paper where premises used for the purposes of a controlled or assisted community home are disposed of or put to alternative use before the home's designation as a community home has been withdrawn. The intention is that the voluntary organisation concerned with the home should repay that proportion of the value of the home that is attributable to public monies paid either by a local authority when the home was a controlled community home, or by grants to an assisted home.[1] This provision (s 58(1)(b)) has effect from 13 January 1987, the date of publication of the White Paper.

1 In an unreported case referred to in the White Paper (para 83), it had been held that under the Child Care Act 1980, s 44 the value to be taken into account for repayment to central or local government was limited to the value of the home as it existed at the time of closure and parts of the home disposed of prior to closure could not be taken into account.

## VOLUNTARY ORGANISATION

**13.5** This is defined in the Act as 'a body (other than a public or local authority) whose activities are not carried on for profit' (s 105(1)). Accordingly, a community home or voluntary home (para 13.6) with which a voluntary organisation is concerned may not be run for profit.

## VOLUNTARY HOMES

**13.6** A home or other institution providing care and accommodation for children which is carried on by a voluntary organisation is known as a 'voluntary home' and is subject to registration under Part VII of the Act (s 60). However, the term 'voluntary home' does not include a nursing home, mental nursing home or residential care home; a school; any home or other institution provided, equipped and maintained by the Secretary of State and any home exempted by regulations made by the Secretary of State (s 60(3)). In particular, 'voluntary home' does not encompass 'any community home' (s 60(3) (d)). Therefore a community home which would otherwise be within the definition of a voluntary home is exempt from the provisions of Part VII and is subject to the requirements of Part VI (community homes).

**13.7** Part VII re-enacts, with amendments, ss 56-57D, 59-61, 64A and 68 of the Child Care Act 1980 and attracted little debate in Parliament, except in relation to the regulation-making powers contained in Sch 5, Part II para 7(2)(f). As originally drafted, the regulations might require the approval of the Secretary of State for the provision and use of secure accommodation in voluntary homes. It was the Government's view that the use of secure accommodation in voluntary homes was unlawful unless approved by the Secretary of State, but it was thought prudent to allow for this eventuality in the regulation-making powers (HL Deb, 23 January

1989, Vol 503, col 503). It appears that as the power in para 7(2)(f), as subsequently amended is merely to prohibit the use of such accommodation, therefore it can never be lawful to use secure accommodation in a voluntary home.

## REGISTRATION

**13.8** Schedule 5 sets out the procedure for registration and para 1 replaces s 57(2)-(5) and (7) of the Child Care Act 1980. Application shall be in the form prescribed by regulations and the Secretary of State may grant or refuse the application or grant it on conditions. He may also cancel a registration where the home is not run in accordance with regulations made as to the conduct of voluntary homes under para 7. Paragraph 2 (1980 Act, s 57A) makes further provisions as to procedure; para 3 (1980 Act, s 57B) provides for the right to make representations; para 4 (1980 Act, s 57C) refers to the decision of the Secretary of State; and para 5 (1980 Act, s 57D) provides for appeals to lie to a Registered Homes Tribunal. A person in charge of any voluntary home must send prescribed particulars to the Secretary of State annually and within three months of the establishment of the home where it is established after the commencement of this Act (para 6). Paragraph 7 re-enacts s 60 of the 1980 Act, whereby the Secretary of State may make regulations as to the conduct of voluntary homes, which include new provisions to align with those for community homes. The regulations made before the commencement of this Act were the Administration of Children's Homes Regulations 1951, SI 1951/1217.

## GENERAL PROVISIONS

### 1 The welfare of a child accommodated by a local authority or voluntary organisation

**13.9** It is the duty of a local authority looking after any child to safeguard and promote his welfare (s 22(3)(a)). This and further duties imposed on local authorities are discussed above (para 5.42).

Section 59 is new and places voluntaty organisations in the same position as local authorities with respect to the provision of accommodation: cf s 23(2). The placing of a child with foster parents by a voluntary organisation is not private fostering and therefore not subject to the provisions of Part IX (ss 66-70 and Sch 8) (see Sch 8, para 2(1)(c)). However, the 'usual fostering limit' will apply and, where more than three children who are not siblings with respect to each other are placed by a voluntary organisation, that placement will be treated as a placement in a children's home unless it is exempted by the local authority (Sch 7). The fostering will bc subject to regulations made under s 59(2) (replacing the Child Care Act 1980, s 61) (and see also s 23(2)(a)). In line with the general strategy, the 1989 Act repeals the procedure in s 64 of the Child Care Act 1980, whereby in certain circumstances a local authority might vest parental rights in a voluntary organisation.

A voluntary organisation has the same duty towards a child accommodated by them as a local authority has towards a child they are looking after, ie, to safeguard and promote his welfare and to make certain services and facilities as available as they are to children cared for by their own parents (s 61)[1]. A local authority has a duty to provide aftercare for children formerly looked after by a voluntary organisation (s 24); and a voluntary organisation now has a duty to prepare each child for the time when he ceases to be accommodated by them or on their behalf (s 61(1)(c)). In making decisions concerning a child's welfare and the services and facilities to be provided, the voluntary organisation shall, so far as is reasonably practicable, ascertain the wishes and feelings of the child, his parents and others referred to in s 61(2), giving due consideration to the factors in s 61(3).

Regulations may provide for a voluntary organisation to review the case of a child provided with accommodation by them and to consider any representations made by a person falling within a prescribed class of person (s 59(4)).

Like local authorities, voluntary organisations may, with leave, seek prohibited steps and specific issue orders under s 8 (see paras 3.19 et seq). The embargo under s 9(2) against local authorities applying for residence or contact orders does not apply to voluntary organisations, but the circumstances in which leave will be given to apply for such orders must be limited.

1 See s 22(3). S 61 replaces the Child Care Act 1980, s 64A, with amendments.

## 2 Supervisory role of the local authority

**13.10** Every local authority must satisfy themselves that any voluntary organisation providing accommodation for children are satisfactorily safeguarding and promoting the welfare of the children provided with accommodation (s 62(1)). Accordingly, the authority must make arrangements for such children to be visited except where a child is in a community home, which then would come under the supervision of the Secretary of State (s 62(2)). A local authority have a right to enter and inspect any such accommodation provided by a voluntary organisation and to inspect any children there and any records (s 62(6)). There are criminal sanctions for obstruction of a person in the exercise of the authority's powers under this section (s 62(9)).

## 3 Supervisory role of the Secretary of State

**13.11** The Secretary of State's existing powers are re-enacted, with amendments, and he may cause establishments and premises specified in s 80(1) to be inspected from time to time. Such places include premises in which a child who is being looked after by a local authority is living, or in which a child is being accommodated by a voluntary organisation, or in which a privately fostered child is living or premises on which any person is acting as a child minder or is registered for day care. Further, persons such as a local authority, voluntary organisation, a person carrying on a voluntary home or children's home, the proprietor of an independent school, a person fostering any privately fostered child, or an occupier of premises used to provide day care may be required to furnish information or allow the inspection of records relating to the child or the premises or the discharge by the Secretary of State of any of his functions under the Act s 80(4) (5). Criminal sanctions are available in the case of an intentional obstruction of the exercise of these powers (s 80(10)).

Where it appears to the Secretary of State that premises used as a community home are unsuitable or that the conduct of a community home is unsatisfactory, he may direct that the premises shall not be used as a community home (s 54(1)).

In the case of a dispute between a local authority which manages a community home and the voluntary organisation by which the home is provided or another local authority who have placed or desire to place in the home a child who is looked after by them, the dispute may be referred to the Secretary of State for his determination (s 55). The Secretary of State may also be involved in the discontinuance by a voluntary organisation of a controlled or assisted community home or in the closure by a local authority of a controlled or assisted community home.

**13.12** The Secretary of State is responsible for the registration and regulation of voluntary homes and voluntary organisations (s 60 and Sch 5) and may grant or refuse applications for registration as he sees fit or grant the application subject to such conditions as he considers appropriate (Sch 5, para 2). He may also cancel registration where it appears to him that the conduct of any voluntary home is unsatisfactory (ibid, para 4).

Chapter 14

# Private placements

## INTRODUCTION

**14.1** Parts VIII (ss 63-65, Schs 6 and 7) and IX (ss 66-70 and Sch 8) regulate the private placement of children either in a children's home or with foster parents. The scheme of Part VIII (registered children's homes) is to control homes or institutions for children which are privately run for profit. The definition of a 'children's home' is drawn so as to exclude both homes which are controlled by other Parts of the Act, such as voluntary homes, or specialised institutions which are subject to other legislation, eg, health service hospitals (para 14.3), and also placements in families (see para 14.13).

The care and accommodation of children in private family placements, which last, or are intended to last, for more than 27 days is regulated by Part IX (private arrangements for fostering children). Private fostering arrangements are normally made for reward, but this is not a prerequisite. Children looked after by a local authority in a family placement will usually be with a 'local authority foster parent' (see Part III, s 23(2)(a), para 5.50), while the fostering of children by a voluntary organisation will be subject to regulations made under s 59(2) (para 13.9). A children's home generally provides care and accommodation for more than three children, whereas private fostering is subject to the 'usual fostering limit' of three children except in the case of siblings, although exceptionally a local authority may exempt a particular private foster parent from the limit and authorise the fostering of children specified in the notice of exemption (see para 14.5). Exemption will depend upon whether the authority consider that the placement should more appropriately be treated as a private fostering arrangement rather than a children's home.

Local authorities have a duty to ensure that the welfare of children accommodated in children's homes and also by private foster parents is safeguarded and promoted. This duty reflects the authorities' obligations in respect of children looked after by itself (s 22(3)) or a voluntary organisation (s 62(1)).

## REGISTERED CHILDREN'S HOMES (Part VIII, ss 63-65 and Schs 6 and 7)

**14.2** Section 63 provides that no child shall be cared for and accommodated in a children's home unless the home is registered under Part VIII. During the Bill's passage through the Commons this section was subject to considerable amendment, with the aim of clarifying the definition of 'children's home' and of safeguarding the welfare of children in independent schools. Accordingly, s 63 now appears in a different guise from its precursor, s 1 of the Children's Homes Act 1982.

## 1 Children's homes

**14.3** A 'children's home' means a home which provides (or usually provides or is intended to provide) care and accommodation wholly or mainly for more than three children at any one time (s 63(3)(a)). Since the definition includes a home which *usually* provides, or is *intended* to provide, accommodation for more than three children, a home may still remain a 'children's home' even though the number of children there temporarily falls below three. Children's homes are essentially homes run by private persons or organisations for a profit. Accordingly, community homes and voluntary homes are exempted from the Part VIII controls (they are regulated in any event by Parts VI and VII) and other institutions providing specialised care are also exempted: residential care homes, nursing and mental nursing homes; health service hospitals; homes provided equipped and maintained by the Secretary of State; and schools (s 63(5)).[1] Regulations made by the Secretary of State may exempt other homes for this purpose (s 63(3) (b)).[2] However, an independent school[3] is a children's home if it provides accommodation for not more than fifty children and is not approved under s 11(3)(a) of the Education Act 1981 as a 'special school' (see para 12.16).[4]

1 These institutions are regulated by other statutory provisions: Registered Homes Act 1984, National Health Service Act 1977 and the Education Acts 1944-1988. For homes provided, equipped and managed by the Secretary of State, see s 82(5).
2 The regulation-making power enables, for example, a 'half way house' for sixteen to seventeen-year-olds who are looked after by authorities to be exempted from this Part in certain circumstances.
3 See s 105(1) and n 1 to para 12.16. Although an independent school must provide education for five or more children, there is no minimum number prescribed for whom accommodation is provided. Therefore, an independent school providing accommodation for fewer than four children will still be a children's home. See also Sch 6, para 1(10) for subsequent change in numbers of children accommodated.
4 Such schools, in addition to being registered with the Department of Education and Science, will now have to register with the relevant local authority. See further for independent schools s 87 (para 12.15).

**14.4** The rule prescribing the care and accommodation of three children, above which a home will be a children's home, is a convenient guideline for distinguishing a children's home from a private fostering placement, although a local authority have power to exempt persons from 'the usual fostering limit' (see para 14.5). While the 'average' family is, according to the statisticians supposed to comprise two adults and 2.4 children, the 'rule of three' would nevertheless include many family homes within the definition of children's home. Therefore, a child is deemed not to be cared for and accommodated in a children's home when cared for and accommodated by a parent, person having parental responsibility for him or a relative (s 63(4)). Even where the child is actually living in a children's home, he is not to be treated as being cared for and accommodated in a children's home when a parent or person having parental responsibility is living at the home or the person caring for him is doing so in his personal capacity and not in the course of carrying out his duties in relation to the home (s 63(7)).

## 2 Exceptions to the 'usual fostering limit' (Sch 7)

**14.5** A person may not generally foster[1] more than three children ('the usual fostering limit') (Sch 7, para 2). However Sch 7 permits the usual fostering limit to be exceeded where all the children concerned are siblings with respect to each other (para 3) or where exemption is provided by a local authority. In deciding whether to grant exemption, the local authority will be concerned whether the proposed placement is more in the nature of fostering rather than in a children's home and whether, if it is treated as fostering, the children's welfare will be safeguarded and promoted.

The local authority must have regard in particular to the number of children the person proposes to foster; the arrangements for their care and accommodation; the intended and likely relationship between the person and the children; the period of time proposed for the fostering, and whether the welfare of the fostered children (and of any other children living in the accommodation) will be safeguarded and promoted (ibid, para 4(2)).

Where exemption is granted, the local authority must inform the person by a notice in writing which describes the children by name whom he may foster and states any conditions to which the exemption is subject. If a child other than one named in the notice is to be fostered, further exemption must be obtained.

The exemption may be varied or cancelled at any time by notice in writing by the local authority.[2] Regulations may provide for cases where children need to be placed with foster parents as a matter of urgency.

A person who exceeds the usual fostering limit or who is in breach of the terms of an exemption is treated as carrying on a children's home (ibid, para 5(1)).

1 For these purposes, a person fosters a child if he is a local authority foster parent, a foster parent with whom a child has been placed by a voluntary organisation or he fosters a child privately.

2 A complaints procedure must be established by every local authority (Sch 7, para 6) and a private foster parent may appeal against a decision regarding exemption (Sch 8, para 8(1)).

## 3 Registration

**14.6** Criminal sanctions are imposed on a person who, without reasonable excuse, carries on a home which is not a registered children's home and where any child is at any time cared for and accommodated. The maximum penalty is a fine not exceeding level 5. Schedule 6 replaces ss 3-8 of the 1982 Act and contains provisions for applications for registration, conditions that may be imposed on registration, procedure, the right to make representations, the decision of the local authority and appeals to a Registered Homes Tribunal. Paragraph 1(5) and (6) are new and regulations may require a local authority to comply with certain requirements, including a pre-registration inspection. The local authority which registered the home must, twelve months after registration and annually thereafter, review the registration in order to determine whether the registration should continue (para 3). Paragraph 9 prohibits a further application for registration within six months of the notification of refusal. Schedule 6, Part II, para 10 authorises the Secretary of State to make regulations as to the placing of children in registered children's homes; the conduct of such homes and for securing the welfare of the children in such homes.

1 The use of secure accommodation in such homes is unlawful: see Sch 6, Part II, para 10(2)(j) and para 13.7.

## 3 Persons disqualified from carrying on, or being employed in, registered homes

**14.7** Section 65 generally corresponds to s 10 of the 1982 Act. However, the opportunity has been taken to align these provisions with those applicable to disqualification from fostering a child privately (s 68). A person who is so disqualified may not carry on, or otherwise be concerned in, the management of a children's home,[1] nor can anyone employ such a person unless he discloses this fact to the local authority and has their written consent. Appeal against a refusal of consent lies to a Registered Homes Tribunal (Sch 6, para 8) and the applicant must be given the reasons for the refusal, notice of his right to appeal and the time within which he may do so. Contravention of the provisions for disqualification carries a criminal penalty of a maximum of six months' imprisonment and/or a fine not exceeding level 5. However, an employer has a defence if he proves (on the balance of probabilities) that he did not know and had no reasonable grounds for believing, that the employee concerned was a disqualified person.

The service of notices under the Act generally is governed by s 105(8)-(10).

1 These provisions are applicable to registered children's homes and to a private children's home which is not currently registered: see para 14.8.

## 4 Welfare of children in children's homes

**14.8** The existing provisions in the Children's Homes Act 1982 (which have not yet been implemented) impose no specific responsibility on the proprietor of a children's home towards children in the home and give a local authority no duties beyond those of registration and inspection.

The person carrying on a children's home must treat children accommodated there in the same way as a local authority would treat children looked after by them (s 64).[1] A local authority have similar powers with respect to children's homes as they do to voluntary homes: to ensure the home is satisfactorily safeguarding and promoting the welfare of the children; to inspect premises, children and records; and to take action if the welfare of the children is not satisfactorily safeguarded or promoted.[2]

1 See ss 22 and 24(1) and paras 5.42 et seq. The provisions of ss 64 and 65 apply where appropriate, whether or not a private children's home is currently registered — for example, during the period when an application for registration is being

considered or where a home should be registered but is not and the welfare of the children in the home is in issue.
2 S 64(4) replaces s 9 of the 1982 Act (inspection of registered homes) by importing the provisions of s 62.

**14.9** A local authority must arrange for children in children's homes to be visited from time to time in the interests of their welfare and the Secretary of State may by regulations require the authority to visit a child in prescribed circumstances and at prescribed times, and meet prescribed requirements in carrying out their functions (s 62(3)). A person authorised by a local authority may enter at any reasonable time and inspect a children's home and any records that may be kept there, and he may apply to court where appropriate for a warrant to authorise a constable to assist in the exercise of those powers (s 102)

**14.10** Where a local authority are not satisfied that the welfare of any child is being satisfactorily safeguarded or promoted, they must take reasonable steps to secure that his care and accommodation is undertaken by a parent, person having parental responsibility for him or a relative and consider whether they should exercise any of their functions with relation to the child, eg, under Part III (local authority support for children and families) or IV (care and supervision). In an emergency, the local authority may apply to the court for an order under Part V, s 44 (order for emergency protection of children). A person under 21 who left the accommodation of a registered children's home at any time after the age of sixteen but while still a child (ie, under eighteen) is a person who qualifies for advice and assistance from a local authority: s 24 (see para 5.42). Further, where a child accommodated in a registered children's home ceases to be accommodated there after reaching the age of sixteen, the person carrying on the home must notify the local authority within whose area the child proposes to live (s 24(12)).

The Secretary of State has power to cause a children's home to be inspected from time to time by a person authorised by him who has powers similar to those of a local authority referred to above but including a power to require a local authority themselves to produce any records they may have in relation to the home (s 80).

## PRIVATE ARRANGEMENTS FOR FOSTERING CHILDREN (Part IX, ss 66-70 and Sch 8)

**14.11** These provisions replace, with amendments, the Foster Children Act 1980 (the '1980 Act'). The White Paper expressed the view that the definition of 'foster parents', and hence of 'foster children' and the exclusions from the requirements were too complex. Accordingly, the Government intended to simplify and restrict the provisions for those placements lasting, or intended to last, for more than 27 days, or aggregated periods of more than 27 days (para 80). In the Act the concept of aggregating periods was rejected. Short-term care of children under eight for reward may be subject to the child-minding provisions of Part X (Chapter 15). The former concept of short-term placement with a 'regular foster parent' (s 2(3) of the 1980 Act) has no relevance to fostering under the 1989 Act. 'Local authority foster parents' are discussed under s 23(2) (see para 5.50)).

**14.12** A privately fostered child is a child who is under the age of sixteen and who is cared for and accommodated by someone other than a parent of his, a person having parental responsibility for him or a relative for a period which is less than 28 days and is not intended to be any longer (s 66(1)). A person caring for more than three such children, if they are not all siblings with respect to each other, would be carrying on a children's home, unless the 'supermum' exemption is obtained from the local authority (see para 14.5).

**14.13** Schedule 8 provides exceptions to the general definition of private fostering in order to ensure that normal domestic arrangements are not within the scope of the Part IX controls and that placements which are more appropriately controlled by other provisions are excluded. Therefore, a child is not a privately fostered child where he is in the care of any person:

(a) in premises where a parent, a person having parental responsibility for him or a relative who has assumed responsibility for him is living;
(b) in a children's home (Part VIII: see para 14.3);
(c) in any accommodation provided by a voluntary organisation, eg, a voluntary home (Part VIII: see para 13.6). The boarding-out of a child with foster parents by a voluntary organisation is to be controlled by regulations made under s 59(2);
(d) in a school (but see para 14.14 for school holidays);
(e) in a health service hospital;
(f) in a residential care home, nursing or mental nursing home (for the duty of the institution or person carrying on the establishment to notify the local authority where the accommodation has been or is intended to be, provided for a consecutive period of at least three months, see ss 85 and 86);
(g) in a home provided, managed and equipped by the Secretary of State under s 82(5).

**14.14** However, where a child is living in one of the establishments referred to in (b)-(g) above and the person caring for him is doing so in a personal capacity and not in the course of carrying out his duties in relation to the establishment, the exemption is not applicable and the normal criteria for determining whether the placement is private fostering will apply (Sch 8, para 2(2)).[1] Children subject to supervision orders in criminal proceedings or subject to the Mental Health Act 1983 or the adoption legislation are not treated as privately fostered children (ibid, paras 3-5).

Although a child cared for and accommodated at a school will not normally be subject to the controls on private fostering, children under sixteen who are pupils at a non-maintained school are treated as privately fostered children if they live at the school during school holidays for more than two weeks (ibid, para 9) (see para 12.18).

1 See, for example, the complementary provision for children's homes: s 63(7).

## 1 Notification of private fostering

**14.15** Regulations will make provision that where a child is, or it is proposed that he be, fostered privately, a person arranging (whether directly or indirectly) the fostering, the person proposing the fostering and the foster parents shall give notice to the local authority.[1] In particular, foster parents must give notice of any convictions that they have and any disqualification under s 68 or prohibition under s 69. Notice must also be given when the private fostering ceases (Sch 8, para 7).

Parents and those with parental responsibility may be required by regulations to give the appropriate authority prior notice of a proposed private fostering arrangement (provided that they are aware that the child is to be fostered and whether or not they are involved in the arrangement). These notice provisions will enable authorities to investigate in advance the suitability of the proposed foster parents and placement. It is expected that authorities, as part of their pre-placement enquiries and duty, will give advice to foster parents on the children's needs arising from their racial origin and cultural background.

1 Whether or not notice has been given to the local authority, a person proposing to foster a child privately, or who is already doing so, may be prohibited from fostering privately under s 69 (see para 14.17)).

## 2 Persons disqualified from being private foster parents

**14.16** A person may not foster a child privately where he is disqualified from doing so under regulations made under the Act and has not obtained the written consent of the local authority (s 68) . Nor without written consent may he foster a child privately in a place where a disqualified person lives or is employed. Where consent is refused, the local authority must inform the applicant by written notice stating their reasons, his right to appeal and the time within which he may do so. Appeals are regulated by Sch 8, para 8 and lie to the court (see s 92 and Sch 11).

1 The former provisions concerning disqualification were contained in s 7 of the Foster Children Act 1980 and stated that a person might not privately foster a child where, for example, a child had previously been removed from his care under the appropriate legislation, eg, CYPA 1969, or he had been convicted of an offence in Sch 1 to the CYPA 1933, or his rights to a child had been vested in a local authority under s 3 of the Child Care Act 1980.

## 3 Power to prohibit private fostering

**14.17** Certain persons are disqualified under s 68 from privately fostering a child. Other persons who are not disqualified from fostering may also be *prohibited* from fostering under s 69. A local authority have power to prohibit a person from fostering if they are of the opinion that he is not a suitable person, the premises are not suitable or it would be prejudicial to the welfare of the child for him to be, or continue to be, accommodated by that person in those premises. A person may be prohibited from fostering privately any child within the area of the authority, any child on the premises in question, or an identified child in specified premises.

The local authority may prohibit a person from fostering privately where he *proposes* to foster a child privately or where he *is* fostering a child privately. Previously, where the fostering had commenced, the power of prohibition existed only where the foster parent had failed to give the authority notice of his proposal to foster. Now the power will exist even where a placement had at first been deemed suitable by an authority but where the circumstances have changed and the authority may need to act to safeguard the child.

**14.18** A prohibition may be cancelled by a local authority if they think fit — either of their own motion or on application if they are satisfied that the prohibition is no longer justified. The requirements for the notice and appeals are the same as for disqualification above (para 14.16).

Where a person is fostering or proposes to foster a child privately, the local authority may impose on him requirements including the number, age and sex of the children who may be fostered by him, the standard of accommodation, arrangements as to their health and safety and particular arrangements for their care (Sch 8, para 6). Similar provisions as to notice in writing of the requirements and the right of appeal apply as for disqualification above (para 14.16).

## 4 Welfare of privately fostered children

**14.19** There is a duty on local authorities to satisfy themselves as to the welfare of privately fostered children and to secure that such advice is given to foster parents as appears to be needed (s 67(1)).[1] The performance of this primary duty is reinforced by duties and powers parallel to those imposed on local authorities in respect of children in voluntary homes (s 62) and registered children's homes (s 64). The requirements of s 67 include a duty to inspect premises where privately fostered children are accommodated or where it is proposed that they be accommodated, and to visit the children in circumstances or on occasions specified by regulations. For the local authority's duty to provide advice and assistance for certain privately fostered children over sixteen on their ceasing to be fostered, see s 24(2)(e).

Where a local authority are not satisfied that the welfare of a privately fostered child is being satisfactorily safeguarded, they may, unless it would not be in the child's interests, take such steps as are reasonably practicable to secure his care by a parent, relative or person with parental responsibility for him and consider whether they should exercise any of their functions under the Act.

1 S 67 corresponds to the former s 3 of the 1980 Act.

Chapter 15

# Child minding and day care for children

**15.1** Part X (ss 71-79 and Sch 9) was introduced at the Committee stage in the Commons.[1] It replaces the Nurseries and Child-Minders Regulation Act 1948 and substantially alters the pre-existing law. Local authorities were concerned that the 1948 Act allowed them little scope to refuse to register and there was felt to be a need to present local authorities with clear powers and the opportunity to refuse to register individuals and organisations that do not meet the criteria. In the 40 years that have passed since the 1948 Act, social conditions had made some of the requirements of that Act inappropriate: three examples are the developing provision for out of school and holiday schemes for school aged children, the increased use of 'nannies' for looking after the children of working mothers and the organising of creches at conferences and other occasions. Such activities might have incurred inappropriate registration requirements under the 1948 Act.

1 The provisions of Part X were drafted in response to two consultation papers issued in England and Wales, and Scotland in October 1985 which in turn led to proposals in the *White Paper, The Law on Child Care and Family Services* (Cm 62 1987).

**15.2** Where immediately before the commencement of this Part of the Act premises were registered as a nursery or a person was registered as a child minder under the Nurseries and Child-Minders Regulation Act 1948, the provisions of the 1948 Act will continue to apply until either the first anniversary of the commencement of the new provisions or until the person concerned is registered (and is also registered with respect to the premises where appropriate) under the 1989 Act, whichever event occurs first (Sch 14, paras 33 and 34).

## DIFFERENCES FROM THE NURSERIES AND CHILD-MINDERS REGULATION ACT 1948

**15.3** (a) ***Age requirements*** The existing legislation requires registration of child-minders caring for children in their own homes up to the age of five and of premises where children are received to be looked after up to the age of sixteen. In the White Paper, the Government proposed that the age be fixed at five years for both categories but, when the new sections were introduced, fixed the age at eight years. While the selection of any age would have been arbitrary, the Government considered that it was the younger children who were most vulnerable and, while it was neither practicable nor desirable for out-of-school and holiday provision for older children up to sixteen to be subject to registration, it was felt desirable to provide reassurance for parents of children between the ages of five and eight that the service has been inspected by the local authority.

**(b) *Nannies*** Nannies were generally not registrable under the 1948 Act. The 1989 Act extends the registration arrangements to cover a domestic nanny except where she is looking after her employer's child in his home. A nanny may work for two families, but the 'peripatetic nanny' who looks after a child in several different places must now register as a child minder.

**(c) *Enforcement procedure*** The former arrangements required registration for all persons acting as child minders within the terms of the Act. Failure to comply was a criminal offence. This was felt to be inappropriate for a person such as, for example, a neighbour providing help, for reward, in an emergency. The new procedure will enable a local authority, where they feel it appropriate, to serve an enforcement notice on the child minder. Only where there is failure to comply with the enforcement notice, will an offence be committed.

**(d) *Institutions*** Those that were exempt from the requirement to register, such as local education authority maintained schools, continue to be so. However, where day-care provision on such premises is run by independent people, such as members of a committee running a playgroup, they must register. Persons providing occasional creche and day nursery facilities at conferences or training courses are exempt, provided these functions are carried on for less than six days a year and they notify the local authority. The former legislation gave local authorities the power to inspect facilities; this power will now include a *duty* to inspect at least once a year.

**(e) *Registration*** Many authorities were apparently worried about the scope of their powers to refuse to register applicants. Registration under the 1989 Act is of 'responsible persons' providing care at specified premises.

**(f) *Requirements imposed on registration*** Local authorities now have a *duty* to impose certain requirements on granting an application instead of the former *discretion* to do so. Furthermore, there is flexibility to add other conditions.

**(g) *Cancellation of registration*** Section 71 clarifies the grounds on which a local authority may cancel registration as being those on which they would be justified in refusing an application, and there is also a new provision justifying cancellation on the grounds that the care provided is seriously inadequate. In addition, a local authority may apply to a court to have a person's registration cancelled or varied as a matter of urgency where it appears that a child is suffering, or is likely to suffer, significant harm.

## REGISTRATION OF CHILD MINDERS AND PERSONS PROVIDING DAY CARE

**15.4** A local authority is required to keep a register of persons who act as child minders on domestic premises and persons who provide day care for children under eight on non-domestic premises (s 71). A child minder is someone who looks after children under eight for reward and for a period or periods in aggregate exceeding two hours on any one day. Section 71(2) makes it clear that the period of two hours is the period for which the child minder is there to look after the children (or during which day care is provided) rather than the time spent there by such child. A distinction is drawn between this 'child minding' in a domestic home and 'day care', which was formerly labelled as a nursery under the 1948 Act. Day care also must amount to a period or periods in aggregate of more than two hours in any one day to require registration under the Act.

**15.5** Whether premises are domestic premises depends upon whether they are wholly or mainly used as a private dwelling. This is a question of fact in each case. In answering this it seems that the word 'mainly' should be given its ordinary dictionary meaning of 'for the most part', 'chiefly', 'principally' (*Miller v Ottilie (Owners)* [1944] KB 188, [1944] 1 All E R 277, CA), and 'private dwelling house' should be construed as meaning private residence (*Bristol Guardians v Bristol Waterworks Co* [1912] 1 Ch 111, 76 JP 17; affirmed [1914] AC 379, 78 JP 217 HL); and see *Barnes v Shore* (1846) 1 Rb Eccl 382; affd (1848) Brod & F 44 PC; although the acts of sleeping upon premises at night and having meals in them by day are facts that are residential in character, they are not conclusive evidence of the use of a house as a dwelling house: see *Macmillan & Co Ltd v Rees* [1946] 1 All E R 675, CA.

**15.6** Certain persons who would otherwise be required to register are specifically exempted: a parent, a relative, a person having parental responsibility for a child and a foster parent are not child minders for the purpose of the Act even though they might be doing so for reward. (This might apply particularly to private foster parents receiving a fee from the natural parents. This situation would be covered by the provisions applying to private fostering (Part IX)).

A nanny will also be exempt where she is looking after a child wholly or mainly in the home of her employer (s 71(5)) or where employed by two employers in the home of either employer (s 71(6)).

Further exemptions are provided for certain schools and other establishments. A school (except an independent nursery school) looking after children under eight is exempted by Sch 9, para 3, provided that the children are being looked after in the school as part of the school's activities by the person carrying on the school or an employee who is authorised to make that provision (ibid). However, the exemption does not apply to an outside body providing child-minding or day care facilities on school premises, such as members of a committee who run a playgroup.

Overlap with statutory provisions regulating the conduct of other forms of residential care, such as a community home or a residential care home, is avoided by exempting (by Sch 9, para 4) such establishments from registration under this Part.

**15.7** Where day care is provided in particular premises on less than six days in any year, such provision is exempted from the requirement for registration, provided the person making it has notified the appropriate local authority in writing before the first occasion on which the premises concerned are so used in that year: Sch 9, para 5(1). This exemption is intended to cover the situation where, for example, a creche is used at premises where a conference or training course is being held. The term 'year' is defined in para 5(2).

**15.8** Despite the above exemptions, the scope of the registration requirements is still wide. They would include the person who helps out in an emergency by looking after a neighbour's child while she goes to work and does so for some reward. Under the former legislation, such a neighbour would automatically have committed an offence of child minding when not registered. Similarly, it is common for teenage girls tc baby sit for some reward. The 1989 Act does not specifically exempt babysitters and it could be argued that the rules relating to premises will exclude most babysitters from the controls of Part X. However, it is a matter for speculation whether a casual babysitter can be described as being 'employed' as a nanny. Even if a babysitter is not exempt and has failed to register, she will not necessarily be guilty of an offence. An unregistered child minder (but not a person who provides day care) will not be guilty of an offence under s 78(3) unless she contravenes an 'enforcement notice'. Accordingly, where it comes to the attention of a local authority that a person is acting as a child minder, they have a discretion whether to serve an enforcement notice on her. If they do, the notice lasts for one year.

## Registration

**15.9** The 1948 Act requires a local authority to keep two registers: a register of premises used as nurseries and a register of persons who receive children into their homes. The 1989 Act replaces this system of registration with a single register of responsible persons providing care at specified premises, although it can be subdivided by the authority into different kinds of facility as appropriate (White Paper, para 72).

The duty to register is found in s 78(1) (day care) and (3) (child minding). Contravention of this duty is a summary offence punishable by a fine of up to £2,000.

Application for registration is made to the appropriate local authority, ie, the authority in whose area the day care premises are situated or where the child minding is to take place (see s 78(1), (3)) in accordance with Sch 9, para 1 and with regulations made by the Secretary of State. Where a person provides day care in different premises situated in the area of the same local authority, he should make a separate application with respect to each of those premises (s 71(3) and Sch 9, para 1(2)). A local authority may charge for registration such charges as may be prescribed (ibid, para 1(3)) and the register is open to inspection by members of the public (s 71(15)(a)). The proposal to charge a fee for registration and inspection aroused great concern, especially in respect of pre-school playgroups. It was seen as a deterrent to the setting-up of such groups, especially self-help groups for working mothers who would need the facilities most. The Minister gave an undertaking that 'if, in order to levy a registration charge on commercial or semi-commercial organisations, it is necessary to make a charge on Pre-School Playgroups Association playgroups, that charge will be purely nominal. I give an undertaking that it would not be more than £10 per annum'[1] The Government is also considering whether certain categories should be exempted altogether.[2] The application for registration must contain a statement with respect to the applicant complying with regulations made for this purpose and also a statement with respect to any person assisting or likely to assist in looking after children on the premises who is living or likely to be living there (Sch 9, para 1). From this information the local authority will determine whether the applicant is disqualified from being registered or whether the application should be refused.

1 HC Deb, 24 October 1989, Vol 158, col 802, per D Mellor.
2 HL Deb, 8 November 1989, Vol 512, col 818, per The Lord Chancellor.

## Disqualification

**15.10** A person may not apply for registration if he is disqualified from doing so by regulations made by the Secretary of State (Sch 9, para 2(1)), which may make particular provision for circumstances set out in para 2(2).

## Refusal to register

**15.11** The new provisions are similar to the old ones, except that a distinction is made between, on the one hand, child minders and people looking after children in day nurseries or playgroups and, on the other, people who live in the same house or premises or who work there. Child minders and persons providing day care are assessed on their fitness to look after children, whereas other people are assessed on their fitness to be in the proximity of children under eight (s 71(7)-(10)). In addition, in the case of child minding and day care provision, the local authority may refuse registration if they are not satisfied that the premises in question are fit to be used for looking after children under the age of eight.

What constitutes a 'fit person' is not elaborated upon but the Government intimated that guidance would be issued as part of the implementation exercise.[2]

1 For procedure and appeals, see para 15.26.
2 HC Deb, Standing Committee B, 6 June 1989, col 406, per D Mellor.

# REQUIREMENTS TO BE COMPLIED WITH BY CHILD MINDERS AND PERSONS PROVIDING DAY CARE FOR YOUNG CHILDREN

**15.12** Where a local authority grant an application for registration, they must issue the applicant with a registration certificate. Under the former legislation there was a *power* for local authorities to impose requirements but no duty to do so. Now local authorities have a *duty* to impose such reasonable requirements on the registered person as they consider appropriate (ss 72(1) and 73(1)). The requirements are to be tailored to each individual case but, in imposing such requirements, the local authority must specify or require the matters set out in ss 72(2) and 73(3). These include the maximum number of children to be looked after, the obligation to secure that the premises concerned and the equipment used are adequately maintained and kept safe, the obligation to keep records, the requirement to notify changes and, in the case of day care providers, the number of assistants. A local authority may at any time add to these requirements or vary or remove them. In commenting on these provisions, the Minister said:

> 'The important difference in these clauses compared with the present law is that local authorities will now have to impose certain requirements with which the registered person will have to comply, but they will also have the flexibility to add other conditions. At present there is no obligation to impose any conditions at all, but if a local authority decides to do so, it may apply only those listed in the Act. We think that that is far too rigid.'[1]

Regulations may provide for those requirements that must be imposed by local authorities in prescribed circumstances and also for requirements that may not be imposed by a local authority (s 72(3) and s 73(4)).

1 HC Deb, Standing Committee B, 6 June 1989, col 394. For procedure and appeals, see para 15.17.

## CANCELLATION OF REGISTRATION[1]

**15.13** A local authority may cancel registration where they would be justified in refusing to grant an application (see s 71(7)-(11)) and also where a requirement under s 72 or 73 has not been complied with or an annual inspection fee has not been paid in time (s 74). An important new provision is the power to cancel registration where the care provided by the child minder or person providing day care is, in the opinion of the authority, seriously inadequate having regard to the needs of the child or children concerned. This provides a form of 'quality control' by local authorities over private provision of care for children under eight. In considering the needs of such a child the local authority shall, in particular, have regard to the child's religious persuasion, racial origin and cultural and linguistic background (s 74(6)).

1 For procedure and appeals, see para 15.19.

### Protection of children in an emergency

**15.14** A local authority may apply to the court for an order to be made as a matter of urgency to have a person's registration cancelled or varied (s 75). Such application can be made ex parte but must then be supported by a written statement of the authority's reasons for making the application (as to which court the application is to be made in, see s 92 and Sch 11). Where the court is satisfied that the child being looked after is suffering or is likely to suffer significant harm, it may make the order and any such cancellation, variation, etc shall have immediate effect. The local authority must then, as soon as reasonably practicable after the making of the order, serve the order and a copy of the authority's reasons for making the application on the registered person.

## INSPECTION

**15.15** A person authorised to do so by a local authority may at any reasonable time enter any domestic premises where child minding takes place or other premises where day care is provided (s 76(1)). Inspection may be of the premises, any children looked after on the premises, arrangements for their welfare and any records required to be kept. An inspector should have documentary authority which he should produce on request (s 76(6)). His title to enter and inspect rests on two conditions being satisfied, namely (i) that the premises are in fact domestic premises where child minding is carried on or are premises on which day care is provided, and (ii) they are not exempt under s 71(4) or (5), Sch 9, para 3, 4 or 5. A mere opinion or belief, or reasonable suspicion, that premises are used for child minding or for the provision of day care will not legally justify an entry, if in fact they are not. In doubtful cases the better course will be not to insist on being allowed to enter, if the right of entry is disputed, but to deal with the matter under s 76(2) if appropriate, so that there may be no risk of entry being a trespass.

**15.16** Section 76(2) provides the power to enter on reasonable belief. The belief must be that of the authority who may then authorise a person to enter premises where it it reasonably believed that children are being looked after in contravention of the Act. This replaces the provision in s 7(2) of the Nurseries and Child-Minders Regulation Act 1948, whereby application was made to a justice of the peace for a warrant of entry.

**15.17** Where a power of entry under s 76(1) or (2) is frustrated by refusal of entry to the premises or access to the child in question, a court may issue a warrant to a constable to assist the person applying for the warrant in the exercise of his power of entry, using reasonable force if necessary (s 102). Where the application relates to a particular child and it is reasonably practicable to do so, the application and warrant shall name the child and, where it does not name him, it shall describe him as clearly as possible (s 76(5)). The constable will normally be accompanied by the applicant and the court may direct that the constable be accompanied by a registered medical practitioner, registered nurse or health visitor if he so chooses.

**15.18** A new requirement placed on local authorities is that they must exercise their power under s 76(1) to inspect premises at least once every year. This was seen by the Government as a minimum requirement: if an authority wish to inspect more often there is nothing to prevent them and the guidance to be issued as part of the implementation of the legislation will make it clear that an annual inspection is the minimum.

The Secretary of State has a general power to inspect premises on which any person is acting as a child minder (s 80(1) (h)). The occupier of such premises may be required to furnish the Secretary of State with information and allow him to inspect records and the children there. Where entry is refused, a warrant may be issued to a constable (see para 15.17).

## APPEALS

**15.19** Section 77 replaces the provisions in the 1948 Act, except that it also gives a right of appeal to registered persons whose application for variation or removal of any requirement is refused.

**15.20** Before refusing an application for registration under s 71 or cancelling any such registration, or refusing consent under Sch 9, para 2, or imposing, removing or varying any requirement under s 72 or 73 or refusing to grant an application for the variation or removal of any such requirement, the local authority must serve a notice of their intention to take the step in question, which states their reasons and informs the person concerned of his rights under s 77. He may object to the proposal and, if the local authority persist in their intention, they shall inform him of their decision in writing. The person aggrieved may then appeal against the decision to the court in accordance with rules of court. Any proposed step specified in s 77(1)(b), (c) will then not take effect until the expiry of the time allowed for appeal or until the appeal is disposed of.

**15.21** These procedures do not apply to measures taken in an emergency which are provided for in s 75. In this situation, the local authority will make their application direct to the Court and the person concerned will be served with a notice of any order and of its terms and a copy of the authority's reasons which supported the application. Appeal from the decision of the Court in either event will be determined by s 94 and Rules of Court.

## OFFENCES

**15.22** Section 78 provides for a summary offence of providing day care without being registered under the Act. A person acting as a child minder without being registered may not be prosecuted unless an enforcement notice has been served on him and he has failed to comply with it. The section also creates offences of contravening without reasonable excuse or failing to comply with requirements imposed under s 72 or 73 and of intentionally obstructing the powers of entry under s 76.

The offences are triable only before a magistrates' criminal court and as summary offences, are subject to the six-month time limit between commission of the offence and institution of proceedings (Magistrates' Courts Act 1980, s 127).

# Children Act 1989

(1989 c 41)

## ARRANGEMENT OF SECTIONS

### Part I

### Introductory



### Part II

### Orders With Respect to Children in Family Proceedings

*General*



*Financial relief*



*Family assistance orders*

Section

## Part VII

### Voluntary Homes and Voluntary Organisations



## Part VIII

### Registered Children's Homes



## Part IX

### Private Arrangements for Fostering Children



## Part X

### Child Minding and Day Care for Young Children



## Part xi

### Secretary of State's Supervisory Functions and Responsibilities

Section

## Part XII

### Miscellaneous and General

An Act to reform the law relating to children; to provide for local authority services for children in need and others; to amend the law with respect to children's homes, community homes, voluntary homes and voluntary organisations; to make provision with respect to fostering, child minding and day care for young children and adoption; and for connected purposes [16 November 1989]

## Part I

## Introductory

### 1 Welfare of the child

(1) When a court determines any question with respect to—

(*a*) the upbringing of a child; or
(*b*) the administration of a child's property or the application of any income arising from it,

the child's welfare shall be the court's paramount consideration.

(2) In any proceedings in which any question with respect to the upbringing of a child arises, the court shall have regard to the general principle that any delay in determining the question is likely to prejudice the welfare of the child.

(3) In the circumstances mentioned in subsection (4), a court shall have regard in particular to—

(*a*) the ascertainable wishes and feelings of the child concerned (considered in the light of his age and understanding);
(*b*) his physical, emotional and educational needs;

(*c*) the likely effect on him of any change in his circumstances;
(*d*) his age, sex, background and any characteristics of his which the court considers relevant;
(*e*) any harm which he has suffered or is at risk of suffering;
(*f*) how capable each of his parents, and any other person in relation to whom the court considers the question to be relevant, is of meeting his needs;
(*g*) the range of powers available to the court under this Act in the proceedings in question.

(4) The circumstances are that—

(*a*) the court is considering whether to make, vary or discharge a section 8 order, and the making, variation or discharge of the order is opposed by any party to the proceedings; or
(*b*) the court is considering whether to make, vary or discharge an order under Part IV.

(5) Where a court is considering whether or not to make one or more orders under this Act with respect to a child, it shall not make the order or any of the orders unless it considers that doing so would be better for the child than making no order at all.

---

**Definitions** For 'court' see s 92 (7); for 'child' and 'upbringing' see s 105 (1); for 'harm' see s 31 (9) as applied to the whole Act by s 105 (1); for 'a section 8 order' see s 8 (2).

**References** See generally para 1.1 ff. For jurisdiction of courts see s 92 and Sch 11, para 9.1 ff. For welfare of the child see para 1.3; for 'parent' see para 2.7. 'Part IV' see ie 31-42 and Sch 3 (care and supervision). For 'family proceedings' under this Act see s 8 (3), (4)(*a*).

---

## 2 Parental responsibility for children

(1) Where a child's father and mother were married to each other at the time of his birth, they shall each have parental responsibility for the child.

(2) Where a child's father and mother were not married to each other at the time of his birth—

(*a*) the mother shall have parental responsibility for the child;
(*b*) the father shall not have parental responsibility for the child, unless he acquires it in accordance with the provisions of this Act.

(3) References in this Act to a child whose father and mother were, or (as the case may be) were not, married to each other at the time of his birth must be read with section 1 of the Family Law Reform Act 1987 (which extends their meaning).

(4) The rule of law that a father is the natural guardian of his legitimate child is abolished.

(5) More than one person may have parental responsibility for the same child at the same time.

(6) A person who has parental responsibility for a child at any time shall not cease to have that responsibility solely because some other person subsequently acquires parental responsibility for the child.

(7) Where more than one person has parental responsibility for a child, each of them may act alone and without the other (or others) in meeting

that responsibility; but nothing in this Part shall be taken to affect the operation of any enactment which requires the consent of more than one person in a matter affecting the child.

(8) The fact that a person has parental responsibility for a child shall not entitle him to act in any way which would be incompatible with any order made with respect to the child under this Act.

(9) A person who has parental responsibility for a child may not surrender or transfer any part of that responsibility to another but may arrange for some or all of it to be met by one or more persons acting on his behalf.

(10) The person with whom any such arrangement is made may himself be a person who already has parental responsibility for the child concerned.

(11) The making of any such arrangement shall not affect any liability of the person making it which may arise from any failure to meet any part of his parental responsibility for the child concerned.

---

**Definitions** For 'child' see s 105(1) ; for 'parental responsibility' see s 3.

**References** See generally para 2.1 ff. For whether a child's father and mother were married to each other at the time of his birth see sub-s (3), and para 2.7. For father acquiring parental responsibility see s 4 and 2.19. For 'this part' see Part I ss 1-7 (introductory).

---

## 3 Meaning of "parental responsibility"

(1) In this Act "parental responsibility" means all the rights, duties, powers, responsibilities and authority which by law a parent of a child has in relation to the child and his property.

(2) It also includes the rights, powers and duties which a guardian of the child's estate (appointed, before the commencement of section 5, to act generally) would have had in relation to the child and his property.

(3) The rights referred to in subsection (2) include, in particular, the right of the guardian to receive or recover in his own name, for the benefit of the child, property of whatever description and wherever situated which the child is entitled to receive or recover.

(4) The fact that a person has, or does not have, parental responsibility for a child shall not affect—

(*a*) any obligation which he may have in relation to the child (such as a statutory duty to maintain the child); or

(*b*) any rights which, in the event of the child's death, he (or any other person) may have in relation to the child's property.

(5) A person who—

(*a*) does not have parental responsibility for a particular child; but

(*b*) has care of the child,

may (subject to the provisions of this Act) do what is reasonable in all the circumstances of the case for the purpose of safeguarding or promoting the child's welfare.

---

**Definitions** For 'parental responsibility' see sub-s (1); for 'child' see s 105 (1).

**References** See generally para 2.1 ff. For 'parent' see para 2.7; for guardians see para 2.34. For the application of 'parental responsibility' to other enactments see s 108 (5), Sch 13.

---

## 4 Acquisition of parental responsibility by father

(1) Where a child's father and mother were not married to each other at the time of his birth—

(*a*) the court may, on the application of the father, order that he shall have parental responsibility for the child; or

(*b*) the father and mother may by agreement ("a parental responsibility agreement") provide for the father to have parental responsibility for the child.

(2) No parental responsibility agreement shall have effect for the purposes of this Act unless—

(*a*) it is made in the form prescribed by regulations made by the Lord Chancellor; and

(*b*) where regulations are made by the Lord Chancellor prescribing the manner in which such agreements must be recorded, it is recorded in the prescribed manner.

(3) Subject to section 12(4), an order under subsection (1)(*a*), or a parental responsibility agreement, may only be brought to an end by an order of the court made on the application—

(*a*) of any person who has parental responsibility for the child; or

(*b*) with leave of the court, of the child himself.

(4) The court may only grant leave under subsection (3)(*b*) if it is satisfied that the child has sufficient understanding to make the proposed application.

---

**Definitions** For 'child' see s 105 (1); for 'court' see s 92 (7); for 'parental responsibility' see s 3; for 'parental responsibility agreement' see sub-s (1)(*b*); for 'prescribed' see sub-s (2).

**References** See generally para 2.19 ff. For jurisdiction of courts see s 92 and Sch 11, para 9.1 ff. For appeals see s 94. For whether a child's father and mother were married to each other at the time of his birth see s 2(3), s 105(2) and para 2.7. For duration of the order see s 12(4) (where residence order made in favour of the father) and generally s 91(7), (8). For 'family proceedings' under this Act see s 8 (3), (4)(*a*).

---

## 5 Appointment of guardians

(1) Where an application with respect to a child is made to the court by any individual, the court may by order appoint that individual to be the child's guardian if—

(*a*) the child has no parent with parental responsibility for him; or

(*b*) a residence order has been made with respect to the child in favour of a parent or guardian of his who has died while the order was in force.

(2) The power conferred by subsection (1) may also be exercised in any family proceedings if the court considers that the order should be made even though no application has been made for it.

(3) A parent who has parental responsibility for his child may appoint another individual to be the child's guardian in the event of his death.

(4) A guardian of a child may appoint another individual to take his place as the child's guardian in the event of his death.

(5) An appointment under subsection (3) or (4) shall not have effect unless

it is made in writing, is dated and is signed by the person making the appointment or—

(*a*) in the case of an appointment made by a will which is not signed by the testator, is signed at the direction of the testator in accordance with the requirements of section 9 of the Wills Act 1837; or

(*b*) in any other case, is signed at the direction of the person making the appointment, in his presence and in the presence of two witnesses who each attest the signature.

(6) A person appointed as a child's guardian under this section shall have parental responsibility for the child concerned.

(7) Where—

(*a*) on the death of any person making an appointment under subsection (3) or (4), the child concerned has no parent with parental responsibility for him; or

(*b*) immediately before the death of any person making such an appointment, a residence order in his favour was in force with respect to the child,

the appointment shall take effect on the death of that person.

(8) Where, on the death of any person making an appointment under subsection (3) or (4)—

(*a*) the child concerned has a parent with parental responsibility for him; and

(*b*) subsection (7)(*b*) does not apply,

the appointment shall take effect when the child no longer has a parent who has parental responsibility for him.

(9) Subsections (1) and (7) do not apply if the residence order referred to in paragraph (*b*) of those subsections was also made in favour of a surviving parent of the child.

(10) Nothing in this section shall be taken to prevent an appointment under subsection (3) or (4) being made by two or more persons acting jointly.

(11) Subject to any provision made by rules of court, no court shall exercise the High Court's inherent jurisdiction to appoint a guardian of the estate of any child.

(12) Where rules of court are made under subsection (11) they may prescribe the circumstances in which, and conditions subject to which, an appointment of such a guardian may be made.

(13) A guardian of a child may only be appointed in accordance with the provisions of this section.

---

**Definitions** For 'child' and 'signed' see s 105 (1). For 'court' see s 92 (7); for 'parental responsibility' see s 3; for 'residence order' see s 8 (1); for a person in whose favour a residence order is in force see s 105 (3).

**References** See generally para 2.34 ff. For jurisdiction of courts see s 92 and Sch 11, 9.1 ff. For duration of order of appointment see s 91 (7), (8) . For transitional provisions see s 108 (6) and Sch 14 para 12. For 'family proceedings' under this Act see s 8 (3), (4)(*a*). For other restrictions on the use of wardship jurisdiction see s 100.

---

## 6 Guardians: revocation and disclaimer

(1) An appointment under section 5(3) or (4) revokes an earlier such appointment (including one made in an unrevoked will or codicil) made by the same person in respect of the same child, unless it is clear (whether as the result of an express provision in the later appointment or by any necessary implication) that the purpose of the later appointment is to appoint an additional guardian.

(2) An appointment under section 5(3) or (4) (including one made in an unrevoked will or codicil) is revoked if the person who made the appointment revokes it by a written and dated instrument which is signed—

(*a*) by him; or
(*b*) at his direction, in his presence and in the presence of two witnesses who each attest the signature.

(3) An appointment under section 5(3) or (4) (other than one made in a will or codicil) is revoked if, with the intention of revoking the appointment, the person who made it—

(*a*) destroys the instrument by which it was made; or
(*b*) has some other person destroy that instrument in his presence.

(4) For the avoidance of doubt, an appointment under section 5(3) or (4) made in a will or codicil is revoked if the will or codicil is revoked.

(5) A person who is appointed as a guardian under section 5(3) or (4) may disclaim his appointment by an instrument in writing signed by him and made within a reasonable time of his first knowing that the appointment has taken effect.

(6) Where regulations are made by the Lord Chancellor prescribing the manner in which such disclaimers must be recorded, no such disclaimer shall have effect unless it is recorded in the prescribed manner.

(7) Any appointment of a guardian under section 5 may be brought to an end at any time by order of the court—

(*a*) on the application of any person who has parental responsibility for the child;
(*b*) on the application of the child concerned, with leave of the court; or
(*c*) in any family proceedings, if the court considers that it should be brought to an end even though no application has been made.

---

**Definitions** For 'child', and 'signed' see s 105 (1); for 'court' see s 94 (7); for 'parental responsibility' see s 3.

**Reference** For jurisdiction of courts see s 92 and Sch 11, para 9.1 ff. For 'family proceedings' under this Act see s 8(3), (4)(a).

---

## 7 Welfare reports

(1) A court considering any question with respect to a child under this Act may—

(*a*) ask a probation officer; or
(*b*) ask a local authority to arrange for—
  (i) an officer of the authority; or

(ii) such other person (other than a probation officer) as the authority considers appropriate,

to report to the court on such matters relating to the welfare of that child as are required to be dealt with in the report.

(2) The Lord Chancellor may make regulations specifying matters which, unless the court orders otherwise, must be dealt with in any report under this section.

(3) The report may be made in writing, or orally, as the court requires.

(4) Regardless of any enactment or rule of law which would otherwise prevent it from doing so, the court may take account of—

(*a*) any statement contained in the report; and

(*b*) any evidence given in respect of the matters referred to in the report,

in so far as the statement or evidence is, in the opinion of the court, relevant to the question which it is considering.

(5) It shall be the duty of the authority or probation officer to comply with any request for a report under this section.

---

**Definitions** For 'court' see s 92(7); for 'child' and 'local authority' see s 105(1).

**References** See generally para 8.1 ff. For jurisdiction of courts see s 92 and Sch 11, para 9.1 ff. For other evidential provisions see s 96.

---

## Part II

## Orders With Respect To Children In Family Proceedings

### *General*

### 8 Residence, contact and other orders with respect to children

(1) In this Act—

"a contact order" means an order requiring the person with whom a child lives, or is to live, to allow the child to visit or stay with the person named in the order, or for that person and the child otherwise to have contact with each other;

"a prohibited steps order" means an order that no step which could be taken by a parent in meeting his parental responsibility for a child, and which is of a kind specified in the order, shall be taken by any person without the consent of the court;

"a residence order" means an order settling the arrangements to be made as to the person with whom a child is to live; and

"a specific issue order" means an order giving directions for the purpose of determining a specific question which has arisen, or which may arise, in connection with any aspect of parental responsibility for a child.

(2) In this Act "a section 8 order" means any of the orders mentioned in subsection (1) and any order varying or discharging such an order.

(3) For the purposes of this Act "family proceedings" means any proceedings—

(*a*) under the inherent jurisdiction of the High Court in relation to children; and (*b*) under the enactments mentioned in subsection (4),

but does not include proceedings on an application for leave under section 100(3).

(4) The enactments are—

(*a*) Parts I, II and IV of this Act;
(*b*) the Matrimonial Causes Act 1973;
(*c*) the Domestic Violence and Matrimonial Proceedings Act 1976;
(*d*) the Adoption Act 1976;
(*e*) the Domestic Proceedings and Magistrates' Courts Act 1978;
(*f*) sections 1 and 9 of the Matrimonial Homes Act 1983;
(*g*) Part III of the Matrimonial and Family Proceedings Act 1984.

---

**Definitions** For 'contact order', 'prohibited steps order', 'residence order', 'specific issue order' see sub-s (1); for 'child' see s 105(1); for 'parental responsibility' see s 3; for 'court' see s 92 (7); for 'a section 8 order' see sub-s (2); for 'family proceedings' see sub-s (3).

**References** See generally para 3.1 ff. For 'parent' see para 2.7. For jurisdiction of courts see s 92 and Sch 11, para 9.1 ff. Part I of this Act: ie ss 1-7 (introductory); Part II ss 8-17 and Sch 1 (orders with respect to children in family and other proceedings); Part IV, ss 31-42 and Sch 3 (care and supervision). For the effects of orders generally see s 91.

---

## 9 Restrictions on making section 8 orders

(1) No court shall make any section 8 order, other than a residence order, with respect to a child who is in the care of a local authority.

(2) No application may be made by a local authority for a residence order or contact order and no court shall make such an order in favour of a local authority.

(3) A person who is, or was at any time within the last six months, a local authority foster parent of a child may not apply for leave to apply for a section 8 order with respect to the child unless—

(*a*) he has the consent of the authority;
(*b*) he is a relative of the child; or
(*c*) the child has lived with him for at least three years preceding the application.

(4) The period of three years mentioned in subsection (3)(*c*) need not be continuous but must have begun not more than five years before the making of the application.

(5) No court shall exercise its powers to make a specific issue order or prohibited steps order—

(*a*) with a view to achieving a result which could be achieved by making a residence or contact order; or
(*b*) in any way which is denied to the High Court (by section 100(2)) in the exercise of its inherent jurisdiction with respect to children.

(6) No court shall make any section 8 order which is to have effect for a period which will end after the child has reached the age of sixteen unless it is satisfied that the circumstances of the case are exceptional.

(7) No court shall make any section 8 order, other than one varying or discharging such an order, with respect to a child who has reached the age of sixteen unless it is satisfied that the circumstances of the case are exceptional.

**Definitions** For 'court' see s 92(7); for 'a section 8 order' see s 8(2); for 'residence order', 'contact order', 'specific issue order' and 'prohibited steps order' see s 8(1); for 'child', 'child who is in the care of a local authority', 'local authority' and 'relative' see s 105(1); for 'local authority foster parent', see s 23(3).

**References** For 'family proceedings' under this Act see s 8(3), (4)(*a*). For jurisdiction of courts see s 92 and Sch 11, para 9.1 ff. For power of court to make section 8 orders, persons who may make an application for such orders and the need for leave to apply see s 10; for the presumption that a delay in determining any question in proceedings concerning the upbringing of a child is likely to prejudice the welfare of the child concerned see s 1(2) for timetable for section 8 proceedings and supplementary provisions see s 11; for provisions connected with residence orders see ss 12,13 and 14.

---

## 10 Power of court to make section 8 orders

(1) In any family proceedings in which a question arises with respect to the welfare of any child, the court may make a section 8 order with respect to the child if—

(*a*) an application for the order has been made by a person who—

(i) is entitled to apply for a section 8 order with respect to the child; or

(ii) has obtained the leave of the court to make the application; or

(*b*) the court considers that the order should be made even though no such application has been made.

(2) The court may also make a section 8 order with respect to any child on the application of a person who—

(*a*) is entitled to apply for a section 8 order with respect to the child; or

(*b*) has obtained the leave of the court to make the application.

(3) This section is subject to the restrictions imposed by section 9.

(4) The following persons are entitled to apply to the court for any section 8 order with respect to a child—

(*a*) any parent or guardian of the child;

(*b*) any person in whose favour a residence order is in force with respect to the child.

(5) The following persons are entitled to apply for a residence or contact order with respect to a child—

(*a*) any party to a marriage (whether or not subsisting) in relation to whom the child is a child of the family;

(*b*) any person with whom the child has lived for a period of at least three years;

(*c*) any person who—

(i) in any case where a residence order is in force with respect to the child, has the consent of each of the persons in whose favour the order was made;

(ii) in any case where the child is in the care of a local authority, has the consent of that authority; or

(iii) in any other case, has the consent of each of those (if any) who have parental responsibility for the child.

(6) A person who would not otherwise be entitled (under the previous

provisions of this section) to apply for the variation or discharge of a section 8 order shall be entitled to do so if—

(*a*) the order was made on his application; or
(*b*) in the case of a contact order, he is named in the order.

(7) Any person who falls within a category of person prescribed by rules of court is entitled to apply for any such section 8 order as may be prescribed in relation to that category of person.

(8) Where the person applying for leave to make an application for a section 8 order is the child concerned, the court may only grant leave if it is satisfied that he has sufficient understanding to make the proposed application for the section 8 order.

(9) Where the person applying for leave to make an application for a section 8 order is not the child concerned, the court shall, in deciding whether or not to grant leave, have particular regard to—

(*a*) the nature of the proposed application for the section 8 order;
(*b*) the applicant's connection with the child;
(*c*) any risk there might be of that proposed application disrupting the child's life to such an extent that he would be harmed by it; and
(*d*) where the child is being looked after by a local authority—
  (i) the authority's plans for the child's future; and
  (ii) the wishes and feelings of the child's parents.

(10) The period of three years mentioned in subsection (5)(*b*) need not be continuous but must not have begun more than five years before, or ended more than three months before, the making of the application.

---

**Definitions** For 'family proceedings' see s 8(3); for 'child', 'guardian', 'child of the family','child in the care of a local authority', 'local authority', 'prescribed' see s 105(1); for 'court' see s 92(7); for 'a section 8 order' see s 8(2); for 'residence order', 'contact order', see s 8(1); for 'a person in whose favour a residence order is in force' see s 105(3)(*b*); for 'parental responsibility' see s 3; for 'harm' see s 31(9) as applied to the whole Act by s 105(1); for 'child looked after by a local authority' see s 22(1) and s 105(4).

**References** See generally para 3.1 ff. For jurisdiction of courts see s 92 and Sch 11, para 9.1 ff. For appeals see s 94. For persons entitled to apply for section 8 orders see sub-ss (4), (5) and (6). For 'parent' see para 2.7; for appointment of guardian ad litem see s 41. For duration of orders made under this section see s 11 (5), (6) and ss 91(10), (11). For 'family proceedings' under this Act see s 8(3), (4)(*a*). For where the leave of the court may be required in order to make an application for an order under this section see s 91(14). For the making of family assistance orders under this Part ie Part II (ss 8-16 and Sch 1) see s 16. For the restrictions on the making of applications for a section 8 order see s 9; for the presumption that a delay in determining any question in proceedings concerning a section 8 order is likely to prejudice the welfare of the child concerned see s 1(2); for the timetable for such proceedings and supplementary provisions see s 11; for other provisions connected with residence orders see ss 12, 13 and 14.

---

### 11 General principles and supplementary provisions

(1) In proceedings in which any question of making a section 8 order, or any other question with respect to such an order, arises, the court shall (in the light of any rules made by virtue of subsection (2))—

(*a*) draw up a timetable with a view to determining the question without delay; and
(*b*) give such directions as it considers appropriate for the purpose of

ensuring, so far as is reasonably practicable, that that timetable is adhered to.

(2) Rules of court may—

(*a*) specify periods within which specified steps must be taken in relation to proceedings in which such questions arise; and

(*b*) make other provision with respect to such proceedings for the purpose of ensuring, so far as is reasonably practicable, that such questions are determined without delay.

(3) Where a court has power to make a section 8 order, it may do so at any time during the course of the proceedings in question even though it is not in a position to dispose finally of those proceedings.

(4) Where a residence order is made in favour of two or more persons who do not themselves all live together, the order may specify the periods during which the child is to live in the different households concerned.

(5) Where—

(*a*) a residence order has been made with respect to a child; and

(*b*) as a result of the order the child lives, or is to live, with one of two parents who each have parental responsibility for him,

the residence order shall cease to have effect if the parents live together for a continuous period of more than six months.

(6) A contact order which requires the parent with whom a child lives to allow the child to visit, or otherwise have contact with, his other parent shall cease to have effect if the parents live together for a continuous period of more than six months.

(7) A section 8 order may—

(*a*) contain directions about how it is to be carried into effect;

(*b*) impose conditions which must be complied with by any person—

(i) in whose favour the order is made;

(ii) who is a parent of the child concerned;

(iii) who is not a parent of his but who has parental responsibility for him; or

(iv) with whom the child is living,

and to whom the conditions are expressed to apply;

(*c*) be made to have effect for a specified period, or contain provisions which are to have effect for a specified period;

(*d*) make such incidental, supplemental or consequential provision as the court thinks fit.

---

**Definitions** For 'a section 8 order' see s 8(2); for 'court' see s 92(7); for 'residence order' and 'contact order' see s 8(1); For 'child' see s 105(1; for a person in whose favour a residence order is made or a person with whom a child lives, or is to live, as the result of the residence order see s 105(3); for 'parental responsibility' see s 3.

**References** See generally para 3.1 ff. For jurisdiction of courts see s 92 and Sch 11, para 9.1 ff. For welfare of the child see para 1.3 ff. For the presumption that a delay in determining any question in proceedings concerning the upbringing of a child is likely to prejudice the welfare of the child concerned see s 1(2); for 'parent' see para 2.7.

---

## 12 Residence orders and parental responsibility

(1) Where the court makes a residence order in favour of the father of a child it shall, if the father would not otherwise have parental responsibility for the child, also make an order under section 4 giving him that responsibility.

(2) Where the court makes a residence order in favour of any person who is not the parent or guardian of the child concerned that person shall have parental responsibility for the child while the residence order remains in force.

(3) Where a person has parental responsibility for a child as a result of subsection (2), he shall not have the right—

(*a*) to consent, or refuse to consent, to the making of an application with respect to the child under section 18 of the Adoption Act 1976;

(*b*) to agree, or refuse to agree, to the making of an adoption order, or an order under section 55 of the Act of 1976, with respect to the child; or

(*c*) to appoint a guardian for the child.

(4) Where subsection (1) requires the court to make an order under section 4 in respect of the father of a child, the court shall not bring that order to an end at any time while the residence order concerned remains in force.

---

**Definitions** For 'court' see s 92(7); for 'residence order' see s 8(1); for 'child' and 'guardian of a child' see s 105(1); for 'parental responsibility' see s 3.

**References** See generally para 3.1 ff. For jurisdiction of courts see s 92 and Sch 11, para 9.1 ff. For 'an order under section 4' see para 2.20; for 'parent' see para 2.7; for the duration of residence orders see s 11(5) and s 91(10), (11). For 'family proceedings' under this Act see s 8(3), (4)(*a*).

---

## 13 Change of child's name or removal from jurisdiction

(1) Where a residence order is in force with respect to a child, no person may—

(*a*) cause the child to be known by a new surname; or

(*b*) remove him from the United Kingdom;

without either the written consent of every person who has parental responsibility for the child or the leave of the court.

(2) Subsection (1)(*b*) does not prevent the removal of a child, for a period of less than one month, by the person in whose favour the residence order is made.

(3) In making a residence order with respect to a child the court may grant the leave required by subsection (1)(*b*), either generally or for specified purposes.

---

**Definitions** For 'residence order' see s 8(1); for 'child' see s 105(1); for 'parental responsibility' see s 3; for 'court' see s 92(7); for 'the person in whose favour a residence order is in force' see s 105(3).

**References** See generally para 3.1 ff. For 'family proceedings' under this Act see s 8(3), (4)(*a*).

---

### 14 Enforcement of residence orders

(1) Where—

(*a*) a residence order is in force with respect to a child in favour of any person; and

(*b*) any other person (including one in whose favour the order is also in force) is in breach of the arrangements settled by that order,

the person mentioned in paragraph (*a*) may, as soon as the requirement in subsection (2) is complied with, enforce the order under section 63(3) of the Magistrates' Courts Act 1980 as if it were an order requiring the other person to produce the child to him.

(2) The requirement is that a copy of the residence order has been served on the other person.

(3) Subsection (1) is without prejudice to any other remedy open to the person in whose favour the residence order is in force.

---

**Definitions** For 'residence order' see s 8(1); for 'child' see s 105(1); for 'the person in whose favour a residence order is in force' see s 105(3).

**Reference** For service of documents under the Act generally see s 105(8)-(10).

---

*Financial relief*

### 15 Orders for financial relief with respect to children

(1) Schedule 1 (which consists primarily of the re-enactment, with consequential amendments and minor modifications, of provisions of the Guardianship of Minors Acts 1971 and 1973, the Children Act 1975 and of sections 15 and 16 of the Family Law Reform Act 1987) makes provision in relation to financial relief for children.

(2) The powers of a magistrates' court under section 60 of the Magistrates' Courts Act 1980 to revoke, revive or vary an order for the periodical payment of money shall not apply in relation to an order made under Schedule 1.

---

**Definition** For 'child' see s 105(1).

**References** See generally para 4.1 ff. For 'family proceedings' under this Act see s 8(3),(4)(*a*).

---

*Family assistance orders*

### 16 Family assistance orders

(1) Where, in any family proceedings, the court has power to make an order under this Part with respect to any child, it may (whether or not it makes such an order) make an order requiring—

(*a*) a probation officer to be made available; or

(*b*) a local authority to make an officer of the authority available,

to advise, assist and (where appropriate) befriend any person named in the order.

(2) The persons who may be named in an order under this section ("a family assistance order") are—

(*a*) any parent or guardian of the child;

(*b*) any person with whom the child is living or in whose favour a contact order is in force with respect to the child;

(*c*) the child himself.

(3) No court may make a family assistance order unless—

(*a*) it is satisfied that the circumstances of the case are exceptional; and

(*b*) it has obtained the consent of every person to be named in the order other than the child.

(4) A family assistance order may direct—

(*a*) the person named in the order; or

(*b*) such of the persons named in the order as may be specified in the order,

to take such steps as may be so specified with a view to enabling the officer concerned to be kept informed of the address of any person named in the order and to be allowed to visit any such person.

(5) Unless it specifies a shorter period, a family assistance order shall have effect for a period of six months beginning with the day on which it is made.

(6) Where—

(*a*) a family assistance order is in force with respect to a child; and

(*b*) a section 8 order is also in force with respect to the child,

the officer concerned may refer to the court the question whether the section 8 order should be varied or discharged.

(7) A family assistance order shall not be made so as to require a local authority to make an officer of theirs available unless—

(*a*) the authority agree; or

(*b*) the child concerned lives or will live within their area.

(8) Where a family assistance order requires a probation officer to be made available, the officer shall be selected in accordance with arrangements made by the probation committee for the area in which the child lives or will live.

(9) If the selected probation officer is unable to carry out his duties, or dies, another probation officer shall be selected in the same manner.

---

**Definitions** For 'family proceedings' see s 8(3), (4)(*a*); for 'court' see s 92(7); for 'child', 'local authority' and 'guardian of a child' see s 105(1); 'family assistance order' see sub-s (2); for 'contact order' see s 8(1) and 'a section 8 order' see s 8(2).

**References** See generally para 3.51 ff. For 'this Part' see Part II ie ss 8-16 and Sch I (orders with respect to children in family and other proceedings). For 'parent' see para 2.7. For the ending of orders see sub-s (5) and for the duration of section 8 orders see s 91 (10), (11).

---

## PART III

## LOCAL AUTHORITY SUPPORT FOR CHILDREN AND FAMILIES

*Provision of services for children and their families*

### 17 Provision of services for children in need, their families and others

(1) It shall be the general duty of every local authority (in addition to the other duties imposed on them by this Part)—

(*a*) to safeguard and promote the welfare of children within their area who are in need; and

(*b*) so far as is consistent with that duty, to promote the upbringing of such children by their families,

by providing a range and level of services appropriate to those children's needs.

(2) For the purpose principally of facilitating the discharge of their general duty under this section, every local authority shall have the specific duties and powers set out in Part 1 of Schedule 2.

(3) Any service provided by an authority in the exercise of functions conferred on them by this section may be provided for the family of a particular child in need or for any member of his family, if it is provided with a view to safeguarding or promoting the child's welfare.

(4) The Secretary of State may by order amend any provision of Part I of Schedule 2 or add any further duty or power to those for the time being mentioned there.

(5) Every local authority—

(*a*) shall facilitate the provision by others (including in particular voluntary organisations) of services which the authority have power to provide by virtue of this section or section 18, 20, 23 or 24; and

(*b*) may make such arrangements as they see fit for any person to act on their behalf in the provision of any such service.

(6) The services provided by a local authority in the exercise of functions conferred on them by this section may include giving assistance in kind or, in exceptional circumstances, in cash.

(7) Assistance may be unconditional or subject to conditions as to the repayment of the assistance or of its value (in whole or in part).

(8) Before giving any assistance or imposing any conditions, a local authority shall have regard to the means of the child concerned and of each of his parents.

(9) No person shall be liable to make any repayment of assistance or of its value at any time when he is in receipt of income support or family credit under the Social Security Act 1986.

(10) For the purposes of this Part a child shall be taken to be in need if—

(*a*) he is unlikely to achieve or maintain, or to have the opportunity of achieving or maintaining, a reasonable standard of health or development without the provision for him of services by a local authority under this Part;

(*b*) his health or development is likely to be significantly impaired, or further impaired, without the provision for him of such services; or
(*c*) he is disabled,

and "family", in relation to such a child, includes any person who has parental responsibility for the child and any other person with whom he has been living.

(11) For the purposes of this Part, a child is disabled if he is blind, deaf or dumb or suffers from mental disorder of any kind or is substantially and permanently handicapped by illness, injury or congenital deformity or such other disability as may be prescribed; and in this Part—

"development" means physical, intellectual, emotional, social or behavioural development; and

"health" means physical or mental health.

---

**Definitions** For 'local authority', 'child', 'upbringing', 'service' 'functions' and 'prescribed' see s 105(1); for 'need' and 'family' see sub-s (10); for voluntary organisation see s 105(1); for 'health', 'development' and 'disabled' see sub-s (11).

**References** See generally para 5.2 ff. For 'this Part' see Part III ie ss 17-30 and Sch 2 (local authority support for children and families). For 'parent' see para 2.7. For the application of sub-ss (7)-(9) in relation to assistance given under s 24 see s 24 (10). For the duty to publish information about the services provided under this section see Sch 2, Pt I; for cooperation between authorities see s 27; for recoupment of the cost of services see s 29; for miscellaneous supplementary provisions see s 30.

---

## 18 Day care for pre-school and other children

(1) Every local authority shall provide such day care for children in need within their area who are—

(*a*) aged five or under; and
(*b*) not yet attending schools,

as is appropriate.

(2) A local authority may provide day care for children within their area who satisfy the conditions mentioned in subsection (1)(*a*) and (*b*) even though they are not in need.

(3) A local authority may provide facilities (including training, advice, guidance and counselling) for those—

(*a*) caring for children in day care; or
(*b*) who at any time accompany such children while they are in day care.

(4) In this section "day care" means any form of care or supervised activity provided for children during the day (whether or not it is provided on a regular basis).

(5) Every local authority shall provide for children in need within their area who are attending any school such care or supervised activities as is appropriate—

(*a*) outside school hours; or
(*b*) during school holidays.

(6) A local authority may provide such care or supervised activities for children within their area who are attending any school even though those children are not in need.

(7) In this section "supervised activity" means an activity supervised by a responsible person.

---

**Definitions** For 'local authority', 'child' and 'school' see s 105(1); for 'a child in need' see s 17(10); for 'day care' see sub-s (4); for 'supervised activity' see sub-s (7).

---

## 19 Review of provision for day care, child minding etc

(1) Every local authority in England and Wales shall review—

(*a*) the provision which they make under section 18;

(*b*) the extent to which the services of child minders are available within their area with respect to children under the age of eight; and

(*c*) the provision for day care within their area made for children under the age of eight by persons, other than the authority, required to register under section 71(1)(*b*).

(2) A review under subsection (1) shall be conducted—

(*a*) together with the appropriate local education authority; and

(*b*) at least once in every review period.

(3) Every local authority in Scotland shall, at least once in every review period, review—

(*a*) the provision for day care within their area made for children under the age of eight by the local authority and by persons required to register under section 71(1)(*b*); and

(*b*) the extent to which the services of child minders are available within their area with respect to children under the age of eight.

(4) In conducting any such review, the two authorities or, in Scotland, the authority shall have regard to the provision made with respect to children under the age of eight in relevant establishments within their area.

(5) In this section—

"relevant establishment" means any establishment which is mentioned in paragraphs 3 and 4 of Schedule 9 (hospitals, schools and other establishments exempt from the registration requirements which apply in relation to the provision of day care); and

"review period" means the period of one year beginning with the commencement of this section and each subsequent period of three years beginning with an anniversary of that commencement.

(6) Where a local authority have conducted a review under this section they shall publish the result of the review—

(*a*) as soon as is reasonably practicable;

(*b*) in such form as they consider appropriate; and

(*c*) together with any proposals they may have with respect to the matters reviewed.

(7) The authorities conducting any review under this section shall have regard to—

(*a*) any representations made to any one of them by any relevant health authority or health board; and

(*b*) any other representations which they consider to be relevant.

(8) In the application of this section to Scotland, "day care" has the same

meaning as in section 79 and "health board" has the same meaning as in the National Health Service (Scotland) Act 1978.

---

**Definitions** For 'local authority', 'child', 'local education authority', 'hospital' and 'health authority' see s 105(1); for 'child minder' see s 71 as applied to the whole Act by s 105(1); for 'day care' see s 18(4) as applied to the whole Act by s 105(1); for 'review period' and 'relevant establishment' see sub-s (5).

**References** See generally para 5.19 ff. For the general duty of local authorities in connection with the welfare of children in need see s 17; for cooperation between authorities see s 27; for recoupment of the cost of services provided see s 29 and for miscellaneous supplementary provisions see s 30. For the registration of child minders and persons providing day care for young children see Part X (ss 71-79 and Sch 9).

---

*Provision of accommodation for children*

## 20 Provision of accommodation for children: general

(1) Every local authority shall provide accommodation for any child in need within their area who appears to them to require accommodation as a result of—

(*a*) there being no person who has parental responsibility for him;
(*b*) his being lost or having been abandoned; or
(*c*) the person who has been caring for him being prevented (whether or not permanently, and for whatever reason) from providing him with suitable accommodation or care.

(2) Where a local authority provide accommodation under subsection (1) for a child who is ordinarily resident in the area of another local authority, that other local authority may take over the provision of accommodation for the child within—

(*a*) three months of being notified in writing that the child is being provided with accommodation; or
(*b*) such other longer period as may be prescribed.

(3) Every local authority shall provide accommodation for any child in need within their area who has reached the age of sixteen and whose welfare the authority consider is likely to be seriously prejudiced if they do not provide him with accommodation.

(4) A local authority may provide accommodation for any child within their area (even though a person who has parental responsibility for him is able to provide him with accommodation) if they consider that to do so would safeguard or promote the child's welfare.

(5) A local authority may provide accommodation for any person who has reached the age of sixteen but is under twenty-one in any community home which takes children who have reached the age of sixteen if they consider that to do so would safeguard or promote his welfare.

(6) Before providing accommodation under this section, a local authority shall, so far as is reasonably practicable and consistent with the child's welfare—

(*a*) ascertain the child's wishes regarding the provision of accommodation; and
(*b*) give due consideration (having regard to his age and understanding) to such wishes of the child as they have been able to ascertain.

(7) A local authority may not provide accommodation under this section for any child if any person who—

(*a*) has parental responsibility for him; and

(*b*) is willing and able to—

(i) provide accommodation for him; or

(ii) arrange for accommodation to be provided for him,

objects.

(8) Any person who has parental responsibility for a child may at any time remove the child from accommodation provided by or on behalf of the local authority under this section.

(9) Subsections (7) and (8) do not apply while any person—

(*a*) in whose favour a residence order is in force with respect to the child; or

(*b*) who has care of the child by virtue of an order made in the exercise of the High Court's inherent jurisdiction with respect to children,

agrees to the child being looked after in accommodation provided by or on behalf of the local authority.

(10) Where there is more than one such person as is mentioned in subsection (9), all of them must agree.

(11) Subsections (7) and (8) do not apply where a child who has reached the age of sixteen agrees to being provided with accommodation under this section.

---

**Definitions** For 'local authority', 'child' and 'prescribed' see s 105(1); for 'a child in need' see s 17(10) as applied to the whole Act by s 105(7); for 'parental responsibility' see s 3; for 'community home' see s 53; for 'residence order' see s 8(1). For a person in whose favour a residence order is in force see s 105(3).

**References** See generally para 5.20 ff. For the determination of the ordinary residence of a child for the purposes of sub-s (2), 21(3) or s 29(7)-(9) see s 30(2) and s 105(6). For the general duties of local authorities in connection with the welfare of children in need see s 17; for review of case of, and representations relating to, child being looked after by local authority see s 26; for cooperation between authorities see s 27; for recoupment for the cost of services provided see s 29; for miscellaneous supplementary provisions see s 30.

---

## 21 Provision of accommodation for children in police protection or detention or on remand, etc

(1) Every local authority shall make provision for the reception and accommodation of children who are removed or kept away from home under Part V.

(2) Every local authority shall receive, and provide accommodation for, children—

(*a*) in police protection whom they are requested to receive under section 46(3)(*f*);

(*b*) whom they are requested to receive under section 38(6) of the Police and Criminal Evidence Act 1984;

(*c*) who are—

(i) on remand under section 23(1) of the Children and Young Persons Act 1969; or

(ii) the subject of a supervision order imposing a residence requirement under section 12AA of that Act,

and with respect to whom they are the designated authority.

(3) Where a child has been—

(*a*) removed under Part V; or

(*b*) detained under section 38 of the Police and Criminal Evidence Act 1984,

and he is not being provided with accommodation by a local authority or in a hospital vested in the Secretary of State, any reasonable expenses of accommodating him shall be recoverable from the local authority in whose area he is ordinarily resident.

---

**Definitions** For 'local authority', 'child' and 'hospital' see s 105(1); for 'in police protection' see s 46(2); for 'supervision order' see s 31(11); for 'designated authority' see s 31(8).

**References** See generally para 5.27. 'Part V' ie ss 43-52 (protection of children). For remand under s 23(1) of the Children and Young Persons Act 1969 see para 5.27. For the determination of the ordinary residence of a child see s 30(2) and s 105(6).

---

*Duties of local authorities in relation to children looked after by them*

## 22 General duty of local authority in relation to children looked after by them

(1) In this Act, any reference to a child who is looked after by a local authority is a reference to a child who is—

(*a*) in their care; or

(*b*) provided with accommodation by the authority in the exercise of any functions (in particular those under this Act) which stand referred to their social services committee under the Local Authority Social Services Act 1970.

(2) In subsection (1) "accommodation" means accommodation which is provided for a continuous period of more than 24 hours.

(3) It shall be the duty of a local authority looking after any child—

(*a*) to safeguard and promote his welfare; and

(*b*) to make such use of services available for children cared for by their own parents as appears to the authority reasonable in his case.

(4) Before making any decision with respect to a child whom they are looking after, or proposing to look after, a local authority shall, so far as is reasonably practicable, ascertain the wishes and feelings of—

(*a*) the child;

(*b*) his parents;

(*c*) any person who is not a parent of his but who has parental responsibility for him; and

(*d*) any other person whose wishes and feelings the authority consider to be relevant,

regarding the matter to be decided.

(5) In making any such decision a local authority shall give due consideration—

(*a*) having regard to his age and understanding, to such wishes and feelings of the child as they have been able to ascertain;
(*b*) to such wishes and feelings of any person mentioned in subsection (4)(*b*) to (*d*) as they have been able to ascertain; and
(*c*) to the child's religious persuasion, racial origin and cultural and linguistic background.

(6) If it appears to a local authority that it is necessary, for the purpose of protecting members of the public from serious injury, to exercise their powers with respect to a child whom they are looking after in a manner which may not be consistent with their duties under this section, they may do so.

(7) If the Secretary of State considers it necessary, for the purpose of protecting members of the public from serious injury, to give directions to a local authority with respect to the exercise of their powers with respect to a child whom they are looking after, he may give such directions to the authority.

(8) Where any such directions are given to an authority they shall comply with them even though doing so is inconsistent with their duties under this section.

---

**Definitions** For 'child', 'local authority' and 'child in the care of a local authority' and 'service' see s 105(1); for 'looked after by a local authority' see sub-s (1); for 'accommodation' see sub-s (2); for 'parental responsibility' see s 3.

**References** See generally para 5.42 ff. For 'parent' see para 2.7. For inspection of premises where a child who is being looked after by a local authority is living by a person authorised to do by the Secretary of State under s 80 see s 80(1)(*b*) and note also s 80(4), (5) as to the information that may by required by the Secretary of State. For the general duty of local authorities in connection with the welfare of children in need, see s 17; for review of case of and representations relating to child being looked after by local authority see s 26; for cooperation between authorities see s 27; for recoupment of the cost of services provided see s 29; for miscellaneous supplementary provisions see s 30. For transitional provisions relating to children in care under repealed enactments see s 108(6) and Sch 14 para 15 ff.

---

### 23 Provision of accommodation and maintenance by local authority for children whom they are looking after

(1) It shall be the duty of any local authority looking after a child—

(*a*) when he is in their care, to provide accommodation for him; and
(*b*) to maintain him in other respects apart from providing accommodation for him.

(2) A local authority shall provide accommodation and maintenance for any child whom they are looking after by—

(*a*) placing him (subject to subsection (5) and any regulations made by the Secretary of State) with—

(i) a family;
(ii) a relative of his; or
(iii) any other suitable person,

on such terms as to payment by the authority and otherwise as the authority may determine;
(*b*) maintaining him in a community home;
(*c*) maintaining him in a voluntary home;
(*d*) maintaining him in a registered children's home;

(*e*) maintaining him in a home provided by the Secretary of State under section 82(5) on such terms as the Secretary of State may from time to time determine; or

(*f*) making such other arrangements as—

(i) seem appropriate to them; and

(ii) comply with any regulations made by the Secretary of State.

(3) Any person with whom a child has been placed under subsection (2)(*a*) is referred to in this Act as a local authority foster parent unless he falls within subsection (4).

(4) A person falls within this subsection if he is—

(*a*) a parent of the child;

(*b*) a person who is not a parent of the child but who has parental responsibility for him; or

(*c*) where the child is in care and there was a residence order in force with respect to him immediately before the care order was made, a person in whose favour the residence order was made.

(5) Where a child is in the care of a local authority, the authority may only allow him to live with a person who falls within subsection (4) in accordance with regulations made by the Secretary of State.

(6) Subject to any regulations made by the Secretary of State for the purposes of this subsection, any local authority looking after a child shall make arrangements to enable him to live with—

(*a*) a person falling within subsection (4); or

(*b*) a relative, friend or other person connected with him,

unless that would not be reasonably practicable or consistent with his welfare.

(7) Where a local authority provide accommodation for a child whom they are looking after, they shall, subject to the provisions of this Part and so far as is reasonably practicable and consistent with his welfare, secure that—

(*a*) the accommodation is near his home; and

(*b*) where the authority are also providing accommodation for a sibling of his, they are accommodated together.

(8) Where a local authority provide accommodation for a child whom they are looking after and who is disabled, they shall, so far as is reasonably practicable, secure that the accommodation is not unsuitable to his particular needs.

(9) Part II of Schedule 2 shall have effect for the purposes of making further provision as to children looked after by local authorities and in particular as to the regulations that may be made under subsections (2)(*a*) and (*f*) and (5).

---

**Definitions** For 'local authority', 'child', 'relative', 'in the care of a local authority' see s 105(1); for 'looked after by a local authority' see s 22(1); for 'community home' see s 53; for 'voluntary home' see s 60; for 'registered children's home' see s 63 (8) and for 'children's home' see s 63(3) as applied to the whole Act by s 105(1); for 'local authority foster parent' see s 23(3); for 'parental responsibility' see s 3; for 'disabled' see s 17(11).

**References** See generally para 5.46 ff. 'This Part' ie Part III (ss 17-30 and Sch 2) (local authority support for children and families). For the general duty of local authorities in connection with the welfare of children in need, see s 17; for review of the case of, and representations relating, to child being looked after by local authority see s 26; for cooperation between authorities see s 27; for recoupment of the cost of services provided see s 29; for miscellaneous supplementary provisions see s 30.

---

*Advice and assistance for certain children*

## 24 Advice and assistance for certain children

(1) Where a child is being looked after by a local authority, it shall be the duty of the authority to advise, assist and befriend him with a view to promoting his welfare when he ceases to be looked after by them.

(2) In this Part "a person qualifying for advice and assistance" means a person within the area of the authority who is under twenty-one and who was, at any time after reaching the age of sixteen but while still a child—

(*a*) looked after by a local authority;
(*b*) accommodated by or on behalf of a voluntary organisation;
(*c*) accommodated in a registered children's home;
(*d*) accommodated—

(i) by any health authority or local education authority; or
(ii) in any residential care home, nursing home or mental nursing home,

for a consecutive period of at least three months; or
(*e*) privately fostered,

but who is no longer so looked after, accommodated or fostered.

(3) Subsection (2)(*d*) applies even if the period of three months mentioned there began before the child reached the age of sixteen.

(4) Where—

(*a*) a local authority know that there is within their area a person qualifying for advice and assistance;
(*b*) the conditions in subsection (5) are satisfied; and
(*c*) that person has asked them for help of a kind which they can give under this section,

they shall (if he was being looked after by a local authority or was accommodated by or on behalf of a voluntary organisation) and may (in any other case) advise and befriend him.

(5) The conditions are that—

(*a*) it appears to the authority that the person concerned is in need of advice and being befriended;
(*b*) where that person was not being looked after by the authority, they are satisfied that the person by whom he was being looked after does not have the necessary facilities for advising or befriending him.

(6) Where as a result of this section a local authority are under a duty, or are empowered, to advise and befriend a person, they may also give him assistance.

(7) Assistance given under subsections (1) to (6) may be in kind or, in exceptional circumstances, in cash.

(8) A local authority may give assistance to any person who qualifies for advice and assistance by virtue of subsection (2)(*a*) by—

(*a*) contributing to expenses incurred by him in living near the place where he is, or will be—

(i) employed or seeking employment; or
(ii) receiving education or training; or

(*b*) making a grant to enable him to meet expenses connected with his education or training.

(9) Where a local authority are assisting the person under subsection (8) by making a contribution or grant with respect to a course of education or training, they may—

(*a*) continue to do so even though he reaches the age of twenty-one before completing the course; and

(*b*) disregard any interruption in his attendance on the course if he resumes it as soon as is reasonably practicable.

(10) Subsections (7) to (9) of section 17 shall apply in relation to assistance given under this section (otherwise than under subsection (8)) as they apply in relation to assistance given under that section.

(11) Where it appears to a local authority that a person whom they have been advising and befriending under this section, as a person qualifying for advice and assistance, proposes to live, or is living, in the area of another local authority, they shall inform that other local authority.

(12) Where a child who is accommodated—

(*a*) by a voluntary organisation or in a registered children's home;
(*b*) by any health authority or local education authority; or
(*c*) in any residential care home, nursing home or mental nursing home,

ceases to be so accommodated, after reaching the age of sixteen, the organisation, authority or (as the case may be) person carrying on the home shall inform the local authority within whose area the child proposes to live.

(13) Subsection (12) only applies, by virtue of paragraph (*b*) or (*c*), if the accommodation has been provided for a consecutive period of at least three months.

---

**Definitions** For 'child', 'local authority', 'voluntary organisation','health authority', 'local education authority' 'residential care home', 'nursing home' and 'mental nursing home' see s 105(1); for 'a child who is being looked after by a local authority' see s 22(1); for 'a person qualifying for advice and assistance' see sub-s (2); for 'a registered children's home' see s 63(8); for 'privately fostered' see s 66 as applied to the whole Act by s 105(1).

**References** See generally para 5.42 ff. 'This Part' ie Part III (ss 17-30 and Sch 2) (local authority support for children and families). For the general duty of local authorities in connection with the welfare of children in need, see s 17; for review of case of, and representations relating to, child being looked after by local authority see s 26; for cooperation between authorities see s 27; for recoupment of the cost of services provided see s 29; for miscellaneous supplementary provisions see s 30. For transitional provisions relating to children in care under repealed enactments see s 108(6) and Sch 14 para 22.

---

*Secure accommodation*

## 25 Use of accommodation for restricting liberty

(1) Subject to the following provisions of this section, a child who is being looked after by a local authority may not be placed, and, if placed,

may not be kept, in accommodation provided for the purpose of restricting liberty ("secure accommodation") unless it appears—

(*a*) that—

(i) he has a history of absconding and is likely to abscond from any other description of accommodation; and

(ii) if he absconds, he is likely to suffer significant harm; or

(*b*) that if he is kept in any other description of accommodation he is likely to injure himself or other persons.

(2) The Secretary of State may by regulations—

(*a*) specify a maximum period—

(i) beyond which a child may not be kept in secure accommodation without the authority of the court; and

(ii) for which the court may authorise a child to be kept in secure accommodation;

(*b*) empower the court from time to time to authorise a child to be kept in secure accommodation for such further period as the regulations may specify; and

(*c*) provide that applications to the court under this section shall be made only by local authorities.

(3) It shall be the duty of a court hearing an application under this section to determine whether any relevant criteria for keeping a child in secure accommodation are satisfied in his case.

(4) If a court determines that any such criteria are satisfied, it shall make an order authorising the child to be kept in secure accommodation and specifying the maximum period for which he may be so kept.

(5) On any adjournment of the hearing of an application under this section, a court may make an interim order permitting the child to be kept during the period of the adjournment in secure accommodation.

(6) No court shall exercise the powers conferred by this section in respect of a child who is not legally represented in that court unless, having been informed of his right to apply for legal aid and having had the opportunity to do so, he refused or failed to apply.

(7) The Secretary of State may by regulations provide that—

(*a*) this section shall or shall not apply to any description of children specified in the regulations;

(*b*) this section shall have effect in relation to children of a description specified in the regulations subject to such modifications as may be so specified;

(*c*) such other provisions as may be so specified shall have effect for the purpose of determining whether a child of a description specified in the regulations may be placed or kept in secure accommodation.

(8) The giving of an authorisation under this section shall not prejudice any power of any court in England and Wales or Scotland to give directions relating to the child to whom the authorisation relates.

(9) This section is subject to section 20(8).

---

**Definitions** For 'child' and 'local authority' see s 105(1); for 'a child who is being looked after by a local authority' see s 22(1); for 'secure accommodation' see sub-s (1); for 'harm' see s 31(9) as applied to the whole Act by s 105(1); as to whether harm is significant see s 31(10) as applied to the whole Act by s 105(1); for 'court' see s 92(7).

**References** See generally para 5.51. For jurisdiction of courts see s 92 and Sch 11, para 9.1 ff. For the general duty of local authorities in connection with the welfare of children in need, see s 17; for review of case of, and representations relating to, child being looked after by local authority see s 26; for cooperation between authorities see s 27; for recoupment of the cost of services provided see s 29; for miscellaneous supplementary provisions see s 30.

---

*Supplemental*

## 26 Review of cases and inquiries into representations

(1) The Secretary of State may make regulations requiring the case of each child who is being looked after by a local authority to be reviewed in accordance with the provisions of the regulations.

(2) The regulations may, in particular, make provision—

(*a*) as to the manner in which each case is to be reviewed;

(*b*) as to the considerations to which the local authority are to have regard in reviewing each case;

(*c*) as to the time when each case is first to be reviewed and the frequency of subsequent reviews;

(*d*) requiring the authority, before conducting any review, to seek the views of—

(i) the child;

(ii) his parents;

(iii) any person who is not a parent of his but who has parental responsibility for him; and

(iv) any other person whose views the authority consider to be relevant,

including, in particular, the views of those persons in relation to any particular matter which is to be considered in the course of the review;

(*e*) requiring the authority to consider, in the case of a child who is in their care, whether an application should be made to discharge the care order;

(*f*) requiring the authority to consider, in the case of a child in accommodation provided by the authority, whether the accommodation accords with the requirements of this Part;

(*g*) requiring the authority to inform the child, so far as is reasonably practicable, of any steps he may take under this Act;

(*h*) requiring the authority to make arrangements, including arrangements with such other bodies providing services as it considers appropriate, to implement any decision which they propose to make in the course, or as a result, of the review;

(*i*) requiring the authority to notify details of the result of the review and of any decision taken by them in consequence of the review to—

(i) the child;

(ii) his parents;

(iii) any person who is not a parent of his but who has parental responsibility for him; and

(iv) any other person whom they consider ought to be notified;

(*j*) requiring the authority to monitor the arrangements which they have made with a view to ensuring that they comply with the regulations.

(3) Every local authority shall establish a procedure for considering any representations (including any complaint) made to them by—

(*a*) any child who is being looked after by them or who is not being looked after by them but is in need;

(*b*) a parent of his;

(*c*) any person who is not a parent of his but who has parental responsibility for him;

(*d*) any local authority foster parent;

(*e*) such other person as the authority consider has a sufficient interest in the child's welfare to warrant his representations being considered by them,

about the discharge by the authority of any of their functions under this Part in relation to the child.

(4) The procedure shall ensure that at least one person who is not a member or officer of the authority takes part in—

(*a*) the consideration; and

(*b*) any discussions which are held by the authority about the action (if any) to be taken in relation to the child in the light of the consideration.

(5) In carrying out any consideration of representations under this section a local authority shall comply with any regulations made by the Secretary of State for the purposes of regulating the procedure to be followed.

(6) The Secretary of State may make regulations requiring local authorities to monitor the arrangements that they have made with a view to ensuring that they comply with any regulations made for the purposes of subsection (5).

(7) Where any representation has been considered under the procedure established by a local authority under this section, the authority shall—

(*a*) have due regard to the findings of those considering the representation; and

(*b*) take such steps as are reasonably practicable to notify (in writing)—

(i) the person making the representation;

(ii) the child (if the authority consider that he has sufficient understanding); and

(iii) such other persons (if any) as appear to the authority to be likely to be affected,

of the authority's decision in the matter and their reasons for taking that decision and of any action which they have taken, or propose to take.

(8) Every local authority shall give such publicity to their procedure for considering representations under this section as they consider appropriate.

---

**Definitions** For 'child' and 'local authority' see s 105(1); for 'a child who is being looked after by a local authority see s 22(1); for 'parental responsibility' see s 3; for 'care order' see s 31(11) and s 105(1); for 'local authority foster parent' see s 23(3).

**References** See generally para 5.52. For 'parent' see para 2.7. 'This Part' ie Part III (ss 17-30 and Sch 2) (local authority support for children and families). For the powers and duties of local authorities under this Part to provide accommodation for children see s 20 (accommodation for certain children eg those lost or abandoned), s 23 (accommodation for and maintenance of children an authority is looking after) and s 25 (use of accommodation for restricting liberty)

## 27 Co-operation between authorities

(1) Where it appears to a local authority that any authority or other person mentioned in subsection (3) could, by taking any specified action, help in the exercise of any of their functions under this Part, they may request the help of that other authority or person, specifying the action in question.

(2) An authority whose help is so requested shall comply with the request if it is compatible with their own statutory or other duties and obligations and does not unduly prejudice the discharge of any of their functions.

(3) The persons are—

(*a*) any local authority;
(*b*) any local education authority;
(*c*) any local housing authority;
(*d*) any health authority; and
(*e*) any person authorised by the Secretary of State for the purposes of this section.

(4) Every local authority shall assist any local education authority with the provision of services for any child within the local authority's area who has special educational needs.

---

**Definitions** For 'local authority', 'functions', 'local education authority', 'local housing authority', 'health authority', 'special educational needs' see s 105(1).

**References** See generally para 5.1 ff. 'This Part' ie Part III (ss 17-30 and Sch 2) (local authority support for children and families). For recovery of reasonable expenses by one local authority from another see s 29(7).

---

## 28 Consultation with local education authorities

(1) Where—

(*a*) a child is being looked after by a local authority; and
(*b*) the authority propose to provide accommodation for him in an establishment at which education is provided for children who are accommodated there,

they shall, so far as is reasonably practicable, consult the appropriate local education authority before doing so.

(2) Where any such proposal is carried out, the local authority shall, as soon as is reasonably practicable, inform the appropriate local education authority of the arrangements that have been made for the child's accommodation.

(3) Where the child ceases to be accommodated as mentioned in subsection (1)(*b*), the local authority shall inform and appropriate local education authority.

(4) In this section "the appropriate local education authority" means—

(*a*) the local education authority within whose area the local authority's area falls; or,
(*b*) where the child has special educational needs and a statement of his needs is maintained under the Education Act 1981, the local education authority who maintain the statement.

---

**Definitions** For 'child', 'local authority' and local education authority' see s 105(1); for 'a child who is being looked after by a local authority' see s 22(1); for 'the appropriate local education authority' see sub-s (4).

---

## 29 Recoupment of cost of providing services etc

(1) Where a local authority provide any service under section 17 or 18, other than advice, guidance or counselling, they may recover from a person specified in subsection (4) such charge for the service as they consider reasonable.

(2) Where the authority are satisfied that the person's means are insufficient for it to be reasonably practicable for him to pay the charge, they shall not require him to pay more than he can reasonably be expected to pay.

(3) No person shall be liable to pay any charge under subsection (1) at any time when he is in receipt of income support or family credit under the Social Security Act 1986.

(4) The persons are—

(*a*) where the service is provided for a child under sixteen, each of his parents;

(*b*) where it is provided for a child who has reached the age of sixteen, the child himself; and

(*c*) where it is provided for a member of the child's family, that member.

(5) Any charge under subsection (1) may, without prejudice to any other method of recovery, be recovered summarily as a civil debt.

(6) Part III of Schedule 2 makes provision in connection with contributions towards the maintenance of children who are being looked after by local authorities and consists of the re-enactment with modifications of provisions in Part V of the Child Care Act 1980.

(7) Where a local authority provide any accommodation under section 20(1) for a child who was (immediately before they began to look after him) ordinarily resident within the area of another local authority, they may recover from that other authority any reasonable expenses incurred by them in providing the accommodation and maintaining him.

(8) Where a local authority provide accommodation under section 21(1) or (2)(*a*) or (*b*) for a child who is ordinarily resident within the area of another local authority and they are not maintaining him in—

(*a*) a community home provided by them;

(*b*) a controlled community home; or

(*c*) a hospital vested in the Secretary of State,

they may recover from that other authority any reasonable expenses incurred by them in providing the accommodation and maintaining him.

(9) Where a local authority comply with any request under section 27(2) in relation to a child or other person who is not ordinarily resident within their area, they may recover from the local authority in whose area the child or person is ordinarily resident any expenses reasonably incurred by them in respect of that person.

---

**Definitions** For 'local authority', 'service', 'child' and 'hospital' see s 105(1); for 'community home' and 'controlled community home' see s 53 as applied to the whole Act by s 105(1).

**References** See generally para 5.59 ff. For 'parent' see para 2.7. For the determination of the ordinary residence of a child for the purposes of sub-s (7)-(9) see s 30(2) and s 105(6). For transitional provisions for contributions for maintenance of children in care under repealed enactments see s 108(6) and Sch 14 para 24.

---

## 30 Miscellaneous

(1) Nothing in this Part shall affect any duty imposed on a local authority by or under any other enactment.

(2) Any question arising under section 20(2), 21(3) or 29(7) to (9) as to the ordinary residence of a child shall be determined by agreement between the local authorities concerned or, in default of agreement, by the Secretary of State.

(3) Where the functions conferred on a local authority by this Part and the functions of a local education authority are concurrent, the Secretary of State may by regulations provide by which authority the functions are to be exercised.

(4) The Secretary of State may make regulations for determining, as respects any local education authority functions specified in the regulations, whether a child who is being looked after by a local authority is to be treated, for purposes so specified, as a child of parents of sufficient resources or as a child of parents without resources.

---

**Definitions** For 'local authority', 'child', 'functions', 'local education authority' see s 105(1); for 'a child who is being looked after by a local authority' see s 22(1).

**References** See generally para 5.1 ff. For determination of ordinary residence of a child see sub-s(2). 'This Part' ie Part III (ss 17-30 and Sch 2) (local authority support for children and families).

---

# Part IV

# Care and Supervision

### *General*

## 31 Care and supervision orders

(1) On the application of any local authority or authorised person, the court may make an order—

(*a*) placing the child with respect to whom the application is made in the care of a designated local authority; or

(*b*) putting him under the supervision of a designated local authority or of a probation officer.

(2) A court may only make a care order or supervision order if it is satisfied—

(*a*) that the child concerned is suffering, or is likely to suffer, significant harm; and

(*b*) that the harm, or likelihood of harm, is attributable to—

(i) the care given to the child, or likely to be given to him if the order were not made, not being what it would be reasonable to expect a parent to give to him; or

(ii) the child's being beyond parental control.

(3) No care order or supervision order may be made with respect to a child who has reached the age of seventeen (or sixteen, in the case of a child who is married).

(4) An application under this section may be made on its own or in any other family proceedings.

(5) The court may—

(*a*) on an application for a care order, make a supervision order;

(*b*) on an application for a supervision order, make a care order.

(6) Where an authorised person proposes to make an application under this section he shall—

(*a*) if it is reasonably practicable to do so; and

(*b*) before making the application,

consult the local authority appearing to him to be the authority in whose area the child concerned is ordinarily resident.

(7) An application made by an authorised person shall not be entertained by the court if, at the time when it is made, the child concerned is—

(*a*) the subject of an earlier application for a care order, or supervision order, which has not been disposed of; or

(*b*) subject to—

(i) a care order or supervision order;

(ii) an order under section 7(7)(*b*) of the Children and Young Persons Act 1969; or

(iii) a supervision requirement within the meaning of the Social Work (Scotland) Act 1968.

(8) The local authority designated in a care order must be—

(*a*) the authority within whose area the child is ordinarily resident; or

(*b*) where the child does not reside in the area of a local authority, the authority within whose area any circumstances arose in consequence of which the order is being made.

(9) In this section—

"authorised person" means—

(*a*) the National Society for the Prevention of Cruelty to Children and any of its officers; and

(*b*) any person authorised by order of the Secretary of State to bring proceedings under this section and any officer of a body which is so authorised;

"harm" means ill-treatment or the impairment of health or development;

"development" means physical, intellectual, emotional, social or behavioural development;

"health" means physical or mental health; and

"ill-treatment" includes sexual abuse and forms of ill-treatment which are not physical.

(10) Where the question of whether harm suffered by a child is significant

turns on the child's health or development, his health or development shall be compared with that which could reasonably be expected of a similar child.

(11) In this Act—

"a care order" means (subject to section 105(1)) an order under subsection (1)(*a*) and (except where express provision to the contrary is made) includes an interim care order made under section 38; and

"a supervision order" means an order under subsection (1)(*b*) and (except where express provision to the contrary is made) includes an interim supervision order made under section 38.

---

**Definitions** For 'local authority','child' see s 105(1); for 'court' see s 92(7); for 'designated local authority' see sub-s (8); for 'care order', 'supervision order' see sub-s(11); for 'harm' see sub-s (9) and as to whether harm is significant see sub-s (10); for 'authorised person', 'development', 'health', 'ill-treatment' see sub-s (9).

**References** See generally para 6.1 ff. For welfare of the child the paramount consideration see s 1. For jurisdiction of courts see s 92 and Sch 11, para 9.1 ff; for appeals see s 94 and orders pending appeals s 40. For 'parent' see para 2.7; for determining the 'ordinary residence' of a child see s 105(6); for 'family proceedings' see s 8(3). For duty of local authority to make inquiries with respect to certain children to enable them to decide whether they should take any action to safeguard or promote the child's welfare see s 47(1). For the appointment of a guardian ad litem see s 41. For interim care and supervision orders see s 38. For attendance of child at hearing see s 95; for evidence given by or with respect of children see s 96; for self incrimination of witness see s 98. For powers of the court when considering whether to make a care or supervision order under this section see s 37. For variation and discharge of care and supervision orders see s 39. For duration of care orders and supervision orders see s 91(12),(13). For effect of orders see generally s 91 and for further provisions relating to care orders see ss 33, 34, and for supervision orders s 35.

---

## 32. Period within which application for order under this Part must be disposed of

(1) A court hearing an application for an order under this Part shall (in the light of any rules made by virtue of subsection (2))—

(*a*) draw up a timetable with a view to disposing of the application without delay; and

(*b*) give such directions as it considers appropriate for the purpose of ensuring, so far as is reasonably practicable, that that timetable is adhered to.

(2) Rules of court may—

(*a*) specify periods within which specified steps must be taken in relation to such proceedings; and

(*b*) make other provision with respect to such proceedings for the purpose of ensuring, so far as is reasonably practicable, that they are disposed of without delay.

---

**Definitions** For 'court' see s 92(7); for 'child' see s 105(1).

**References** See generally 6.43 ff. For jurisdiction of courts see s 92 and Sch 11, para 9.1 ff. 'This Part' ie Part IV (ss 31-42 and Sch 3) (care and supervision). For welfare of the child the paramount consideration see s 1(1). For family proceedings see s 8(3).

---

*Care orders*

## 33 Effect of care order

(1) Where a care order is made with respect to a child it shall be the duty of the local authority designated by the order to receive the child into their care and to keep him in their care while the order remains in force.

(2) Where—

(*a*) a care order has been made with respect to a child on the application of an authorised person; but

(*b*) the local authority designated by the order was not informed that that person proposed to make the application,

the child may be kept in the care of that person until received into the care of the authority.

(3) While a care order is in force with respect to a child, the local authority designated by the order shall—

(*a*) have parental responsibility for the child; and

(*b*) have the power (subject to the following provisions of this section) to determine the extent to which a parent or guardian of the child may meet his parental responsibility for him.

(4) The authority may not exercise the power in subsection (3)(*b*) unless they are satisfied that it is necessary to do so in order to safeguard or promote the child's welfare.

(5) Nothing in subsection (3)(*b*) shall prevent a parent or guardian of the child who has care of him from doing what is reasonable in all the circumstances of the case for the purpose of safeguarding or promoting his welfare.

(6) While a care order is in force with respect to a child, the local authority designated by the order shall not—

(*a*) cause the child to be brought up in any religious persuasion other than that in which he would have been brought up if the order had not been made; or

(*b*) have the right—

(i) to consent or refuse to consent to the making of an application with respect to the child under section 18 of the Adoption Act 1976;

(ii) to agree or refuse to agree to the making of an adoption order, or an order under section 55 of the Act of 1976, with respect to the child; or

(iii) to appoint a guardian for the child.

(7) While a care order is in force with respect to a child, no person may—

(*a*) cause the child to be known by a new surname; or

(*b*) remove him from the United Kingdom,

without either the written consent of every person who has parental responsibility for the child or the leave of the court.

(8) Subsection (7)(*b*) does not—

(*a*) prevent the removal of such a child, for a period of less than one month, by the authority in whose care he is; or (*b*) apply to arrangements for such a child to live outside England and Wales (which are governed by paragraph 19 of Schedule 2).

(9) The power in subsection (3)(*b*) is subject (in addition to being subject to the provisions of this section) to any right, duty, power, responsibility or authority which a parent or guardian of the child has in relation to the child and his property by virtue of any other enactment.

---

**Definitions** For 'care order' see s 31(11) and s 105(1); for 'child', 'local authority' and 'guardian of a child' see s 105(1); for 'designated local authority' see s 31(8); for 'authorised person' see s 31(9); for 'parental responsibility' see s 3; for 'court' see s 92(7).

**References** See generally para 6.22 ff. For appointment of guardian ad litem see s 41. For duration of care orders see s 91(12). For care and supervision orders generally see s 31; for further provisions in connection with care orders see s 34 and in connection with supervision orders see ss 35 and 36; for interim care and supervision orders see s 38; for the discharge and variation of care and supervision orders see s 39. For jurisdiction of courts see s 92 and Sch 11, para 9.1 ff.

---

## 34 Parental contact etc with children in care

(1) Where a child is in the care of a local authority, the authority shall (subject to the provisions of this section) allow the child reasonable contact with—

(*a*) his parents;
(*b*) any guardian of his;
(*c*) where there was a residence order in force with respect to the child immediately before the care order was made, the person in whose favour the order was made; and
(*d*) where, immediately before the care order was made, a person had care of the child by virtue of an order made in the exercise of the High Court's inherent jurisdiction with respect to children, that person.

(2) On an application made by the authority or the child, the court may make such order as it considers appropriate with respect to the contact which is to be allowed between the child and any named person.

(3) On an application made by—

(*a*) any person mentioned in paragraphs (*a*) to (*d*) of subsection (1); or
(*b*) any person who has obtained the leave of the court to make the application,

the court may make such order as it considers appropriate with respect to the contact which is to be allowed between the child and that person.

(4) On an application made by the authority or the child, the court may make an order authorising the authority to refuse to allow contact between the child and any person who is mentioned in paragraphs (*a*) to (d) of subsection (1) and named in the order.

(5) When making a care order with respect to a child, or in any family proceedings in connection with a child who is in the care of a local authority, the court may make an order under this section, even though no application for such an order has been made with respect to the child, if it considers that the order should be made.

(6) An authority may refuse to allow the contact that would otherwise be required by virtue of subsection (1) or an order under this section if—

(*a*) they are satisfied that it is necessary to do so in order to safeguard or promote the child's welfare; and

(*b*) the refusal—

(i) is decided upon as a matter of urgency; and

(ii) does not last for more than seven days.

(7) An order under this section may impose such conditions as the court considers appropriate.

(8) The Secretary of State may by regulations make provision as to—

(*a*) the steps to be taken by a local authority who have exercised their powers under subsection (6);

(*b*) the circumstances in which, and conditions subject to which, the terms of any order under this section may be departed from by agreement between the local authority and the person in relation to whom the order is made;

(*c*) notification by a local authority of any variation or suspension of arrangements made (otherwise than under an order under this section) with a view to affording any person contact with a child to whom this section applies.

(9) The court may vary or discharge any order made under this section on the application of the authority, the child concerned or the person named in the order.

(10) An order under this section may be made either at the same time as the care order itself or later.

(11) Before making a care order with respect to any child the court shall—

(*a*) consider the arrangements which the authority have made, or propose to make, for affording any person contact with a child to whom this section applies; and

(*b*) invite the parties to the proceedings to comment on those arrangements.

---

**Definitions** For 'child', 'local authority', 'guardian of a child' and 'child in the care of a local authority' see s 105(1). For 'care order' see s 31(11) and s 105(1); for 'residence order' see s 8(1); for 'a person in whose favour a residence order is in force' see s 105(3); for 'court' see s 92(7) ; for 'the local authority designated in a care order' see s 31(8).

**References** See generally para 6.52 ff. For welfare of the child the paramount consideration see s 1(1). For 'parent' see para 2.7. For appointment of a guardian ad litem see s 41. For care and supervision orders generally see s 31; for further provisions in connection with supervision orders see s 35 and 36; for interim care and supervision orders see s 38; for the discharge and variation of care and supervisions orders see s 39. For jurisdiction of courts see s 92 and Sch 11, para 9.1 ff.

---

*Supervision orders*

**35 Supervision orders**

(1) While a supervision order is in force it shall be the duty of the supervisor—

(*a*) to advise, assist and befriend the supervised child;

(*b*) to take such steps as are reasonably necessary to give effect to the order; and

(*c*) where—

(i) the order is not wholly complied with; or

(ii) the supervisor considers that the order may no longer be necessary,

to consider whether or not to apply to the court for its variation or discharge.

(2) Parts I and II of Schedule 3 make further provision with respect to supervision orders.

---

**Definitions** For 'supervision order' see s 31(11); for 'supervisor', 'supervised child' see s 105(1).

**References** See generally para 6.28 ff. For duration of supervision orders see s 91(13) and Sch 3, Para 6(1). For care and supervisions orders generally see s 31; for further provisions in connection with supervision orders see s 36; for interim care and supervision orders see s 38; for the discharge and variation of care and supervision orders see s 39. For transitional provisions for supervision orders made under repealed enactments see s 108(6) and Sch 14 para 25 ff.

---

### 36 Education supervision orders

(1) On the application of any local education authority, the court may make an order putting the child with respect to whom the application is made under the supervision of a designated local education authority.

(2) In this Act "an education supervision order" means an order under subsection (1).

(3) A court may only make an education supervision order if it is satisfied that the child concerned is of compulsory school age and is not being properly educated.

(4) For the purposes of this section, a child is being properly educated only if he is receiving efficient full-time education suitable to his age, ability and aptitude and any special educational needs he may have.

(5) Where a child is—

(*a*) the subject of a school attendance order which is in force under section 37 of the Education Act 1944 and which has not been complied with; or

(*b*) a registered pupil at a school which he is not attending regularly within the meaning of section 39 of that Act,

then, unless it is proved that he is being properly educated, it shall be assumed that he is not.

(6) An education supervision order may not be made with respect to a child who is in the care of a local authority.

(7) The local education authority designated in an education supervision order must be—

(*a*) the authority within whose area the child concerned is living or will live; or

(*b*) where—

(i) the child is a registered pupil at a school; and

(ii) the authority mentioned in paragraph (*a*) and the authority within whose area the school is situated agree,

the latter authority.

(8) Where a local education authority propose to make an application for an education supervision order they shall, before making the application,

consult the social services committee (within the meaning of the Local Authority Social Services Act 1970) of the appropriate local authority.

(9) The appropriate local authority is—

(*a*) in the case of a child who is being provided with accommodation by, or on behalf of, a local authority, that authority; and

(*b*) in any other case, the local authority within whose area the child concerned lives, or will live.

(10) Part III of Schedule 3 makes further provision with respect to education supervision orders.

---

**Definitions** For 'local education authority', 'child', 'child who is in the care of a local authority', 'local authority' see s 105(1); for 'court' see s 92(7); for 'designated local authority' see sub-s (7); for 'education supervision order' see sub-s (2); for 'being properly educated' see sub-s (4), (5); for 'registered pupil' see s 105(1) and Education Act 1944 s 114(1); for 'special educational needs' see s 105(1) and Education Act 1981 s 1(1); for 'appropriate local authority' see sub-s (9); for 'accommodation provided by or on behalf of a local authority' see s 105(5).

**References** See generally para 12.5 ff. For jurisdiction of courts see s 92 and Sch 11, para 9.1 ff. For attendance of child at hearing see s 95; for evidence given by or with respect to children see s 96; for self incrimination of witness see s 98. For 'full time education' see Education (No 2) Act 1986, s 21 (as amended) for the fixing of school sessions and terms. For 'family proceedings' under this Act see s 8(3), (4)(*a*).

---

*Powers of court*

## 37 Powers of court in certain family proceedings

(1) Where, in any family proceedings in which a question arises with respect to the welfare of any child, it appears to the court that it may be appropriate for a care or supervision order to be made with respect to him, the court may direct the appropriate authority to undertake an investigation of the child's circumstances.

(2) Where the court gives a direction under this section the local authority concerned shall, when undertaking the investigation, consider whether they should—

(*a*) apply for a care order or for a supervision order with respect to the child;

(*b*) provide services or assistance for the child or his family; or

(*c*) take any other action with respect to the child.

(3) Where a local authority undertake an investigation under this section, and decide not to apply for a care order or supervision order with respect to the child concerned, they shall inform the court of—

(*a*) their reasons for so deciding;

(*b*) any service or assistance which they have provided, or intend to provide, for the child and his family; and

(*c*) any other action which they have taken, or propose to take, with respect to the child.

(4) The information shall be given to the court before the end of the period of eight weeks beginning with the date of the direction, unless the court otherwise directs.

(5) The local authority named in a direction under subsection (1) must be—

(*a*) the authority in whose area the child is ordinarily resident; or
(*b*) where the child does not reside in the area of a local authority, the authority within whose area any circumstances arose in consequence of which the direction is being given.

(6) If, on the conclusion of any investigation or review under this section, the authority decide not to apply for a care order or supervision order with respect to the child—

(*a*) they shall consider whether it would be appropriate to review the case at a later date; and
(*b*) if they decide that it would be, they shall determine the date on which that review is to begin.

---

**Definitions** For 'family proceedings' see s 8(3), (4)(*a*); for 'child', 'local authority' see s 105(1); for 'court' see s 92(7); for 'care order' see s 31(11) and s 105(1); for 'supervision order' see s 31(11); for 'appropriate authority' see sub-s (5); for 'ordinary residence' see s 105(6).

**References** See generally para 3.1 ff. For welfare of the child as paramount consideration see s 1(1). For jurisdiction of courts see s 92 and Sch 11, para 9.1 ff. For the bringing to an end of an interim order made under s 38 as a result of a direction by the court under sub-s (1) see s 38(4). For the appointment of a guardian ad litem see s 41. For the provision of services and assistance by local authorities see Part III ie ss 17-30 and Sch 2 (local authority support for children and families). For interim orders see s 38. For 'family proceedings' under this Act see s 8(3), (4)(*a*).

---

## 38 Interim orders

(1) Where—

(*a*) in any proceedings on an application for a care order or supervision order, the proceedings are adjourned; or
(*b*) the court gives a direction under section 37(1),

the court may make an interim care order or an interim supervision order with respect to the child concerned.

(2) A court shall not make an interim care order or interim supervision order under this section unless it is satisfied that there are reasonable grounds for believing that the circumstances with respect to the child are as mentioned in section 31(2).

(3) Where, in any proceedings on an application for a care order or supervision order, a court makes a residence order with respect to the child concerned, it shall also make an interim supervision order with respect to him unless satisfied that his welfare will be satisfactorily safeguarded without an interim order being made.

(4) An interim order made under or by virtue of this section shall have effect for such period as may be specified in the order, but shall in any event cease to have effect on whichever of the following events first occurs—

(*a*) the expiry of the period of eight weeks beginning with the date on which the order is made;
(*b*) if the order is the second or subsequent such order made with respect to the same child in the same proceedings, the expiry of the relevant period;
(*c*) in a case which falls within subsection (1)(*a*), the disposal of the application;
(*d*) in a case which falls within subsection (1)(*b*), the disposal of an

application for a care order or supervision order made by the authority with respect to the child;

(*e*) in a case which falls within subsection (1)(*b*) and in which—

(i) the court has given a direction under section 37(4), but

(ii) no application for a care order or supervision order has been made with respect to the child,

the expiry of the period fixed by that direction.

(5) In subsection (4)(*b*) "the relevant period" means—

(*a*) the period of four weeks beginning with the date on which the order in question is made; or

(*b*) the period of eight weeks beginning with the date on which the first order was made if that period ends later than the period mentioned in paragraph (*a*).

(6) Where the court makes an interim care order, or interim supervision order, it may give such directions (if any) as it considers appropriate with regard to the medical or psychiatric examination or other assessment of the child; but if the child is of sufficient understanding to make an informed decision he may refuse to submit to the examination or other assessment.

(7) A direction under subsection (6) may be to the effect that there is to be—

(*a*) no such examination or assessment; or

(*b*) no such examination or assessment unless the court directs otherwise.

(8) A direction under subsection (6) may be—

(*a*) given when the interim order is made or at any time while it is in force; and

(*b*) varied at any time on the application of any person falling within any class of person prescribed by rules of court for the purposes of this subsection.

(9) Paragraphs 4 and 5 of Schedule 3 shall not apply in relation to an interim supervision order.

(10) Where a court makes an order under or by virtue of this section it shall, in determining the period for which the order is to be in force, consider whether any party who was, or might have been, opposed to the making of the order was in a position to argue his case against the order in full.

---

**Definitions** For 'care order' see s 31(11) and s 105(1); for 'supervision order' see s 31(11); for 'court' see s 92(7); for 'child' see s 105(1); for 'residence order' see s 8(1); for 'the relevant period' see sub-s (5); for 'the authority' see s 37(1), (5).

**References** See generally para 6.35 ff. For application for care order or supervision order see s 31. For jurisdiction of courts see s 92 and Sch 11, para 9.1 ff. For attendance of child at hearing see s 95; for evidence given by or with respect to children see s 96; for self incrimination of witness see s 98.

---

## 39 Discharge and variation etc of care orders and supervision orders

(1) A care order may be discharged by the court on the application of—

(*a*) any person who has parental responsibility for the child;

(*b*) the child himself; or

(*c*) the local authority designated by the order.

(2) A supervision order may be varied or discharged by the court on the application of—

(*a*) any person who has parental responsibility for the child;
(*b*) the child himself; or
(*c*) the supervisor.

(3) On the application of a person who is not entitled to apply for the order to be discharged, but who is a person with whom the child is living, a supervision order may be varied by the court in so far as it imposes a requirement which affects that person.

(4) Where a care order is in force with respect to a child the court may, on the application of any person entitled to apply for the order to be discharged, substitute a supervision order for the care order.

(5) When a court is considering whether to substitute one order for another under subsection (4) any provision of this Act which would otherwise require section 31(2) to be satisfied at the time when the proposed order is substituted or made shall be disregarded.

---

**Definitions** For 'care order' see s 31(11) and s 105(1); for 'court' see s 92(7); for parental responsibility see s 3; for 'child', 'local authority', 'supervision' see s 105(1). For 'supervision order' see s 31(11).

**References** See generally para 6.46 ff. For jurisdiction of courts see s 92 and Sch 11, para 9.1 ff. For attendance of child at hearing see s 95; for evidence given by or with respect to children see s 96; for self incrimination of witness see s 98. For 'family proceedings' under this Act see s 8(3), (4)(*a*). For limitation on repeated applications see s 91(14) (15).

---

### 40 Orders pending appeals in cases about care or supervision orders

(1) Where—

(*a*) a court dismisses an application for a care order; and
(*b*) at the time when the court dismisses the application, the child concerned is the subject of an interim care order,

the court may make a care order with respect to the child to have effect subject to such directions (if any) as the court may see fit to include in the order.

(2) Where—

(*a*) a court dismisses an application for a care order, or an application for a supervision order; and
(*b*) at the time when the court dismisses the application, the child concerned is the subject of an interim supervision order,

the court may make a supervision order with respect to the child to have effect subject to such directions (if any) as the court may see fit to include in the order.

(3) Where a court grants an application to discharge a care order or supervision order, it may order that—

(*a*) its decision is not to have effect; or
(*b*) the care order, or supervision order, is to continue to have effect but subject to such directions as the court sees fit to include in the order.

(4) An order made under this section shall only have effect for such period, not exceeding the appeal period, as may be specified in the order.

(5) Where—

(*a*) an appeal is made against any decision of a court under this section; or

(*b*) any application is made to the appellate court in connection with a proposed appeal against that decision,

the appellate court may extend the period for which the order in question is to have effect, but not so as to extend it beyond the end of the appeal period.

(6) In this section "the appeal period" means—

(*a*) where an appeal is made against the decision in question, the period between the making of that decision and the determination of the appeal; and

(*b*) otherwise, the period during which an appeal may be made against the decision.

---

**Definitions** For 'court' see s 92(7); for 'care order' see s 31 (11) and s 105(1); for 'child' see s 105(1); for 'supervision order' see s 31(11); for 'appeal period' see sub-s (6).

**References** For interim care and supervision orders see s 38; for discharge of care or supervision orders see s 39.

---

*Guardians ad litem*

### 41 Representation of child and of his interests in certain proceedings

(1) For the purpose of any specified proceedings, the court shall appoint a guardian ad litem for the child concerned unless satisfied that it is not necessary to do so in order to safeguard his interests.

(2) The guardian ad litem shall—

(*a*) be appointed in accordance with rules of court; and

(*b*) be under a duty to safeguard the interests of the child in the manner prescribed by such rules.

(3) Where—

(*a*) the child concerned is not represented by a solicitor; and

(*b*) any of the conditions mentioned in subsection (4) is satisfied,

the court may appoint a solicitor to represent him.

(4) The conditions are that—

(*a*) no guardian ad litem has been appointed for the child;

(*b*) the child has sufficient understanding to instruct a solicitor and wishes to do so;

(*c*) it appears to the court that it would be in the child's best interests for him to be represented by a solicitor.

(5) Any solicitor appointed under or by virtue of this section shall be appointed, and shall represent the child, in accordance with rules of court.

(6) In this section "specified proceedings" means any proceedings—

(*a*) on an application for a care order or supervision order;

(*b*) in which the court has given a direction under section 37(1) and has made, or is considering whether to make, an interim care order;

(*c*) on an application for the discharge of a care order or the variation or discharge of a supervision order;

(*d*) on an application under section 39(4);

(*e*) in which the court is considering whether to make a residence order with respect to a child who is the subject of a care order;

(*f*) with respect to contact between a child who is the subject of a care order and any other person;

(*g*) under Part V;

(*h*) on an appeal against—

(i) the making of, or refusal to make, a care order, supervision order or any order under section 34;

(ii) the making of, or refusal to make, a residence order with respect to a child who is the subject of a care order; or

(iii) the variation or discharge, or refusal of an application to vary or discharge, an order of a kind mentioned in sub-paragraph (i) or (ii);

(iv) the refusal of an application under section 39(4);

(v) the making of, or refusal to make, an order under Part V; or

(*i*) which are specified for the time being, for the purposes of this section, by rules of court.

(7) The Secretary of State may by regulations provide for the establishment of panels of persons from whom guardians ad litem appointed under this section must be selected.

(8) Subsection (7) shall not be taken to prejudice the power of the Lord Chancellor to confer or impose duties on the Official Solicitor under section 90(3) of the Supreme Court Act 1981.

(9) The regulations may, in particular, make provision—

(*a*) as to the constitution, administration and procedures of panels;

(*b*) requiring two or more specified local authorities to make arrangements for the joint management of a panel;

(*c*) for the defrayment by local authorities of expenses incurred by members of panels;

(*d*) for the payment by local authorities of fees and allowances for members of panels;

(*e*) as to the qualifications for membership of a panel;

(*f*) as to the training to be given to members of panels;

(*g*) as to the co-operation required of specified local authorities in the provision of panels in specified areas; and

(*h*) for monitoring the work of guardians ad litem.

(10) Rules of court may make provision as to—

(*a*) the assistance which any guardian ad litem may be required by the court to give to it;

(*b*) the consideration to be given by any guardian ad litem, where an order of a specified kind has been made in the proceedings in question, as to whether to apply for the variation or discharge of the order;

(*c*) the participation of guardians ad litem in reviews, of a kind specified in the rules, which are conducted by the court.

(11) Regardless of any enactment or rule of law which would otherwise prevent it from doing so, the court may take account of—

(*a*) any statement contained in a report made by a guardian ad litem who is appointed under this section for the purpose of the proceedings in question; and

(*b*) any evidence given in respect of the matters referred to in the report,

in so far as the statement or evidence is, in the opinion of the court, relevant to the question which the court is considering.

---

**Definitions** For 'specified proceedings' see sub-s (6); for 'court' see s 92(7); for 'child', 'prescribed', 'local authority' see s 105(1); for 'care order' see s 31(11) and s 105(1); for 'supervision order' see s 31(11); for 'residence order' see s 8(1).

**References** See generally para 8.12 ff. For jurisdiction of courts see s 92 and Sch 11, para 9.1 ff. For the power to make interim care orders see s 38(1). Part V ie ss 43-52 (protection of children).

---

### 42 Right of guardian ad litem to have access to local authority records

(1) Where a person has been appointed as a guardian ad litem under this Act he shall have the right at all reasonable times to examine and take copies of—

(*a*) any records of, or held by, a local authority which were compiled in connection with the making, or proposed making, by any person of any application under this Act with respect to the child concerned; or

(*b*) any other records of, or held by, a local authority which were compiled in connection with any functions which stand referred to their social services committee under the Local Authority Social Services Act 1970, so far as those records relate to that child.

(2) Where a guardian ad litem takes a copy of any record which he is entitled to examine under this section, that copy or any part of it shall be admissible as evidence of any matter referred to in any—

(*a*) report which he makes to the court in the proceedings in question; or

(*b*) evidence which he gives in those proceedings.

(3) Subsection (2) has effect regardless of any enactment or rule of law which would otherwise prevent the record in question being admissible in evidence.

---

**Definitions** For 'local authority' and 'child' see s 105(1).

**Reference** For other evidential provisions see s 96.

---

## PART V

## PROTECTION OF CHILDREN

### 43 Child assessment orders

(1) On the application of a local authority or authorised person for an order to be made under this section with respect to a child, the court may make the order if, but only if, it is satisfied that—

(*a*) the applicant has reasonable cause to suspect that the child is suffering, or is likely to suffer, significant harm;

(*b*) an assessment of the state of the child's health or development, or of the way in which he has been treated, is required to enable the applicant to determine whether or not the child is suffering, or is likely to suffer, significant harm; and
(*c*) it is unlikely that such an assessment will be made, or be satisfactory, in the absence of an order under this section.

(2) In this Act "a child assessment order" means an order under this section.

(3) A court may treat an application under this section as an application for an emergency protection order.

(4) No court shall make a child assessment order if it is satisfied—

(*a*) that there are grounds for making an emergency protection order with respect to the child; and
(*b*) that it ought to make such an order rather than a child assessment order.

(5) A child assessment order shall—

(*a*) specify the date by which the assessment is to begin; and
(*b*) have effect for such period, not exceeding 7 days beginning with that date, as may be specified in the order.

(6) Where a child assessment order is in force with respect to a child it shall be the duty of any person who is in a position to produce the child—

(*a*) to produce him to such person as may be named in the order; and
(*b*) to comply with such directions relating to the assessment of the child as the court thinks fit to specify in the order.

(7) A child assessment order authorises any person carrying out the assessment, or any part of the assessment, to do so in accordance with the terms of the order.

(8) Regardless of subsection (7), if the child is of sufficient understanding to make an informed decision he may refuse to submit to a medical or psychiatric examination or other assessment.

(9) The child may only be kept away from home—

(*a*) in accordance with directions specified in the order;
(*b*) if it is necessary for the purposes of the assessment; and
(*c*) for such period or periods as may be specified in the order.

(10) Where the child is to be kept away from home, the order shall contain such directions as the court thinks fit with regard to the contact that he must be allowed to have with other persons while away from home.

(11) Any person making an application for a child assessment order shall take such steps as are reasonably practicable to ensure that notice of the application is given to—

(*a*) the child's parents;
(*b*) any person who is not a parent of his but who has parental responsibility for him;
(*c*) any other person caring for the child;
(*d*) any person in whose favour a contact order is in force with respect to the child;
(*e*) any person who is allowed to have contact with the child by virtue of an order under section 34; and

(*f*) the child,

before the hearing of the application.

(12) Rules of court may make provision as to the circumstances in which—

(*a*) any of the persons mentioned in subsection (11); or

(*b*) such other person as may be specified in the rules,

may apply to the court for a child assessment order to be varied or discharged.

(13) In this section "authorised person" means a person who is an authorised person for the purposes of section 31.

---

**Definitions** For 'local authority' and 'child' see s 105(1); for 'authorised person' see sub-s (13); for 'court' see s 92(7); for 'harm' see s 31(9) as applied to the whole Act by s 105(1) and as to whether harm is significant see s 31(10) as applied to the whole Act by s 105(1); for 'a child assessment order' see sub-s (2); for 'emergency protection order' see s 44(4) as applied to the whole Act by s 105(1); for 'parental responsibility' see s 3; for 'contact order' see s 8(1).

**References** See generally para 7.8 ff. For jurisdiction of courts see s 92 and Sch 11, para 9.1 ff. For attendance of child at hearing see s 95; for evidence given by or with respect to children see s 96; for self incrimination of witness see s 98.

---

## 44 Orders for emergency protection of children

(1) Where any person ("the applicant") applies to the court for an order to be made under this section with respect to a child, the court may make the order if, but only if it is satisfied that—

(*a*) there is reasonable cause to believe that the child is likely to suffer significant harm if—

(i) he is not removed to accommodation provided by or on behalf of the applicant; or

(ii) he does not remain in the place in which he is then being accommodated;

(*b*) in the case of an application made by a local authority—

(i) enquiries are being made with respect to the child under section 47(1)(*b*); and

(ii) those enquiries are being frustrated by access to the child being unreasonably refused to a person authorised to seek access and that the applicant has reasonable cause to believe that access to the child is required as a matter of urgency; or

(*c*) in the case of an application made by an authorised person—

(i) the applicant has reasonable cause to suspect that a child is suffering, or is likely to suffer, significant harm;

(ii) the applicant is making enquiries with respect to the child's welfare; and

(iii) those enquiries are being frustrated by access to the child being unreasonably refused to a person authorised to seek access and the applicant has reasonable cause to believe that access to the child is required as a matter of urgency.

(2) In this section—

(*a*) "authorised person" means a person who is an authorised person for the purposes of section 31; and

(*b*) "a person authorised to seek access" means—

(i) in the case of an application by a local authority, an officer of the local authority or a person authorised by the authority to act on their behalf in connection with the enquiries; or

(ii) in the case of an application by an authorised person, that person.

(3) Any person—

(*a*) seeking access to a child in connection with enquiries of a kind mentioned in subsection (1); and

(*b*) purporting to be a person authorised to do so,

shall, on being asked to do so, produce some duly authenticated document as evidence that he is such a person.

(4) While an order under this section ("an emergency protection order") is in force it—

(*a*) operates as a direction to any person who is in a position to do so to comply with any request to produce the child to the applicant;

(*b*) authorises—

(i) the removal of the child at any time to accommodation provided by or on behalf of the applicant and his being kept there; or

(ii) the prevention of the child's removal from any hospital, or other place, in which he was being accommodated immediately before the making of the order; and

(*c*) gives the applicant parental responsibility for the child.

(5) Where an emergency protection order is in force with respect to a child, the applicant—

(*a*) shall only exercise the power given by virtue of subsection (4)(*b*) in order to safeguard the welfare of the child;

(*b*) shall take, and shall only take, such action in meeting his parental responsibility for the child as is reasonably required to safeguard or promote the welfare of the child, (having regard in particular to the duration of the order); and

(*c*) shall comply with the requirements of any regulations made by the Secretary of State for the purposes of this subsection.

(6) Where the court makes an emergency protection order, it may give such directions (if any) as it considers appropriate with respect to—

(*a*) the contact which is, or is not, to be allowed between the child and any named person;

(*b*) the medical or psychiatric examination or other assessment of the child.

(7) Where any direction is given under subsection (6)(*b*), the child may, if he is of sufficient understanding to make an informed decision, refuse to submit to the examination or other assessment.

(8) A direction under subsection (6)(*a*) may impose conditions and one under subsection (6)(*b*) may be to the effect that there is to be—

(*a*) no such examination or assessment; or

(*b*) no such examination or assessment unless the court directs otherwise.

(9) A direction under subsection (6) may be—

(*a*) given when the emergency protection order is made or at any time while it is in force; and

(*b*) varied at any time on the application of any person falling within any class of person prescribed by rules of court for the purposes of this subsection.

(10) Where an emergency protection order is in force with respect to a child and—

(*a*) the applicant has exercised the power given by subsection (4)(*b*)(i) but it appears to him that it is safe for the child to be returned; or

(*b*) the applicant has exercised the power given by subsection (4)(*b*)(ii) but it appears to him that it is safe for the child to be allowed to be removed from the place in question,

he shall return the child or (as the case may be) allow him to be removed.

(11) Where he is required by subsection (10) to return the child the applicant shall—

(*a*) return him to the care of the person from whose care he was removed; or

(*b*) if that is not reasonably practicable, return him to the care of—

(i) a parent of his;

(ii) any person who is not a parent of his but who has parental responsibility for him; or

(iii) such other person as the applicant (with the agreement of the court) considers appropriate.

(12) Where the applicant has been required by subsection (10) to return the child, or to allow him to be removed, he may again exercise his powers with respect to the child (at any time while the emergency protection order remains in force) if it appears to him that a change in the circumstances of the case makes it necessary for him to do so.

(13) Where an emergency protection order has been made with respect to a child, the applicant shall, subject to any direction given under subsection (6), allow the child reasonable contact with—

(*a*) his parents;

(*b*) any person who is not a parent of his but who has parental responsibility for him;

(*c*) any person with whom he was living immediately before the making of the order;

(*d*) any person in whose favour a contact order is in force with respect to him;

(*e*) any person who is allowed to have contact with the child by virtue of an order under section 34; and

(*f*) any person acting on behalf of any of those persons.

(14) Wherever it is reasonably practicable to do so, an emergency protection order shall name the child; and where it does not name him it shall describe him as clearly as possible.

(15) A person shall be guilty of an offence if he intentionally obstructs any person exercising the power under subsection (4)(*b*) to remove, or prevent the removal of, a child.

(16) A person guilty of an offence under subsection (15) shall be liable on summary conviction to a fine not exceeding level 3 on the standard scale.

---

**Definitions** For 'court' see s 92(7); for 'child', 'local authority', 'hospital' see s 105(1); for 'harm' see s 31(9) as applied to the whole Act by s 105(1) and as to whether harm is significant see s 31(10) as applied to the whole Act by s 105(1); for 'applicant' see sub-s (1); for 'a person authorised to seek access' see sub-s (2)(b); for 'authorised person' see sub-s (2)(a); for 'emergency protection order' see sub-s (4); for 'parental responsibility' see s 3; for 'contact order' see s 8(1).

**References** See generally para 7.23 ff. For welfare of the child as paramount consideration see s 1(1). For jurisdiction of courts see s 92 and Sch 11, para 9.1 ff. For attendance of child at hearing see s 95; for evidence given by or with respect to children see s 96; for self incrimination of witness see s 98. For application by the police when child is in police protection see s 46(7),(8). For duration of an emergency protection order see s 45; for duty of local authority to make inquiries with respect to certain children to enable them to decide whether they should take any action to safeguard or promote the child's welfare see s 47 (1). For powers to assist in discovery of children who may be in need of emergency protection see s 48. For local authority responsibility in relation to accommodation see s 21. For 'the standard scale' see the Criminal Justice Act 1982 s 37(2),(3) as amended; 'level 3' ie £400.

---

## 45 Duration of emergency protection orders and other supplemental provisions

(1) An emergency protection order shall have effect for such period, not exceeding eight days, as may be specified in the order.

(2) Where—

(*a*) the court making an emergency protection order would, but for this subsection, specify a period of eight days as the period for which the order is to have effect; but

(*b*) the last of those eight days is a public holiday (that is to say, Christmas Day, Good Friday, a bank holiday or a Sunday),

the court may specify a period which ends at noon on the first later day which is not such a holiday.

(3) Where an emergency protection order is made on an application under section 46(7), the period of eight days mentioned in subsection (1) shall begin with the first day on which the child was taken into police protection under section 46.

(4) Any person who—

(*a*) has parental responsibility for a child as the result of an emergency protection order; and

(*b*) is entitled to apply for a care order with respect to the child,

may apply to the court for the period during which the emergency protection order is to have effect to be extended.

(5) On an application under subsection (4) the court may extend the period during which the order is to have effect by such period, not exceeding seven days, as it thinks fit, but may do so only if it has reasonable cause to believe that the child concerned is likely to suffer significant harm if the order is not extended.

(6) An emergency protection order may only be extended once.

(7) Regardless of any enactment or rule of law which would otherwise prevent it from doing so, a court hearing an application for, or with respect to, an emergency protection order may take account of—

(*a*) any statement contained in any report made to the court in the course of, or in connection with, the hearing; or
(*b*) any evidence given during the hearing,

which is, in the opinion of the court, relevant to the application.

(8) Any of the following may apply to the court for an emergency protection order to be discharged—

(*a*) the child;
(*b*) a parent of his;
(*c*) any person who is not a parent of his but who has parental responsibility for him; or
(*d*) any person with whom he was living immediately before the making of the order.

(9) No application for the discharge of an emergency protection order shall be heard by the court before the expiry of the period of 72 hours beginning with the making of the order.

(10) No appeal may be made against the making of, or refusal to make, an emergency protection order or against any direction given by the court in connection with such an order.

(11) Subsection (8) does not apply—

(*a*) where the person who would otherwise be entitled to apply for the emergency protection order to be discharged—
 (i) was given notice (in accordance with rules of court) of the hearing at which the order was made; and
 (ii) was present at that hearing; or
(*b*) to any emergency protection order the effective period of which has been extended under subsection (5).

(12) A court making an emergency protection order may direct that the applicant may, in exercising any powers which he has by virtue of the order, be accompanied by a registered medical practitioner, registered nurse or registered health visitor, if he so chooses.

---

**Definitions** For 'emergency protection order' see s 44(4); for 'court' see s 92(7); for 'bank holiday', 'child' see s 105(1); for 'parental responsibility' see s 3; for 'care order' see s 31(11); for 'harm' see s 31(9) as applied to the whole Act by s 105(1); and as to whether harm is significant see s 31(10) as applied to the whole Act by s 105(1); for 'applicant' see s 44(1).

**References** See generally para 7.31 ff. For persons entitled to apply for care order see s 31(1)(9). For 'parent' see para 2.7. For further provisions see note to s 44. For jurisdiction of courts see s 92(7) and Sch 11, para 9.1 ff.

---

## 46 Removal and accommodation of children by police in cases of emergency

(1) Where a constable has reasonable cause to believe that a child would otherwise be likely to suffer significant harm, he may—

(*a*) remove the child to suitable accommodation and keep him there; or
(*b*) take such steps as are reasonable to ensure that the child's removal from any hospital, or other place, in which he is then being accommodated is prevented.

(2) For the purposes of this Act, a child with respect to whom a constable

has exercised his powers under this section is referred to as having been taken into police protection.

(3) As soon as is reasonably practicable after taking a child into police protection, the constable concerned shall—

(*a*) inform the local authority within whose area the child was found of the steps that have been, and are proposed to be, taken with respect to the child under this section and the reasons for taking them;

(*b*) give details to the authority within whose area the child is ordinarily resident ("the appropriate authority") of the place at which the child is being accommodated;

(*c*) inform the child (if he appears capable of understanding)—

(i) of the steps that have been taken with respect to him under this section and of the reasons for taking them; and

(ii) of the further steps that may be taken with respect to him under this section;

(*d*) take such steps as are reasonably practicable to discover the wishes and feelings of the child;

(*e*) secure that the case is inquired into by an officer designated for the purposes of this section by the chief officer of the police area concerned; and

(*f*) where the child was taken into police protection by being removed to accommodation which is not provided—

(i) by or on behalf of a local authority; or

(ii) as a refuge, in compliance with the requirements of section 51,

secure that he is moved to accommodation which is so provided.

(4) As soon as is reasonably practicable after taking a child into police protection, the constable concerned shall take such steps as are reasonably practicable to inform—

(*a*) the child's parents;

(*b*) every person who is not a parent of his but who has parental responsibility for him; and

(*c*) any other person with whom the child was living immediately before being taken into police protection,

of the steps that he has taken under this section with respect to the child, the reasons for taking them and the further steps that may be taken with respect to him under this section.

(5) On completing any inquiry under subsection (3)(*e*), the officer conducting it shall release the child from police protection unless he considers that there is still reasonable cause for believing that the child would be likely to suffer significant harm if released.

(6) No child may be kept in police protection for more than 72 hours.

(7) While a child is being kept in police protection, the designated officer may apply on behalf of the appropriate authority for an emergency protection order to be made under section 44 with respect to the child.

(8) An application may be made under subsection (7) whether or not the authority know of it or agree to its being made.

(9) While a child is being kept in police protection—

(*a*) neither the constable concerned nor the designated officer shall have parental responsibility for him; but

(*b*) the designated officer shall do what is reasonable in all the circumstances of the case for the purpose of safeguarding or promoting the child's welfare (having regard in particular to the length of the period during which the child will be so protected).

(10) Where a child has been taken into police protection, the designated officer shall allow—

(*a*) the child's parents;

(*b*) any person who is not a parent of the child but who has parental responsibility for him;

(*c*) any person with whom the child was living immediately before he was taken into police protection;

(*d*) any person in whose favour a contact order is in force with respect to the child;

(*e*) any person who is allowed to have contact with the child by virtue of an order under section 34; and

(*f*) any person acting on behalf of any of those persons,

to have such contact (if any) with the child as, in the opinion of the designated officer, is both reasonable and in the child's best interests.

(11) Where a child who has been taken into police protection is in accommodation provided by, or on behalf of, the appropriate authority, subsection (10) shall have effect as if it referred to the authority rather than to the designated officer.

---

**Definitions** For 'child', 'hospital' and 'local authority' see s 105(1); for 'harm' see s 31(9) as applied to the whole Act by s 105(1) and as to whether harm is significant see s 31(10) as applied to the whole Act by s 105(1); for 'police protection' see sub-s (2); for 'ordinary residence' see s 105(6); for 'appropriate authority' see sub-s (3)(*b*); for 'emergency protection order' see s 44(4); for 'designated officer' see sub-s (3)(*e*). For 'parental responsibility' see s 3; for 'contact order' see s 8(1);

**References** See generally para 7.39 ff. For 'parent' see para 2.7. For the maximum duration of an emergency protection order taken under sub-s (7) see s 45(3). For the welfare of the child the paramount consideration see s 1(1). For duty of local authority to make inquiries with respect to certain children to enable them to decide whether they should take any action to safeguard or promote the child's welfare see s 47(1). For powers to assist in discovery of children who may be in need of emergency protection see s 48. For local authority responsibility in relation to accommodation see s 21. For refuges for children at risk see s 51.

---

## 47 Local authority's duty to investigate

(1) Where a local authority—

(*a*) are informed that a child who lives, or is found, in their area—

(i) is the subject of an emergency protection order; or

(ii) is in police protection; or

(*b*) have reasonable cause to suspect that a child who lives, or is found, in their area is suffering, or is likely to suffer, significant harm,

the authority shall make, or cause to be made, such enquiries as they consider necessary to enable them to decide whether they should take any action to safeguard or promote the child's welfare.

(2) Where a local authority have obtained an emergency protection order

with respect to a child, they shall make, or cause to be made, such enquiries as they consider necessary to enable them to decide what action they should take to safeguard or promote the child's welfare.

(3) The enquiries shall, in particular, be directed towards establishing—

(*a*) whether the authority should make any application to the court, or exercise any of their other powers under this Act, with respect to the child;

(*b*) whether, in the case of a child—

(i) with respect to whom an emergency protection order has been made; and

(ii) who is not in accommodation provided by or on behalf of the authority,

it would be in the child's best interests (while an emergency protection order remains in force) for him to be in such accommodation; and

(*c*) whether, in the case of a child who has been taken into police protection, it would be in the child's best interests for the authority to ask for an application to be made under section 46(7).

(4) Where enquiries are being made under subsection (1) with respect to a child, the local authority concerned shall (with a view to enabling them to determine what action, if any, to take with respect to him) take such steps as are reasonably practicable—

(*a*) to obtain access to him; or

(*b*) to ensure that access to him is obtained, on their behalf, by a person authorised by them for the purpose,

unless they are satisfied that they already have sufficient information with respect to him.

(5) Where, as a result of any such enquiries, it appears to the authority that there are matters connected with the child's education which should be investigated, they shall consult the relevant local education authority.

(6) Where, in the course of enquiries made under this section—

(*a*) any officer of the local authority concerned; or

(*b*) any person authorised by the authority to act on their behalf in connection with those enquiries—

(i) is refused access to the child concerned; or

(ii) is denied information as to his whereabouts,

the authority shall apply for an emergency protection order, a child assessment order, a care order or a supervision order with respect to the child unless they are satisfied that his welfare can be satisfactorily safeguarded without their doing so.

(7) If, on the conclusion of any enquiries or review made under this section, the authority decide not to apply for an emergency protection order, a child assessment order, a care order or a supervision order they shall—

(*a*) consider whether it would be appropriate to review the case at a later date; and

(*b*) if they decide that it would be, determine the date on which that review is to begin.

(8) Where, as a result of complying with this section, a local authority conclude that they should take action to safeguard or promote the child's

welfare they shall take that action (so far as it is both within their power and reasonably practicable for them to do so).

(9) Where a local authority are conducting enquiries under this section, it shall be the duty of any person mentioned in subsection (11) to assist them with those enquiries (in particular by providing relevant information and advice) if called upon by the authority to do so.

(10) Subsection (9) does not oblige any person to assist a local authority where doing so would be unreasonable in all the circumstances of the case.

(11) The persons are—

(*a*) any local authority;
(*b*) any local education authority;
(*c*) any local housing authority;
(*d*) any health authority; and
(*e*) any person authorised by the Secretary of State for the purposes of this section.

(12) Where a local authority are making enquiries under this section with respect to a child who appears to them to be ordinarily resident within the area of another authority, they shall consult that other authority, who may undertake the necessary enquiries in their place.

---

**Definitions** For 'local authority', 'child', 'local education authority', 'local housing authority', 'health authority' see s 105(1); for 'emergency protection order' see s 44(4); for 'police protection' see s 46(2); for 'harm' see s 31(9) as applied to the whole Act by s 105(1) as to whether harm is significant see s 31(10) as applied to the whole Act by s 105(1); for 'court' see s 92(7); for 'accommodation provided by or on behalf of a local authority' see s 105 (5); for 'care order', 'supervision order' see s 31(11); for ordinary residence see s 105(6). For 'child assessment order' see s 43(2).

**References** See generally para 7.3 ff. For welfare of the child the paramount consideration see s 1(1). For emergency protection orders see s 44 and for child assessment orders see s 43. For jurisdiction of courts see s 92 and Sch 11, para 9.1 ff.

---

## 48 Powers to assist in discovery of children who may be in need of emergency protection

(1) Where it appears to a court making an emergency protection order that adequate information as to the child's whereabouts—

(*a*) is not available to the applicant for the order; but
(*b*) is available to another person,

it may include in the order a provision requiring that other person to disclose, if asked to do so by the applicant, any information that he may have as to the child's whereabouts.

(2) No person shall be excused from complying with such a requirement on the ground that complying might incriminate him or his spouse of an offence; but a statement or admission made in complying shall not be admissible in evidence against either of them in proceedings for any offence other than perjury.

(3) An emergency protection order may authorise the applicant to enter premises specified by the order and search for the child with respect to whom the order is made.

(4) Where the court is satisfied that there is reasonable cause to believe

that there may be another child on those premises with respect to whom an emergency protection order ought to be made, it may make an order authorising the applicant to search for that other child on those premises.

(5) Where—

(*a*) an order has been made under subsection (4);

(*b*) the child concerned has been found on the premises; and

(*c*) the applicant is satisfied that the grounds for making an emergency protection order exist with respect to him,

the order shall have effect as if it were an emergency protection order.

(6) Where an order has been made under subsection (4), the applicant shall notify the court of its effect.

(7) A person shall be guilty of an offence if he intentionally obstructs any person exercising the power of entry and search under subsection (3) or (4).

(8) A person guilty of an offence under subsection (7) shall be liable on summary conviction to a fine not exceeding level 3 on the standard scale.

(9) Where, on an application made by any person for a warrant under this section, it appears to the court—

(*a*) that a person attempting to exercise powers under an emergency protection order has been prevented from doing so by being refused entry to the premises concerned or access to the child concerned; or

(*b*) that any such person is likely to be so prevented from exercising any such powers,

it may issue a warrant authorising any constable to assist the person mentioned in paragraph (*a*) or (*b*) in the exercise of those powers, using reasonable force if necessary.

(10) Every warrant issued under this section shall be addressed to, and executed by, a constable who shall be accompanied by the person applying for the warrant if—

(*a*) that person so desires; and

(*b*) the court by whom the warrant is issued does not direct otherwise.

(11) A court granting an application for a warrant under this section may direct that the constable concerned may, in executing the warrant, be accompanied by a registered medical practitioner, registered nurse or registered health visitor if he so chooses.

(12) An application for a warrant under this section shall be made in the manner and form prescribed by rules of court.

(13) Wherever it is reasonably practicable to do so, an order under subsection (4), an application for a warrant under this section and any such warrant shall name the child; and where it does not name him it shall describe him as clearly as possible.

---

**Definitions** For 'court' see s 92(7); for 'emergency protection order' see s 44(4); for 'child' see s 105(1); for 'applicant' see s 44(1).

**References** See generally para 7.43 ff. For grounds for making an emergency protection order see s 44(1). For jurisdiction of courts see s 92 and Sch 11, para 9.1 ff. For 'the standard scale' see the Criminal Justice Act 1982 s 37(2) (3) as amended; 'level 3' ie £400.

---

## 49 Abduction of children in care etc

(1) A person shall be guilty of an offence if, knowingly and without lawful authority or reasonable excuse, he—

(*a*) takes a child to whom this section applies away from the responsible person;
(*b*) keeps such a child away from the responsible person; or
(*c*) induces, assists of incites such a child to run away or stay away from the responsible person.

(2) This section applies in relation to a child who is—

(*a*) in care;
(*b*) the subject of an emergency protection order; or
(*c*) in police protection,

and in this section "the responsible person" means any person who for the time being has care of him by virtue of the care order, the emergency protection order, or section 46, as the case may be.

(3) A person guilty of an offence under this section shall be liable on summary conviction to imprisonment for a term not exceeding six months, or to a fine not exceeding level 5 on the standard scale, or to both.

---

**Definitions** For 'child' and 'child who is in care' see s 105(1); for 'the responsible person' see sub-s (2); for 'emergency protection order' see s 44(4); for 'in police protection' see s 46(2).

**References** See generally para 7.47. For 'the standard scale' see the Criminal Justice Act 1982 s 37(2) (3) as amended; 'level 5' ie £2,000.

---

## 50 Recovery of abducted children etc

(1) Where it appears to the court that there is reason to believe that a child to whom this section applies—

(*a*) has been unlawfully taken away or is being unlawfully kept away from the responsible person;
(*b*) has run away or is staying away from the responsible person; or
(*c*) is missing,

the court may make an order under this section ("a recovery order").

(2) This section applies to the same children to whom section 49 applies and in this section "the responsible person" has the same meaning as in section 49.

(3) A recovery order—

(*a*) operates as a direction to any person who is in a position to do so to produce the child on request to any authorised person;
(*b*) authorises the removal of the child by any authorised person;
(*c*) requires any person who has information as to the child's whereabouts to disclose that information, if asked to do so, to a constable or an officer of the court;
(*d*) authorises a constable to enter any premises specified in the order and search for the child, using reasonable force if necessary.

(4) The court may make a recovery order only on the application of—

(*a*) any person who has parental responsibility for the child by virtue of a care order or emergency protection order; or
(*b*) where the child is in police protection, the designated officer.

(5) A recovery order shall name the child and—

(*a*) any person who has parental responsibility for the child by virtue of a care order or emergency protection order; or
(*b*) where the child is in police protection, the designated officer.

(6) Premises may only be specified under subsection (3)(*d*) if it appears to the court that there are reasonable grounds for believing the child to be on them.

(7) In this section—
"an authorised person" means—

(*a*) any person specified by the court;
(*b*) any constable;
(*c*) any person who is authorised—
  (i) after the recovery order is made; and
  (ii) by a person who has parental responsibility for the child by virtue of a care order or an emergency protection order,

to exercise any power under a recovery order; and
"the designated officer" means the officer designated for the purposes of section 46.

(8) Where a person is authorised as mentioned in subsection (7)(*c*)—

(*a*) the authorisation shall identify the recovery order; and
(*b*) any person claiming to be so authorised shall, if asked to do so, produce some duly authenticated document showing that he is so authorised.

(9) A person shall be guilty of an offence if he intentionally obstructs an authorised person exercising the power under subsection (3)(*b*) to remove a child.

(10) A person guilty of an offence under this section shall be liable on summary conviction to a fine not exceeding level 3 on the standard scale.

(11) No person shall be excused from complying with any request made under subsection (3)(*c*) on the ground that complying with it might incriminate him or his spouse of an offence; but a statement or admission made in complying shall not be admissible in evidence against either of them in proceedings for an offence other than perjury.

(12) Where a child is made the subject of a recovery order whilst being looked after by a local authority, any reasonable expenses incurred by an authorised person in giving effect to the order shall be recoverable from the authority.

(13) A recovery order shall have effect in Scotland as if it had been made by the Court of Session and as if that court had had jurisdiction to make it.

(14) In this section "the court", in relation to Northern Ireland, means a magistrates' court within the meaning of the Magistrates' Courts (Northern Ireland) Order 1981.

---

**Definitions** For 'court' see s 92(7) and sub-ss (13) (Scotland) and (14) (Northern Ireland); for 'child' and 'local authority' see s 105(1); for 'the responsible person' see sub-s (2) and s 49(2); for 'a recovery order' see sub-s (1); for 'authorised person' and 'designated officer' see sub-s (7); for 'parental responsibility' see s 3; for 'care order' see s 31(11) and s 105(1); for 'emergency protection order' see s 44(4); for 'in police protection' see s 46(2); for 'child looked after by a local authority' see s 22(1).

**References** See generally para 7.47. For jurisdiction of courts see s 92 and Sch 11, para 9.1 ff. For 'the standard scale' see the Criminal Justice Act 1982 s 37(2) (3) as amended; 'level 3' ie £400.

---

## 51 Refuges for children at risk

(1) Where it is proposed to use a voluntary home or registered children's home to provide a refuge for children who appear to be at risk of harm, the Secretary of State may issue a certificate under this section with respect to that home.

(2) Where a local authority or voluntary organisation arrange for a foster parent to provide such a refuge, the Secretary of State may issue a certificate under this section with respect to that foster parent.

(3) In subsection (2) "foster parent" means a person who is, or who from time to time is, a local authority foster parent or a foster parent with whom children are placed by a voluntary organisation.

(4) The Secretary of State may by regulations—

(*a*) make provision as to the manner in which certificates may be issued;

(*b*) impose requirements which must be complied with while any certificate is in force; and

(*c*) provide for the withdrawal of certificates in prescribed circumstances.

(5) Where a certificate is in force with respect to a home, none of the provisions mentioned in subsection (7) shall apply in relation to any person providing a refuge for any child in that home.

(6) Where a certificate is in force with respect to a foster parent, none of those provisions shall apply in relation to the provision by him of a refuge for any child in accordance with arrangements made by the local authority or voluntary organisation.

(7) The provisions are—

(*a*) section 49;

(*b*) section 71 of the Social Work (Scotland) Act 1968 (harbouring children who have absconded from residential establishments etc), so far as it applies in relation to anything done in England and Wales;

(*c*) section 32(3) of the Children and Young Persons Act 1969 (compelling, persuading, inciting or assisting any person to be absent from detention, etc), so far as it applies in relation to anything done in England and Wales;

(*d*) section 2 of the Child Abduction Act 1984.

---

**Definitions** For 'voluntary home' see s 60(3); for 'registered children's home' see s 63(8); for 'child', 'local authority' and 'voluntary organisation' see s 105(1); for 'harm' see s 31(9) as applied to the whole Act by s 105(1); for 'foster parent' see sub-s (3); for 'local authority foster parent' see s 23(3).

---

## 52 Rules and regulations

(1) Without prejudice to section 93 or any other power to make such rules, rules of court may be made with respect to the procedure to be followed in connection with proceedings under this Part.

(2) The rules may, in particular make provision—

(*a*) as to the form in which any application is to be made or direction is to be given;

(*b*) prescribing the persons who are to be notified of—

(i) the making, or extension, of an emergency protection order; or

(ii) the making of an application under section 45(4) or (8) or 46(7); and

(*c*) as to the content of any such notification and the manner in which, and person by whom, it is to be given.

(3) The Secretary of State may by regulations provide that, where—

(*a*) an emergency protection order has been made with respect to a child;

(*b*) the applicant for the order was not the local authority within whose area the child is ordinarily resident; and

(*c*) that local authority are of the opinion that it would be in the child's best interests for the applicant's responsibilities under the order to be transferred to them,

that authority shall (subject to their having complied with any requirements imposed by the regulations) be treated, for the purposes of this Act, as though they and not the original applicant had applied for, and been granted, the order.

(4) Regulations made under subsection (3) may, in particular, make provision as to—

(*a*) the considerations to which the local authority shall have regard in forming an opinion as mentioned in subsection (3)(*c*); and

(*b*) the time at which responsibility under any emergency protection order is to be treated as having been transferred to a local authority.

---

**Definitions** For 'emergency protection order' see s 44(4); for 'child' and 'local authority' see s 105(1); for 'ordinary residence' see s 105(6).

**References** See generally 7.1 ff. 'This Part' ie Part V (ss 43-52) (protection of children).

---

# Part VI

# Community Homes

## 53 Provision of community homes by local authorities

(1) Every local authority shall make such arrangements as they consider appropriate for securing that homes ("community homes") are available—

(*a*) for the care and accommodation of children looked after by them; and

(*b*) for purposes connected with the welfare of children (whether or not looked after by them),

and may do so jointly with one or more other local authorities.

(2) In making such arrangements, a local authority shall have regard to the need for ensuring the availability of accommodation—

(*a*) of different descriptions; and

(*b*) which is suitable for different purposes and the requirements of different descriptions of children.

(3) A community home may be a home—

(*a*) provided, managed, equipped and maintained by a local authority; or

(*b*) provided by a voluntary organisation but in respect of which a local authority and the organisation—

(i) propose that, in accordance with an instrument of management, the management, equipment and maintenance of the home shall be the responsibility of the local authority; or

(ii) so propose that the management, equipment and maintenance of the home shall be the responsibility of the voluntary organisation.

(4) Where a local authority are to be responsible for the management of a community home provided by a voluntary organisation, the authority shall designate the home as a controlled community home.

(5) Where a voluntary organisation are to be responsible for the management of a community home provided by the organisation, the local authority shall designate the home as an assisted community home.

(6) Schedule 4 shall have effect for the purpose of supplementing the provisions of this Part.

---

**Definitions** For 'local authority', 'child', 'voluntary organisation' see s 105(1); for 'child who is looked after by a local authority' see s 22(1); for 'controlled community home' see sub-s (4) and 'assisted community home' see sub-s (5).

**References** See generally para 13.2 ff. 'This Part' ie Part VI (ss 53-58 and Sch 4) (community homes).

---

## 54 Directions that premises be no longer used for community home

(1) Where it appears to the Secretary of State that—

(*a*) any premises used for the purposes of a community home are unsuitable for those purposes; or

(*b*) the conduct of a community home—

(i) is not in accordance with regulations made by him under paragraph 4 of Schedule 4; or

(ii) is otherwise unsatisfactory,

he may, by notice in writing served on the responsible body, direct that as from such date as may be specified in the notice the premises shall not be used for the purposes of a community home.

(2) Where—

(*a*) the Secretary of State has given a direction under subsection (1); and

(*b*) the direction has not been revoked,

he may at any time by order revoke the instrument of management for the home concerned.

(3) For the purposes of subsection (1), the responsible body—

(*a*) in relation to a community home provided by a local authority, is that local authority;

(*b*) in relation to a controlled community home, is the local authority specified in the home's instrument of management; and

(*c*) in relation to an assisted community home, is the voluntary organisation by which the home is provided.

---

**Definitions** For 'community home' see s 53; for 'the responsible body' see sub-s (3); for 'local authority' see s 105(1); for 'controlled community home' see s 53(4); for 'assisted community home' see s 53(5).

**References** See generally para 13.2 ff. For service of notices under the Act generally see s 105(8)-(10). For instruments of management see Sch 4 Pt I. For the financial provisions which apply on the cessation of a community home see s 58.

---

## 55 Determination of disputes relating to controlled and assisted community homes

(1) Where any dispute relating to a controlled community home arises between the local authority specified in the home's instrument of management and—

(*a*) the voluntary organisation by which the home is provided; or

(*b*) any other local authority who have placed, or desire or are required to place, in the home a child who is looked after by them,

the dispute may be referred by either party to the Secretary of State for his determination.

(2) Where any dispute relating to an assisted community home arises between the voluntary organisation by which the home is provided and any local authority who have placed, or desire to place, in the home a child who is looked after by them, the dispute may be referred by either party to the Secretary of State for his determination.

(3) Where a dispute is referred to the Secretary of State under this section he may, in order to give effect to his determination of the dispute, give such directions as he thinks fit to the local authority or voluntary organisation concerned.

(4) This section applies even though the matter in dispute may be one which, under or by virtue of Part II of Schedule 4, is reserved for the decision, or is the responsibility, of—

(*a*) the local authority specified in the home's instrument of management; or

(*b*) (as the case may be) the voluntary organisation by which the home is provided.

(5) Where any trust deed relating to a controlled or assisted community home contains provision whereby a bishop or any other ecclesiastical or denominational authority has power to decide questions relating to religious instruction given in the home, no dispute which is capable of being dealt with in accordance with that provision shall be referred to the Secretary of State under this section.

(6) In this Part "trust deed", in relation to a voluntary home, means any instrument (other than an instrument of management) regulating—

(*a*) the maintenance, management or conduct of the home; or (*b*) the constitution of a body of managers or trustees of the home.

---

**Definitions** For 'controlled community home' see s 53(4). For 'local authority', 'voluntary organisation', 'child' see s 105(1); for 'child who is looked after by a local authority' see s 22(1); for 'assisted community home' see s 53(5); for 'trust deed see sub-s (6).

**References** See generally para 13.2 ff. For instruments of management see Sch 4 Pt I. 'This Part' ie Part VI (ss 53-58 and Sch 4) (community homes).

---

## 56 Discontinuance by voluntary organisation of controlled or assisted community home

(1) The voluntary organisation by which a controlled or assisted community home is provided shall not cease to provide the home except after giving to the Secretary of State and the local authority specified in the home's instrument of management not less than two years' notice in writing of their intention to do so.

(2) A notice under subsection (1) shall specify the date from which the voluntary organisation intend to cease to provide the home as a community home.

(3) Where such a notice is given and is not withdrawn before the date specified in it, the home's instrument of management shall cease to have effect on that date and the home shall then cease to be a controlled or assisted community home.

(4) Where a notice is given under subsection (1) and the home's managers give notice in writing to the Secretary of State that they are unable or unwilling to continue as its managers until the date specified in the subsection (1) notice, the Secretary of State may by order—

(*a*) revoke the home's instrument of management; and
(*b*) require the local authority who were specified in that instrument to conduct the home until—
  (i) the date specified in the subsection (1) notice; or
  (ii) such earlier date (if any) as may be specified for the purposes of this paragraph in the order,

as if it were a community home provided by the local authority.

(5) Where the Secretary of State imposes a requirement under subsection (4)(*b*)—

(*a*) nothing in the trust deed for the home shall affect the conduct of the home by the local authority;
(*b*) the Secretary of State may by order direct that for the purposes of any provision specified in the direction and made by or under any enactment relating to community homes (other than this section) the home shall, until the date or earlier date specified as mentioned in subsection (4)(*b*), be treated as a controlled or assisted community home;
(*c*) except in so far as the Secretary of State so directs, the home shall until that date be treated for the purposes of any such enactment as a community home provided by the local authority; and
(*d*) on the date or earlier date specified as mentioned in subsection (4)(*b*) the home shall cease to be a community home.

**Definitions** For 'voluntary organisation', 'local authority' see s 105(1); for 'controlled community home' see s 53(4); for 'assisted community home' see s 53(5); for 'trust deed' see s 55(6).

**References** See generally para 13.2 ff. For instruments of management see Sch 4 Pt I. For service of notices under the Act generally see s 105(8)-(10). For the financial provisions which apply on the cessation of a community home see s 58.

## 57 Closure by local authority of controlled or assisted community home

(1) The local authority specified in the instrument of management for a controlled or assisted community home may give—

(*a*) the Secretary of State; and
(*b*) the voluntary organisation by which the home is provided,

not less than two years' notice in writing of their intention to withdraw their designation of the home as a controlled or assisted community home.

(2) A notice under subsection (1) shall specify the date ("the specified date") on which the designation is to be withdrawn.

(3) Where—

(*a*) a notice is given under subsection (1) in respect of a controlled or assisted community home;
(*b*) the home's managers give notice in writing to the Secretary of State that they are unable or unwilling to continue as managers until the specified date; and
(*c*) the managers' notice is not withdrawn,

the Secretary of State may by order revoke the home's instrument of management from such date earlier than the specified date as may be specified in the order.

(4) Before making an order under subsection (3), the Secretary of State shall consult the local authority and the voluntary organisation.

(5) Where a notice has been given under subsection (1) and is not withdrawn, the home's instrument of management shall cease to have effect on—

(*a*) the specified date; or
(*b*) where an earlier date has been specified under subsection (3), that earlier date,

and the home shall then cease to be a community home.

**Definitions** For 'local authority', 'voluntary organisation' see s 105(1); for 'community home' see s 53; for 'controlled community home' see s 53(4); for 'assisted community home' see s 53(5); for 'the specified date' see sub-s (2).

**References** See generally para 13.00 ff. For instruments of management see Sch 4 Pt I. For service of notices under the Act generally see s 105(8)-(10). For the financial provisions which apply on the cessation of a community home see s 58.

**58 Financial provisions applicable on cessation of controlled or assisted community home or disposal etc of premises**

(1) Where—

(*a*) the instrument of management for a controlled or assisted community home is revoked or otherwise ceases to have effect under section 54(2), 56(3) or (4)(*a*) or 57(3) or (5); or

(*b*) any premises used for the purposes of such a home are (at any time after 13th January 1987) disposed of, or put to use otherwise than for those purposes,

the proprietor shall become liable to pay compensation ("the appropriate compensation") in accordance with this section.

(2) Where the instrument of management in force at the relevant time relates—

(*a*) to a controlled community home; or

(*b*) to an assisted community home which, at any time before the instrument came into force, was a controlled community home,

the appropriate compensation is a sum equal to that part of the value of any premises which is attributable to expenditure incurred in relation to the premises, while the home was a controlled community home, by the authority who were then the responsible authority.

(3) Where the instrument of management in force at the relevant time relates—

(*a*) to an assisted community home; or

(*b*) to a controlled community home which, at any time before the instrument came into force, was an assisted community home,

the appropriate compensation is a sum equal to that part of the value of the premises which is attributable to the expenditure of money provided by way of grant under section 82, section 65 of the Children and Young Persons Act 1969 or section 82 of the Child Care Act 1980.

(4) Where the home is, at the relevant time, conducted in premises which formerly were used as an approved school or were an approved probation hostel or home, the appropriate compensation is a sum equal to that part of the value of the premises which is attributable to the expenditure—

(*a*) of sums paid towards the expenses of the managers of an approved school under section 104 of the Children and Young Persons Act 1933; or

(*b*) of sums paid under section 51(3)(*c*) of the Powers of Criminal Courts Act 1973 in relation to expenditure on approved probation hostels or homes.

(5) The appropriate compensation shall be paid—

(*a*) in the case of compensation payable under subsection (2), to the authority who were the responsible authority at the relevant time; and

(*b*) in any other case, to the Secretary of State.

(6) In this section—

"disposal" includes the grant of a tenancy and any other conveyance, assignment, transfer, grant, variation or extinguishment of an interest in or right over land, whether made by instrument or otherwise;

"premises" means any premises or part of premises (including land) used for the purposes of the home and belonging to the proprietor;

"the proprietor" means—

(*a*) the voluntary organisation by which the home is, at the relevant time, provided; or

(*b*) if the premises are not, at the relevant time, vested in that organisation, the persons in whom they are vested;

"the relevant time" means the time immediately before the liability to pay arises under subsection (1); and

"the responsible authority" means the local authority specified in the instrument of management in question.

(7) For the purposes of this section an event of a kind mentioned in subsection (1)(*b*) shall be taken to have occurred—

(*a*) in the case of a disposal, on the date on which the disposal was completed or, in the case of a disposal which is effected by a series of transactions, the date on which the last of those transactions was completed;

(*b*) in the case of premises which are put to different use, on the date on which they first begin to be put to their new use.

(8) The amount of any sum payable under this section shall be determined in accordance with such arrangements—

(*a*) as may be agreed between the voluntary organisation by which the home is, at the relevant time, provided and the responsible authority or (as the case may be) the Secretary of State; or

(*b*) in default of agreement, as may be determined by the Secretary of State.

(9) With the agreement of the responsible authority or (as the case may be) the Secretary of State, the liability to pay any sum under this section may be discharged, in whole or in part, by the transfer of any premises.

(10) This section has effect regardless of—

(*a*) anything in any trust deed for a controlled or assisted community home;

(*b*) the provisions of any enactment or instrument governing the disposition of the property of a voluntary organisation.

---

**Definitions** For 'controlled community home' see s 53(4); for 'assisted community home' see s 53(5); for 'appropriate compensation', see sub-s (1); for 'the relevant time', 'disposal', 'premises', 'the proprietor', 'relevant premises', 'the responsible authority', see sub-s (6); for 'trust deed' see s 55(6).

**References** See generally para 13.4 ff. For instruments of management see Sch 4 Pt I. For disposal or change of use of premises see sub-s (7). For the amount of any sum payable under this section see sub-s (8) and for the payment of such funds into the Consolidated Fund see s 106(2).

---

## PART VII

## VOLUNTARY HOMES AND VOLUNTARY ORGANISATIONS

### 59 Provision of accommodation by voluntary organisations

(1) Where a voluntary organisation provide accommodation for a child, they shall do so by—

(*a*) placing him (subject to subsection (2)) with—

(i) a family;
(ii) a relative of his; or
(iii) any other suitable person,

on such terms as to payment by the organisation and otherwise as the organisation may determine;

(*b*) maintaining him in a voluntary home;
(*c*) maintaining him in a community home;
(*d*) maintaining him in a registered children's home;
(*e*) maintaining him in a home provided by the Secretary of State under section 82(5) on such terms as the Secretary of State may from time to time determine; or
(*f*) making such other arrangements (subject to subsection (3)) as seem appropriate to them.

(2) The Secretary of State may make regulations as to the placing of children with foster parents by voluntary organisations and the regulations may, in particular, make provision which (with any necessary modifications) is similar to the provision that may be made under section 23(2)(*a*).

(3) The Secretary of State may make regulations as to the arrangements which may be made under subsection (1)(*f*) and the regulations may in particular make provision which (with any necessary modifications) is similar to the provision that may be made under section 23(2)(*f*).

(4) The Secretary of State may make regulations requiring any voluntary organisation who are providing accommodation for a child—

(*a*) to review his case; and
(*b*) to consider any representations (including any complaint) made to them by any person falling within a prescribed class of person,

in accordance with the provisions of the regulations.

(5) Regulations under subsection (4) may in particular make provision which (with any necessary modifications) is similar to the provision that may be made under section 26.

(6) Regulations under subsections (2) to (4) may provide that any person who, without reasonable excuse, contravenes or fails to comply with a regulation shall be guilty of an offence and liable on summary conviction to a fine not exceeding level 4 on the standard scale.

---

**Definitions** For 'voluntary organisation', 'child' and 'relative' see s 105(1); for 'voluntary home' see s 60(3); for 'community home' see s 53 for 'registered children's home' see s 63(8).

**References** See generally para 13.5 ff. For 'the standard scale' see the Criminal Justice Act 1982 s 37(2) (3) as amended; 'level 4' ie £1000.

---

## 60 Registration and regulation of voluntary homes

(1) No voluntary home shall be carried on unless it is registered in a register to be kept for the purposes of this section by the Secretary of State.

(2) The register may be kept by means of a computer.

(3) In this Act "voluntary home" means any home or other institution providing care and accommodation for children which is carried on by a voluntary organisation but does not include—

(*a*) a nursing home, mental nursing home or residential care home;

(*b*) a school;
(*c*) any health service hospital;
(*d*) any community home;
(*e*) any home or other institution provided, equipped and maintained by the Secretary of State; or
(*f*) any home which is exempted by regulations made for the purposes of this section by the Secretary of State.

(4) Schedule 5 shall have effect for the purpose of supplementing the provisions of this Part.

---

**Definitions** For 'voluntary home' see sub-s (3); for 'child', 'voluntary organisation', 'nursing home', 'mental nursing home', 'residential care home', 'school', 'health service hospital', 'local authority' see s 105(1); for 'community home' see s 53.

**References** See generally para 13.6 ff. 'This Part' ie Part VII (ss 59-62 and Sch 5) (voluntary homes and voluntary organisations). For the circumstances in which the Secretary of State may make a grant to a voluntary organisation in connection with a voluntary home see s 82(4). For the power to inspect a voluntary home and to hold inquiries into any matter connected with a voluntary home see ss 80 and 81.

---

## 61 Duties of voluntary organisations

(1) Where a child is accommodated by or on behalf of a voluntary organisation, it shall be the duty of the organisation—

(*a*) to safeguard and promote his welfare;
(*b*) to make such use of the services and facilities available for children cared for by their own parents as appears to the organisation reasonable in his case; and
(*c*) to advise, assist and befriend him with a view to promoting his welfare when he ceases to be so accommodated.

(2) Before making any decision with respect to any such child the organisation shall, so far as is reasonably practicable, ascertain the wishes and feelings of—

(*a*) the child;
(*b*) his parents;
(*c*) any person who is not a parent of his but who has parental responsibility for him; and
(*d*) any other person whose wishes and feelings the organisation consider to be relevant,

regarding the matter to be decided.

(3) In making any such decision the organisation shall give due consideration—

(*a*) having regard to the child's age and understanding, to such wishes and feelings of his as they have been able to ascertain;
(*b*) to such other wishes and feelings mentioned in subsection (2) as they have been able to ascertain; and
(*c*) to the child's religious persuasion, racial origin and cultural and linguistic background.

---

**Definitions** For 'child' and 'voluntary organisation' see s 105(1); for 'parental responsibility' see s 3.

**References** See generally para 13.9 ff. For 'parent' see para 2.7.

---

## 62 Duties of local authorities

(1) Every local authority shall satisfy themselves that any voluntary organisation providing accommodation—

(*a*) within the authority's area for any child; or

(*b*) outside that area for any child on behalf of the authority,

are satisfactorily safeguarding and promoting the welfare of the children so provided with accommodation.

(2) Every local authority shall arrange for children who are accommodated within their area by or on behalf of voluntary organisations to be visited, from time to time, in the interests of their welfare.

(3) The Secretary of State may make regulations—

(*a*) requiring every child who is accommodated within a local authority's area, by or on behalf of a voluntary organisation, to be visited by an officer of the authority—

(i) in prescribed circumstances; and

(ii) on specified occasions or within specified periods; and

(*b*) imposing requirements which must be met by any local authority, or officer of a local authority, carrying out functions under this section.

(4) Subsection (2) does not apply in relation to community homes.

(5) Where a local authority are not satisfied that the welfare of any child who is accommodated by or on behalf of a voluntary organisation is being satisfactorily safeguarded or promoted they shall—

(*a*) unless they consider that it would not be in the best interests of the child, take such steps as are reasonably practicable to secure that the care and accommodation of the child is undertaken by—

(i) a parent of his;

(ii) any person who is not a parent of his but who has parental responsibility for him; or

(iii) a relative of his; and

(*b*) consider the extent to which (if at all) they should exercise any of their functions with respect to the child.

(6) Any person authorised by a local authority may, for the purpose of enabling the authority to discharge their duties under this section—

(*a*) enter, at any reasonable time, and inspect any premises in which children are being accommodated as mentioned in subsection (1) or (2);

(*b*) inspect any children there;

(*c*) require any person to furnish him with such records of a kind required to be kept by regulations made under paragraph 7 of Schedule 5 (in whatever form they are held), or allow him to inspect such records, as he may at any time direct.

(7) Any person exercising the power conferred by subsection (6) shall, if asked to do so, produce some duly authenticated document showing his authority to do so.

(8) Any person authorised to exercise the power to inspect records conferred by subsection (6)—

(*a*) shall be entitled at any reasonable time to have access to, and inspect and check the operation of, any computer and any associated apparatus or material which is or has been in use in connection with the records in question; and

(*b*) may require—

(i) the person by whom or on whose behalf the computer is or has been so used; or

(ii) any person having charge of, or otherwise concerned with the operation of, the computer, apparatus or material,

to afford him such assistance as he may reasonably require.

(9) Any person who intentionally obstructs another in the exercise of any power conferred by subsections (6) or (8) shall be guilty of an offence and liable on summary conviction to a fine not exceeding level 3 on the standard scale.

---

**Definitions** For 'local authority', 'voluntary organisation', 'child', 'functions' and 'relative' see s 105(1); for 'community home' see s 53; for 'parental responsibility' see s 3.

**References** See generally para 13.10 ff. For 'parent' see para 2.00. For power to issue warrant to authorise a constable to assist in exercising the power under sub-ss (6) or (8) see s 102. For 'the standard scale' see the Criminal Justice Act 1982 s 37(2) (3) as amended; 'level 3' ie £400.

---

## Part VIII

## Registered Children's Homes

### 63 Children not to be cared for and accommodated in unregistered children's homes

(1) No child shall be cared for and provided with accommodation in a children's home unless the home is registered under this Part.

(2) The register may be kept by means of a computer.

(3) For the purposes of this Part, "a children's home"—

(*a*) means a home which provides (or usually provides or is intended to provide) care and accommodation wholly or mainly for more than three children at any one time; but

(*b*) does not include a home which is exempted by or under any of the following provisions of this section or by regulations made for the purposes of this subsection by the Secretary of State.

(4) A child is not cared for and accommodated in a children's home when he is cared for and accommodated by—

(*a*) a parent of his;

(*b*) a person who is not a parent of his but who has parental responsibility for him; or

(*c*) any relative of his.

(5) A home is not a children's home for the purposes of this Part if it is—

(*a*) a community home;

(*b*) a voluntary home;

(*c*) a residential care home, nursing home or mental nursing home;

(*d*) a health service hospital;

(*e*) a home provided, equipped and maintained by the Secretary of State; or

(*f*) a school (but subject to subsection (6)).

(6) An independent school is a children's home if—

(*a*) it provides accommodation for not more than fifty children; and

(*b*) it is not approved by the Secretary of State under section 11(3)(*a*) of the Education Act 1981.

(7) A child shall not be treated as cared for and accommodated in a children's home when—

(*a*) any person mentioned in subsection (4)(*a*) or (*b*) is living at the home; or

(*b*) the person caring for him is doing so in his personal capacity and not in the course of carrying out his duties in relation to the home.

(8) In this Act "a registered children's home" means a children's home registered under this Part.

(9) In this section "home" includes any institution.

(10) Where any child is at any time cared for and accommodated in a children's home which is not a registered children's home, the person carrying on the home shall be—

(*a*) guilty of an offence; and

(*b*) liable to a fine not exceeding level 5 on the standard scale,

unless he has a reasonable excuse.

(11) Schedule 6 shall have effect with respect to children's homes.

(12) Schedule 7 shall have effect for the purpose of setting out the circumstances in which a person may foster more than three children without being treated as carrying on a children's home.

---

**Definitions** For 'child', 'local authority', 'residential care home', 'nursing home', 'mental nursing home', 'health service hospital', 'school', 'independent school', 'relative' see s 105(1); for 'a children's home' see sub-s (3); for 'home' see sub-s (9); for 'parental responsibility' see s 3; for 'community home' see s 53; for 'voluntary home' see s 60(3); for 'registered children's home' see sub-s (8).

**References** See generally para 14.3 ff. For 'parent' see para 2.7. For 'the standard scale' see the Criminal Justice Act 1982 s 37(2) (3) as amended; 'level 5' ie £2,000. For the inspection of Registered Children's homes see s 80(1)(a). For the power to hold inquiries into any matter connected with a registered children's home see s 81. For transitional provisions see s 108(6) and Sch 14 para 32.

---

### 64 Welfare of children in children's homes

(1) Where a child is accommodated in a children's home, it shall be the duty of the person carrying on the home to—

(*a*) safeguard and promote the child's welfare;

(*b*) make such use of the services and facilities available for children cared for by their own parents as appears to that person reasonable in the case of the child; and

(*c*) advise, assist and befriend him with a view to promoting his welfare when he ceases to be so accommodated.

(2) Before making any decision with respect to any such child the person

carrying on the home shall, so far as is reasonably practicable, ascertain the wishes and feelings of—

(*a*) the child;
(*b*) his parents;
(*c*) any other person who is not a parent of his but who has parental responsibility for him; and
(*d*) any person whose wishes and feelings the person carrying on the home considers to be relevant,

regarding the matter to be decided.

(3) In making any such decision the person concerned shall give due consideration—

(*a*) having regard to the child's age and understanding, to such wishes and feelings of his as he has been able to ascertain;
(*b*) to such other wishes and feelings mentioned in subsection (2) as he has been able to ascertain; and
(*c*) to the child's religious persuasion, racial origin and cultural and linguistic background.

(4) Section 62, except subsection (4), shall apply in relation to any person who is carrying on a children's home as it applies in relation to any voluntary organisation.

---

**Definitions** For 'child' and 'voluntary organisation' see s 105(1); for 'children's home' see s 63(3); for 'parental responsibility' see s 3.

**References** See generally para 14.8 ff. For 'parent' see para 2.7. For power to issue a warrant to authorise a constable to assist in exercising the power under sub-s (4) see s 102.

---

## 65 Persons disqualified from carrying on, or being employed in, children's homes

(1) A person who is disqualified (under section 68) from fostering a child privately shall not carry on, or be otherwise concerned in the management of, or have any financial interest in, a children's home unless he has—

(*a*) disclosed to the responsible authority the fact that he is so disqualified; and
(*b*) obtained their written consent.

(2) No person shall employ a person who is so disqualified in a children's home unless he has—

(*a*) disclosed to the responsible authority the fact that that person is so disqualified; and
(*b*) obtained their written consent.

(3) Where an authority refuse to give their consent under this section, they shall inform the applicant by a written notice which states—

(*a*) the reason for the refusal;
(*b*) the applicant's right to appeal against the refusal to a Registered Homes Tribunal under paragraph 8 of Schedule 6; and
(*c*) the time within which he may do so.

(4) Any person who contravenes subsection (1) or (2) shall be guilty of an offence and liable on summary conviction to imprisonment for a term

not exceeding six months or to a fine not exceeding level 5 on the standard scale or to both.

(5) Where a person contravenes subsection (2) he shall not be guilty of an offence if he proves that he did not know, and had no reasonable grounds for believing, that the person whom he was employing was disqualified under section 68.

---

**Definitions** For 'fostering a child privately' see s 66(1)(b) as applied to the whole Act by s 105(1); for 'children's home' see s 63(3); for 'the responsible authority' see Sch 6 Pt I para 3(1).

**References** See generally para 14.7. For service of notices under the Act generally see s 105(8)-(10). For 'the standard scale' see the Criminal Justice Act 1982 s 37(2) (3) as amended; level 5 ie £2,000.

---

## PART IX

## PRIVATE ARRANGEMENTS FOR FOSTERING CHILDREN

### 66 Privately fostered children

(1) In this Part—

(*a*) "a privately fostered child" means a child who is under the age of sixteen and who is cared for, and provided with accommodation by, someone other than—

(i) a parent of his;

(ii) a person who is not a parent of his but who has parental responsibility for him; or

(iii) a relative of his; and

(*b*) "to foster a child privately" means to look after the child in circumstances in which he is a privately fostered child as defined by this section.

(2) A child is not a privately fostered child if the person caring for and accommodating him—

(*a*) has done so for a period of less than 28 days; and

(*b*) does not intend to do so for any longer period.

(3) Subsection (1) is subject to—

(*a*) the provisions of section 63; and

(*b*) the exceptions made by paragraphs 1 to 5 of Schedule 8.

(4) In the case of a child who is disabled, subsection (1)(*a*) shall have effect as if for "sixteen" there were substituted "eighteen".

(5) Schedule 8 shall have effect for the purposes of supplementing the provision made by this Part.

---

**Definitions** For 'a privately fostered child' see sub-s(1)(a); for 'parental responsibility' see s 3; for 'relative' see s 105(1); for 'to foster a child privately' see sub-s (1)(b); for 'disabled' see s 17(11) as applied to the whole Act by s 105(1).

**References** See generally para 14.11 ff. 'This Part' ie Part IX ss 66-70 and Sch 8 (private arrangements for fostering children). For 'parent' see para 2.7. For transitional provisions see s 108(6) and Sch 14 para 32.

---

## 67 Welfare of privately fostered children

(1) It shall be the duty of every local authority to satisfy themselves that the welfare of children who are privately fostered within their area is being satisfactorily safeguarded and promoted and to secure that such advice is given to those caring for them as appears to the authority to be needed.

(2) The Secretary of State may make regulations—

(*a*) requiring every child who is privately fostered within a local authority's area to be visited by an officer of the authority—

(i) in prescribed circumstances; and

(ii) on specified occasions or within specified periods; and

(*b*) imposing requirements which are to be met by any local authority, or officer of a local authority, in carrying out functions under this section.

(3) Where any person who is authorised by a local authority to visit privately fostered children has reasonable cause to believe that—

(*a*) any privately fostered child is being accommodated in premises within the authority's area; or

(*b*) it is proposed to accommodate any such child in any such premises,

he may at any reasonable time inspect those premises and any children there.

(4) Any person exercising the power under subsection (3) shall, if so required, produce some duly authenticated document showing his authority to do so.

(5) Where a local authority are not satisfied that the welfare of any child who is privately fostered within their area is being satisfactorily safeguarded or promoted they shall—

(*a*) unless they consider that it would not be in the best interests of the child, take such steps as are reasonably practicable to secure that the care and accommodation of the child is undertaken by—

(i) a parent of his;

(ii) any person who is not a parent of his but who has parental responsibility for him; or

(iii) a relative of his; and

(*b*) consider the extent to which (if at all) they should exercise any of their functions under this Act with respect to the child.

---

**Definitions** For 'local authority', 'child', 'relative', 'functions' see s 105(1); for 'a privately fostered child' see s 66(1)(a); for 'parental responsibility' see s 3.

**References** See generally para 14.19 ff. For 'parent' see para 2.7. For the offence of intentionally obstructing a person exercising the power under sub-s (3) see s 70(1)(c) in particular and s 70(4) concerning the punishment for such offence. For the inspection of premises where a foster child is living see s 80(1)(g). For power to issue a warrant to authorise a constable to assist in exercising the power under sub-s (3) see s 102.

---

## 68 Persons disqualified from being private foster parents

(1) Unless he has disclosed the fact to the appropriate local authority and obtained their written consent, a person shall not foster a child privately if he is disqualified from doing so by regulations made by the Secretary of State for the purposes of this section.

(2) The regulations may, in particular, provide for a person to be so disqualified where—

(*a*) an order of a kind specified in the regulations has been made at any time with respect to him;

(*b*) an order of a kind so specified has been made at any time with respect to any child who has been in his care;

(*c*) a requirement of a kind so specified has been imposed at any time with respect to any such child, under or by virtue of any enactment;

(*d*) he has been convicted of any offence of a kind so specified, or has been placed on probation or discharged absolutely or conditionally for any such offence;

(*e*) a prohibition has been imposed on him at any time under section 69 or under any other specified enactment;

(*f*) his rights and powers with respect to a child have at any time been vested in a specified authority under a specified enactment.

(3) Unless he has disclosed the fact to the appropriate local authority and obtained their written consent, a person shall not foster a child privately if—

(*a*) he lives in the same household as a person who is himself prevented from fostering a child by subsection (1); or

(*b*) he lives in a household at which any such person is employed.

(4) Where an authority refuse to give their consent under this section, they shall inform the applicant by a written notice which states—

(*a*) the reason for the refusal;

(*b*) the applicant's right under paragraph 8 of Schedule 8 to appeal against the refusal; and

(*c*) the time within which he may do so.

(5) In this section—

"the appropriate authority" means the local authority within whose area it is proposed to foster the child in question; and

"enactment" means any enactment having effect, at any time, in any part of the United Kingdom.

---

**Definitions** For 'the appropriate local authority' and 'enactment' see sub-s (5); for 'to foster a child privately' see s 66(1)(b); for 'child', 'local authority' see s 105(1).

**References** See generally para 14.16 ff. For appeal to the court by a person aggrieved by a refusal of consent under this section see Sch 8 para 8. For offences see s 70.

---

## 69 Power to prohibit private fostering

(1) This section applies where a person—

(*a*) proposes to foster a child privately; or

(*b*) is fostering a child privately.

(2) Where the local authority for the area within which the child is proposed to be, or is being, fostered are of the opinion that—

(*a*) he is not a suitable person to foster a child;

(*b*) the premises in which the child will be, or is being, accommodated are not suitable; or

(*c*) it would be prejudicial to the welfare of the child for him to be, or continue to be, accommodated by that person in those premises, the authority may impose a prohibition on him under subsection (3).

(3) A prohibition imposed on any person under this subsection may prohibit him from fostering privately—

(*a*) any child in any premises within the area of the local authority; or
(*b*) any child in premises specified in the prohibition;
(*c*) a child identified in the prohibition, in premises specified in the prohibition.

(4) A local authority who have imposed a prohibition on any person under subsection (3) may, if they think fit, cancel the prohibition—

(*a*) of their own motion; or
(*b*) on an application made by that person,

if they are satisfied that the prohibition is no longer justified.

(5) Where a local authority impose a requirement of any person under paragraph 6 of Schedule 8, they may also impose a prohibition on him under subsection (3).

(6) Any prohibition imposed by virtue of subsection (5) shall not have effect unless—

(*a*) the time specified for compliance with the requirement has expired; and
(*b*) the requirement has not been complied with.

(7) A prohibition imposed under this section shall be imposed by notice in writing addressed to the person on whom it is imposed and informing him of—

(*a*) the reason for imposing the prohibition;
(*b*) his right under paragraph 8 of Schedule 8 to appeal against the prohibition; and
(*c*) the time within which he may do so.

---

**Definitions** For 'child', 'local authority' see s 105(1); for 'to foster a child privately' see s 66(1)(b).

**References** See generally para 14.17 ff. For 'required notice' see Sch 8 para 7. For service of notices under this Act generally see s 105(8)-(10). For appeal to the court by a person aggrieved by a prohibition imposed under this section see Sch 8 para 8. For offences see s 70. For inspection of premises where a child is privately fostered see s 67(3).

---

### 70 Offences

(1) A person shall be guilty of an offence if—

(*a*) being required, under any provision made by or under this Part, to give any notice or information—
  (i) he fails without reasonable excuse to give the notice within the time specified in that provision; or
  (ii) he fails without reasonable excuse to give the information within a reasonable time; or
  (iii) he makes, or causes or procures another person to make, any statement in the notice or information which he knows to be false or misleading in a material particular;
(*b*) he refuses to allow a privately fostered child to be visited by a duly authorised officer of a local authority;

(*c*) he intentionally obstructs another in the exercise of the power conferred by section 67(3);
(*d*) he contravenes section 68;
(*e*) he fails without reasonable excuse to comply with any requirement imposed by a local authority under this Part;
(*f*) he accommodates a privately fostered child in any premises in contravention of a prohibition imposed by a local authority under this Part;
(*g*) he knowingly causes to be published, or publishes, an advertisement which he knows contravenes paragraph 10 of Schedule 8.

(2) Where a person contravenes section 68(3), he shall not be guilty of an offence under this section if he proves that he did not know, and had no reasonable ground for believing, that any person to whom section 68(1) applied was living or employed in the premises in question.

(3) A person guilty of an offence under subsection (1)(*a*) shall be liable on summary conviction to a fine not exceeding level 5 on the standard scale.

(4) A person guilty of an offence under subsection (1)(*b*), (*c*) or (*g*) shall be liable on summary conviction to a fine not exceeding level 3 on the standard scale.

(5) A person guilty of an offence under subsection (1)(*d*) or (*f*) shall be liable on summary conviction to imprisonment for a term not exceeding six months, or to a fine not exceeding level 5 on the standard scale, or to both.

(6) A person guilty of an offence under subsection (1)(*e*) shall be liable on summary conviction to a fine not exceeding level 4 on the standard scale.

(7) If any person who is required, under any provision of this Part, to give a notice fails to give the notice within the time specified in that provision, proceedings for the offence may be brought at any time within six months from the date when evidence of the offence came to the knowledge of the local authority.

(8) Subsection (7) is not affected by anything in section 127(1) of the Magistrates' Courts Act 1980 (time limit for proceedings).

---

**Definitions** For 'a privately fostered child' see s 66(1)(a); for 'local authority' see s 105(1).

**References** 'This Part' ie Part IX s 66-70 and Sch 8 (private arrangements for fostering children). For 'the standard scale' see the Criminal Justice Act 1982 s 37(2) (3) as amended; 'level 5' ie £2,000; 'level 4' ie £1000; 'level 3' ie £400.

---

## Part X

## Child Minding and Day Care for Young Children

### 71 Registration

(1) Every local authority shall keep a register of—

(*a*) persons who act as child minders on domestic premises within the authority's area; and
(*b*) persons who provide day care for children under the age of eight on premises (other than domestic premises) within that area.

(2) For the purposes of this Part—

(*a*) a person acts as a child minder if—

(i) he looks after one or more children under the age of eight, for reward; and

(ii) the period, or the total of the periods, which he spends so looking after children in any day exceeds two hours; and

(*b*) a person does not provide day care for children unless the period, or the total of the periods, during which children are looked after exceeds two hours in any day.

(3) Where a person provides day care for children under the age of eight on different premises situated within the area of the same local authority, that person shall be separately registered with respect to each of those premises.

(4) A person who—

(*a*) is the parent, or a relative, of a child;

(*b*) has parental responsibility for a child; or

(*c*) is a foster parent of a child,

does not act as a child minder for the purposes of this Part when looking after that child.

(5) Where a person is employed as a nanny for a child, she does not act as a child minder when looking after that child wholly or mainly in the home of the person so employing her.

(6) Where a person is so employed by two different employers, she does not act as a child minder when looking after any of the children concerned wholly or mainly in the home or either of her employers.

(7) A local authority may refuse to register an applicant for registration under subsection (1)(*a*) if they are satisfied that—

(*a*) the applicant; or

(*b*) any person looking after, or likely to be looking after, any children on any premises on which the applicant is, or is likely to be, child minding,

is not fit to look after children under the age of eight.

(8) A local authority may refuse to register an applicant for registration under subsection (1)(*a*) if they are satisfied that—

(*a*) any person living, or likely to be living, at any premises on which the applicant is, or is likely to be, child minding; or

(*b*) any person employed, or likely to be employed, on those premises,

is not fit to be in the proximity of children under the age of eight.

(9) A local authority may refuse to register an applicant for registration under subsection (1)(*b*) if they are satisfied that any person looking after, or likely to be looking after, any children on the premises to which the application relates is not fit to look after children under the age of eight.

(10) A local authority may refuse to register an applicant for registration under subsection (1)(*b*) if they are satisfied that—

(*a*) any person living, or likely to be living, at the premises to which the application relates; or

(*b*) any person employed, or likely to be employed, on those premises,

is not fit to be in the proximity of children under the age of eight.

(11) A local authority may refuse to register an applicant for registration under this section if they are satisfied—

(*a*) in the case of an application under subsection (1)(*a*), that any premises on which the applicant is, or is likely to be, child minding; or

(*b*) in the case of an application under subsection (1)(*b*), that the premises to which the application relates,

are not fit to be used for looking after children under the age of eight, whether because of their condition or the condition of any equipment used on the premises or for any reason connected with their situation, construction or size.

(12) In this section—

"domestic premises" means any premises which are wholly or mainly used as a private dwelling;

"premises" includes any vehicle.

(13) For the purposes of this Part a person acts as a nanny for a child if she is employed to look after the child by—

(*a*) a parent of the child;

(*b*) a person who is not a parent of the child but who has parental responsibility for him; or

(*c*) a person who is a relative of the child and who has assumed responsibility for his care.

(14) For the purposes of this section, a person fosters a child if—

(*a*) he is a local authority foster parent in relation to the child;

(*b*) he is a foster parent with whom the child has been placed by a voluntary organisation; or

(*c*) he fosters the child privately.

(15) Any register kept under this section—

(*a*) shall be open to inspection by members of the public at all reasonable times; and

(*b*) may be kept by means of a computer.

(16) Schedule 9 shall have effect for the purpose of making further provision with respect to registration under this section including, in particular, further provision for exemption from the requirement to be registered and provision for disqualification.

---

**Definitions** For 'local authority', 'relative' see s 105(1); for 'child minder' see sub-s (2)(*a*); for 'domestic premises', 'premises' see sub-s (12); for 'day care' see sub-s (2)(*b*) and s 18(4) as applied to the whole Act by s 105(1); for 'parental responsibility' see s 3; for 'fostering a child see sub-s (14); for 'nanny' see sub-s (13); for local authority foster parent' see s 23(3) as applied to the whole Act by s 105(1); for 'to foster a child privately' see s 66(1)(b) as applied to the whole Act by s 105(1).

**References** See generally para 15.1 ff. 'This Part' ie Part X ss 71-79 and Sch 9 (child minding and day care for young children). For 'parent' see para 2.7. For disqualification from registration see Sch 9 para 2; for exemption for certain schools and other establishments see Sch 9 paras 3 and 4, and for occasional facilities see para 5. For requirements to be complied with by child minders see s 72, and by persons providing day care see s 73; for cancellation of registration see s 74; for protection of children in an emergency see s 75; for inspection of premises used for child minding or to provide day care see s 76; for appeals see s 77 and for offences see s 78. For transitional provisions see s 108(6) and Sch 14 para 33.

---

## 72 Requirements to be complied with by child minders

(1) Where a local authority register a person under section 71(1)(*a*), they shall impose such reasonable requirements on him as they consider appropriate in his case.

(2) In imposing requirements on him, the authority shall—

(*a*) specify the maximum number of children, or the maximum number of children within specified age groups, whom he may look after when acting as a child minder;

(*b*) require him to secure that any premises on which he so looks after any child, and the equipment used in those premises, are adequately maintained and kept safe;

(*c*) require him to keep a record of the name and address of—

- (i) any child so looked after by him on any premises within the authority's area;
- (ii) any person who assists in looking after any such child; and
- (iii) any person living, or likely at any time to be living, at those premises;

(*d*) require him to notify the authority in writing of any change in the persons mentioned in paragraph (*c*)(ii) and (iii).

(3) The Secretary of State may by regulations make provision as to—

(*a*) requirements which must be imposed by local authorities under this section in prescribed circumstances;

(*b*) requirements of such descriptions as may be prescribed which must not be imposed by local authorities under this section.

(4) In determining the maximum number of children to be specified under subsection (2)(*a*), the authority shall take account of the number of other children who may at any time be on any premises on which the person concerned acts, or is likely to act, as a child minder.

(5) Where, in addition to the requirements mentioned in subsection (2), a local authority impose other requirements, those other requirements must not be incompatible with any of the subsection (2) requirements.

(6) A local authority may at any time vary any requirement imposed under this section, impose any additional requirement or remove any requirement.

---

**Definitions** For 'local authority' see s 105(1); for 'child minder' see s 71(2)(*a*).

**Reference** For 'premises' see definition of domestic premises in s 71 (12) as applied to the whole Act by s 105(1).

---

## 73 Requirements to be complied with by persons providing day care for young children

(1) Where a local authority register a person under section 71(1)(*b*) they shall impose such reasonable requirements on him as they consider appropriate in his case.

(2) Where a person is registered under section 71(1)(*b*) with respect to different premises within the area of the same authority, this section applies separately in relation to each registration.

(3) In imposing requirements on him, the authority shall—

(*a*) specify the maximum number of children, or the maximum number of children within specified age groups, who may be looked after on the premises;
(*b*) require him to secure that the premises, and the equipment used in them, are adequately maintained and kept safe;
(*c*) require him to notify the authority of any change in the facilities which he provides or in the period during which he provides them;
(*d*) specify the number of persons required to assist in looking after children on the premises;
(*e*) require him to keep a record of the name and address of—
  (i) any child looked after on the registered premises;
  (ii) any person who assists in looking after any such child; and
  (iii) any person who lives, or is likely at any time to be living, at those premises;
(*f*) require him to notify the authority of any change in the persons mentioned in paragraph (*e*)(ii) and (iii).

(4) The Secretary of State may by regulations make provision as to—
(*a*) requirements which must be imposed by local authorities under this section in prescribed circumstances;
(*b*) requirements of such descriptions as may be prescribed which must not be imposed by local authorities under this section.

(5) In subsection (3), references to children looked after are to children looked after in accordance with the provision of day care made by the registered person.

(6) In determining the maximum number of children to be specified under subsection (3)(*a*), the authority shall take account of the number of other children who may at any time be on the premises.

(7) Where, in addition to the requirements mentioned in subsection (3), a local authority impose other requirements, those other requirements must not be incompatible with any of the subsection (3) requirements.

(8) A local authority may at any time vary any requirement imposed under this section, impose any additional requirement or remove any requirement.

---

**Definitions** For 'local authority' see 105(1); for 'children looked after' see sub-s (5); for 'day care' see s 71(2)(b) and s 18(4) as applied to the whole Act by s 105(1).

**Reference** For 'premises' see the note to s 72.

---

## 74 Cancellation of registration

(1) A local authority may at any time cancel the registration of any person under section 71(1)(*a*) if—
(*a*) it appears to them that the circumstances of the case are such that they would be justified in refusing to register that person as a child minder;
(*b*) the care provided by that person when looking after any child as a child minder is, in the opinion of the authority, seriously inadequate having regard to the needs of that child; or
(*c*) that person has—

(i) contravened, or failed to comply with, any requirement imposed on him under section 72; or

(ii) failed to pay any annual fee under paragraph 7 of Schedule 9 within the prescribed time.

(2) A local authority may at any time cancel the registration of any person under section 71(1)(*b*) with respect to particular premises if—

(*a*) it appears to them that the circumstances of the case are such that they would be justified in refusing to register that person with respect to those premises;

(*b*) the day care provided by that person on those premises is, in the opinion of the authority, seriously inadequate having regard to the needs of the children concerned; or

(*c*) that person has—

(i) contravened, or failed to comply with, any requirement imposed on him under section 73; or

(ii) failed to pay an annual fee under paragraph 7 of Schedule 9 within the prescribed time.

(3) A local authority may at any time cancel all registrations of any person under section 71(1)(*b*) if it appears to them that the circumstances of the case are such that they would be justified in refusing to register that person with respect to any premises.

(4) Where a requirement to carry out repairs or make alterations or additions has been imposed on a registered person under section 72 or 73, his registration shall not be cancelled on the ground that the premises are not fit to be used for looking after children if—

(*a*) the time set for complying with the requirements has not expired, and

(*b*) it is shown that the condition of the premises is due to the repairs not having been carried out or the alterations or additions not having been made.

(5) Any cancellation under this section must be in writing.

(6) In considering the needs of any child for the purposes of subsection (1)(*b*) or (2)(*b*), a local authority shall, in particular, have regard to the child's religious persuasion, racial origin and cultural and linguistic background.

---

**Definitions** For 'local authority s 105(1); for 'child minder' see s 71(2)(a); for 'needs of any child' see sub-s (6).

**Reference** For 'premises' see the note to s 72.

---

## 75 Protection of children in an emergency

(1) If—

(*a*) a local authority apply to the court for an order—

(i) cancelling a registered person's registration;

(ii) varying any requirement imposed on a registered person under section 72 or 73; or

(iii) removing a requirement or imposing an additional requirement on such a person; and

(*b*) it appears to the court that a child who is being, or may be, looked after by that person, or (as the case may be) in accordance with the provision for day care made by that person, is suffering, or is likely to suffer, significant harm,

the court may make the order.

(2) Any such cancellation, variation, removal or imposition shall have effect from the date on which the order is made.

(3) An application under subsection (1) may be made *ex parte* and shall be supported by a written statement of the authority's reasons for making it.

(4) Where an order is made under this section, the authority shall serve on the registered person, as soon as is reasonably practicable after the making of the order—

(*a*) notice of the order and of its terms; and

(*b*) a copy of the statement of the authority's reasons which supported their application for the order.

(5) Where the court imposes or varies any requirement under subsection (1), the requirement, or the requirement as varied, shall be treated for all purposes, other than those of section 77, as if it had been imposed under section 72 or (as the case may be) 73 by the authority concerned.

---

**Definitions** For 'local authority' and 'child' see s 105(1); for 'court' see s 92(7); for 'harm' see s 31(9) as applied to the whole Act by s 105(1) and as to whether harm is significant see s 31(10) as applied to the whole Act by s 105(1).

**Reference** For jurisdiction of courts see s 92 and Sch 11, 9.1 ff. For service of notices under the Act generally see s 105(8)-(10).

---

### 76 Inspection

(1) Any person authorised to do so by a local authority may at any reasonable time enter—

(*a*) any domestic premises within the authority's area on which child minding is at any time carried on; or

(*b*) any premises within their area on which day care for children under the age of eight is at any time provided.

(2) Where a local authority have reasonable cause to believe that a child is being looked after on any premises within their area in contravention of this Part, any person authorised to do so by the authority may enter those premises at any reasonable time.

(3) Any person entering premises under this section may inspect—

(*a*) the premises;

(*b*) any children being looked after on the premises;

(*c*) the arrangements made for their welfare; and

(*d*) any records relating to them which are kept as a result of this Part.

(4) Every local authority shall exercise their power to inspect the premises mentioned in subsection (1) at least once every year.

(5) Any person inspecting any records under this section—

(*a*) shall be entitled at any reasonable time to have access to, and inspect and check the operation of, any computer and any associated apparatus or material which is, or has been, in use in connection with the records in question; and

(*b*) may require—

(i) the person by whom or on whose behalf the computer is or has been so used; or

(ii) any person having charge of, or otherwise concerned with the operation of, the computer, apparatus or material,

to afford him such reasonable assistance as he may require.

(6) A person exercising any power conferred by this section shall, if so required, produce some duly authenticated document showing his authority to do so.

(7) Any person who intentionally obstructs another in the exercise of any such power shall be guilty of an offence and liable on summary conviction to a fine not exceeding level 3 on the standard scale.

---

**Definitions** For 'local authority' and 'child' see s 105(1); for 'domestic premises', see s 71(12) as applied to the whole Act by s 105(1); for 'child minder' see s 71(2)(a); for 'day care' see s 71(2)(b).

**References** 'This Part' ie Part X ss 71-79 and Sch 9 (child minding and day care for young children). For power to issue warrant to authorise a constable to assist in exercising the power under sub-ss (1) and (2) see s 102. For 'the standard scale see the Criminal Justice Act 1982 s 37(2) (3) as amended; 'level 3' ie £400.

---

## 77 Appeals

(1) Not less than 14 days before—

(*a*) refusing an application for registration under section 71;

(*b*) cancelling any such registration;

(*c*) refusing consent under paragraph 2 of Schedule 9;

(*d*) imposing, removing or varying any requirement under section 72 or 73; or

(*e*) refusing to grant any application for the variation or removal of any such requirement,

the authority concerned shall send to the applicant, or (as the case may be) registered person, notice in writing of their intention to take the step in question ("the step").

(2) Every such notice shall—

(*a*) give the authority's reasons for proposing to take the step; and

(*b*) inform the person concerned of his rights under this section.

(3) Where the recipient of such a notice informs the authority in writing of his desire to object to the step being taken, the authority shall afford him an opportunity to do so.

(4) Any objection made under subsection (3) may be made in person or by a representative.

(5) If the authority, after giving the person concerned an opportunity to object to the step being taken, decide nevertheless to take it they shall send him written notice of their decision.

(6) A person aggrieved by the taking of any step mentioned in subsection (1) may appeal against it to the court.

(7) Where the court imposes or varies any requirement under subsection (8) or (9) the requirement, or the requirement as varied, shall be treated for all purposes (other than this section) as if it had been imposed by the authority concerned.

(8) Where the court allows an appeal against the refusal or cancellation of any registration under section 71 it may impose requirements under section 72 or (as the case may be) 73.

(9) Where the court allows an appeal against such a requirement it may, instead of cancelling the requirement, vary it.

(10) In Scotland, an appeal under subsection (6) shall be by summary application to the sheriff and shall be brought within 21 days from the date of the step to which the appeal relates.

(11) A step of a kind mentioned in subsection (1)(*b*) or (*d*) shall not take effect until the expiry of the time within which an appeal may be brought under this section or, where such an appeal is brought, before its determination.

---

**Definitions** For 'local authority' see s 105(1); for 'the step' see sub-s(1). For 'court' see s 92(7).

**Reference** For jurisdiction of courts see s 92 and Sch 11, para 9.1 ff.

---

## 78 Offences

(1) No person shall provide day care for children under the age of eight on any premises within the area of a local authority unless he is registered by the authority under section 71(1)(*b*) with respect to those premises.

(2) If any person contravenes subsection (1) without reasonable excuse, he shall be guilty of an offence.

(3) No person shall act as a child minder on domestic premises within the area of a local authority unless he is registered by the authority under section 71(1)(*a*).

(4) Where it appears to a local authority that a person has contravened subsection (3), they may serve a notice ("an enforcement notice") on him.

(5) An enforcement notice shall have effect for a period of one year beginning with the date on which it is served.

(6) If a person with respect to whom an enforcement notice is in force contravenes subsection (3) without reasonable excuse, he shall be guilty of an offence.

(7) Subsection (6) applies whether or not the subsequent contravention occurs within the area of the authority who served the enforcement notice.

(8) Any person who without reasonable excuse contravenes, or otherwise fails to comply with, any requirement imposed on him under section 72 or 73 shall be guilty of an offence.

(9) If any person—

(*a*) acts as a child minder on domestic premises at any time when he is disqualified by regulations made under paragraph 2 of Schedule 9; or

(*b*) contravenes any of sub-paragraphs (3) to (5) of paragraph 2, he shall be guilty of an offence.

(10) Where a person contravenes sub-paragraph (3) of paragraph 2 he shall not be guilty of an offence under this section if he proves that he did not know, and had no reasonable grounds for believing, that the person in question was living or employed in the household.

(11) Where a person contravenes sub-paragraph (5) of paragraph 2 he shall not be guilty of an offence under this section if he proves that he did not know, and had no reasonable grounds for believing, that the person whom he was employing was disqualified.

(12) A person guilty of an offence under this section shall be liable on summary conviction—

(*a*) in the case of an offence under subsection (8), to a fine not exceeding level 4 on the standard scale;
(*b*) in the case of an offence under subsection (9), to imprisonment for a term not exceeding six months, or to a fine not exceeding level 5 on the standard scale, or to both; and
(*c*) in the case of any other offence, to a fine not exceeding level 5 on the standard scale.

---

**Definitions** For 'day care' see s 71(2)(b) and s 18(4) as applied to the whole Act by s 105(1); for 'premises', 'domestic premises' see s 71(12) as applied to the whole Act by s 105(1); for 'local authority' see s 105(1); for 'child minder' see s 71(2)(a) for 'enforcement notice' see sub-s (4).

**Reference** For 'the standard scale' see the Criminal Justice Act 1982 s 37(2) (3) as amended; 'level 4' ie £1000; 'level 5' ie £2,000.

---

## 79 Application of this Part to Scotland

In the application to Scotland of this Part—

(*a*) "the court" means the sheriff;
(*b*) "day care" means any form of care or activity supervised by a responsible person provided for children during the day (whether or not it is provided on a regular basis);
(*c*) "education authority" has the same meaning as in the Education (Scotland) Act 1980;
(*d*) "local authority foster parent" means a foster parent with whom a child is placed by a local authority;
(*e*) for references to a person having parental responsibility for a child there shall be substituted references to a person in whom parental rights and duties relating to the child are vested; and
(*f*) for references to fostering a child privately there shall be substituted references to maintaining a foster child within the meaning of the Foster Children (Scotland) Act 1984.

## Part XI

### Secretary of State's Supervisory Functions and Responsibilities

**80 Inspection of children's homes etc by persons authorised by Secretary of State**

(1) The Secretary of State may cause to be inspected from time to time any—

(*a*) children's home;

(*b*) premises in which a child who is being looked after by a local authority is living;

(*c*) premises in which a child who is being accommodated by or on behalf of a local education authority or voluntary organisation is living;

(*d*) premises in which a child who is being accommodated by or on behalf of a health authority is living;

(*e*) premises in which a child is living with a person with whom he has been placed by an adoption agency;

(*f*) premises in which a child who is a protected child is, or will be, living;

(*g*) premises in which a privately fostered child, or child who is treated as a foster child by virtue of paragraph 9 of Schedule 8, is living or in which it is proposed that he will live;

(*h*) premises on which any person is acting as a child minder;

(*i*) premises with respect to which a person is registered under section 71(1)(*b*);

(*j*) residential care home, nursing home or mental nursing home required to be registered under the Registered Homes Act 1984 and used to accommodate children;

(*k*) premises which are provided by a local authority and in which any service is provided by that authority under Part III;

(*l*) independent school providing accommodation for any child.

(2) An inspection under this section shall be conducted by a person authorised to do so by the Secretary of State.

(3) An officer of a local authority shall not be so authorised except with the consent of that authority.

(4) The Secretary of State may require any person of a kind mentioned in subsection (5) to furnish him with such information, or allow him to inspect such records (in whatever form they are held), relating to—

(*a*) any premises to which subsection (1) or, in relation to Scotland, subsection (1)(*h*) or (*i*) applies;

(*b*) any child who is living in any such premises;

(*c*) the discharge by the Secretary of State of any of his functions under this Act; or

(*d*) the discharge by any local authority of any of their functions under this Act,

as the Secretary of State may at any time direct.

(5) The persons are any—

(*a*) local authority;

(*b*) voluntary organisation;

(*c*) person carrying on a children's home;

(*d*) proprietor of an independent school;

(*e*) person fostering any privately fostered child or providing accommodation for a child on behalf of a local authority, local education authority, health authority or voluntary organisation;

(*f*) local education authority providing accommodation for any child;

(*g*) person employed in a teaching or administrative capacity at any educational establishment (whether or not maintained by a local education authority) at which a child is accommodated on behalf of a local authority or local education authority;

(*h*) person who is the occupier of any premises in which any person acts as a child minder (within the meaning of Part X) or provides day care for young children (within the meaning of that Part);

(*i*) person carrying on any home of a kind mentioned in subsection (1)(*j*).

(6) Any person inspecting any home or other premises under this section may—

(*a*) inspect the children there; and

(*b*) make such examination into the state and management of the home or premises and the treatment of the children there as he thinks fit.

(7) Any person authorised by the Secretary of State to exercise the power to inspect records conferred by subsection (4)—

(*a*) shall be entitled at any reasonable time to have access to, and inspect and check the operation of, any computer and any associated apparatus or material which is or has been in use in connection with the records in question; and

(*b*) may require—

(i) the person by whom or on whose behalf the computer is or has been so used; or

(ii) any person having charge of, or otherwise concerned with the operation of, the computer, apparatus or material,

to afford him such reasonable assistance as he may require.

(8) A person authorised to inspect any premises under this section shall have a right to enter the premises for that purpose, and for any purpose specified in subsection (4), at any reasonable time.

(9) Any person exercising that power shall, if so required, produce some duly authenticated document showing his authority to do so.

(10) Any person who intentionally obstructs another in the exercise of that power shall be guilty of an offence and liable on summary conviction to a fine not exceeding level 3 on the standard scale.

(11) The Secretary of State may by order provide for subsections (1), (4) and (6) not to apply in relation to such homes, or other premises, as may be specified in the order.

(12) Without prejudice to section 104, any such order may make different provision with respect to each of those subsections.

---

**Definitions** For 'children's home' see s 63(3) as applied to the whole Act by s 105(1); for 'child', 'local authority', 'local education authority', 'voluntary organisation', 'health authority', 'adoption agency', 'protected child', 'residential care home', 'nursing home', 'mental nursing home', 'independent school', 'school' and 'service' see s 105(1); for 'child who is looked after by a local authority' see s 22(1); for 'accommodation provided by or on behalf of a local authority' see s 105(5); for 'privately fostered child' see s 66(1) as applied to the whole Act by s 105(1); for 'child minder' see s 71(2)(a) as applied to the whole Act by s 105(1).

**References** 'Part III' ie ss 17-30 and Sch 2 (local authority support for children and families).

For 'premises' see the note to s 72. 'Part X' ie ss 71-79 and Sch 9 (child minding and day care for young children). For proprietor of an independent school see Education Act 1944 s 114(1). For power to issue warrant to authorise a constable to assist in exercising the power under this section see s 102. For 'the standard scale' see the Criminal Justice Act 1982 s 37(2) (3) as amended; 'level 3' ie £400.

---

## 81 Inquiries

(1) The Secretary of State may cause an inquiry to be held into any matter connected with—

(*a*) the functions of the social services committee of a local authority, in so far as those functions relate to children;
(*b*) the functions of an adoption agency;
(*c*) the functions of a voluntary organisation, in so far as those functions relate to children;
(*d*) a registered children's home or voluntary home;
(*e*) a residential care home, nursing home or mental nursing home, so far as it provides accommodation for children;
(*f*) a home provided by the Secretary of State under section 82(5);
(*g*) the detention of a child under section 53 of the Children and Young Persons Act 1933.

(2) Before an inquiry is begun, the Secretary of State may direct that it shall be held in private.

(3) Where no direction has been given, the person holding the inquiry may if he thinks fit hold it, or any part of it, in private.

(4) Subsections (2) to (5) of section 250 of the Local Government Act 1972 (powers in relation to local inquiries) shall apply in relation to an inquiry under this section as they apply in relation to a local inquiry under that section.

(5) In this section "functions" includes powers and duties which a person has otherwise than by virtue of any enactment.

---

**Definitions** For 'functions' see sub-s (5); for 'local authority', 'child', 'adoption agency', 'voluntary organisation', 'residential care home', 'nursing home', 'mental nursing home', see s 105(1); for 'registered children's home' see s 63(8); for 'voluntary home' see s 60(3).

---

## 82 Financial support by Secretary of State

(1) The Secretary of State may (with the consent of the Treasury) defray or contribute towards—

(*a*) any fees or expenses incurred by any person undergoing approved child care training;
(*b*) any fees charged, or expenses incurred, by any person providing approved child care training or preparing material for use in connection with such training; or
(*c*) the cost of maintaining any person undergoing such training.

(2) The Secretary of State may make grants to local authorities in respect of expenditure incurred by them in providing secure accommodation in community homes other than assisted community homes.

(3) Where—

(*a*) a grant has been made under subsection (2) with respect to any secure accommodation; but

(*b*) the grant is not used for the purpose for which it was made or the accommodation is not used as, or ceases to be used as, secure accommodation,

the Secretary of State may (with the consent of the Treasury) require the authority concerned to repay the grant, in whole or in part.

(4) The Secretary of State may make grants to voluntary organisations towards—

(*a*) expenditure incurred by them in connection with the establishment, maintenance or improvement of voluntary homes which, at the time when the expenditure was incurred—

(i) were assisted community homes; or

(ii) were designated as such; or

(*b*) expenses incurred in respect of the borrowing of money to defray any such expenditure.

(5) The Secretary of State may arrange for the provision, equipment and maintenance of homes for the accommodation of children who are in need of particular facilities and services which—

(*a*) are or will be provided in those homes; and

(*b*) in the opinion of the Secretary of State, are unlikely to be readily available in community homes.

(6) In this Part—

"child care training" means training undergone by any person with a view to, or in the course of—

(*a*) his employment for the purposes of any of the functions mentioned in section 83(9) or in connection with the adoption of children or with the accommodation of children in a residential care home, nursing home or mental nursing home; or

(*b*) his employment by a voluntary organisation for similar purposes;

"approved child care training" means child care training which is approved by the Secretary of State; and

"secure accommodation" means accommodation provided for the purpose of restricting the liberty of children.

(7) Any grant made under this section shall be of such amount, and shall be subject to such conditions, as the Secretary of State may (with the consent of the Treasury) determine.

---

**Definitions** For 'child care training', 'approved child care training', 'secure accommodation' see sub-s(6); for 'local authority', 'voluntary organisation' see s 105(1); for 'community home' and 'assisted community home' see s 53 as applied to the whole Act by s 105(1); for 'voluntary home' see s 60(3).

**Reference** 'This Part' ie Part XI ss 80-84 (Secretary of State's supervisory functions and responsibilities).

---

## 83 Research and returns of information

(1) The Secretary of State may conduct, or assist other persons in conducting, research into any matter connected with—

(*a*) his functions, or the functions of local authorities, under the enactments mentioned in subsection (9);
(*b*) the adoption of children; or
(*c*) the accommodation of children in a residential care home, nursing home or mental nursing home.

(2) Any local authority may conduct, or assist other persons in conducting, research into any matter connected with—

(*a*) their functions under the enactments mentioned in subsection (9);
(*b*) the adoption of children; or
(*c*) the accommodation of children in a residential care home, nursing home or mental nursing home.

(3) Every local authority shall, at such times and in such form as the Secretary of State may direct, transmit to him such particulars as he may require with respect to—

(*a*) the performance by the local authority of all or any of their functions—
  (i) under the enactments mentioned in subsection (9); or
  (ii) in connection with the accommodation of children in a residential care home, nursing home or mental nursing home; and
(*b*) the children in relation to whom the authority have exercised those functions.

(4) Every voluntary organisation shall, at such times and in such form as the Secretary of State may direct, transmit to him such particulars as he may require with respect to children accommodated by them or on their behalf.

(5) The Secretary of State may direct the clerk of each magistrates' court to which the direction is expressed to relate to transmit—

(*a*) to such person as may be specified in the direction; and
(*b*) at such times and in such form as he may direct,

such particulars as he may require with respect to proceedings of the court which relate to children.

(6) The Secretary of State shall in each year lay before Parliament a consolidated and classified abstract of the information transmitted to him under subsections (3) to (5).

(7) The Secretary of State may institute research designed to provide information on which requests for information under this section may be based.

(8) The Secretary of State shall keep under review the adequacy of the provision of child care training and for the purpose shall receive and consider any information from or representations made by—

(*a*) the Central Council for Education and Training in Social Work;
(*b*) such representatives of local authorities as appear to him to be appropriate; or
(*c*) such other persons or organisations as appear to him to be appropriate,

concerning the provision of such training.

(9) The enactments are—

(*a*) this Act;

(*b*) the Children and Young Persons Acts 1933 to 1969;

(*c*) section 116 of the Mental Health Act 1983 (so far as it relates to children looked after by local authorities);

(*d*) section 10 of the Mental Health (Scotland) Act 1984 (so far as it relates to children for whom local authorities have responsibility).

---

**Definitions** For 'functions', 'local authority', 'child', 'residential care home', 'nursing home', 'mental nursing home' ,'voluntary organisation' see s 105(1); for 'child care training' see s 82(6).

---

## 84 Local authority failure to comply with statutory duty: default power of Secretary of State

(1) If the Secretary of State is satisfied that any local authority has failed, without reasonable excuse, to comply with any of the duties imposed on them by or under this Act he may make an order declaring that authority to be in default with respect to that duty.

(2) An order under subsection (1) shall give the Secretary of State's reasons for making it.

(3) An order under subsection (1) may contain such directions for the purpose of ensuring that the duty is complied with, within such period as may be specified in the order, as appears to the Secretary of State to be necessary.

(4) Any such directions shall, on the application of the Secretary of State, be enforceable by mandamus.

---

**Definition** For 'local authority' see s 105(1).
**Reference** See generally para 5.54.

---

# PART XII

## MISCELLANEOUS AND GENERAL

*Notification of children accommodated in certain establishments*

## 85 Children accommodated by health authorities and local education authorities

(1) Where a child is provided with accommodation by any health authority or local education authority ("the accommodating authority")—

(*a*) for a consecutive period of at least three months; or

(*b*) with the intention, on the part of that authority, of accommodating him for such a period,

the accommodating authority shall notify the responsible authority.

(2) Where subsection (1) applies with respect to a child, the accommodating authority shall also notify the responsible authority when they cease to accommodate the child.

(3) In this section "the responsible authority" means—

(*a*) the local authority appearing to the accommodating authority to be the authority within whose area the child was ordinarily resident immediately before being accommodated; or

(*b*) where it appears to the accommodating authority that a child was not ordinarily resident within the area of any local authority, the local authority within whose area the accommodation is situated.

(4) Where a local authority have been notified under this section, they shall—

(*a*) take such steps as are reasonably practicable to enable them to determine whether the child's welfare is adequately safeguarded and promoted while he is accommodated by the accommodating authority; and

(*b*) consider the extent to which (if at all) they should exercise any of their functions under this Act with respect to the child.

---

**Definitions** For 'child', 'health authority', 'local education authority', 'local authority' see s 105(1); for 'the accommodating authority' see sub-s (1); for 'the responsible authority' see sub-s (3); for 'ordinary residence' see s 105(6).

---

**86 Children accommodated in residential care, nursing or mental nursing homes**

(1) Where a child is provided with accommodation in any residential care home, nursing home or mental nursing home—

(*a*) for a consecutive period of at least three months; or

(*b*) with the intention, on the part of the person taking the decision to accommodate him, of accommodating him for such period,

the person carrying on the home shall notify the local authority within whose area the home is carried on.

(2) Where subsection (1) applies with respect to a child, the person carrying on the home shall also notify that authority when he ceases to accommodate the child in the home.

(3) Where a local authority have been notified under this section, they shall—

(*a*) take such steps as are reasonably practicable to enable them to determine whether the child's welfare is adequately safeguarded and promoted while he is accommodated in the home; and

(*b*) consider the extent to which (if at all) they should exercise any of their functions under this Act with respect to the child.

(4) If the person carrying on any home fails, without reasonable excuse, to comply with this section he shall be guilty of an offence.

(5) A person authorised by a local authority may enter any residential care home, nursing home or mental nursing home within the authority's area for the purpose of establishing whether the requirements of this section have been complied with.

(6) Any person who intentionally obstructs another in the exercise of the power of entry shall be guilty of an offence.

(7) Any person exercising the power of entry shall, if so required, produce some duly authenticated document showing his authority to do so.

(8) Any person committing an offence under this section shall be liable on summary conviction to a fine not exceeding level 3 on the standard scale.

---

**Definitions** For 'child', 'residential care home', 'nursing home', 'mental nursing home', 'local authority' see s 105(1).

**References** For power to issue warrant to authorise a constable to assist in exercising the power under this section see s 102. For 'the standard scale' see the Criminal Justice Act 1982 s 37(2) (3) as amended; 'level 3' ie £400.

---

## 87 Welfare of children accommodated in independent schools

(1) It shall be the duty of—

(*a*) the proprietor of any independent school which provides accommodation for any child; and

(*b*) any person who is not the proprietor of such a school but who is responsible for conducting it,

to safeguard and promote the child's welfare.

(2) Subsection (1) does not apply in relation to a school which is a children's home or a residential care home.

(3) Where accommodation is provided for a child by an independent school within the area of a local authority, the authority shall take such steps as are reasonably practicable to enable them to determine whether the child's welfare is adequately safeguarded and promoted while he is accommodated by the school.

(4) Where a local authority are of the opinion that there has been a failure to comply with subsection (1) in relation to a child provided with accommodation by a school within their area, they shall notify the Secretary of State.

(5) Any person authorised by a local authority may, for the purpose of enabling the authority to discharge their duty under this section, enter at any reasonable time any independent school within their area which provides accommodation for any child.

(6) Any person entering an independent school in exercise of the power conferred by subsection (5) may carry out such inspection of premises, children and records as is prescribed by regulations made by the Secretary of State for the purposes of this section.

(7) Any person exercising that power shall, if asked to do so, produce some duly authenticated document showing his authority to do so.

(8) Any person authorised by the regulations to inspect records—

(*a*) shall be entitled at any reasonable time to have access to, and inspect and check the operation of, any computer and any associated apparatus or material which is or has been in use in connection with the records in question; and

(*b*) may require—

- (i) the person by whom or on whose behalf the computer is or has been so used; or
- (ii) any person having charge of, or otherwise concerned with the operation of, the computer, apparatus or material,

to afford him such assistance as he may reasonably require.

(9) Any person who intentionally obstructs another in the exercise of any power conferred by this section or the regulations shall be guilty of an offence

and liable on summary conviction to a fine not exceeding level 3 on the standard scale.

(10) In this section "proprietor" has the same meaning as in the Education Act 1944.

---

**Definitions** For 'proprietor' see sub-s (10); for 'independent school', 'school', 'child', 'residential care home' and 'local authority' see s 105(1).

**References** See generally para 12.15. For independent schools which are children's homes see s 63(6). For power to issue warrant to authorise a constable to assist in exercising the power under this section see s 102. For 'the standard scale' see the Criminal Justice Act 1982 s 37(2) (3) as amended: 'level 3' ie £400.

---

*Adoption*

## 88 Amendments of adoption legislation

(1) The Adoption Act 1976 shall have effect subject to the amendments made by Part I of Schedule 10.

(2) The Adoption (Scotland) Act 1978 shall have effect subject to the amendments made by Part II of Schedule 10.

*Paternity tests*

## 89 Tests to establish paternity

In section 20 of the Family Law Reform Act 1969 (power of court to require use of tests to determine paternity), the following subsections shall be inserted after subsection (1)—

"(1A) Where—

(*a*) an application is made for a direction under this section; and
(*b*) the person whose paternity is in issue is under the age of eighteen when the application is made,

the application shall specify who is to carry out the tests.

(1B) In the case of a direction made on an application to which subsection (1A) applies the court shall—

(*a*) specify, as the person who is to carry out the tests, the person specified in the application; or
(*b*) where the court considers that it would be inappropriate to specify that person (whether because to specify him would be incompatible with any provision made by or under regulations made under section 22 of this Act or for any other reason), decline to give the direction applied for."

---

**Date in force** 16th November 1989

---

*Criminal care and supervision orders*

## 90 Care and supervision orders in criminal proceedings

(1) The power of a court to make an order under subsection (2) of section 1 of the Children and Young Persons Act 1969 (care proceedings in juvenile

courts) where it is of the opinion that the condition mentioned in paragraph (*f*) of that subsection ("the offence condition") is satisfied is hereby abolished.

(2) The powers of the court to make care orders—

(*a*) under section 7(7)(*a*) of the Children and Young Persons Act 1969 (alteration in treatment of young offenders etc); and

(*b*) under section 15(1) of that Act, on discharging a supervision order made under section 7(7)(*b*) of that Act,

are hereby abolished.

(3) The powers given by that Act to include requirements in supervision orders shall have effect subject to amendments made by Schedule 12.

*Effect and duration of orders etc*

**91 Effect and duration of orders etc**

(1) The making of a residence order with respect to a child who is the subject of a care order discharges the care order.

(2) The making of a care order with respect to a child who is the subject of any section 8 order discharges that order.

(3) The making of a care order with respect to a child who is the subject of a supervision order discharges that other order.

(4) The making of a care order with respect to a child who is a ward of court brings that wardship to an end.

(5) The making of a care order with respect to a child who is the subject of a school attendance order made under section 37 of the Education Act 1944 discharges the school attendance order.

(6) Where an emergency protection order is made with respect to a child who is in care, the care order shall have effect subject to the emergency protection order.

(7) Any order made under section 4(1) or 5(1) shall continue in force until the child reaches the age of eighteen, unless it is brought to an end earlier.

(8) Any—

(*a*) agreement under section 4; or

(*b*) appointment under section 5(3) or (4),

shall continue in force until the child reaches the age of eighteen, unless it is brought to an end earlier.

(9) An order under Schedule 1 has effect as specified in that Schedule.

(10) A section 8 order shall, if it would otherwise still be in force, cease to have effect when the child reaches the age of sixteen, unless it is to have effect beyond that age by virtue of section 9(6).

(11) Where a section 8 order has effect with respect to a child who has reached the age of sixteen, it shall, if it would otherwise still be in force, cease to have effect when he reaches the age of eighteen.

(12) Any care order, other than an interim care order, shall continue in force until the child reaches the age of eighteen, unless it is brought to an end earlier.

(13) Any order made under any other provision of this Act in relation to a child shall, if it would otherwise still be in force, cease to have effect when he reaches the age of eighteen.

(14) On disposing of any application for an order under this Act, the court may (whether or not it makes any other order in response to the application) order that no application for an order under this Act of any specified kind may be made with respect to the child concerned by any person named in the order without leave of the court.

(15) Where an application ("the previous application") has been made for—

(*a*) the discharge of a care order;
(*b*) the discharge of a supervision order;
(*c*) the discharge of an education supervision order;
(*d*) the substitution of a supervision order for a care order; or
(*e*) a child assessment order,

no further application of a kind mentioned in paragraphs (*a*) to (*e*) may be made with respect to the child concerned, without leave of the court, unless the period between the disposal of the previous application and the making of the further application exceeds six months.

(16) Subsection (15) does not apply to applications made in relation to interim orders.

(17) Where—

(*a*) a person has made an application for an order under section 34;
(*b*) the application has been refused; and
(*c*) a period of less than six months has elapsed since the refusal,

that person may not make a further application for such an order with respect to the same child, unless he has obtained the leave of the court.

---

**Definitions** For 'residence order' see s 8(1); for 'child' see s 105(1); for 'care order' see s 31(11) and s 105(1); for 'a section 8 order see s 8(2); for 'supervision order' see s 31(11); for 'emergency protection order' see s 44 as applied to the whole Act by s 105(1); for 'court' see s 92(7); for 'education supervision order' see s 36; for 'child assessment order' see s 43(2).

**References** For the duration of supervision orders see also Sch 3 Pt II para 6. For the discharge and variation of care and supervision orders see s 39. For interim orders see s 38.

---

*Jurisdiction and procedure etc*

## 92 Jurisdiction of courts

(1) The name "domestic proceedings", given to certain proceedings in magistrates' courts, is hereby changed to "family proceedings" and the names "domestic court" and "domestic court panel" are hereby changed to "family proceedings court" and "family panel", respectively.

(2) Proceedings under this Act shall be treated as family proceedings in relation to magistrates' courts.

(3) Subsection (2) is subject to the provisions of section 65(1) and (2) of the Magistrates' Courts Act 1980 (proceedings which may be treated as not being family proceedings), as amended by this Act.

(4) A magistrates' court shall not be competent to entertain any application, or make any order, involving the administration or application of—

(*a*) any property belonging to or held in trust for a child; or
(*b*) the income of any such property.

(5) The powers of a magistrates' court under section 63(2) of the Act of 1980 to suspend or rescind orders shall not apply in relation to any order made under this Act.

(6) Part I of Schedule 11 makes provision, including provision for the Lord Chancellor to make orders, with respect to the jurisdiction of courts and justices of the peace in relation to—

(*a*) proceedings under this Act; and
(*b*) proceedings under certain other enactments.

(7) For the purposes of this Act "the court" means the High Court, a county court or a magistrates' court.

(8) Subsection (7) is subject to the provision made by or under Part I of Schedule 11 and to any express provision as to the jurisdiction of any court made by any other provision of this Act.

(9) The Lord Chancellor may by order make provision for the principal registry of the Family Division of the High Court to be treated as if it were a county court for such purposes of this Act, or of any provision made under this Act, as may be specified in the order.

(10) Any order under subsection (9) may make such provision as the Lord Chancellor thinks expedient for the purpose of applying (with or without modifications) provisions which apply in relation to the procedure in county courts to the principal registry when it acts as if it were a county court.

(11) Part II of Schedule 11 makes amendments consequential on this section.

### 93 Rules of court

(1) An authority having power to make rules of court may make such provision for giving effect to—

(*a*) this Act;
(*b*) the provisions of any statutory instrument made under this Act; or
(*c*) any amendment made by this Act in any other enactment,

as appears to that authority to be necessary or expedient.

(2) The rules may, in particular, make provision—

(*a*) with respect to the procedure to be followed in any relevant proceedings (including the manner in which any application is to be made or other proceedings commenced);
(*b*) as to the persons entitled to participate in any relevant proceedings, whether as parties to the proceedings or by being given the opportunity to make representations to the court;
(*c*) with respect to the documents and information to be furnished, and notices to be given, in connection with any relevant proceedings;
(*d*) applying (with or without modification) enactments which govern the procedure to be followed with respect to proceedings brought on a complaint made to a magistrates' court to relevant proceedings in such a court brought otherwise than on a complaint;
(*e*) with respect to preliminary hearings;
(*f*) for the service outside the United Kingdom, in such circumstances

and in such manner as may be prescribed, of any notice of proceedings in a magistrates' court;

(*g*) for the exercise by magistrates' courts, in such circumstances as may be prescribed, of such powers as may be prescribed (even though a party to the proceedings in question is outside England and Wales);

(*h*) enabling the court, in such circumstances as may be prescribed, to proceed on any application even though the respondent has not been given notice of the proceedings;

(*i*) authorising a single justice to discharge the functions of a magistrates' court with respect to such relevant proceedings as may be prescribed;

(*j*) authorising a magistrates' court to order any of the parties to such relevant proceedings as may be prescribed, in such circumstances as may be prescribed, to pay the whole or part of the costs of all or any of the other parties.

(3) In subsection (2)—

"notice of proceedings" means a summons or such other notice of proceedings as is required; and "given", in relation to a summons, means "served";

"prescribed" means prescribed by the rules; and

"relevant proceedings" means any application made, or proceedings brought, under any of the provisions mentioned in paragraphs (*a*) to (*c*) of subsection (1) and any part of such proceedings.

(4) This section and any other power in this Act to make rules of court are not to be taken as in any way limiting any other power of the authority in question to make rules of court.

(5) When making any rules under this section an authority shall be subject to the same requirements as to consultation (if any) as apply when the authority makes rules under its general rule making power.

---

**Definitions** For 'notice of proceedings', 'prescribed' and 'relevant proceedings' see sub-s (3).

---

## 94 Appeals

(1) An appeal shall lie to the High Court against—

(*a*) the making by a magistrates' court of any order under this Act; or

(*b*) any refusal by a magistrates' court to make such an order.

(2) Where a magistrates' court has power, in relation to any proceedings under this Act, to decline jurisdiction because it considers that the case can more conveniently be dealt with by another court, no appeal shall lie against any exercise by that magistrates' court of that power.

(3) Subsection (1) does not apply in relation to an interim order for periodical payments made under Schedule 1.

(4) On an appeal under this section, the High Court may make such orders as may be necessary to give effect to its determination of the appeal.

(5) Where an order is made under subsection (4) the High Court may also make such incidental or consequential orders as appear to it to be just.

(6) Where an appeal from a magistrates' court relates to an order for the making of periodical payments, the High Court may order that its

determination of the appeal shall have effect from such date as it thinks fit to specify in the order.

(7) The date so specified must not be earlier than the earliest date allowed in accordance with rules of court made for the purposes of this section.

(8) Where, on an appeal under this section in respect of an order requiring a person to make periodical payments, the High Court reduces the amount of those payments or discharges the order—

(*a*) it may order the person entitled to the payments to pay to the person making them such sum in respect of payments already made as the High Courts thinks fit; and

(*b*) if any arrears are due under the order for periodical payments, it may remit payment of the whole, or part, of those arrears.

(9) Any order of the High Court made on an appeal under this section (other than one directing that an application be re-heard by a magistrates' court) shall, for the purposes—

(*a*) of the enforcement of the order; and

(*b*) of any power to vary, revive or discharge orders,

be treated as if it were an order of the magistrates' court from which the appeal was brought and not an order of the High Court.

(10) The Lord Chancellor may by order make provision as to the circumstances in which appeals may be made against decisions taken by courts on questions arising in connection with the transfer, or proposed transfer, of proceedings by virtue of any order under paragraph 2 of Schedule 11.

(11) Except to the extent provided for in any order made under subsection (10), no appeal may be made against any decision of a kind mentioned in that subsection.

**95 Attendance of child at hearing under Part IV or V**

(1) In any proceedings in which a court is hearing an application for an order under Part IV or V, or is considering whether to make any such order, the court may order the child concerned to attend such stage or stages of the proceedings as may be specified in the order.

(2) The power conferred by subsection (1) shall be exercised in accordance with rules of court.

(3) Subsections (4) to (6) apply where—

(*a*) an order under subsection (1) has not been not complied with; or

(*b*) the court has reasonable cause to believe that it will not be complied with.

(4) The court may make an order authorising a constable, or such person as may be specified in the order—

(*a*) to take charge of the child and to bring him to the court; and

(*b*) to enter and search any premises specified in the order if he has reasonable cause to believe that the child may be found on the premises.

(5) The court may order any person who is in a position to do so to bring the child to the court.

(6) Where the court has reason to believe that a person has information

about the whereabouts of the child it may order him to disclose it to the court.

---

**Definitions** For 'court' see s 92(7); for 'child' see s 105(1).

**References** Part IV ie ss 31-42 and Sch 3 (care and supervision). Part V ie ss 43-52 (protection of children).

---

### 96 Evidence given by, or with respect to, children

(1) Subsection (2) applies where a child who is called as a witness in any civil proceedings does not, in the opinion of the court, understand the nature of an oath.

(2) The child's evidence may be heard by the court if, in its opinion—

(*a*) he understands that it is his duty to speak the truth; and

(*b*) he has sufficient understanding to justify his evidence being heard.

(3) The Lord Chancellor may by order make provision for the admissibility of evidence which would otherwise be inadmissible under any rule of law relating to hearsay.

(4) An order under subsection (3) may only be made with respect to—

(*a*) civil proceedings in general or such civil proceedings, or class of civil proceedings, as may be prescribed; and

(*b*) evidence in connection with the upbringing, maintenance or welfare of a child.

(5) An order under subsection (3)—

(*a*) may, in particular, provide for the admissibility of statements which are made orally or in a prescribed form or which are recorded by any prescribed method of recording;

(*b*) may make different provision for different purposes and in relation to different descriptions of court; and

(*c*) may make such amendments and repeals in any enactment relating to evidence (other than in this Act) as the Lord Chancellor considers necessary or expedient in consequence of the provision made by the order.

(6) Subsection (5)(*b*) is without prejudice to section 104(4).

(7) In this section—

"civil proceedings" and "court" have the same meaning as they have in the Civil Evidence Act 1968 by virtue of section 18 of that Act; and

"prescribed" means prescribed by an order under subsection (3).

---

**Date in force** sub-ss (3)-(7): 16 November 1989.

**Definitions** For 'child' see s 105(1); for 'court', 'civil proceedings' and 'prescribed' see sub-s (7).

---

### 97 Privacy for children involved in certain proceedings

(1) Rules made under section 144 of the Magistrates' Courts Act 1980 may make provision for a magistrates' court to sit in private in proceedings

in which any powers under this Act may be exercised by the court with respect to any child.

(2) No person shall publish any material which is intended, or likely, to identify—

(*a*) any child as being involved in any proceedings before a magistrates' court in which any power under this Act may be exercised by the court with respect to that or any other child; or

(*b*) an address or school as being that of a child involved in any such proceedings.

(3) In any proceedings for an offence under this section it shall be a defence for the accused to prove that he did not know, and had no reason to suspect, that the published material was intended, or likely, to identify the child.

(4) The court or the Secretary of State may, if satisfied that the welfare of the child requires it, by order dispense with the requirements of subsection (2) to such extent as may be specified in the order.

(5) For the purposes of this section—

"publish" includes—

(*a*) broadcast by radio, television or cable television; or

(*b*) cause to be published; and

"material" includes any picture or representation.

(6) Any person who contravenes this section shall be guilty of an offence and liable, on summary conviction, to a fine not exceeding level 4 on the standard scale.

(7) Subsection (1) is without prejudice to—

(*a*) the generality of the rule making power in section 144 of the Act of 1980; or

(*b*) any other power of a magistrates' court to sit in private.

(8) Section 71 of the Act of 1980 (newspaper reports of certain proceedings) shall apply in relation to any proceedings to which this section applies subject to the provisions of this section.

---

**Definitions** Definition For 'child' and 'school' see 105(1); for 'publish' and 'material' see sub-s (5).

**References** For 'the standard scale' see the Criminal Justice Act 1982 s 37(2) (3) as amended; 'level 4' ie £1000.

---

### 98 Self-incrimination

(1) In any proceedings in which a court is hearing an application for an order under Part IV or V, no person shall be excused from—

(*a*) giving evidence on any matter; or

(*b*) answering any question put to him in the course of his giving evidence,

on the ground that doing so might incriminate him or his spouse of an offence.

(2) A statement or admission made in such proceedings shall not be admissible in evidence against the person making it or his spouse in proceedings for an offence other than perjury.

---

**Defintion** Definition For 'court' see s 92(7).

**References** 'Part IV' ie ss 31-42 and Sch 3 (care and supervision). 'Part V' ie ss 43-52 (protection of children).

---

### 99 Legal aid

(1) The Legal Aid Act 1988 is amended as mentioned in subsections (2) to (4).

(2) In section 15 (availability of, and payment for, representation under provisions relating to civil legal aid), for the words "and (3)" in subsection (1) there shall be substituted "to (3B)"; and the following subsections shall be inserted after subsection (3)—

"(3A) Representation under this Part shall not be available—

(*a*) to any local authority; or

(*b*) to any other body which falls within a prescribed description,

for the purposes of any proceedings under the Children Act 1989.

(3B) Regardless of subsection (2) or (3), representation under this Part must be granted where a child who is brought before a court under section 25 of the 1989 Act (use of accommodation for restricting liberty) is not, but wishes to be, legally represented before the court."

(3) In section 19(5) (scope of provisions about criminal legal aid), at the end of the definition of "criminal proceedings" there shall be added "and also includes proceedings under section 15 of the Children and Young Persons Act 1969 (variation and discharge of supervision orders) and section 16(8) of that Act (appeals in such proceedings)".

(4) Sections 27, 28 and 30(1) and (2) (provisions about legal aid in care, and other, proceedings in relation to children) shall cease to have effect.

(5) The Lord Chancellor may by order make such further amendments in the Legal Aid Act 1988 as he considers necessary or expedient in consequence of any provision made by or under this Act.

### 100 Restrictions on use of wardship jurisdiction

(1) Section 7 of the Family Law Reform Act 1969 (which gives the High Court power to place a ward of court in the care, or under the supervision, of a local authority) shall cease to have effect.

(2) No court shall exercise the High Court's inherent jurisdiction with respect to children—

(*a*) so as to require a child to be placed in the care, or put under the supervision, of a local authority;

(*b*) so as to require a child to be accommodated by or on behalf of a local authority;

(*c*) so as to make a child who is the subject of a care order a ward of court; or

(*d*) for the purpose of conferring on any local authority power to determine any question which has arisen, or which may arise, in connection with any aspect of parental responsibility for a child.

(3) No application for any exercise of the court's inherent jurisdiction

with respect to children may be made by a local authority unless the authority have obtained the leave of the court.

(4) The court may only grant leave if it is satisfied that—

(*a*) the result which the authority wish to achieve could not be achieved through the making of any order of a kind to which subsection (5) applies; and

(*b*) there is reasonable cause to believe that if the court's inherent jurisdiction is not exercised with respect to the child he is likely to suffer significant harm.

(5) This subsection applies to any order—

(*a*) made otherwise than in the exercise of the court's inherent jurisdiction; and

(*b*) which the local authority is entitled to apply for (assuming, in the case of any application which may only be made with leave, that leave is granted).

---

**Definitions** For 'local authority', 'child' see s 105(1); for 'care order' see s 31(11) and s 105(1); for 'parental responsibility' see s 3; for 'harm' see s 31(9) as applied to the whole Act by s 105(1) and as to whether harm is significant see s 31(10) as applied to the whole Act by s 105(1).

**References** See generally para 10.1 ff. For exclusion of applications under s 100 (3) from the definition of 'family proceedings' under this Act see s 8(3).

---

### 101 Effect of orders as between England and Wales and Northern Ireland, the Channel Islands or the Isle of Man

(1) The Secretary of State may make regulations providing—

(*a*) for prescribed orders which—

(i) are made by a court in Northern Ireland; and

(ii) appear to the Secretary of State to correspond in their effect to orders which may be made under any provision of this Act,

to have effect in prescribed circumstances, for prescribed purposes of this Act, as if they were orders of a prescribed kind made under this Act;

(*b*) for prescribed orders which—

(i) are made by a court in England and Wales; and

(ii) appear to the Secretary of State to correspond in their effect to orders which may be made under any provision in force in Northern Ireland,

to have effect in prescribed circumstances, for prescribed purposes of the law of Northern Ireland, as if they were orders of a prescribed kind made in Northern Ireland.

(2) Regulations under subsection (1) may provide for the order concerned to cease to have effect for the purposes of the law of Northern Ireland, or (as the case may be) the law of England and Wales, if prescribed conditions are satisfied.

(3) The Secretary of State may make regulations providing for prescribed orders which—

(*a*) are made by a court in the Isle of Man or in any of the Channel Islands; and

(*b*) appear to the Secretary of State to correspond in their effect to orders which may be made under this Act,

to have effect in prescribed circumstances for prescribed purposes of this Act, as if they were orders of a prescribed kind made under this Act.

(4) Where a child who is in the care of a local authority is lawfully taken to live in Northern Ireland, the Isle of Man or any of the Channel Islands, the care order in question shall cease to have effect if the conditions prescribed in regulations made by the Secretary of State are satisfied.

(5) Any regulations made under this section may—

(*a*) make such consequential amendments (including repeals) in—

- (i) section 25 of the Children and Young Persons Act 1969 (transfers between England and Wales and Northern Ireland); or
- (ii) section 26 (transfers between England and Wales and Channel Islands or Isle of Man) of that Act,

as the Secretary of State considers necessary or expedient; and

(*b*) modify any provision of this Act, in its application (by virtue of the regulations) in relation to an order made otherwise than in England and Wales.

---

**Definitions** For 'court' see s 92(7); for 'prescribed' see s 105(1); for 'care order' see s 31(11) and s 105(1).

---

*Search warrants*

## 102 Power of constable to assist in exercise of certain powers to search for children or inspect premises

(1) Where, on an application made by any person for a warrant under this section, it appears to the court—

(*a*) that a person attempting to exercise powers under any enactment mentioned in subsection (6) has been prevented from doing so by being refused entry to the premises concerned or refused access to the child concerned; or

(*b*) that any such person is likely to be so prevented from exercising any such powers,

it may issue a warrant authorising any constable to assist that person in the exercise of those powers, using reasonable force if necessary.

(2) Every warrant issued under this section shall be addressed to, and executed by, a constable who shall be accompanied by the person applying for the warrant if—

(*a*) that person so desires; and

(*b*) the court by whom the warrant is issued does not direct otherwise.

(3) A court granting an application for a warrant under this section may direct that the constable concerned may, in executing the warrant, be accompanied by a registered medical practitioner, registered nurse or registered health visitor if he so chooses.

(4) An application for a warrant under this section shall be made in the manner and form prescribed by rules of court.

(5) Where—

(*a*) an application for a warrant under this section relates to a particular child; and

(*b*) it is reasonably practicable to do so,

the application and any warrant granted on the application shall name the child; and where it does not name him it shall describe him as clearly as possible.

(6) The enactments are—

(*a*) sections 62, 64, 67, 76, 80, 86 and 87;

(*b*) paragraph 8(1)(*b*) and (2)(*b*) of Schedule 3;

(*c*) section 33 of the Adoption Act 1976 (duty of local authority to secure that protected children are visited from time to time).

---

**Definitions** For 'court' see s 92(7); for 'child', 'prescribed' see s 105(1).

**Reference** For 'premises' see the note to s 72.

---

*General*

### 103 Offences by bodies corporate

(1) This section applies where any offence under this Act is committed by a body corporate.

(2) If the offence is proved to have been committed with the consent or connivance of or to be attributable to any neglect on the part of any director, manager, secretary or other similar officer of the body corporate, or any person who was purporting to act in any such capacity, he (as well as the body corporate) shall be guilty of the offence and shall be liable to be proceeded against and punished accordingly.

### 104 Regulations and orders

(1) Any power of the Lord Chancellor or the Secretary of State under this Act to make an order, regulations, or rules, except an order under section 54(2), 56(4)(*a*), 57(3), 84 or 97(4) or paragraph 1(1) of Schedule 4, shall be exercisable by statutory instrument.

(2) Any such statutory instrument, except one made under section 17(4), 107 or 108(2), shall be subject to annulment in pursuance of a resolution of either House of Parliament.

(3) An order under section 17(4) shall not be made unless a draft of it has been laid before, and approved by a resolution of, each House of Parliament.

(4) Any statutory instrument made under this Act may—

(*a*) make different provision for different cases;

(*b*) provide for exemptions from any of its provisions; and

(*c*) contain such incidental, supplemental and transitional provisions as the person making it considers expedient.

## 105 Interpretation

(1) In this Act—

"adoption agency" means a body which may be referred to as an adoption agency by virtue of section 1 of the Adoption Act 1976;

"bank holiday" means a day which is a bank holiday under the Banking and Financial Dealings Act 1971;

"care order" has the meaning given by section 31(11) and also includes any order which by or under any enactment has the effect of, or is deemed to be, a care order for the purposes of this Act; and any reference to a child who is in the care of an authority is a reference to a child who is in their care by virtue of a care order;

"child" means, subject to paragraph 16 of Schedule 1, a person under the age of eighteen;

"child assessment order" has the meaning given by section 43(2);

"child minder" has the meaning given by section 71;

"child of the family", in relation to the parties to a marriage, means—

(*a*) a child of both of those parties;

(*b*) any other child, not being a child who is placed with those parties as foster parents by a local authority or voluntary organisation, who has been treated by both of those parties as a child of their family;

"children's home" has the same meaning as in section 63;

"community home" has the meaning given by section 53;

"contact order" has the meaning given by section 8(1);

"day care" has the same meaning as in section 18;

"disabled", in relation to a child, has the same meaning as in section 17(11);

"district health authority" has the same meaning as in the National Health Service Act 1977;

"domestic premises" has the meaning given by section 71(12);

"education supervision order" has the meaning given in section 36;

"emergency protection order" means an order under section 44;

"family assistance order" has the meaning given in section 16(2);

"family proceedings" has the meaning given by section 8(3);

"functions" includes powers and duties;

"guardian of a child" means a guardian (other than a guardian of the estate of a child) appointed in accordance with the provisions of section 5;

"harm" has the same meaning as in section 31(9) and the question of whether harm is significant shall be determined in accordance with section 31(10);

"health authority" means any district health authority and any special health authority established under the National Health Service Act 1977;

"health service hospital" has the same meaning as in the National Health Service Act 1977;

"hospital" has the same meaning as in the Mental Health Act 1983, except that it does not include a special hospital within the meaning of that Act;

"ill-treatment" has the same meaning as in section 31(9);

"independent school" has the same meaning as in the Education Act 1944;

"local authority" means, in relation to England and Wales, the council of a county, a metropolitan district, a London Borough or the Common Council of the City of London and, in relation to Scotland, a local authority within the meaning of section 1(2) of the Social Work (Scotland) Act 1968;

"local authority foster parent" has the same meaning as in section 23(3);

"local education authority" has the same meaning as in the Education Act 1944;

"local housing authority" has the same meaning as in the Housing Act 1985;

"mental nursing home" has the same meaning as in the Registered Homes Act 1984;

"nursing home" has the same meaning as in the Act of 1984;

"parental responsibility" has the meaning given in section 3;

"parental responsibility agreement" has the meaning given in section 4(1);

"prescribed" means prescribed by regulations made under this Act;

"privately fostered child" and "to foster a child privately" have the same meaning as in section 66;

"prohibited steps order" has the meaning given by section 8(1);

"protected child" has the same meaning as in Part III of the Adoption Act 1976;

"registered children's home" has the same meaning as in section 63;

"registered pupil" has the same meaning as in the Education Act 1944;

"relative", in relation to a child, means a grandparent, brother, sister, uncle or aunt (whether of the full blood or half blood or by affinity) or step-parent;

"residence order" has the meaning given by section 8(1);

"residential care home" has the same meaning as in the Registered Homes Act 1984;

"responsible person", in relation to a child who is the subject of a supervision order, has the meaning given in paragraph 1 of Schedule 3;

"school" has the same meaning as in the Education Act 1944 or, in relation to Scotland, in the Education (Scotland) Act 1980;

"service", in relation to any provision made under Part III, includes any facility;

"signed", in relation to any person, includes the making by that person of his mark;

"special educational needs" has the same meaning as in the Education Act 1981;

"special health authority" has the same meaning as in the National Health Service Act 1977;

"specific issue order" has the meaning given by section 8(1);

"supervision order" has the meaning given by section 31(11);

"supervised child" and "supervisor", in relation to a supervision order or an education supervision order, mean respectively the child who is (or is to be) under supervision and the person under whose supervision he is (or is to be) by virtue of the order;

"upbringing", in relation to any child, includes the care of the child but not his maintenance;

"voluntary home" has the meaning given by section 60;

"voluntary organisation" means a body (other than a public or local authority) whose activities are not carried on for profit.

(2) References in this Act to a child whose father and mother were, or (as the case may be) were not, married to each other at the time of his birth must be read with section 1 of the Family Law Reform Act 1987 (which extends the meaning of such references).

(3) References in this Act to—

(*a*) a person with whom a child lives, or is to live, as the result of a residence order; or

(*b*) a person in whose favour a residence order is in force,

shall be construed as references to the person named in the order as the person with whom the child is to live.

(4) References in this Act to a child who is looked after by a local authority have the same meaning as they have (by virtue of section 22) in Part III.

(5) References in this Act to accommodation provided by or on behalf of a local authority are references to accommodation so provided in the exercise of functions which stand referred to the social services committee of that or any other local authority under the Land Authority Social Services Act 1970.

(6) In determining the "ordinary residence" of a child for any purpose of this Act, there shall be disregarded any period in which he lives in any place—

(*a*) which is a school or other institution;

(*b*) in accordance with the requirements of a supervision order under this Act or an order under section 7(7)(*b*) of the Children and Young Persons Act 1969; or

(*c*) while he is being provided with accommodation by or on behalf of a local authority.

(7) References in this Act to children who are in need shall be construed in accordance with section 17.

(8) Any notice or other document required under this Act to be served on any person may be served on him by being delivered personally to him, or being sent by post to him in a registered letter or by the recorded delivery service at his proper address.

(9) Any such notice or other document required to be served on a body corporate or a firm shall be duly served if it is served on the secretary or clerk of that body or a partner of that firm.

(10) For the purposes of this section, and of section 7 of the Interpretation Act 1978 in its application to this section, the proper address of a person—

(*a*) in the case of a secretary or clerk of a body corporate, shall be that of the registered or principal office of that body;

(*b*) in the case of a partner of a firm, shall be that of the principal office of the firm; and

(*c*) in any other case, shall be the last known address of the person to be served.

### 106 Financial provisions

(1) Any—

(*a*) grants made by the Secretary of State under this Act; and (*b*) any other expenses incurred by the Secretary of State under this Act,

shall be payable out of money provided by Parliament.

(2) Any sums received by the Secretary of State under section 58, or by way of the repayment of any grant made under section 82(2) or (4) shall be paid into the Consolidated Fund.

### 107 Application to Channel Islands

Her Majesty may by Order in Council direct that any of the provisions of this Act shall extend to any of the Channel Islands with such exceptions and modifications as may be specified in the Order.

### 108 Short title, commencement, extent etc

(1) This Act may be cited as the Children Act 1989.

(2) Sections 89 and 96(3) to (7), and paragraph 35 of Schedule 12, shall come into force on the passing of this Act and paragraph 36 of Schedule 12 shall come into force at the end of the period of two months beginning with the day on which this Act is passed but otherwise this Act shall come into force on such date as may be appointed by order made by the Lord Chancellor or the Secretary of State, or by both acting jointly.

(3) Different dates may be appointed for different provisions of this Act and in relation to different cases.

(4) The minor amendments set out in Schedule 12 shall have effect.

(5) The consequential amendments set out in Schedule 13 shall have effect.

(6) The transitional provisions and savings set out in Schedule 14 shall have effect.

(7) The repeals set out in Schedule 15 shall have effect.

(8) An order under subsection (2) may make such transitional provisions or savings as appear to the person making the order to be necessary or expedient in connection with the provisions brought into force by the order, including—

(*a*) provisions adding to or modifying the provisions of Schedule 14; and

(*b*) such adaptations—

(i) of the provisions brought into force by the order; and

(ii) of any provisions of this Act then in force,

as appear to him necessary or expedient in consequence of the partial operation of this Act.

(9) The Lord Chancellor may by order make such amendments or repeals, in such enactments as may be specified in the order, as appear to him to be necessary or expedient in consequence of any provision of this Act.

(10) This Act shall, in its application to the Isles of Scilly, have effect subject to such exceptions, adaptations and modifications as the Secretary of State may by order prescribe.

(11) The following provisions of this Act extend to Scotland—

section 19;

section 25(8);

section 50(13);

Part X;

section 80(1)(*h*) and (*i*), (2) to (4), (5)(*a*), (*b*) and (*h*) and (6) to (12);

section 88;

section 104 (so far as necessary);

section 105 (so far as necessary);

subsections (1) to (3), (8) and (9) and this subsection;

in Schedule 2, paragraph 24;

in Schedule 12, paragraphs 1, 7 to 10, 18, 27, 30(*a*) and 41 to 44;

in Schedule 13, paragraphs 18 to 23, 32, 46, 47, 50, 57, 62, 63, 68(*a*) and (*b*) and 71;

in Schedule 14, paragraphs 1, 33 and 34;

in Schedule 15, the entries relating to—

(*a*) the Custody of Children Act 1891;
(*b*) the Nurseries and Child Minders Regulation Act 1948;
(*c*) section 53(3) of the Children and Young Persons Act 1963;
(*d*) section 60 of the Health Services and Public Health Act 1968;
(*e*) the Social Work (Scotland) Act 1968;
(*f*) the Adoption (Scotland) Act 1978;
(*g*) the Child Care Act 1980;
(*h*) the Foster Children (Scotland) Act 1984;
(*i*) the Child Abduction and Custody Act 1985; and
(*j*) the Family Law Act 1986.

(12) The following provisions of this Act extend to Northern Ireland—

section 50;

section 101(1)(*b*), (2) and (5)(*a*)(i);

subsections (1) to (3), (8) and (9) and this subsection;

in Schedule 2, paragraph 24;

in Schedule 12, paragraphs 7 to 10, 18 and 27;

in Schedule 13, paragraphs 21, 22, 46, 47, 57, 62, 63, 68(*c*) to (*e*) and 69 to 71;

in Schedule 14, paragraphs 18, 28 to 30 and 38(*a*); and

in Schedule 15, the entries relating to the Guardianship of Minors Act 1971, the Children Act 1975, the Child Care Act 1980, and the Family Law Act 1986.

# SCHEDULES

## SCHEDULE 1

Section 15(1)

FINANCIAL PROVISION FOR CHILDREN

*Orders for financial relief against parents*

1.—(1) On an application made by a parent or guardian of a child, or by any person in whose favour a residence order is in force with respect to a child, the court may—

(*a*) in the case of an application to the High Court or a county court, make one or more of the orders mentioned in sub-paragraph (2);
(*b*) in the case of an application to a magistrates' court, make one or both of the orders mentioned in paragraphs (*a*) and (*c*) of that sub-paragraph.

(2) The orders referred to in sub-paragraph (1) are—

(*a*) an order requiring either or both parents of a child—

(i) to make to the applicant for the benefit of the child; or
(ii) to make to the child himself,

such periodical payments, for such term, as may be specified in the order;
(*b*) an order requiring either or both parents of a child—

(i) to secure to the applicant for the benefit of the child; or
(ii) to secure to the child himself,

such periodical payments, for such term, as may be so specified;
(*c*) an order requiring either or both parents of a child—

(i) to pay to the applicant for the benefit of the child; or
(ii) to pay to the child himself,

such lump sum as may be so specified;
(*d*) an order requiring a settlement to be made for the benefit of the child, and to the satisfaction of the court, of property—

(i) to which either parent is entitled (either in possession or in reversion); and
(ii) which is specified in the order;

(*e*) an order requiring either or both parents of a child—

(i) to transfer to the applicant, for the benefit of the child; or
(ii) to transfer to the child himself,

such property to which the parent is, or the parents are, entitled (either in possession or in reversion) as may be specified in the order.

(3) The powers conferred by this paragraph may be exercised at any time.

(4) An order under sub-paragraph (2)(*a*) or (*b*) may be varied or discharged by a subsequent order made on the application of any person by or to whom payments were required to be made under the previous order.

(5) Where a court makes an order under this paragraph—

(*a*) it may at any time make a further such order under sub-paragraph (2)(*a*), (*b*) or (*c*) with respect to the child concerned if he has not reached the age of eighteen;
(*b*) it may not make more than one order under sub-paragraph (2)(*d*) or (*e*) against the same person in respect of the same child.

(6) On making, varying or discharging a residence order the court may exercise

any of its powers under this Schedule even though no application has been made to it under this Schedule.

*Orders for financial relief for persons over eighteen*

2.—(1) If, on an application by a person who has reached the age of eighteen, it appears to the court—

(*a*) that the applicant is, will be or (if an order were made under this paragraph) would be receiving instruction at an educational establishment or undergoing training for a trade, profession or vocation, whether or not while in gainful employment; or

(*b*) that there are special circumstances which justify the making of an order under this paragraph,

the court may make one or both of the orders mentioned in sub-paragraph (2).

(2) The orders are—

(*a*) an order requiring either or both of the applicant's parents to pay to the applicant such periodical payments, for such term, as may be specified in the order;

(*b*) an order requiring either or both of the applicant's parents to pay to the applicant such lump sum as may be so specified.

(3) An application may not be made under this paragraph by any person if, immediately before he reached the age of sixteen, a periodical payments order was in force with respect to him.

(4) No order shall be made under this paragraph at a time when the parents of the applicant are living with each other in the same household.

(5) An order under sub-paragraph (2)(*a*) may be varied or discharged by a subsequent order made on the application of any person by or to whom payments were required to be made under the previous order.

(6) In sub-paragraph (3) "periodical payments order" means an order made under—

(*a*) this Schedule;

(*b*) section 6(3) of the Family Law Reform Act 1969;

(*c*) section 23 or 27 of the Matrimonial Causes Act 1973;

(*d*) Part I of the Domestic Proceedings and Magistrates' Courts Act 1978,

for the making or securing of periodical payments.

(7) The powers conferred by this paragraph shall be exercisable at any time.

(8) Where the court makes an order under this paragraph it may from time to time while that order remains in force make a further such order.

*Duration of orders for financial relief*

3.—(1) The term to be specified in an order for periodical payments made under paragraph 1(2)(*a*) or (*b*) in favour of a child may begin with the date of the making of an application for the order in question or any later date but—

(*a*) shall not in the first instance extend beyond the child's seventeenth birthday unless the court thinks it right in the circumstances of the case to specify a later date; and

(*b*) shall not in any event extend beyond the child's eighteenth birthday.

(2) Paragraph (*b*) of sub-paragraph (1) shall not apply in the case of a child if it appears to the court that—

(*a*) the child is, or will be or (if an order were made without complying with that paragraph) would be receiving instruction at an educational establishment or undergoing training for a trade, profession or vocation, whether or not while in gainful employment; or (*b*) there are special circumstances which justify the making of an order without complying with that paragraph.

(3) An order for periodical payments made under paragraph 1(2)(*a*) or 2(2)(*a*) shall, notwithstanding anything in the order, cease to have effect on the death of the person liable to make payments under the order.

(4) Where an order is made under paragraph 1(2)(*a*) or (*b*) requiring periodical payments to be made or secured to the parent of a child, the order shall cease to have effect if—

(*a*) any parent making or securing the payments; and
(*b*) any parent to whom the payments are made or secured,

live together for a period of more than six months.

*Matters to which court is to have regard in making orders for financial relief*

4.—(1) In deciding whether to exercise its powers under paragraph 1 or 2, and if so in what manner, the court shall have regard to all the circumstances including—

(*a*) the income, earning capacity, property and other financial resources which each person mentioned in sub-paragraph (3) has or is likely to have in the foreseeable future;
(*b*) the financial needs, obligations and responsibilities which each person mentioned in sub-paragraph (3) has or is likely to have in the foreseeable future;
(*c*) the financial needs of the child;
(*d*) the income, earning capacity (if any), property and other financial resources of the child;
(*e*) any physical or mental disability of the child;
(*f*) the manner in which the child was being, or was expected to be, educated or trained.

(2) In deciding whether to exercise its powers under paragraph 1 against a person who is not the mother or father of the child, and if so in what manner, the court shall in addition have regard to—

(*a*) whether that person had assumed responsibility for the maintenance of the child and, if so, the extent to which and basis on which he assumed that responsibility and the length of the period during which he met that responsibility;
(*b*) whether he did so knowing that the child was not his child;
(*c*) the liability of any other person to maintain the child.

(3) Where the court makes an order under paragraph 1 against a person who is not the father of the child, it shall record in the order that the order is made on the basis that the person against whom the order is made is not the child's father.

(4) The persons mentioned in sub-paragraph (1) are—

(*a*) in relation to a decision whether to exercise its powers under paragraph 1, any parent of the child;
(*b*) in relation to a decision whether to exercise its powers under paragraph 2, the mother and father of the child;
(*c*) the applicant for the order;
(*d*) any other person in whose favour the court proposes to make the order.

*Provisions relating to lump sums*

5.—(1) Without prejudice to the generality of paragraph 1, an order under that paragraph for the payment of a lump sum may be made for the purpose of enabling any liabilities or expenses—

(*a*) incurred in connection with the birth of the child or in maintaining the child; and
(*b*) reasonably incurred before the making of the order,

to be met.

(2) The amount of any lump sum required to be paid by an order made by a magistrates' court under paragraph 1 or 2 shall not exceed ;bp1000 or such larger amount as the Secretary of State may from time to time by order fix for the purposes of this sub-paragraph.

(3) The power of the court under paragraph 1 or 2 to vary or discharge an order for the making or securing of periodical payments by a parent shall include power to make an order under that provision for the payment of a lump sum by that parent.

(4) The amount of any lump sum which a parent may be required to pay by virtue of sub-
paragraph (3) shall not, in the case of an order made by a magistrates' court, exceed the maximum amount that may at the time of the making of the order be required to be paid under sub-paragraph (2), but a magistrates' court may make an order for the payment of a lump sum not exceeding that amount even though the parent was required to pay a lump sum by a previous order under this Act.

(5) An order made under paragraph 1 or 2 for the payment of a lump sum may provide for the payment of that sum by instalments.

(6) Where the court provides for the payment of a lump sum by instalments the court, on an application made either by the person liable to pay or the person entitled to receive that sum, shall have power to vary that order by varying—

(*a*) the number of instalments payable;
(*b*) the amount of any instalment payable;
(*c*) the date on which any instalment becomes payable.

*Variation etc of orders for periodical payments*

6.—(1) In exercising its powers under paragraph 1 or 2 to vary or discharge an order for the making or securing of periodical payments the court shall have regard to all the circumstances of the case, including any change in any of the matters to which the court was required to have regard when making the order.

(2) The power of the court under paragraph 1 or 2 to vary an order for the making or securing of periodical payments shall include power to suspend any provision of the order temporarily and to revive any provision so suspended.

(3) Where on an application under paragraph 1 or 2 for the variation or discharge of an order for the making or securing of periodical payments the court varies the payments required to be made under that order, the court may provide that the payments as so varied shall be made from such date as the court may specify, not being earlier than the date of the making of the application.

(4) An application for the variation of an order made under paragraph 1 for the making or securing of periodical payments to or for the benefit of a child may, if the child has reached the age of sixteen, be made by the child himself.

(5) Where an order for the making or securing of periodical payments made under paragraph 1 ceases to have effect on the date on which the child reaches the age of sixteen, or at any time after that date but before or on the date on which he reaches the age of eighteen, the child may apply to the court which made the order for an order for its revival.

(6) If on such an application it appears to the court that—

(*a*) the child is, will be or (if an order were made under this sub-paragraph) would be receiving instruction at an educational establishment or undergoing training for a trade, profession or vocation, whether or not while in gainful employment; or

(*b*) there are special circumstances which justify the making of an order under this paragraph,

the court shall have power by order to revive the order from such date as the court may specify, not being earlier than the date of the making of the application.

(7) Any order which is revived by an order under sub-paragraph (5) may be varied or discharged under that provision, on the application of any person by whom or to whom payments are required to be made under the revived order.

(8) An order for the making or securing of periodical payments made under paragraph 1 may be varied or discharged, after the death of either parent, on the application of a guardian of the child concerned.

*Variation of orders for secured periodical payments after death of parent*

7.—(1) Where the parent liable to make payments under a secured periodical payments order has died, the persons who may apply for the variation or discharge of the order shall include the personal representatives of the deceased parent.

(2) No application for the variation of the order shall, except with the permission of the court, be made after the end of the period of six months from the date on which representation in regard to the estate of that parent is first taken out.

(3) The personal representatives of a deceased person against whom a secured periodical payments order was made shall not be liable for having distributed any part of the estate of the deceased after the end of the period of six months referred to in sub-paragraph (2) on the ground that they ought to have taken into account the possibility that the court might permit an application for variation to be made after that period by the person entitled to payments under the order.

(4) Sub-paragraph (3) shall not prejudice any power to recover any part of the estate so distributed arising by virtue of the variation of an order in accordance with this paragraph.

(5) Where an application to vary a secured periodical payments order is made after the death of the parent liable to make payments under the order, the circumstances to which the court is required to have regard under paragraph 6(1) shall include the changed circumstances resulting from the death of the parent.

(6) In considering for the purposes of sub-paragraph (2) the question when representation was first taken out, a grant limited to settled land or to trust property shall be left out of account and a grant limited to real estate or to personal estate shall be left out of account unless a grant limited to the remainder of the estate has previously been made or is made at the same time.

(7) In this paragraph "secured periodical payments order" means an order for secured periodical payments under paragraph 1(2)(*b*).

*Financial relief under other enactments*

8.—(1) This paragraph applies where a residence order is made with respect to a child at a time when there is in force an order ("the financial relief order") made under any enactment other than this Act and requiring a person to contribute to the child's maintenance.

(2) Where this paragraph applies, the court may, on the application of—

(*a*) any person required by the financial relief order to contribute to the child's maintenance; or

(*b*) any person in whose favour a residence order with respect to the child is in force, make an order revoking the financial relief order, or varying it by altering the amount of any sum payable under that order or by substituting the applicant for the person to whom any such sum is otherwise payable under that order.

*Interim orders*

9.—(1) Where an application is made under paragraph 1 or 2 the court may, at any time before it disposes of the application, make an interim order—

(*a*) requiring either or both parents to make such periodical payments, at such times and for such term as the court thinks fit; and
(*b*) giving any direction which the court thinks fit.

(2) An interim order made under this paragraph may provide for payments to be made from such date as the court may specify, not being earlier than the date of the making of the application under paragraph 1 or 2.

(3) An interim order made under this paragraph shall cease to have effect when the application is disposed of or, if earlier, on the date specified for the purposes of this paragraph in the interim order.

(4) An interim order in which a date has been specified for the purposes of sub-paragraph (3) may be varied by substituting a later date.

*Alteration of maintenance agreements*

10.—(1) In this paragraph and in paragraph 11 "maintenance agreement" means any agreement in writing made with respect to a child, whether before or after the commencement of this paragraph, which—

(*a*) is or was made between the father and mother of the child; and
(*b*) contains provision with respect to the making or securing of payments, or the disposition or use of any property, for the maintenance or education of the child,

and any such provisions are in this paragraph, and paragraph 11, referred to as "financial arrangements".

(2) Where a maintenance agreement is for the time being subsisting and each of the parties to the agreement is for the time being either domiciled or resident in England and Wales, then, either party may apply to the court for an order under this paragraph.

(3) If the court to which the application is made is satisfied either—

(*a*) that, by reason of a change in the circumstances in the light of which any financial arrangements contained in the agreement were made (including a change foreseen by the parties when making the agreement), the agreement should be altered so as to make different financial arrangements; or
(*b*) that the agreement does not contain proper financial arrangements with respect to the child,

then that court may by order make such alterations in the agreement by varying or revoking any financial arrangements contained in it as may appear to it to be just having regard to all the circumstances.

(4) If the maintenance agreement is altered by an order under this paragraph, the agreement shall have effect thereafter as if the alteration had been made by agreement between the parties and for valuable consideration.

(5) Where a court decides to make an order under this paragraph altering the maintenance agreement—

(*a*) by inserting provision for the making or securing by one of the parties to the agreement of periodical payments for the maintenance of the child; or (*b*) by increasing the rate of periodical payments required to be made or secured by one of the parties for the maintenance of the child,

then, in deciding the term for which under the agreement as altered by the order the payments or (as the case may be) the additional payments attributable to the increase are to be made or secured for the benefit of the child, the court shall apply the provisions of sub-paragraphs (1) and (2) of paragraph 3 as if the order were an order under paragraph 1(2)(*a*) or (*b*).

(6) A magistrates' court shall not entertain an application under sub-paragraph (2) unless both the parties to the agreement are resident in England and Wales and at least one of the parties is resident in the commission area (within the meaning of the Justices of the Peace Act 1979) for which the court is appointed, and shall not have power to make any order on such an application except—

(*a*) in a case where the agreement contains no provision for periodical payments by either of the parties, an order inserting provision for the making by one of the parties of periodical payments for the maintenance of the child;
(*b*) in a case where the agreement includes provision for the making by one of the parties of periodical payments, an order increasing or reducing the rate of, or terminating, any of those payments.

(7) For the avoidance of doubt it is hereby declared that nothing in this paragraph affects any power of a court before which any proceedings between the parties to a maintenance agreement are brought under any other enactment to make an order containing financial arrangements or any right of either party to apply for such an order in such proceedings.

11.—(1) Where a maintenance agreement provides for the continuation, after the death of one of the parties, of payments for the maintenance of a child and that party dies domiciled in England and Wales, the surviving party or the personal representatives of the deceased party may apply to the High Court or a county court for an order under paragraph 10.

(2) If a maintenance agreement is altered by a court on an application under this paragraph, the agreement shall have effect thereafter as if the alteration had been made, immediately before the death, by agreement between the parties and for valuable consideration.

(3) An application under this paragraph shall not, except with leave of the High Court or a county court, be made after the end of the period of six months beginning with the day on which representation in regard to the estate of the deceased is first taken out.

(4) In considering for the purposes of sub-paragraph (3) the question when representation was first taken out, a grant limited to settled land or to trust property shall be left out of account and a grant limited to real estate or to personal estate shall be left out of account unless a grant limited to the remainder of the estate has previously been made or is made at the same time.

(5) A county court shall not entertain an application under this paragraph, or an application for leave to make an application under this paragraph, unless it would have jurisdiction to hear and determine proceedings for an order under section 2 of the Inheritance (Provision for Family and Dependants) Act 1975 in relation to the deceased's estate by virtue of section 25 of the County Courts Act 1984 (jurisdiction under the Act of 1975).

(6) The provisions of this paragraph shall not render the personal representatives of the deceased liable for having distributed any part of the estate of the deceased after the expiry of the period of six months referred to in sub-paragraph (3) on the ground that they ought to have taken into account the possibility that a court might grant leave for an application by virtue of this paragraph to be made by the surviving party after that period.

(7) Sub-paragraph (6) shall not prejudice any power to recover any part of the estate so distributed arising by virtue of the making of an order in pursuance of this paragraph.

*Enforcement of orders for maintenance*

12.—(1) Any person for the time being under an obligation to make payments in pursuance of any order for the payment of money made by a magistrates' court under this Act shall give notice of any change of address to such person (if any) as may be specified in the order.

(2) Any person failing without reasonable excuse to give such a notice shall be guilty of an offence and liable on summary conviction to a fine not exceeding level 2 on the standard scale.

(3) An order for the payment of money made by a magistrates' court under this Act shall be enforceable as a magistrates' court maintenance order within the meaning of section 150(1) of the Magistrates' Courts Act 1980.

*Direction for settlement of instrument by conveyancing counsel*

13. Where the High Court or a county court decides to make an order under this Act for the securing of periodical payments or for the transfer or settlement of property, it may direct that the matter be referred to one of the conveyancing counsel of the court to settle a proper instrument to be executed by all necessary parties.

*Financial provision for child resident in country outside England and Wales*

14.—(1) Where one parent of a child lives in England and Wales and the child lives outside England and Wales with—

(*a*) another parent of his;
(*b*) a guardian of his; or
(*c*) a person in whose favour a residence order is in force with respect to the child,

the court shall have power, on an application made by any of the persons mentioned in paragraphs (*a*) to (*c*), to make one or both of the orders mentioned in paragraph 1(2)(*a*) and (*b*) against the parent living in England and Wales.

(2) Any reference in this Act to the powers of the court under paragraph 1(2) or to an order made under paragraph 1(2) shall include a reference to the powers which the court has by virtue of sub-paragraph (1) or (as the case may be) to an order made by virtue of sub-paragraph (1).

*Local authority contribution to child's maintenance*

15.—(1) Where a child lives, or is to live, with a person as the result of a residence order, a local authority may make contributions to that person towards the cost of the accommodation and maintenance of the child.

(2) Sub-paragraph (1) does not apply where the person with whom the child lives, or is to live, is a parent of the child or the husband or wife of a parent of the child.

*Interpretation*

16.—(1) In this Schedule "child" includes, in any case where an application is made under paragraph 2 or 6 in relation to a person who has reached the age of eighteen, that person.

(2) In this Schedule, except paragraphs 2 and 15, "parent" includes any party to a marriage (whether or not subsisting) in relation to whom the child concerned

is a child of the family; and for this purpose any reference to either parent or both parents shall be construed as references to any parent of his and to all of his parents.

---

**Definitions** For 'child' and 'guardian of a child' see s 105(1) but note (for applications under paras 2 or 6) para 16; for 'court' see s 92(7) and 9.1 ff; for 'periodical payments order' see para 2; for 'secured periodical payments order' see para 7(7); for 'the financial relief order' see para 8(1); for 'a person in whose favour a residence order is in force' see s 105(3)(b); for 'maintenance agreement', 'financial arrangements', see para 10(1); for 'local authority' see s 105(1).

**References** See generally para 4.41 ff and s 15 (financial relief). For 'parent' see para 2.7 and para 16; for appointment of guardian see s 5(1). For 'the standard scale' see the Criminal Justice Act 1982 s 37(2) (3) as amended; 'level 2' ie £100.

---

## SCHEDULE 2

Sections 17, 23 and 29

## Local Authority Support for Children and Families

### Part I

### Provision of Services for Families

*Identification of children in need and provision of information*

1.—(1) Every local authority shall take reasonable steps to identify the extent to which there are children in need within their area.

(2) Every local authority shall—

(*a*) publish information—

(i) about services provided by them under sections 17, 18, 20 and 24; and

(ii) where they consider it appropriate, about the provision by others (including, in particular, voluntary organisations) of services which the authority have power to provide under those sections; and

(*b*) take such steps as are reasonably practicable to ensure that those who might benefit from the services receive the information relevant to them.

*Maintenance of a register of disabled children*

2.—(1) Every local authority shall open and maintain a register of disabled children within their area.

(2) The register may be kept by means of a computer.

*Assessment of children's needs*

3. Where it appears to a local authority that a child within their area is in need, the authority may assess his needs for the purposes of this Act at the same time as any assessment of his needs is made under—

(*a*) the Chronically Sick and Disabled Persons Act 1970;
(*b*) the Education Act 1981;
(*c*) the Disabled Persons (Services, Consultation and Representation) Act 1986; or
(*d*) any other enactment.

*Prevention of neglect and abuse*

4.—(1) Every local authority shall take reasonable steps, through the provision of services under Part III of this Act, to prevent children within their area suffering ill-treatment or neglect.

(2) Where a local authority believe that a child who is at any time within their area—

(*a*) is likely to suffer harm; but
(*b*) lives or proposes to live in the area of another local authority

they shall inform that other local authority.

(3) When informing that other local authority they shall specify—

(*a*) the harm that they believe he is likely to suffer; and
(*b*) (if they can) where the child lives or proposes to live.

*Provision of accommodation in order to protect child*

5.—(1) Where—

(*a*) it appears to a local authority that a child who is living on particular premises is suffering, or is likely to suffer, ill treatment at the hands of another person who is living on those premises; and
(*b*) that other person proposes to move from the premises,

the authority may assist that other person to obtain alternative accommodation.

(2) Assistance given under this paragraph may be in cash.

(3) Subsections (7) to (9) of section 17 shall apply in relation to assistance given under this paragraph as they apply in relation to assistance given under that section.

*Provision for disabled children*

6. Every local authority shall provide services designed—

(*a*) to minimise the effect on disabled children within their area of their disabilities; and
(*b*) to give such children the opportunity to lead lives which are as normal as possible.

*Provision to reduce need for care proceedings etc*

7. Every local authority shall take reasonable steps designed—

(*a*) to reduce the need to bring—

(i) proceedings for care or supervision orders with respect to children within their area;
(ii) criminal proceedings against such children;
(iii) any family or other proceedings with respect to such children which might lead to them being placed in the authority's care; or
(iv) proceedings under the inherent jurisdiction of the High Court with respect to children;

(*b*) to encourage children within their area not to commit criminal offences; and
(*c*) to avoid the need for children within their area to be placed in secure accommodation.

*Provision for children living with their families*

8. Every local authority shall make such provision as they consider appropriate for the following services to be available with respect to children in need within their area while they are living with their families—

(*a*) advice, guidance and counselling;
(*b*) occupational, social, cultural or recreational activities;
(*c*) home help (which may include laundry facilities);
(*d*) facilities for, or assistance with, travelling to and from home for the purpose

of taking advantage of any other service provided under this Act or of any similar service;

(*e*) assistance to enable the child concerned and his family to have a holiday.

*Family centres*

9.—(1) Every local authority shall provide such family centres as they consider appropriate in relation to children within their area.

(2) "Family centre" means a centre at which any of the persons mentioned in sub-paragraph (3) may—

(*a*) attend for occupational, social, cultural or recreational activities;
(*b*) attend for advice, guidance or counselling; or
(*c*) be provided with accommodation while he is receiving advice, guidance or counselling.

(3) The persons are—

(*a*) a child;
(*b*) his parents;
(*c*) any person who is not a parent of his but who has parental responsibility for him;
(*d*) any other person who is looking after him.

*Maintenance of the family home*

10. Every local authority shall take such steps as are reasonably practicable, where any child within their area who is in need and whom they are not looking after is living apart from his family—

(*a*) to enable him to live with his family; or
(*b*) to promote contact between him and his family,

if, in their opinion, it is necessary to do so in order to safeguard or promote his welfare.

*Duty to consider racial groups to which children in need belong*

11. Every local authority shall, in making any arrangements—

(*a*) for the provision of day care within their area; or
(*b*) designed to encourage persons to act as local authority foster parents,

have regard to the different racial groups to which children within their area who are in need belong.

---

**Definitions** For 'local authority', 'child', 'voluntary organisation', 'service' see s 105(1); for 'child in need' and 'family' see s 17(10); for 'disabled' see s 17(11); for 'ill-treatment', 'harm' see s 31(9) as applied to the whole Act by s 105(1); for 'care order', 'supervision order' see s 31(11); for 'family proceedings' see s 8(3) (4)(a); for secure accommodation see s 25(1); for 'family centre' see para (9); for 'parental responsibility' see s 3.

**References** 'Part III of this Act' ie ss 17-30 and Sch 2 (local authority support for children and families). For 'parent' see para 2.7.

---

## PART II

## CHILDREN LOOKED AFTER BY LOCAL AUTHORITIES

*Regulations as to placing of children with local authority foster parents*

12. Regulations under section 23(2)(*a*) may, in particular, make provision—

(*a*) with regard to the welfare of children placed with local authority foster parents;

(*b*) as to the arrangements to be made by local authorities in connection with the health and education of such children;
(*c*) as to the records to be kept by local authorities;
(*d*) for securing that a child is not placed with a local authority foster parent unless that person is for the time being approved as a local authority foster parent by such local authority as may be prescribed;
(*e*) for securing that where possible the local authority foster parent with whom a child is to be placed is—
 (i) of the same religious persuasion as the child; or
 (ii) gives an undertaking that the child will be brought up in that religious persuasion;
(*f*) for securing that children placed with local authority foster parents, and the premises in which they are accommodated, will be supervised and inspected by a local authority and that the children will be removed from those premises if their welfare appears to require it;
(*g*) as to the circumstances in which local authorities may make arrangements for duties imposed on them by the regulations to be discharged, on their behalf.

*Regulations as to arrangements under section 23(2)(f)*

13. Regulations under section 23(2)(*f*) may, in particular, make provision as to—

(*a*) the persons to be notified of any proposed arrangements;
(*b*) the opportunities such persons are to have to make representations in relation to the arrangements proposed;
(*c*) the persons to be notified of any proposed changes in arrangements;
(*d*) the records to be kept by local authorities;
(*e*) the supervision by local authorities of any arrangements made.

*Regulations as to conditions under which child in care is allowed to live with parent, etc*

14. Regulations under section 23(5) may, in particular, impose requirements on a local authority as to—

(*a*) the making of any decision by a local authority to allow a child to live with any person falling within section 23(4) (including requirements as to those who must be consulted before the decision is made, and those who must be notified when it has been made);
(*b*) the supervision or medical examination of the child concerned;
(*c*) the removal of the child, in such circumstances as may be prescribed, from the care of the person with whom he has been allowed to live.

*Promotion and maintenance of contact between child and family*

15.—(1) Where a child is being looked after by a local authority, the authority shall, unless it is not reasonably practicable or consistent with his welfare, endeavour to promote contact between the child and—

(*a*) his parents;
(*b*) any person who is not a parent of his but who has parental responsibility for him; and
(*c*) any relative, friend or other person connected with him.

(2) Where a child is being looked after by a local authority—

(*a*) the authority shall take such steps as are reasonably practicable to secure that—
 (i) his parents; and
 (ii) any person who is not a parent of his but who has parental responsibility for him,

are kept informed of where he is being accommodated; and

(*b*) every such person shall secure that the authority are kept informed of his or her address.

(3) Where a local authority ("the receiving authority") take over the provision of accommodation for a child from another local authority ("the transferring authority") under section 20(2)—

(*a*) the receiving authority shall (where reasonably practicable) inform—

(i) the child's parents; and
(ii) any person who is not a parent of his but who has parental responsibility for him;

(*b*) sub-paragraph (2)(*a*) shall apply to the transferring authority, as well as the receiving authority, until at least one such person has been informed of the change; and
(*c*) sub-paragraph (2)(*b*) shall not require any person to inform the receiving authority of his address until he has been so informed.

(4) Nothing in this paragraph requires a local authority to inform any person of the whereabouts of a child if—

(*a*) the child is in the care of the authority; and
(*b*) the authority has reasonable cause to believe that informing the person would prejudice the child's welfare.

(5) Any person who fails (without reasonable excuse) to comply with sub-paragraph (2)(*b*) shall be guilty of an offence and liable on summary conviction to a fine not exceeding level 2 on the standard scale.

(6) It shall be a defence in any proceedings under sub-paragraph (5) to prove that the defendant was residing at the same address as another person who was the child's parent or had parental responsibility for the child and had reasonable cause to believe that the other person had informed the appropriate authority that both of them were residing at that address.

*Visits to, or by, children: expenses*

16.—(1) This paragraph applies where—

(*a*) a child is being looked after by a local authority; and
(*b*) the conditions mentioned in sub-paragraph (3) are satisfied.

(2) The authority may—

(*a*) make payments to—

(i) a parent of the child;
(ii) any person who is not a parent of his but who has parental responsibility for him; or
(iii) any relative, friend or other person connected with him,

in respect of travelling, subsistence or other expenses incurred by that person visiting the child; or

(*b*) make payments to the child, or to any person on his behalf, in respect of travelling, subsistence or other expenses incurred by or on behalf of the child in his visiting—

(i) a parent of his;
(ii) any person who is not a parent of his but who has parental responsibility for him; or
(iii) any relative, friend or other person connected with him.

(3) The conditions are that—

(*a*) it appears to the authority that the visit in question could not otherwise be made without undue financial hardship; and
(*b*) the circumstances warrant the making of the payments.

*Appointment of visitor for child who is not being visited*

17.—(1) Where it appears to a local authority in relation to any child that they are looking after that—

(*a*) communication between the child and—

(i) a parent of his, or

(ii) any person who is not a parent of his but who has parental responsibility for him,

has been infrequent; or

(*b*) he has not visited or been visited by (or lived with) any such person during the preceding twelve months,

and that it would be in the child's best interests for an independent person to be appointed to be his visitor for the purposes of this paragraph, they shall appoint such a visitor.

(2) A person so appointed shall—

(*a*) have the duty of visiting, advising and befriending the child; and

(*b*) be entitled to recover from the authority who appointed him any reasonable expenses incurred by him for the purposes of his functions under this paragraph.

(3) A person's appointment as a visitor in pursuance of this paragraph shall be determined if—

(*a*) he gives notice in writing to the authority who appointed him that he resigns the appointment; or

(*b*) the authority give him notice in writing that they have terminated it.

(4) The determination of such an appointment shall not prejudice any duty under this paragraph to make a further appointment.

(5) Where a local authority propose to appoint a visitor for a child under this paragraph, the appointment shall not be made if—

(*a*) the child objects to it; and

(*b*) the authority are satisfied that he has sufficient understanding to make an informed decision.

(6) Where a visitor has been appointed for a child under this paragraph, the local authority shall determine the appointment if—

(*a*) the child objects to its continuing; and

(*b*) the authority are satisfied that he has sufficient understanding to make an informed decision.

(7) The Secretary of State may make regulations as to the circumstances in which a person appointed as a visitor under this paragraph is to be regarded as independent of the local authority appointing him.

*Power to guarantee apprenticeship deeds etc*

18.—(1) While a child is being looked after by a local authority, or is a person qualifying for advice and assistance, the authority may undertake any obligation by way of guarantee under any deed of apprenticeship or articles of clerkship which he enters into.

(2) Where a local authority have undertaken any such obligation under any deed or articles they may at any time (whether or not they are still looking after the person concerned) undertake the like obligation under any supplemental deed or articles.

*Arrangements to assist children to live abroad*

19.—(1) A local authority may only arrange for, or assist in arranging for, any child in their care to live outside England and Wales with the approval of the court.

(2) A local authority may, with the approval of every person who has parental responsibility for the child arrange for, or assist in arranging for, any other child looked after by them to live outside England and Wales.

(3) The court shall not give its approval under sub-paragraph (1) unless it is satisfied that—

(*a*) living outside England and Wales would be in the child's best interests;
(*b*) suitable arrangements have been, or will be, made for his reception and welfare in the country in which he will live;
(*c*) the child has consented to living in that country; and
(*d*) every person who has parental responsibility for the child has consented to his living in that country.

(4) Where the court is satisfied that the child does not have sufficient understanding to give or withhold his consent, it may disregard sub-paragraph (3)(*c*) and give its approval if the child is to live in the country concerned with a parent, guardian, or other suitable person.

(5) Where a person whose consent is required by sub-paragraph (3)(*d*) fails to give his consent, the court may disregard that provision and give its approval if it is satisfied that that person—

(*a*) cannot be found;
(*b*) is incapable of consenting; or
(*c*) is withholding his consent unreasonably.

(6) Section 56 of the Adoption Act 1976 (which requires authority for the taking or sending abroad for adoption of a child who is a British subject) shall not apply in the case of any child who is to live outside England and Wales with the approval of the court given under this paragraph.

(7) Where a court decides to give its approval under this paragraph it may order that its decision is not to have effect during the appeal period.

(8) In sub-paragraph (7) "the appeal period" means—

(*a*) where an appeal is made against the decision, the period between the making of the decision and the determination of the appeal; and
(*b*) otherwise, the period during which an appeal may be made against the decision.

*Death of children being looked after by local authorities*

20.—(1) If a child who is being looked after by a local authority dies, the authority—

(*a*) shall notify the Secretary of State;
(*b*) shall, so far as is reasonably practicable, notify the child's parents and every person who is not a parent of his but who has parental responsibility for him;
(*c*) may, with the consent (so far as it is reasonably practicable to obtain it) of every person who has parental responsibility for the child, arrange for the child's body to be buried or cremated; and
(*d*) may, if the conditions mentioned in sub-paragraph (2) are satisfied, make payments to any person who has parental responsibility for the child, or any relative, friend or other person connected with the child, in respect of travelling, subsistence or other expenses incurred by that person in attending the child's funeral.

(2) The conditions are that—

(*a*) it appears to the authority that the person concerned could not otherwise attend the child's funeral without undue financial hardship; and (*b*) that the circumstances warrant the making of the payments.

(3) Sub-paragraph (1) does not authorise cremation where it does not accord with the practice of the child's religious persuasion.

(4) Where a local authority have exercised their power under sub-paragraph (1)(*c*) with respect to a child who was under sixteen when he died, they may recover from any parent of the child any expenses incurred by them.

(5) Any sums so recoverable shall, without prejudice to any other method of recovery, be recoverable summarily as a civil debt.

(6) Nothing in this paragraph affects any enactment regulating or authorising the burial, cremation or anatomical examination of the body of a deceased person.

---

**Definitions** For 'a child who is looked after by a local authority' see s 22(1). For 'child', 'local authority', 'relative', 'child who is in the care of a local authority' see s 105(1); for 'local authority foster parent' see s 23(3); for 'parental responsibility' see s 3; for 'the receiving authority', 'the transferring authority' see para 15(3); for 'court' see s 92(7) and para 9.1 ff; for 'appeal period' see para 19(8).

**References** For 'parent' see para 2.7; for 'welfare of the child' see para 1.1 ff. For 'the standard scale' see the Criminal Justice Act 1982 s 37(2), (3) as amended; 'level 2' ie £100.

---

## Part III

## Contributions Towards Maintenance of Children Looked After by Local Authorities

### *Liability to contribute*

21.—(1) Where a local authority are looking after a child (other than in the cases mentioned in sub-paragraph (7)) they shall consider whether they should recover contributions towards the child's maintenance from any person liable to contribute ("a contributor").

(2) An authority may only recover contributions from a contributor if they consider it reasonable to do so.

(3) The persons liable to contribute are—

(*a*) where the child is under sixteen, each of his parents;
(*b*) where he has reached the age of sixteen, the child himself.

(4) A parent is not liable to contribute during any period when he is in receipt of income support or family credit under the Social Security Act 1986.

(5) A person is not liable to contribute towards the maintenance of a child in the care of a local authority in respect of any period during which the child is allowed by the authority (under section 23(5)) to live with a parent of his.

(6) A contributor is not obliged to make any contribution towards a child's maintenance except as agreed or determined in accordance with this Part of this Schedule.

(7) The cases are where the child is looked after by a local authority under—

(*a*) section 21;
(*b*) an interim care order;
(*c*) section 53 of the Children and Young Persons Act 1933.

### *Agreed contributions*

22.—(1) Contributions towards a child's maintenance may only be recovered if the local authority have served a notice ("a contribution notice") on the contributor specifying—

(*a*) the weekly sum which they consider that he should contribute; and (*b*) arrangements for payment.

(2) The contribution notice must be in writing and dated.

(3) Arrangements for payment shall, in particular, include—

(*a*) the date on which liability to contribute begins (which must not be earlier than the date of the notice);
(*b*) the date on which liability under the notice will end (if the child has not before that date ceased to be looked after by the authority); and
(*c*) the date on which the first payment is to be made.

(4) The authority may specify in a contribution notice a weekly sum which is a standard contribution determined by them for all children looked after by them.

(5) The authority may not specify in a contribution notice a weekly sum greater than that which they consider—

(*a*) they would normally be prepared to pay if they had placed a similar child with local authority foster parents; and
(*b*) it is reasonably practicable for the contributor to pay (having regard to his means).

(6) An authority may at any time withdraw a contribution notice (without prejudice to their power to serve another).

(7) Where the authority and the contributor agree—

(*a*) the sum which the contributor is to contribute; and
(*b*) arrangements for payment,

(whether as specified in the contribution notice or otherwise) and the contributor notifies the authority in writing that he so agrees, the authority may recover summarily as a civil debt any contribution which is overdue and unpaid.

(8) A contributor may, by serving a notice in writing on the authority, withdraw his agreement in relation to any period of liability falling after the date of service of the notice.

(9) Sub-paragraph (7) is without prejudice to any other method of recovery.

*Contribution orders*

23.-(1) Where a contributor has been served with a contribution notice and has—

(*a*) failed to reach any agreement with the local authority as mentioned in paragraph 22(7) within the period of one month beginning with the day on which the contribution notice was served; or
(*b*) served a notice under paragraph 22(8) withdrawing his agreement,

the authority may apply to the court for an order under this paragraph.

(2) On such an application the court may make an order ("a contribution order") requiring the contributor to contribute a weekly sum towards the child's maintenance in accordance with arrangements for payment specified by the court.

(3) A contribution order—

(*a*) shall not specify a weekly sum greater than that specified in the contribution notice; and
(*b*) shall be made with due regard to the contributor's means.

(4) A contribution order shall not—

(*a*) take effect before the date specified in the contribution notice; or
(*b*) have effect while the contributor is not liable to contribute (by virtue of paragraph 21); or
(*c*) remain in force after the child has ceased to be looked after by the authority who obtained the order.

(5) An authority may not apply to the court under sub-paragraph (1) in relation to a contribution notice which they have withdrawn.

(6) Where—

(*a*) a contribution order is in force;
(*b*) the authority serve another contribution notice; and
(*c*) the contributor and the authority reach an agreement under paragraph 22(7) in respect of that other contribution notice,

the effect of the agreement shall be to discharge the order from the date on which it is agreed that the agreement shall take effect.

(7) Where an agreement is reached under sub-paragraph (6) the authority shall notify the court—

(*a*) of the agreement; and
(*b*) of the date on which it took effect.

(8) A contribution order may be varied or revoked on the application of the contributor or the authority.

(9) In proceedings for the variation of a contribution order, the authority shall specify—

(*a*) the weekly sum which, having regard to paragraph 22, they propose that the contributor should contribute under the order as varied; and
(*b*) the proposed arrangements for payment.

(10) Where a contribution order is varied, the order—

(*a*) shall not specify a weekly sum greater than that specified by the authority in the proceedings for variation; and
(*b*) shall be made with due regard to the contributor's means.

(11) An appeal shall lie in accordance with rules of court from any order made under this paragraph.

*Enforcement of contribution orders etc*

24.—(1) A contribution order made by a magistrates' court shall be enforceable as a magistrates' court maintenance order (within the meaning of section 150(1) of the Magistrates' Courts Act 1980).

(2) Where a contributor has agreed, or has been ordered, to make contributions to a local authority, any other local authority within whose area the contributor is for the time being living may—

(*a*) at the request of the local authority who served the contribution notice; and
(*b*) subject to agreement as to any sum to be deducted in respect of services rendered,

collect from the contributor any contributions due on behalf of the authority who served the notice.

(3) In sub-paragraph (2) the reference to any other local authority includes a reference to—

(*a*) a local authority within the meaning of section 1(2) of the Social Work (Scotland) Act 1968; and
(*b*) a Health and Social Services Board established under Article 16 of the Health and Personal Social Services (Northern Ireland) Order 1972.

(4) The power to collect sums under sub-paragraph (2) includes the power to—

(*a*) receive and give a discharge for any contributions due; and
(*b*) (if necessary) enforce payment of any contributions,

even though those contributions may have fallen due at a time when the contributor was living elsewhere.

(5) Any contribution collected under sub-paragraph (2) shall be paid (subject to any agreed deduction) to the local authority who served the contribution notice.

(6) In any proceedings under this paragraph, a document which purports to be—

(*a*) a copy of an order made by a court under or by virtue of paragraph 23; and
(*b*) certified as a true copy by the clerk of the court,

shall be evidence of the order.

(7) In any proceedings under this paragraph, a certificate which—

(*a*) purports to be signed by the clerk or some other duly authorised officer of the local authority who obtained the contribution order; and
(*b*) states that any sum due to the authority under the order is overdue and unpaid,

shall be evidence that the sum is overdue and unpaid.

*Regulations*

25. The Secretary of State may make regulations—

(*a*) as to the considerations which a local authority must take into account in deciding—
  (i) whether it is reasonable to recover contributions; and
  (ii) what the arrangements for payment should be;
(*b*) as to the procedures they must follow in reaching agreements with—
  (i) contributors (under paragraphs 22 and 23); and
  (ii) any other local authority (under paragraph 23).

---

**Definitions** For 'local authority', 'child' see s 105(1); for 'a child who is looked after by a local authority' see s 22(1); for 'a contributor' see para 21(1); for 'a contribution notice' see para 22(1); for 'local authority foster parent' see s 23(3); for 'court' see s 92(7) and para 9.1 ff; for 'a contribution order' see para 23(2).

**References** For 'parent' see para 2.7. 'This Part of this Schedule' ie Part III paras 21-25. For interim care orders see s 38. For service of notices generally under the Act see s 105(8)-(10).

---

## SCHEDULE 3

Sections 35 and 36

## Supervision Orders

### Part I

### General

*Meaning of "responsible person"*

1. In this Schedule, "the responsible person", in relation to a supervised child, means—

(*a*) any person who has parental responsibility for the child; and
(*b*) any other person with whom the child is living.

*Power of supervisor to give directions to supervised child*

2.—(1) A supervision order may require the supervised child to comply with any directions given from time to time by the supervisor which require him to do all or any of the following things—

(*a*) to live at a place or places specified in the directions for a period or periods so specified;

(*b*) to present himself to a person or persons specified in the directions at a place or places and on a day or days so specified;
(*c*) to participate in activities specified in the directions on a day or days so specified.

(2) It shall be for the supervisor to decide whether, and to what extent, he exercises his power to give directions and to decide the form of any directions which he gives.

(3) Sub-paragraph (1) does not confer on a supervisor power to give directions in respect of any medical or psychiatric examination or treatment (which are matters dealt with in paragraphs 4 and 5).

*Imposition of obligations on responsible person*

3.—(1) With the consent of any responsible person, a supervision order may include a requirement—

(*a*) that he take all reasonable steps to ensure that the supervised child complies with any direction given by the supervisor under paragraph 2;
(*b*) that he take all reasonable steps to ensure that the supervised child complies with any requirement included in the order under paragraph 4 or 5;
(*c*) that he comply with any directions given by the supervisor requiring him to attend at a place specified in the directions for the purpose of taking part in activities so specified.

(2) A direction given under sub-paragraph (1)(*c*) may specify the time at which the responsible person is to attend and whether or not the supervised child is required to attend with him.

(3) A supervision order may require any person who is a responsible person in relation to the supervised child to keep the supervisor informed of his address, if it differs from the child's.

*Psychiatric and medical examinations*

4.—(1) A supervision order may require the supervised child—

(*a*) to submit to a medical or psychiatric examination; or
(*b*) to submit to any such examination from time to time as directed by the supervisor.

(2) Any such examination shall be required to be conducted—

(*a*) by, or under the direction of, such registered medical practitioner as may be specified in the order;
(*b*) at a place specified in the order and at which the supervised child is to attend as a non-
resident patient; or
(*c*) at—

(i) a health service hospital; or
(ii) in the case of a psychiatric examination, a hospital or mental nursing home,

at which the supervised child is, or is to attend as, a resident patient.

(3) A requirement of a kind mentioned in sub-paragraph (2)(*c*) shall not be included unless the court is satisfied, on the evidence of a registered medical practitioner, that—

(*a*) the child may be suffering from a physical or mental condition that requires, and may be susceptible to, treatment; and
(*b*) a period as a resident patient is necessary if the examination is to be carried out properly.

(4) No court shall include a requirement under this paragraph in a supervision order unless it is satisfied that—

(*a*) where the child has sufficient understanding to make an informed decision, he consents to its inclusion; and
(*b*) satisfactory arrangements have been, or can be, made for the examination.

*Psychiatric and medical treatment*

5.—(1) Where a court which proposes to make or vary a supervision order is satisfied, on the evidence of a registered medical practitioner approved for the purposes of section 12 of the Mental Health Act 1983, that the mental condition of the supervised child—

(*a*) is such as requires, and may be susceptible to, treatment; but
(*b*) is not such as to warrant his detention in pursuance of a hospital order under Part III of that Act,

the court may include in the order a requirement that the supervised child shall, for a period specified in the order, submit to such treatment as is so specified.

(2) The treatment specified in accordance with sub-paragraph (1) must be—

(*a*) by, or under the direction of, such registered medical practitioner as may be specified in the order;
(*b*) as a non-resident patient at such a place as may be so specified; or
(*c*) as a resident patient in a hospital or mental nursing home.

(3) Where a court which proposes to make or vary a supervision order is satisfied, on the evidence of a registered medical practitioner, that the physical condition of the supervised child is such as requires, and may be susceptible to, treatment, the court may include in the order a requirement that the supervised child shall, for a period specified in the order, submit to such treatment as is so specified.

(4) The treatment specified in accordance with sub-paragraph (3) must be—

(*a*) by, or under the direction of, such registered medical practitioner as may be specified in the order;
(*b*) as a non-resident patient at such place as may be so specified; or
(*c*) as a resident patient in a health service hospital.

(5) No court shall include a requirement under this paragraph in a supervision order unless it is satisfied—

(*a*) where the child has sufficient understanding to make an informed decision, that he consents to its inclusion; and
(*b*) that satisfactory arrangements have been, or can be, made for the treatment.

(6) If a medical practitioner by whom or under whose direction a supervised person is being treated in pursuance of a requirement included in a supervision order by virtue of this paragraph is unwilling to continue to treat or direct the treatment of the supervised child or is of the opinion that—

(*a*) the treatment should be continued beyond the period specified in the order;
(*b*) the supervised child needs different treatment;
(*c*) he is not susceptible to treatment; or
(*d*) he does not require further treatment,

the practitioner shall make a report in writing to that effect to the supervisor.

(7) On receiving a report under this paragraph the supervisor shall refer it to the court, and on such a reference the court may make an order cancelling or varying the requirement.

---

**Definitions** For 'the responsible person' see para 1; for 'supervised child', 'child', 'supervisor', 'health service hospital', 'hospital', 'mental nursing home' see s 105(1); for 'parental responsibility' see s 3; for 'court' see s 92(7) and para 9.1 ff.

---

PART II

MISCELLANEOUS

*Life of supervision order*

6.—(1) Subject to sub-paragraph (2) and section 91, a supervision order shall cease to have effect at the end of the period of one year beginning with the date on which it was made.

(2) A supervision order shall also cease to have effect if an event mentioned in section 25(1)(*a*) or (*b*) of the Child Abduction and Custody Act 1985 (termination of existing orders) occurs with respect to the child.

(3) Where the supervisor applies to the court to extend, or further extend, a supervision order the court may extend the order for such period as it may specify.

(4) A supervision order may not be extended so as to run beyond the end of the period of three years beginning with the date on which it was made.

*Limited life of directions*

7.—(1) The total number of days in respect of which a supervised child or (as the case may be) responsible person may be required to comply with directions given under paragraph 2 or 3 shall not exceed 90 or such lesser number (if any) as the supervision order may specify.

(2) For the purpose of calculating that total number of days, the supervisor may disregard any day in respect of which directions previously given in pursuance of the order were not complied with.

*Information to be given to supervisor etc*

8.—(1) A supervision order may require the supervised child—

(*a*) to keep the supervisor informed of any change in his address; and
(*b*) to allow the supervisor to visit him at the place where he is living.

(2) The responsible person in relation to any child with respect to whom a supervision order is made shall—

(*a*) if asked by the supervisor, inform him of the child's address (if it is known to him); and
(*b*) if he is living with the child, allow the supervisor reasonable contact with the child.

*Selection of supervisor*

9.—(1) A supervision order shall not designate a local authority as the supervisor unless—

(*a*) the authority agree; or
(*b*) the supervised child lives or will live within their area.

(2) A court shall not place a child under the supervision of a probation officer unless—

(*a*) the appropriate authority so request; and
(*b*) a probation officer is already exercising or has exercised, in relation to another member of the household to which the child belongs, duties imposed on probation officers—

(i) by paragraph 8 of Schedule 3 to the Powers of Criminal Courts Act 1973; or
(ii) by rules under paragraph 18(1)(*b*) of that Schedule.

(3) In sub-paragraph (2) "the appropriate authority" means the local authority

appearing to the court to be the authority in whose area the supervised child lives or will live.

(4) Where a supervision order places a person under the supervision of a probation officer, the officer shall be selected in accordance with arrangements made by the probation committee for the area in question.

(5) If the selected probation officer is unable to carry out his duties, or dies, another probation officer shall be selected in the same manner.

*Effect of supervision order on earlier orders*

10. The making of a supervision order with respect to any child brings to an end any earlier care or supervision order which—

(*a*) was made with respect to that child; and
(*b*) would otherwise continue in force.

*Local authority functions and expenditure*

11.—(1) The Secretary of State may make regulations with respect to the exercise by a local authority of their functions where a child has been placed under their supervision by a supervision order.

(2) Where a supervision order requires compliance with directions given by virtue of this section, any expenditure incurred by the supervisor for the purposes of the directions shall be defrayed by the local authority designated in the order.

---

**Definitions** For 'supervision order' see s 31(11); for 'supervisor', 'supervised child', 'local authority', 'functions' see s 105(1); for 'court' see s 92(7) and para 9.1 ff; for 'the responsible person' see para 1; for 'the appropriate authority' see para 9(3). For power to issue a warrant to authorise a constable to assist in exercising the power under para 8(1)(b), (2)(b) see s 102.

---

## PART III

### EDUCATION SUPERVISION ORDERS

*Effect of orders*

12.—(1) Where an education supervision order is in force with respect to a child, it shall be the duty of the supervisor—

(*a*) to advise, assist and befriend, and give directions to—

(i) the supervised child; and
(ii) his parents;

in such a way as will, in the opinion of the supervisor, secure that he is properly educated;

(*b*) where any such directions given to—

(i) the supervised child; or
(ii) a parent of his,

have not been complied with, to consider what further steps to take in the exercise of the supervisor's powers under this Act.

(2) Before giving any directions under sub-paragraph (1) the supervisor shall, so far as is reasonably practicable, ascertain the wishes and feelings of—

(*a*) the child; and
(*b*) his parents,

including, in particular, their wishes as to the place at which the child should be educated.

(3) When settling the terms of any such directions, the supervisor shall give due consideration—

(*a*) having regard to the child's age and understanding, to such wishes and feelings of his as the supervisor has been able to ascertain; and

(*b*) to such wishes and feelings of the child's parents as he has been able to ascertain.

(4) Directions may be given under this paragraph at any time while the education supervision order is in force.

13.—(1) Where an education supervision order is in force with respect to a child, the duties of the child's parents under sections 36 and 39 of the Education Act 1944 (duty to secure education of children and to secure regular attendance of registered pupils) shall be superseded by their duty to comply with any directions in force under the education supervision order.

(2) Where an education supervision order is made with respect to a child—

(*a*) any school attendance order—

(i) made under section 37 of the Act of 1944 with respect to the child; and

(ii) in force immediately before the making of the education supervision order,

shall cease to have effect; and

(*b*) while the education supervision order remains in force, the following provisions shall not apply with respect to the child—

(i) section 37 of that Act (school attendance orders);

(ii) section 76 of that Act (pupils to be educated in accordance with wishes of their parents);

(iii) sections 6 and 7 of the Education Act 1980 (parental preference and appeals against admission decisions);

(*c*) a supervision order made with respect to the child in criminal proceedings, while the education supervision order is in force, may not include an education requirement of the kind which could otherwise be included under section 12C of the Children and Young Persons Act 1969;

(*d*) any education requirement of a kind mentioned in paragraph (*c*), which was in force with respect to the child immediately before the making of the education supervision order, shall cease to have effect.

*Effect where child also subject to supervision order*

14.—(1) This paragraph applies where an education supervision order and a supervision order, or order under section 7(7)(*b*) of the Children and Young Persons Act 1969, are in force at the same time with respect to the same child.

(2) Any failure to comply with a direction given by the supervisor under the education supervision order shall be disregarded if it would not have been reasonably practicable to comply with it without failing to comply with a direction given under the other order.

*Duration of orders*

15.—(1) An education supervision order shall have effect for a period of one year, beginning with the date on which it is made.

(2) An education supervision order shall not expire if, before it would otherwise have expired, the court has (on the application of the authority in whose favour the order was made) extended the period during whith it is in force.

(3) Such an application may not be made earlier than three months before the date on which the order would otherwise expire.

(4) The period during which an education supervision order is in force may be extended under sub-paragraph (2) on more than one occasion.

(5) No one extension may be for a period of more than three years.

(6) An education supervision order shall cease to have effect on—

(*a*) the child's ceasing to be of compulsory school age; or
(*b*) the making of a care order with respect to the child;

and sub-paragraphs (1) to (4) are subject to this sub-paragraph.

*Information to be given to supervisor etc*

16.—(1) An education supervision order may require the child—

(*a*) to keep the supervisor informed of any change in his address; and
(*b*) to allow the supervisor to visit him at the place where he is living.

(2) A person who is the parent of a child with respect to whom an education supervision order has been made shall—

(*a*) if asked by the supervisor, inform him of the child's address (if it is known to him); and
(*b*) if he is living with the child, allow the supervisor reasonable contact with the child.

*Discharge of orders*

17.—(1) The court may discharge any education supervision order on the application of—

(*a*) the child concerned;
(*b*) a parent of his; or
(*c*) the local education authority concerned.

(2) On discharging an education supervision order, the court may direct the local authority within whose area the child lives, or will live, to investigate the circumstances of the child.

*Offences*

18.—(1) If a parent of a child with respect to whom an education supervision order is in force persistently fails to comply with a direction given under the order he shall be guilty of an offence.

(2) It shall be a defence for any person charged with such an offence to prove that—

(*a*) he took all reasonable steps to ensure that the direction was complied with;
(*b*) the direction was unreasonable; or
(*c*) he had complied with—

(i) a requirement included in a supervision order made with respect to the child; or
(ii) directions given under such a requirement,

and that it was not reasonably practicable to comply both with the direction and with the requirement or directions mentioned in this paragraph.

(3) A person guilty of an offence under this paragraph shall be liable on summary conviction to a fine not exceeding level 3 on the standard scale.

*Persistent failure of child to comply with directions*

19.—(1) Where a child with respect to whom an education supervision order is in force persistently fails to comply with any direction given under the order, the local education authority concerned shall notify the appropriate local authority.

(2) Where a local authority have been notified under sub-paragraph (1) they shall investigate the circumstances of the child.

(3) In this paragraph "the appropriate local authority" has the same meaning as in section 36.

*Miscellaneous*

20. The Secretary of State may by regulations make provision modifying, or displacing, the provisions of any enactment about education in relation to any child with respect to whom an education supervision order is in force to such extent as appears to the Secretary of State to be necessary or expedient in consequence of the provision made by this Act with respect to such orders.

*Interpretation*

21. In this Part of this Schedule "parent" has the same meaning as in the Education Act 1944 (as amended by Schedule 13).

---

**Definitions** For 'education supervision order' see s 36(2); for 'child', 'supervisor', 'supervised child', 'local education authority' see s 105(1); for 'parent' see para 21; for 'registered pupil' see s 105(1) and Education Act 1944 s 114; for 'court' see s 92(7) and para 9.1 ff; for 'care order' see s 31(11) and s 105(1); for 'compulsory school age' see Education Act 1944 s 114; for 'the appropriate local authority' see para 19 (3).

**References** For 'the standard scale' see the Criminal Justice Act 1982 s 37(2) (3) as amended; 'level 3' ie £400.

---

## SCHEDULE 4

Section 53(6)

### MANAGEMENT AND CONDUCT OF COMMUNITY HOMES

### PART I

### INSTRUMENTS OF MANAGEMENT

*Instruments of management for controlled and assisted community homes*

1.—(1) The Secretary of State may by order make an instrument of management providing for the constitution of a body of managers for any voluntary home which is designated as a controlled or assisted community home.

(2) Sub-paragraph (3) applies where two or more voluntary homes are designated as controlled community homes or as assisted community homes.

(3) If—

(*a*) those homes are, or are to be, provided by the same voluntary organisation; and

(*b*) the same local authority is to be represented on the body of managers for those homes,

a single instrument of management may be made by the Secretary of State under this paragraph constituting one body of managers for those homes or for any two or more of them.

(4) The number of persons who, in accordance with an instrument of management, constitute the body of managers for a voluntary home shall be such number (which must be a multiple of three) as may be specified in the instrument.

(5) The instrument shall provide that the local authority specified in the instrument shall appoint—

(*a*) in the case of a voluntary home which is designated as a controlled community home, two-thirds of the managers; and

(*b*) in the case of a voluntary home which is designated as an assisted community home, one-third of them.

(6) An instrument of management shall provide that the foundation managers shall be appointed, in such manner and by such persons as may be specified in the instrument—

(*a*) so as to represent the interests of the voluntary organisation by which the home is, or is to be, provided; and

(*b*) for the purpose of securing that—

(i) so far as is practicable, the character of the home as a voluntary home will be preserved; and

(ii) subject to paragraph 2(3), the terms of any trust deed relating to the home are observed.

(7) An instrument of management shall come into force on such date as it may specify.

(8) If an instrument of management is in force in relation to a voluntary home the home shall be (and be known as) a controlled community home or an assisted community home, according to its designation.

(9) In this paragraph—

"foundation managers", in relation to a voluntary home, means those of the managers of the home who are not appointed by a local authority in accordance with sub-paragraph (5); and

"designated" means designated in accordance with section 53.

2.—(1) An instrument of management shall contain such provisions as the Secretary of State considers appropriate.

(2) Nothing in the instrument of management shall affect the purposes for which the premises comprising the home are held.

(3) Without prejudice to the generality of sub-paragraph (1), an instrument of management may contain provisions—

(*a*) specifying the nature and purpose of the home (or each of the homes) to which it relates;

(*b*) requiring a specified number or proportion of the places in that home (or those homes) to be made available to local authorities and to any other body specified in the instrument; and

(*c*) relating to the management of that home (or those homes) and the charging of fees with respect to—

(i) children placed there; or

(ii) places made available to any local authority or other body.

(4) Subject to sub-paragraphs (1) and (2), in the event of any inconsistency between the provisions of any trust deed and an instrument of management, the instrument of management shall prevail over the provisions of the trust deed in so far as they relate to the home concerned.

(5) After consultation with the voluntary organisation concerned and with the local authority specified in its instrument of management, the Secretary of State may by order vary or revoke any provisions of the instrument.

---

**Definitions** For 'voluntary home' see s 60(3); for 'designated' and 'foundation managers' see para 1(9); for 'controlled community home' see s 53(4); for 'assisted community home' see s 53(5); for 'voluntary organisation', 'local authority', 'child' see s 105(1); for 'trust deed' see s 55(6).

---

## Part II

### Management of Controlled and Assisted Community Homes

3.—(1) The management, equipment and maintenance of a controlled community home shall be the responsibility of the local authority specified in its instrument of management.

(2) The management, equipment and maintenance of an assisted community home shall be the responsibility of the voluntary organisation by which the home is provided.

(3) In this paragraph—

"home" means a controlled community home or (as the case may be) assisted community home; and

"the managers", in relation to a home, means the managers constituted by its instrument of management; and

"the responsible body", in relation to a home, means the local authority or (as the case may be) voluntary organisation responsible for its management, equipment and maintenance.

(4) The functions of a home's responsible body shall be exercised through the managers.

(5) Anything done, liability incurred or property acquired by a home's managers shall be done, incurred or acquired by them as agents of the responsible body.

(6) In so far as any matter is reserved for the decision of a home's responsible body by—

(*a*) sub-paragraph (8);
(*b*) the instrument of management;
(*c*) the service by the body on the managers, or any of them, of a notice reserving any matter,

that matter shall be dealt with by the body and not by the managers.

(7) In dealing with any matter so reserved, the responsible body shall have regard to any representations made to the body by the managers.

(8) The employment of persons at a home shall be a matter reserved for the decision of the responsible body.

(9) Where the instrument of management of a controlled community home so provides, the responsible body may enter into arrangements with the voluntary organisation by which that home is provided whereby, in accordance with such terms as may be agreed between them and the voluntary organisation, persons who are not in the employment of the responsible body shall undertake duties at that home.

(10) Subject to sub-paragraph (11)—

(*a*) where the responsible body for an assisted community home proposes to engage any person to work at that home or to terminate without notice the employment of any person at that home, it shall consult the local authority specified in the instrument of management and, if that authority so direct, the responsible body shall not carry out its proposal without their consent; and
(*b*) that local authority may, after consultation with the responsible body, require that body to terminate the employment of any person at that home.

(11) Paragraphs (*a*) and (*b*) of sub-paragraph (10) shall not apply—

(*a*) in such cases or circumstances as may be specified by notice in writing given by the local authority to the responsible body; and
(*b*) in relation to the employment of any persons or class of persons specified in the home's instrument of management.

(12) The accounting year of the managers of a home shall be such as may be specified by the responsible body.

(13) Before such date in each accounting year as may be so specified, the managers of a home shall submit to the responsible body estimates, in such form as the body may require, of expenditure and receipts in respect of the next accounting year.

(14) Any expenses incurred by the managers of a home with the approval of the responsible body shall be defrayed by that body.

(15) The managers of a home shall keep—

(*a*) proper accounts with respect to the home; and
(*b*) proper records in relation to the accounts.

(16) Where an instrument of management relates to more than one home, one set of accounts and records may be kept in respect of all the homes to which it relates.

---

**Definitions** For 'controlled community home' see s 53(4); for 'local authority', 'voluntary organisation', 'functions' see s 105(1); for 'assisted community home' see s 53(5); for 'home', 'the managers', 'the responsible body' see para 3(3).

**References** For service of notices under the Act generally see s 105(8)-(10).

---

## Part III

### Regulations

4.—(1) The Secretary of State may make regulations—

(*a*) as to the placing of children in community homes;
(*b*) as to the conduct of such homes; and
(*c*) for securing the welfare of children in such homes.

(2) The regulations may, in particular—

(*a*) prescribe standards to which the premises used for such homes are to conform;
(*b*) impose requirements as to the accommodation, staff and equipment to be provided in such homes, and as to the arrangements to be made for protecting the health of children in such homes;
(*c*) provide for the control and discipline of children in such homes;
(*d*) impose requirements as to the keeping of records and giving of notices in respect of children in such homes;
(*e*) impose requirements as to the facilities which are to be provided for giving religious instruction to children in such homes;
(*f*) authorise the Secretary of State to give and revoke directions requiring—

(i) the local authority by whom a home is provided or who are specified in the instrument of management for a controlled community home, or
(ii) the voluntary organisation by which an assisted community home is provided,

to accommodate in the home a child looked after by a local authority for whom no places are made available in that home or to take such action in relation to a child accommodated in the home as may be specified in the directions;

(*g*) provide for consultation with the Secretary of State as to applicants for appointment to the charge of a home;
(*h*) empower the Secretary of State to prohibit the appointment of any particular applicant except in the cases (if any) in which the regulations dispense with such consultation by reason that the person to be appointed possesses such qualifications as may be prescribed;
(*i*) require the approval of the Secretary of State for the provision and use of

accommodation for the purpose of restricting the liberty of children in such homes and impose other requirements (in addition to those imposed by section 25) as to the placing of a child in accommodation provided for that purpose, including a requirement to obtain the permission of any local authority who are looking after the child;

(*j*) provide that, to such extent as may be provided for in the regulations, the Secretary of State may direct that any provision of regulations under this paragraph which is specified in the direction and makes any such provision as is referred to in paragraph (*a*) or (*b*) shall not apply in relation to a particular home or the premises used for it, and may provide for the variation or revocation of any such direction by the Secretary of State.

(3) Without prejudice to the power to make regulations under this paragraph conferring functions on—

(*a*) the local authority or voluntary organisation by which a community home is provided; or

(*b*) the managers of a controlled or assisted community home,

regulations under this paragraph may confer functions in relation to a controlled or assisted community home on the local authority named in the instrument of management for the home.

---

**Definitions** For 'child', 'local authority', 'voluntary organisation', see s 105(1). For 'community home' see s 53. For 'assisted community home' see s 53(5). For 'a child who is looked after by a local authority' see s 22(1). For 'controlled community home' see s 53(4).

---

## SCHEDULE 5

Section 60(4)

### Voluntary Homes and Voluntary Organisations

### Part I

### Registration of Voluntary Homes

*General*

1.—(1) An application for registration under this paragraph shall—

(*a*) be made by the persons intending to carry on the home to which the application relates; and

(*b*) be made in such manner, and be accompanied by such particulars, as the Secretary of State may prescribe.

(2) On an application duly made under sub-paragraph (1) the Secretary of State may—

(*a*) grant or refuse the application, as he thinks fit; or

(*b*) grant the application subject to such conditions as he considers appropriate.

(3) The Secretary of State may from time to time—

(*a*) vary any condition for the time being in force with respect to a voluntary home by virtue of this paragraph; or

(*b*) impose an additional condition,

either on the application of the person carrying on the home or without such an application.

(4) Where at any time it appears to the Secretary of State that the conduct of any voluntary home—

(*a*) is not in accordance with regulations made under paragraph 7; or

(*b*) is otherwise unsatisfactory,

he may cancel the registration of the home and remove it from the register.

(5) Any person who, without reasonable excuse, carries on a voluntary home in contravention of—

(*a*) section 60; or
(*b*) a condition to which the registration of the home is for the time being subject by virtue of this Part,

shall be guilty of an offence.

(6) Any person guilty of such an offence shall be liable on summary conviction to a fine not exceeding—

(*a*) level 5 on the standard scale, if his offence is under sub-paragraph (5)(*a*); or
(*b*) level 4, if it is under sub-paragraph (5)(*b*).

(7) Where the Secretary of State registers a home under this paragraph, or cancels the registration of a home, he shall notify the local authority within whose area the home is situated.

*Procedure*

2.—(1) Where—

(*a*) a person applies for registration of a voluntary home; and
(*b*) the Secretary of State proposes to grant his application,

the Secretary of State shall give him written notice of his proposal and of the conditions subject to which he proposes to grant the application.

(2) The Secretary of State need not give notice if he proposes to grant the application subject only to conditions which—

(*a*) the applicant specified in the application; or
(*b*) the Secretary of State and the applicant have subsequently agreed.

(3) Where the Secretary of State proposes to refuse such an application he shall give notice of his proposal to the applicant.

(4) The Secretary of State shall give any person carrying on a voluntary home notice of a proposal to—

(*a*) cancel the registration of the home;
(*b*) vary any condition for the time being in force with respect to the home by virtue of paragraph 1; or
(*c*) impose any additional condition.

(5) A notice under this paragraph shall give the Secretary of State's reasons for his proposal.

*Right to make representations*

3.—(1) A notice under paragraph 2 shall state that within 14 days of service of the notice any person on whom it is served may (in writing) require the Secretary of State to give him an opportunity to make representations to the Secretary of State concerning the matter.

(2) Where a notice has been served under paragraph 2, the Secretary of State shall not determine the matter until either—

(*a*) any person on whom the notice was served has made representations to him concerning the matter; or
(*b*) the period during which any such person could have required the Secretary of State to give him an opportunity to make representations has elapsed without the Secretary of State being required to give such an opportunity; or
(*c*) the conditions specified in sub-paragraph (3) are satisfied.

(3) The conditions are that—

(*a*) a person on whom the notice was served has required the Secretary of State to give him an opportunity to make representations to the Secretary of State;
(*b*) the Secretary of State has allowed him a reasonable period to make his representations; and
(*c*) he has failed to make them within that period.

(4) The representations may be made, at the option of the person making them, either in writing or orally.

(5) If he informs the Secretary of State that he desires to make oral representations, the Secretary of State shall give him an opportunity of appearing before, and of being heard by, a person appointed by the Secretary of State.

*Decision of Secretary of State*

4.—(1) If the Secretary of State decides to adopt the proposal, he shall serve notice in writing of his decision on any person on whom he was required to serve notice of his proposal.

(2) A notice under this paragraph shall be accompanied by a notice explaining the right of appeal conferred by paragraph 5.

(3) A decision of the Secretary of State, other than a decision to grant an application for registration subject only to such conditions as are mentioned in paragraph 2(2) or to refuse an application for registration, shall not take effect—

(*a*) if no appeal is brought, until the end of the period of 28 days referred to in paragraph 5(3); and
(*b*) if an appeal is brought, until it is determined or abandoned.

*Appeals*

5.—(1) An appeal against a decision of the Secretary of State under Part VII shall lie to a Registered Homes Tribunal.

(2) An appeal shall be brought by notice in writing given to the Secretary of State.

(3) No appeal may be brought by a person more than 28 days after service on him of notice of the decision.

(4) On an appeal, the Tribunal may confirm the Secretary of State's decision or direct that it shall not have effect.

(5) A Tribunal shall also have power on an appeal to—

(*a*) vary any condition for the time being in force by virtue of Part VII with respect to the home to which the appeal relates;
(*b*) direct that any such condition shall cease to have effect; or
(*c*) direct that any such condition as it thinks fit shall have effect with respect to the home.

*Notification of particulars with respect to voluntary homes*

6.—(1) It shall be the duty of the person in charge of any voluntary home established after the commencement of this Act to send to the Secretary of State within three months from the establishment of the home such particulars with respect to the home as the Secretary of State may prescribe.

(2) It shall be the duty of the person in charge of any voluntary home (whether established before or after the commencement of this Act) to send to the Secretary of State such particulars with respect to the home as may be prescribed.

(3) The particulars must be sent—

(*a*) in the case of a home established before the commencement of this Act, in every year, or
(*b*) in the case of a home established after the commencement of this Act, in every year subsequent to the year in which particulars are sent under sub-paragraph (1),

by such date as the Secretary of State may prescribe.

(4) Where the Secretary of State by regulations varies the particulars which are to be sent to him under sub-paragraph (1) or (2) by the person in charge of a voluntary home—

(*a*) that person shall send to the Secretary of State the prescribed particulars within three months from the date of the making of the regulations;
(*b*) where any such home was established before, but not more than three months before, the making of the regulations, compliance with paragraph (*a*) shall be sufficient compliance with the requirement of sub-paragraph (1) to send the prescribed particulars within three months from the establishment of the home;
(*c*) in the year in which the particulars are varied, compliance with paragraph (*a*) by the person in charge of any voluntary home shall be sufficient compliance with the requirement of sub-paragraph (2) to send the prescribed particulars before the prescribed date in that year.

(5) If the person in charge of a voluntary home fails, without resasonable excuse, to comply with any of the requirements of this paragraph he shall be guilty of an offence.

(6) Any person guilty of such an offence shall be liable on summary conviction to a fine not exceeding level 2 on the standard scale.

---

**Definitions** For 'voluntary home' see s 60(3); for 'local authority' see s 105(1).

**References** 'This Part' ie Part VII ss 59-62 and this schedule. For 'the standard scale' see the Criminal Justice Act 1982 s 37(2), (3) as amended; 'level 5' ie £2,000, 'level 4' ie £1,000, 'level 2' ie £100. For service of notices generally under the Act see s 105(8)-(10).

---

## Part II

## Regulations as to Voluntary Homes

### *Regulations as to conduct of voluntary homes*

7.—(1) The Secretary of State may make regulations—

(*a*) as to the placing of children in voluntary homes;
(*b*) as to the conduct of such homes; and
(*c*) for securing the welfare of children in such homes.

(2) The regulations may, in particular—

(*a*) prescribe standards to which the premises used for such homes are to conform;
(*b*) impose requirements as to the accommodation, staff and equipment to be provided in such homes, and as to the arrangements to be made for protecting the health of children in such homes;
(*c*) provide for the control and discipline of children in such homes;
(*d*) require the furnishing to the Secretary of State of information as to the facilities provided for—

(i) the parents of children in the homes; and
(ii) persons who are not parents of such children but who have parental responsibility for them; and
(iii) other persons connected with such children,

to visit and communicate with the children;

(*e*) authorise the Secretary of State to limit the number of children who may be accommodated in any particular voluntary home;

(*f*) prohibit the use of accommodation for the purposes of restricting the liberty of children in such homes;

(*g*) impose requirements as to the keeping of records and giving of notices with respect to children in such homes;

(*h*) impose requirements as to the facilities which are to be provided for giving religious instruction to children in such homes;

(*i*) require notice to be given to the Secretary of State of any change of the person carrying on or in charge of a voluntary home or of the premises used by such a home.

(3) The regulations may provide that a contravention of, or failure to comply with, any specified provision of the regulations without reasonable excuse shall be an offence against the regulations.

(4) Any person guilty of such an offence shall be liable to a fine not exceeding level 4 on the standard scale.

*Disqualification*

8. The Secretary of State may by regulation make provision with respect to the disqualification of persons in relation to voluntary homes of a kind similar to that made in relation to children's homes by section 65.

---

**Definitions** For 'child', 'local authority' see s 105(1); for 'voluntary home' see s 60(3); for 'parental responsibility' see s 3.

**References** For 'parent' see para 2.7. For 'the standard scale' see the Criminal Justice Act 1988 s 37(2), (3) as amended; 'level 4' ie £1,000.

---

## SCHEDULE 6

Section 63(11)

### Registered Children's Homes

### Part I

### Registration

*Application for registration*

1.—(1) An application for the registration of a children's home shall be made—

(*a*) by the person carrying on, or intending to carry on, the home; and

(*b*) to the local authority for the area in which the home is, or is to be, situated.

(2) The application shall be made in the prescribed manner and shall be accompanied by—

(*a*) such particulars as may be prescribed; and

(*b*) such reasonable fee as the local authority may determine.

(3) In this Schedule "prescribed" means prescribed by regulations made by the Secretary of State.

(4) If a local authority are satisfied that a children's home with respect to which an application has been made in accordance with this Schedule complies or (as the case may be) will comply—

(*a*) with such requirements as may be prescribed, and

(*b*) with such other requirements (if any) as appear to them to be appropriate, they shall grant the application, either unconditionally or subject to conditions imposed under paragraph 2.

(5) Before deciding whether or not to grant an application a local authority shall comply with any prescribed requirements.

(6) Regulations made for the purposes of sub-paragraph (5) may, in particular, make provision as to the inspection of the home in question.

(7) Where an application is granted, the authority shall notify the applicant that the home has been registered under this Act as from such date as may be specified in the notice.

(8) If the authority are not satisfied as mentioned in sub-paragraph (4), they shall refuse the application.

(9) For the purposes of this Act, an application which has not been granted or refused within the period of twelve months beginning with the date when it is served on the authority shall be deemed to have been refused by them, and the applicant shall be deemed to have been notified of their refusal at the end of that period.

(10) Where a school to which section 63(1) applies is registered it shall not cease to be a registered children's home by reason only of a subsequent change in the number of children for whom it provides accommodation.

*Conditions imposed on registration*

2.—(1) A local authority may grant an application for registration subject to such conditions relating to the conduct of the home as they think fit.

(2) A local authority may from time to time—

(*a*) vary any condition for the time being in force with respect to a home by virtue of this paragraph; or

(*b*) impose an additional condition,

either on the application of the person carrying on the home or without such an application.

(3) If any condition imposed or varied under this paragraph is not complied with, the person carrying on the home shall, if he has no reasonable excuse, be guilty of an offence and liable on summary conviction to a fine not exceeding level 4 on the standard scale.

*Annual review of registration*

3.—(1) In this Part "the responsible authority", in relation to a registered children's home means the local authority who registered it.

(2) The responsible authority for a registered children's home shall, at the end of the period of twelve months beginning with the date of registration, and annually thereafter, review its registration for the purpose of determining whether the registration should continue in force or be cancelled under paragraph 4(3).

(3) If on any such annual review the responsible authority are satisfied that the home is being carried on in accordance with the relevant requirements they shall determine that, subject to sub-paragraph (4), the registration should continue in force.

(4) The responsible authority shall give to the person carrying on the home notice of their determination under sub-paragraph (3) and the notice shall require him to pay to the authority with respect to the review such reasonable fee as the authority may determine.

(5) It shall be a condition of the home's continued registration that the fee is so paid before the expiry of the period of twenty-eight days beginning with the date on which the notice is received by the person carrying on the home.

(6) In this Schedule "the relevant requirements" means any requirements of Part VIII and of any regulations made under paragraph 10, and any conditions imposed under paragraph 2.

*Cancellation of registration*

4.—(1) The person carrying on a registered children's home may at any time make an application, in such manner and including such particulars as may be prescribed, for the cancellation by the responsible authority of the registration of the home.

(2) If the authority are satisfied, in the case of a school registered by virtue of section 63(6), that it is no longer a school to which that provision applies, the authority shall give to the person carrying on the home notice that the registration of the home has been cancelled as from the date of the notice.

(3) If on any annual review under paragraph 3, or at any other time, it appears to the responsible authority that a registered home is being carried on otherwise than in accordance with the relevant requirements, they may determine that the registration of the home should be cancelled.

(4) The responsible authority may at any time determine that the registration of a home should be cancelled on the ground—

(*a*) that the person carrying on the home has been convicted of an offence under this Part or any regulations made under paragraph 10; or
(*b*) that any other person has been convicted of such an offence in relation to the home.

*Procedure*

5.—(1) Where—

(*a*) a person applies for the registration of a children's home; and
(*b*) the local authority propose to grant his application,

they shall give him written notice of their proposal and of the conditions (if any) subject to which they propose to grant his application.

(2) The authority need not give notice if they propose to grant the application subject only to conditions which—

(*a*) the applicant specified in the application; or
(*b*) the authority and the applicant have subsequently agreed.

(3) The authority shall give an applicant notice of a proposal to refuse his application.

(4) The authority shall give any person carrying on a registered children's home notice of a proposal—

(*a*) to cancel the registration;
(*b*) to vary any condition for the time being in force with respect to the home by virtue of Part VIII; or
(*c*) to impose any additional condition.

(5) A notice under this paragraph shall give the local authority's reasons for their proposal.

*Right to make representations*

6.—(1) A notice under paragraph 5 shall state that within 14 days of service of the notice any person on whom it is served may in writing require the local authority to give him an opportunity to make representations to them concerning the matter.

(2) Where a notice has been served under paragraph 5, the local authority shall not determine the matter until—

(*a*) any person on whom the notice was served has made representations to them concerning the matter;
(*b*) the period during which any such person could have required the local authority to give him an opportunity to make representations has elapsed without their being required to give such an opportunity; or
(*c*) the conditions specified in sub-paragraph (3) below are satisfied.

(3) The conditions are—

(*a*) that a person on whom the notice was served has required the local authority to give him an opportunity to make representations to them concerning the matter;
(*b*) that the authority have allowed him a reasonable period to make his representations; and
(*c*) that he has failed to make them within that period.

(4) The representations may be made, at the option of the person making them, either in writing or orally.

(5) If he informs the local authority that he desires to make oral representations, the authority shall give him an opportunity of appearing before and of being heard by a committee or sub-committee of theirs.

*Decision of local authority*

7.—(1) If the local authority decide to adopt a proposal of theirs to grant an application, they shall serve notice in writing of their decision on any person on whom they were required to serve notice of their proposal.

(2) A notice under this paragraph shall be accompanied by an explanation of the right of appeal conferred by paragraph 8.

(3) A decision of a local authority, other than a decision to grant an application for registration subject only to such conditions as are mentioned in paragraph 5(2) or to refuse an application for registration, shall not take effect—

(*a*) if no appeal is brought, until the end of the period of 28 days referred to in paragraph 8(3); and
(*b*) if an appeal is brought, until it is determined or abandoned.

*Appeals*

8.—(1) An appeal against a decision of a local authority under Part VIII shall lie to a Registered Homes Tribunal.

(2) An appeal shall be brought by notice in writing given to the local authority.

(3) No appeal shall be brought by a person more than 28 days after service on him of notice of the decision.

(4) On an appeal the Tribunal may confirm the local authority's decision or direct that it shall not have effect.

(5) A Tribunal shall also have power on an appeal—

(*a*) to vary any condition in force with respect to the home to which the appeal relates by virtue of paragraph 2;
(*b*) to direct that any such condition shall cease to have effect; or
(*c*) to direct that any such condition as it thinks fit shall have effect with respect to the home.

(6) A local authority shall comply with any direction given by a Tribunal under this paragraph.

*Prohibition on further applications*

9.—(1) Where an application for the registration of a home is refused, no further application may be made within the period of six months beginning with the date when the applicant is notified of the refusal.

(2) Sub-paragraph (1) shall have effect, where an appeal against the refusal of an application is determined or abandoned, as if the reference to the date when the applicant is notified of the refusal were a reference to the date on which the appeal is determined or abandoned.

(3) Where the registration of a home is cancelled, no application for the registration of the home shall be made within the period of six months beginning with the date of cancellation.

(4) Sub-paragraph (3) shall have effect, where an appeal against the cancellation of the registration of a home is determined or abandoned, as if the reference to the date of cancellation were a reference to the date on which the appeal is determined or abandoned.

---

**Definitions** For children's home see s 63(3). For 'child', 'local authority', 'school' see s 105(1); for 'prescribed' see para 1(3);for 'the responsible authority' see para 3(1); for 'the relevant requirements' see para 3(6); for 'registered children's home' see s 63(8).

**References** For 'the standard scale' see the Criminal Justice Act 1982 s 37(2), (3) as amended; 'level 4' ie £1,000. 'This Part' ie Part VIII ss 63-65, Schs 6 and 7 (registered children's homes). For service of notices under the Act generally see s 105(8)-(10).

---

## Part II

### Regulations

10.—(1) The Secretary of State may make regulations—

(*a*) as to the placing of children in registered children's homes;
(*b*) as to the conduct of such homes; and
(*c*) for securing the welfare of the children in such homes.

(2) The regulations may in particular—

(*a*) prescribe standards to which the premises used for such homes are to conform;
(*b*) impose requirements as to the accommodation, staff and equipment to be provided in such homes;
(*c*) impose requirements as to the arrangements to be made for protecting the health of children in such homes;
(*d*) provide for the control and discipline of children in such homes;
(*e*) require the furnishing to the responsible authority of information as to the facilities provided for—

 (i) the parents of children in such homes;
 (ii) persons who are not parents of such children but who have parental responsibility for them; and
 (iii) other persons connected with such children;

 to visit and communicate with the children.

(*f*) impose requirements as to the keeping of records and giving of notices with respect to children in such homes;
(*g*) impose requirements as to the facilities which are to be provided for giving religious instruction to children in such homes;
(*h*) make provision as to the carrying out of annual reviews under paragraph 3;
(*i*) authorise the responsible authority to limit the number of children who may be accommodated in any particular registered home;
(*j*) prohibit the use of accommodation for the purposes of restricting the liberty of children in such homes;

(*k*) require notice to be given to the responsible authority of any change of the person carrying on or in charge of a registered home or of the premises used by such a home;

(*l*) make provision similar to that made by regulations under section 26.

(3) The regulations may provide that a contravention of or failure to comply with any specified provision of the regulations, without reasonable excuse, shall be an offence against the regulations.

(4) Any person guilty of such an offence shall be liable on summary conviction to a fine not exceeding level 4 on the standard scale.

---

**Definitions** For 'child' see s 105(1); for 'registered children's home' see s 63(8); for 'the responsible authority' see para 3(1); for 'a child who is looked after by a local authority' see s 22(1).

**Reference** For 'the standard scale' see the Criminal Justice Act 1982 s 37(2), (3) as amended; 'level 4' ie £1,000.

---

## SCHEDULE 7

Section 63(12)

### Foster Parents: Limits on Number of Foster Children

*Interpretation*

1. For the purposes of this Schedule, a person fosters a child if—

(*a*) he is a local authority foster parent in relation to the child;

(*b*) he is a foster parent with whom the child has been placed by a voluntary organisation; or

(*c*) he fosters the child privately.

*The usual fostering limit*

2. Subject to what follows, a person may not foster more than three children ("the usual fostering limit").

*Siblings*

3. A person may exceed the usual fostering limit if the children concerned are all siblings with respect to each other.

*Exemption by local authority*

4.—(1) A person may exceed the usual fostering limit if he is exempted from it by the local authority within whose area he lives.

(2) In considering whether to exempt a person, a local authority shall have regard, in particular, to—

(*a*) the number of children whom the person proposes to foster;

(*b*) the arrangements which the person proposes for the care and accommodation of the fostered children;

(*c*) the intended and likely relationship between the person and the fostered children;

(*d*) the period of time for which he proposes to foster the children; and

(*e*) whether the welfare of the fostered children (and of any other children who are or will be living in the accommodation) will be safeguarded and promoted.

(3) Where a local authority exempt a person, they shall inform him by notice in writing—

(*a*) that he is so exempted;
(*b*) of the children, described by name, whom he may foster; and
(*c*) of any condition to which the exemption is subject.

(4) A local authority may at any time by notice in writing—

(*a*) vary of cancel an exemption; or
(*b*) impose, vary or cancel a condition to which the exemption is subject,

and, in considering whether to do so, they shall have regard in particular to the considerations mentioned in sub-paragraph (2).

(5) The Secretary of State may make regulations amplifying or modifying the provisions of this paragraph in order to provide for cases where children need to be placed with foster parents as a matter of urgency.

*Effect of exceeding fostering limit*

5.—(1) A person shall cease to be treated as fostering and shall be treated as carrying on a children's home if—

(*a*) he exceeds the usual fostering limit; or
(*b*) where he is exempted under paragraph 4,—

(i) he fosters any child not named in the exemption; and
(ii) in so doing, he exceeds the usual fostering limit.

(2) Sub-paragraph (1) does not apply if the children concerned are all siblings in respect of each other.

*Complaints etc*

6.—(1) Every local authority shall establish a procedure for considering any representations (including any complaint) made to them about the discharge of their functions under paragraph 4 by a person exempted or seeking to be exempted under that paragraph.

(2) In carrying out any consideration or representations under sub-paragraph (1), a local authority shall comply with any regulations made by the Secretary of State for the purposes of this paragraph.

---

**Definitions** For 'local authority foster parent' see s 23(3); for 'child', 'local authority', and 'voluntary organisation' see s 105(1); for 'to foster a child privately' see s 66(1)(b); for 'the usual fostering limit' see para 2.

**Reference** See generally para 14.3. For service of notices under the Act generally see s 105(8)-(10). For duty to register a children's home see s 63.

---

## SCHEDULE 8

Section 66(5)

### Privately Fostered Children

*Exemptions*

1. A child is not a privately fostered child while he is being looked after by a local authority.

2.—(1) A child is not a privately fostered child while he is in the care of any person—

(*a*) in premises in which any—

(i) parent of his;
(ii) person who is not a parent of his but who has parental responsibility for him; or

(iii) person who is a relative of his and who has assumed responsibility for his care,

is for the time being living;

(*b*) in any children's home;
(*c*) in accommodation provided by or on behalf of any voluntary organisation;
(*d*) in any school in which he is receiving full-time education;
(*e*) in any health service hospital;
(*f*) in any residential care home, nursing home or mental nursing home; or
(*g*) in any home or institution not specified in this paragraph but provided, equipped and maintained by the Secretary of State.

(2) Sub-paragraph (1)(*b*) to (*g*) does not apply where the person caring for the child is doing so in his personal capacity and not in the course of carrying out his duties in relation to the establishment mentioned in the paragraph in question.

3. A child is not a privately fostered child while he is in the care of any person in compliance with—

(*a*) an order under section 7(7)(*b*) of the Children and Young Persons Act 1969; or
(*b*) a supervision requirement within the meaning of the Social Work (Scotland) Act 1968.

4. A child is not a privately fostered child while he is liable to be detained, or subject to guardianship, under the Mental Health Act 1983.

5. A child is not a privately fostered child while—

(*a*) he is placed in the care of a person who proposes to adopt him under arrangements made by an adoption agency within the meaning of—
   (i) section 1 of the Adoption Act 1976;
   (ii) section 1 of the Adoption (Scotland) Act 1978; or
   (iii) Article 3 of the Adoption (Northern Ireland) Order 1987; or
(*b*) he is a protected child.

*Power of local authority to impose requirements*

6.—(1) Where a person is fostering any child privately, or proposes to foster any child privately, the appropriate local authority may impose on him requirements as to—

(*a*) the number, age and sex of the children who may be privately fostered by him;
(*b*) the standard of the accommodation and equipment to be provided for them;
(*c*) the arrangements to be made with respect to their health and safety; and
(*d*) particular arrangements which must be made with respect to the provision of care for them,

and it shall be his duty to comply with any such requirement before the end of such period as the authority may specify unless, in the case of a proposal, the proposal is not carried out.

(2) A requirement may be limited to a particular child, or class of child.

(3) A requirement (other than one imposed under sub-paragraph (1)(*a*)) may be limited by the authority so as to apply only when the number of children fostered by the person exceeds a specified number.

(4) A requirement shall be imposed by notice in writing addressed to the person on whom it is imposed and informing him of—

(*a*) the reason for imposing the requirement;
(*b*) his right under paragraph 8 to appeal against it; and
(*c*) the time within which he may do so.

(5) A local authority may at any time vary any requirement, impose any additional requirement or remove any requirement.

(6) In this Schedule—

(*a*) "the appropriate local authority" means—

(i) the local authority within whose area the child is being fostered; or

(ii) in the case of a proposal to foster a child, the local authority within whose area it is proposed that he will be fostered; and

(*b*) "requirement", in relation to any person, means a requirement imposed on him under this paragraph.

*Regulations requiring notification of fostering etc*

7.—(1) The Secretary of State may by regulations make provision as to—

(*a*) the circumstances in which notification is required to be given in connection with children who are, have been or are proposed to be fostered privately; and

(*b*) the manner and form in which such notification is to be given.

(2) The regulations may, in particular—

(*a*) require any person who is, or proposes to be, involved (whether or not directly) in arranging for a child to be fostered privately to notify the appropriate authority;

(*b*) require any person who is—

(i) a parent of a child; or

(ii) a person who is not a parent of his but who has parental responsibility for a child,

and who knows that it is proposed that the child should be fostered privately, to notify the appropriate authority;

(*c*) require any parent of a privately fostered child, or person who is not a parent of such a child but who has parental responsibility for him, to notify the appropriate authority of any change in his address;

(*d*) require any person who proposes to foster a child privately, to notify the appropriate authority of his proposal;

(*e*) require any person who is fostering a child privately, or proposes to do so, to notify the appropriate authority of—

(i) any offence of which he has been convicted;

(ii) any disqualification imposed on him under section 68; or

(iii) any prohibition imposed on him under section 69;

(*f*) require any person who is fostering a child privately, to notify the appropriate authority of any change in his address;

(*g*) require any person who is fostering a child privately to notify the appropriate authority in writing of any person who begins, or ceases, to be part of his household;

(*h*) require any person who has been fostering a child privately, but has ceased to do so, to notify the appropriate authority (indicating, where the child has died, that that is the reason).

*Appeals*

8.—(1) A person aggrieved by—

(*a*) a requirement imposed under paragraph 6;

(*b*) a refusal of consent under section 68;

(*c*) a prohibition imposed under section 69;

(*d*) a refusal to cancel such a prohibition;

(*e*) a refusal to make an exemption under paragraph 4 of Schedule 7;

(*f*) a condition imposed in such an exemption; or
(*g*) a variation or cancellation of such an exemption,

may appeal to the court.

(2) The appeal must be made within fourteen days from the date on which the person appealing is notified of the requirement, refusal, prohibition, condition, variation or cancellation.

(3) Where the appeal is against—

(*a*) a requirement imposed under paragraph 6;
(*b*) a condition of an exemption imposed under paragraph 4 of Schedule 7; or
(*c*) a variation or cancellation of such an exemption,

the requirement, condition, variation or cancellation shall not have effect while the appeal is pending.

(4) Where it allows an appeal against a requirement or prohibition, the court may, instead of cancelling the requirement or prohibition—

(*a*) vary the requirement, or allow more time for compliance with it; or
(*b*) if an absolute prohibition has been imposed, substitute for it a prohibition on using the premises after such time as the court may specify unless such specified requirements as the local authority had power to impose under paragraph 6 are complied with.

(5) Any requirement or prohibition specified or substituted by a court under this paragraph shall be deemed for the purposes of Part IX (other than this paragraph) to have been imposed by the local authority under paragraph 6 or (as the case may be) section 69.

(6) Where it allows an appeal against a refusal to make an exemption, a condition imposed in such an exemption or a variation or cancellation of such an exemption, the court may—

(*a*) make an exemption;
(*b*) impose a condition; or
(*c*) vary the exemption.

(7) Any exemption made or varied under sub-paragraph (6), or any condition imposed under that sub-paragraph, shall be deemed for the purposes of Schedule 7 (but not for the purposes of this paragraph) to have been made, varied or imposed under that Schedule.

(8) Nothing in sub-paragraph (1)(*e*) to (*g*) confers any right of appeal on—

(*a*) a person who is, or would be if exempted under Schedule 7, a local authority foster parent; or
(*b*) a person who is, or would be if so exempted, a person with whom a child is placed by a voluntary organisation.

*Extension of Part IX to certain school children during holidays*

9.—(1) Where a child under sixteen who is a pupil at a school which is not maintained by a local education authority lives at the school during school holidays for a period of more than two weeks, Part IX shall apply in relation to the child as if—

(*a*) while living at the school, he were a privately fostered child; and
(*b*) paragraphs 2(1)(*d*) and 6 were omitted.

(2) Sub-paragraph (3) applies to any person who proposes to care for and accommodate one or more children at a school in circumstances in which some or all of them will be treated as private foster children by virtue of this paragraph.

(3) That person shall, not less than two weeks before the first of those children

is treated as a private foster child by virtue of this paragraph during the holiday in question, give written notice of his proposal to the local authority within whose area the child is ordinarily resident ("the appropriate authority"), stating the estimated number of the children.

(4) A local authority may exempt any person from the duty of giving notice under sub-
paragraph (3).

(5) Any such exemption may be granted for a special period or indefinitely and may be revoked at any time by notice in writing given to the person exempted.

(6) Where a child who is treated as a private foster child by virtue of this paragraph dies, the person caring for him at the school shall, not later than 48 hours after the death, give written notice of it—

(*a*) to the appropriate local authority; and
(*b*) where reasonably practicable, to each parent of the child and to every person who is not a parent of his but who has parental responsibility for him.

(7) Where a child who is treated as a foster child by virtue of this paragraph ceases for any other reason to be such a child, the person caring for him at the school shall give written notice of the fact to the appropriate local authority.

*Prohibition of advertisements relating to fostering*

10. No advertisement indicating that a person will undertake, or will arrange for, a child to be privately fostered shall be published, unless it states that person's name and address.

*Avoidance of insurances on lives of privately fostered children*

11. A person who fosters a child privately and for reward shall be deemed for the purposes of the Life Assurance Act 1774 to have no interest in the life of the child.

---

**Definitions** For 'child', 'local authority', 'relative', 'voluntary organisation', 'health service hospital', 'residential care home', 'nursing home', 'mental nursing home', 'protected child', 'local education authority', 'school' see s 105(1); for 'children's home' see s 63(3) as applied to the whole Act by s 105(1); for ' child who is looked after by a local authority' see s 22(1); for 'privately fostered child' see s 66(1)(a); for 'parental responsibility' see s 3; for 'court' see s 92(7) and para 9.1 ff. For 'requirement' see para 6(6)(b); for 'the appropriate authority' see para 6(6)(a); for 'pupil', 'maintained' see Education Act 1944 s 114; for 'ordinarily resident' see s 105(6).

**References** For 'parent' see para 2.7. For 'premises' see the note to s 72. For service of notices generally under the Act see s 105(8)-(10).

---

## SCHEDULE 9

Section 71(16)

### Child Minding and Day Care for Young Children

*Applications for registration*

1.—(1) An application for registration under section 71 shall be of no effect unless it contains—

(*a*) a statement with respect to the applicant which complies with the requirements of regulations made for the purposes of this paragraph by the Secretary of State; and
(*b*) a statement with respect to any person assisting or likely to be assisting in looking after children on the premises in question, or living or likely to be living there, which complies with the requirements of such regulations.

(2) Where a person provides, or proposes to provide, day care for children under the age of eight on different premises situated within the area of the same local authority, he shall make a separate application with respect to each of those premises.

(3) An application under section 71 shall be accompanied by such fee as may be prescribed.

(4) On receipt of an application for registration under section 71 from any person who is acting, or proposes to act, in any way which requires him to be registered under that section, a local authority shall register him if the application is properly made and they are not otherwise entitled to refuse to do so.

*Disqualification from registration*

2.—(1) A person may not be registered under section 71 if he is disqualified by regulations made by the Secretary of State for the purposes of this paragraph.

(2) The regulations may, in particular, provide for a person to be disqualified where—

(*a*) an order of a prescribed kind has been made at any time with respect to him;
(*b*) an order of a prescribed kind has been made at any time with respect to any child who has been in his care;
(*c*) a requirement of a prescribed kind has been imposed at any time with respect to such a child, under or by virtue of any enactment;
(*d*) he has at any time been refused registration under Part X or any other prescribed enactment or had any such registration cancelled;
(*e*) he has been convicted of any offence of a prescribed kind, or has been placed on probation or discharged absolutely or conditionally for any such offence;
(*f*) he has at any time been disqualified from fostering a child privately;
(*g*) a prohibition has been imposed on him at any time under section 61, section 10 of the Foster Children (Scotland) Act 1984 or any other prescribed enactment;
(*h*) his rights and powers with respect to a child have at any time been vested in a prescribed authority under a prescribed enactment.

(3) A person who lives—

(*a*) in the same household as a person who is himself disqualified by the regulations; or
(*b*) in a household at which any such person is employed,

shall be disqualified unless he has disclosed the fact to the appropriate local authority and obtained their written consent.

(4) A person who is disqualified shall not provide day care, or be concerned in the management of, or have any financial interest in, any provision of day care unless he has—

(*a*) disclosed the fact to the appropriate local authority; and
(*b*) obtained their written consent.

(5) No person shall employ, in connection with the provision of day care, a person who is disqualified, unless he has—

(*a*) disclosed to the appropriate local authority the fact that that person is so disqualified; and
(*b*) obtained their written consent.

(6) In this paragraph "enactment" means any enactment having effect, at any time, in any part of the United Kingdom.

*Exemption of certain schools*

3.—(1) Section 71 does not apply in relation to any child looked after in any—

(*a*) school maintained or assisted by a local education authority;
(*b*) school under the management of an education authority;
(*c*) school in respect of which payments are made by the Secretary of State under section 100 of the Education Act 1944;
(*d*) independent school;
(*e*) grant-aided school;
(*f*) grant maintained school;
(*g*) self-governing school;
(*h*) play centre maintained or assisted by a local education authority under section 53 of the Act of 1944, or by an education authority under section 6 of the Education (Scotland) Act 1980.

(2) The exemption provided by sub-paragraph (1) only applies where the child concerned is being looked after in accordance with provision for day care made by—

(*a*) the person carrying on the establishment in question as part of the establishment's activities; or
(*b*) a person employed to work at that establishment and authorised to make that provision as part of the establishment's activities.

(3) In sub-paragraph (1)—

"assisted" and "maintained" have the same meanings as in the Education Act 1944;

"grant maintained" has the same meaning as in section 52(3) of the Education Reform Act 1988; and

"grant-aided school", "self-governing school" and (in relation to Scotland) "independent school" have the same meaning as in the Education (Scotland) Act 1980.

*Exemption for other establishments*

4.—(1) Section 71(1)(*b*) does not apply in relation to any child looked after in—

(*a*) a registered children's home;
(*b*) a voluntary home;
(*c*) a community home;
(*d*) a residential care home, nursing home or mental nursing home required to be registered under the Registered Homes Act 1984;
(*e*) a health service hospital;
(*f*) a home provided, equipped and maintained by the Secretary of State; or
(*g*) an establishment which is required to be registered under section 61 of the Social Work (Scotland) Act 1968.

(2) The exemption provided by sub-paragraph (1) only applies where the child concerned is being looked after in accordance with provision for day care made by—

(*a*) the department, authority or other person carrying on the establishment in question as part of the establishment's activities; or
(*b*) a person employed to work at that establishment and authorised to make that provision as part of the establishment's activities.

(3) In this paragraph "a health service hospital" includes a health service hospital within the meaning of the National Health Service (Scotland) Act 1978.

*Exemption for occasional facilities*

5.—(1) Where day care for children under the age of eight is provided in particular premises on less than six days in any year, that provision shall be disregarded for the purposes of section 71 if the person making it has notified the appropriate local authority in writing before the first occasion on which the premises concerned are so used in that year.

(2) In sub-paragraph (1) "year" means the year beginning with the day on which the day care in question is (after the commencement of this paragraph) first provided in the premises concerned and any subsequent year.

*Certificates of registration*

6.—(1) Where a local authority register a person under section 71 they shall issue him with a certificate of registration.

(2) The certificate shall specify—

(*a*) the registered person's name and address;

(*b*) in a case falling within section 71(1)(*b*), the address or situation of the premises concerned; and

(*c*) any requirements imposed under section 72 or 73;

(3) Where, due to a change of circumstances, any part of the certificate requires to be amended, the authority shall issue an amended certificate.

(4) Where the authority are satisfied that the certificate has been lost or destroyed, they shall issue a copy, on payment by the registered person of such fee as may be prescribed.

*Fees for annual inspection of premises*

7.—(1) Where—

(*a*) a person is registered under section 71, and

(*b*) the local authority concerned make an annual inspection of the premises in question under section 76,

they shall serve on that person a notice informing him that the inspection is to be carried out and requiring him to pay to them such fee as may be prescribed.

(2) It shall be a condition of the continued registration of that person under section 71 that the fee is so paid before the expiry of the period of twenty-eight days beginning with the date on which the inspection is carried out.

*Co-operation between authorities*

8.—(1) Where it appears to a local authority that any local education authority or, in Scotland, education authority could, by taking any specified action, help in the exercise of any of their functions under Part X, they may request the help of that local education authority, or education authority, specifying the action in question.

(2) An authority whose help is so requested shall comply with the request if it is compatible with their own statutory or other duties and obligations and does not unduly prejudice the discharge of any of their functions.

---

**Definitions** For 'day care' see s 71(2)(b) and s 18(4) as applied to the whole Act by s 105(1); for 'to foster a child privately' see s 66(1)(*b*); for 'local education authority', 'local authority', 'residential care home', 'nursing home', 'mental nursing home', 'health service hospital', see s 105(1); for 'assisted', 'maintained', 'grant maintained', 'education authority', 'grant aided school', 'self-governing school', 'independent school' see para 3(3); for 'children's home' see s 63(3); for 'voluntary home' see s 60(3); for 'community home' see s 53 and s 105(1).

**Reference** For 'premises' see the note to s 72.

---

## SCHEDULE 10

Section 88

### AMENDMENTS OF ADOPTION LEGISLATION

### PART I

### AMENDMENTS OF ADOPTION ACT (1976 c 36)

1. In section 2 (local authorities' social services) for the words from "relating to" to the end there shall be substituted—

"(*a*) under the Children Act 1989, relating to family assistance orders, local authority support for children and families, care and supervision and emergency protection of children, community homes, voluntary homes and organisations, registered children's homes, private arrangements for fostering children, child minding and day care for young children and children accommodated by health authorities and local education authorities or in residential care, nursing or mental nursing homes or in independent schools; and

(*b*) under the National Health Service Act 1977, relating to the provision of care for expectant and nursing mothers."

2. In section 11 (restrictions on arranging adoptions and placing of children) for subsection (2) there shall be substituted—

"(2) An adoption society which is—

(*a*) approved as respects Scotland under section 3 of the Adoption (Scotland) Act 1978; or

(*b*) registered as respects Northern Ireland under Article 4 of the Adoption (Northern Ireland) Order 1987,

but which is not approved under section 3 of this Act, shall not act as an adoption society in England and Wales except to the extent that the society considers it necessary to do so in the interests of a person mentioned in section 1 of the Act of 1978 or Article 3 of the Order of 1987."

3.—(1) In section 12 (adoption orders), in subsection (1) for the words "vesting the parental rights and duties relating to a child in" there shall be substituted "giving parental responsibility for a child to".

(2) In subsection (2) of that section for the words "the parental rights and duties so far as they relate" there shall be substituted "parental responsibility so far as it relates".

(3) In subsection (3) of that section for paragraph (*a*) there shall be substituted—

"(*a*) the parental responsibility which any person has for the child immediately before the making of the order;

(*aa*) any order under the Children Act 1989";

and in paragraph (*b*) for the words from "for any period" to the end there shall be substituted "or upbringing for any period after the making of the order."

4. For section 14(1) (adoption by married couple) there shall be substituted—

"(1) An adoption order shall not be made on the application of more than one person except in the circumstances specified in subsections (1A) and (1B).

(1A) An adoption order may be made on the application of a married couple where both the husband and the wife have attained the age of 21 years.

(1B) An adoption order may be made on the application of a married couple where—

(*a*) the husband or the wife—

"(i) is the father or mother of the child; and
(ii) has attained the age of 18 years:

and

(*b*) his or her spouse has attained the age of 21 years."

5.—(1) In section 16 (parental agreement), in subsection (1) for the words from "in England" to "Scotland)" there shall be substituted—

"(i) in England and Wales, under section 18;
(ii) in Scotland, under section 18 of the Adoption (Scotland) Act 1978; or
(iii) in Northern Ireland, under Article 17(1) or 18(1) of the Adoption (Northern Ireland) Order 1987."

(2) In subsection (2)(*c*) of that section for the words "the parental duties in relation to" there shall be substituted "his parental responsibility for".

6.—(1) In section 18 (freeing child for adoption), after subsection (2) there shall be inserted—

"(2A) For the purposes of subsection (2) a child is in the care of an adoption agency if the adoption agency is a local authority and he is in their care."

(2) In subsection (5) of that section, for the words from "the parental rights" to "vest in" there shall be substituted "parental responsibility for the child is given to", and for the words "and (3)" there shall be substituted "to (4)".

(3) For subsections (7) and (8) of that section there shall be substituted—

"(7) Before making an order under this section in the case of a child whose father does not have parental responsibility for him, the court shall satisfy itself in relation to any person claiming to be the father that—

(*a*) he has no intention of applying for—

(i) an order under section 4(1) of the Children Act 1989, or
(ii) a residence order under section 10 of that Act, or

(*b*) if he did make any such application, it would be likely to be refused.

(8) Subsections (5) and (7) of section 12 apply in relation to the making of an order under this section as they apply in relation to the making of an order under that section."

7. In section 19(2) (progress reports to former parents) for the words "in which the parental rights and duties were vested" there shall be substituted "to which parental responsibility was given".

8.—(1) In section 20 (revocation of section 18 order), in subsections (1) and (2) for the words "the parental rights and duties", in both places where they occur, there shall be substituted "parental responsibility".

(2) For subsection (3) of that section there shall be substituted—

"(3) The revocation of an order under section 18 ("a section 18 order") operates—

(*a*) to extinguish the parental responsibility given to the adoption agency under the section 18 order;

(*b*) to give parental responsibility for the child to—

(i) the child's mother; and
(ii) where the child's father and mother were married to each other at the time of his birth, the father; and

(*c*) to revive—

(i) any parental responsibility agreement,
(ii) any order under section 4(1) of the Children Act 1989, and

(iii) any apportionment of a guardian in respect of the child (whether made by a court or otherwise),

extinguished by the making of the section 18 order.

(3A) Subject to subsection (3)(*c*), the revocation does not—

(*a*) operate to revive—

(i) any order under the Children Act 1989, or
(ii) any duty referred to in section 12(3)(*b*)

extinguished by the making of the section 18 order; or

(*b*) affect any person's parental responsibility so far as it relates to the period between the making of the section 18 order and the date of revocation of that order."

9. For section 21 (transfer of parental rights and duties between adoption agencies) there shall be substituted—

**"21 Variation of section 18 order so as to substitute one adoption agency for another**

(1) On an application to which this section applies, an authorised court may vary an order under section 18 so as to give parental responsibility for the child to another adoption agency ('the substitute agency') in place of the agency for the time being having parental responsbility for the child under the order ('the existing agency').

(2) This section applies to any application made jointly by—

(*a*) the existing agency; and
(*b*) the would-be substitute agency.

(3) Where an order under section 18 is varied under this section, section 19 shall apply as if the substitute agency had been given responsibility for the child on the making of the order."

10.—(1) In section 22 (notification to local authority of adoption application), after subsection (1) there shall be inserted the following subsections—

"(1A) An application for such an adoption order shall not be made unless the person wishing to make the application has, within the period of two years preceding the making of the application, given notice as mentioned in subsection (1).

(1B) In subsections (1) and (1A) the references to the area in which the applicant or person has his home are references to the area in which he has his home at the time of giving the notice."

(2) In subsection (4) of that section for the word "receives" there shall be substituted "receive" and for the words "in the care of" there shall be substituted "looked after by".

11. In section 25(1) (interim orders) for the words "vesting the legal custody of the child in" there shall be substituted "giving parental responsibility for the child to".

12. In—

(*a*) section 27(1) and (2) (restrictions on removal where adoption agreed or application made under section 18); and
(*b*) section 28(1) and (2) (restrictions on removal where applicant has provided home for 5 years),

for the words "actual custody", in each place where they occur, there shall be substituted "home".

13. After section 27(2) there shall be inserted—

"(2A) For the purposes of subsection (2) a child is in the care of an adoption agency if the adoption agency is a local authority and he is in their care."

14. (1) After section 28(2) there shall be inserted—

"(2A) The reference in subsections (1) and (2) to any enactment does not include a reference to section 20(8) of the Children Act 1989".

(2) For subsection (3) of that section there shall be substituted—

"(3) In any case where subsection (1) or (2) applies and—

(*a*) the child was being looked after by a local authority before he began to have his home with the applicant or, as the case may be, the prospective adopter, and

(*b*) the child is still being looked after by a local authority,

the authority which are looking after the child shall not remove him from the home of the applicant or the prospective adopter except in accordance with section 30 or 31 or with the leave of a court."

(3) In subsection (5) of that section—

(*a*) for the word "receives" there shall be substituted "receive"; and

(*b*) for the words "in the care of another local authority or of a voluntary organisation" there shall be substituted "looked after by another local authority".

15. In section 29 (return of child taken away in breach of section 27 or 28) for subsections (1) and (2) there shall be substituted—

"(1) An authorised court may, on the application of a person from whose home a child has been removed in breach of—

(*a*) section 27 or 28,

(*b*) section 27 or 28 of the Adoption (Scotland) Act 1978, or

(*c*) Article 28 or 29 of the Adoption (Northern Ireland) Order 1987,

order the person who has so removed the child to return the child to the applicant.

(2) An authorised court may, on the application of a person who has reasonable grounds for believing that another person is intending to remove a child from his home in breach of—

(*a*) section 27 or 28,

(*b*) section 27 or 28 of the Adoption (Scotland) Act 1978, or

(*c*) Article 28 or 29 of the Adoption (Northern Ireland) Order 1987,

by order direct that other person not to remove the child from the applicant's home in breach of any of those provisions."

16.—(1) In section 30 (return of children placed for adoption by adoption agencies), in subsection (1) there shall be substituted—

(*a*) for the words "delivered into the actual custody of" the words "placed with";

(*b*) in paragraph (*a*) for the words "retain the actual custody of the child" the words "give the child a home"; and

(*c*) in paragraph (*b*) for the words "actual custody" the word "home".

(2) In subsection (3) of that section for the words "in his actual custody" there shall be substituted "with him".

17.—(1) In section 31 (application of section 30 where child not placed for adoption), in subsection (1) for the words from "child", where it first occurs, to "except" there shall be substituted "child—

(*a*) who is (when the notice is given) being looked after by a local authority; but (*b*) who was placed with that person otherwise than in pursuance of such arrangements as are mentioned in section 30(1),

that section shall apply as if the child had been placed in pursuance of such arrangements".

(2) In subsection (2) of that section for the words "for the time being in the care of" there shall be substituted "(when the notice is given) being looked after by".

(3) In subsection (3) of that section—

(*a*) for the words "remains in the actual custody of" there shall be substituted "has his home with"; and

(*b*) for the words "section 45 of the Child Care Act 1980" there shall be substituted "Part III of Schedule 2 to the Children Act 1989".

(4) At the end of that section there shall be added—

"(4) Nothing in this section affects the right of any person who has parental responsibility for a child to remove him under section 20(8) of the Children Act 1989".

18.—(1) In section 32 (meaning of "protected child"), in subsection (2) for the words "section 37 of the Adoption Act 1958" there shall be substituted—

"(*a*) section 32 of the Adoption (Scotland) Act 1978; or

(*b*) Article 33 of the Adoption (Northern Ireland) Order 1987."

(2) In subsection (3) of that section for paragraph (*a*) there shall be substituted—

"(*a*) he is in the care of any person—

(i) in any community home, voluntary home or registered children's home;

(ii) in any school in which he is receiving full-time education;

(iii) in any health service hospital";

and at the end of that subsection there shall be added—

"(*d*) he is in the care of any person in any home or institution not specified in this subsection but provided, equipped and maintained by the Secretary of State."

(3) After that subsection there shall be inserted—

"(3A) In subsection (3) "community home", "voluntary home", "registered children's home", "school" and "health service hospital" have the same meaning as in the Children Act 1989."

(4) For subsection (4) of that section there shall be substituted—

"(4) A protected child ceases to be a protected child—

(*a*) on the grant or refusal of the application for an adoption order;

(*b*) on the notification to the local authority for the area where the child has his home that the application for an adoption order has been withdrawn;

(*c*) in a case where no application is made for an adoption order, on the expiry of the period of two years from the giving of the notice;

(*d*) on the making of a residence order, a care order or a supervision order under the Children Act 1989 in respect of the child;

(*e*) on the appointment of a guardian for him under that Act;

(*f*) on his attaining the age of 18 years; or

(*g*) on his marriage,

whichever first occurs.

(5) In subsection (4)(*d*) the references to a care order and a supervision order do not include references to an interim care order or interim supervision order."

19.—(1) In section 35 (notices and information to be given to local authorities), in subsection (1) for the words "who has a protected child in his actual custody" there shall be substituted "with whom a protected child has his home".

(2) In subsection (2) of that section for the words "in whose actual custody he was" there shall be substituted "with whom he had his home".

20.—(1) In section 51 (disclosure of birth records of adopted children), in subsection (1) for the words "subsections (4) and (6)" there shall be substituted "what follows".

(2) For subsections (3) to (7) of that section there shall be substituted—

"(3) Before supplying any information to an applicant under subsection (1), the Registrar General shall inform the applicant that counselling services are available to him—

(*a*) if he is in England and Wales—

(i) at the General Register Office;
(ii) from the local authority in whose area he is living;
(iii) where the adoption order relating to him was made in England and Wales, from the local authority in whose area the court which made the order sat; or
(iv) from any other local authority;

(*b*) if he is in Scotland—

(i) from the regional or islands council in whose area he is living;
(ii) where the adoption order relating to him was made in Scotland, from the council in whose area the court which made the order sat; or
(iii) from any other regional or islands council;

(*c*) if he is in Northern Ireland—

(i) from the Board in whose area he is living;
(ii) where the adoption order relating to him was made in Northern Ireland, from the Board in whose area the court which made the order sat; or
(iii) from any other Board;

(*d*) if he is in the United Kingdom and his adoption was arranged by an adoption society—

(i) approved under section 3,
(ii) approved under section 3 of the Adoption (Scotland) Act 1978,
(iii) registered under Article 4 of the Adoption (Northern Ireland) Order 1987,

from that society.

(4) Where an adopted person who is in England and Wales—

(*a*) applies for information under—

(i) subsection (1), or
(ii) Article 54 of the Adoption (Northern Ireland) Order 1987, or

(*b*) is supplied with information under section 45 of the Adoption (Scotland) Act 1978,

it shall be the duty of the persons and bodies mentioned in subsection (5) to provide counselling for him if asked by him to do so.

(5) The persons and bodies are—

(*a*) the Registrar General;
(*b*) any local authority falling within subsection (3)(*a*)(ii) to (iv);
(*c*) any adoption society falling within subsection (3)(*d*) in so far as it is acting as an adoption society in England and Wales.

(6) If the applicant chooses to receive counselling from a person or body falling within subsection (3), the Registrar General shall send to the person or body the information to which the applicant is entitled under subsection (1).

(7) Where a person—

(*a*) was adopted before 12th November 1975, and
(*b*) applies for information under subsection (1),

the Registrar General shall not supply the information to him unless he has attended an interview with a counsellor arranged by a person or body from whom counselling services are available as mentioned in subsection (3).

(8) Where the Registrar General is prevented by subsection (7) from supplying information to a person who is not living in the United Kingdom, he may supply the information to any body which—

(*a*) the Registrar General is satisfied is suitable to provide counselling to that person, and
(*b*) has notified the Registrar General that it is prepared to provide such counselling.

(9) In this section—

"a Board" means a Health and Social Services Board established under Article 16 of the Health and Personal Social Services (Northern Ireland) Order 1972; and

"prescribed" means prescribed by regulations made by the Registrar General."

21. After section 51 there shall be inserted—

**"51A Adoption Contact Register**

(1) The Registrar General shall maintain at the General Register Office a register to be called the Adoption Contact register.

(2) The register shall be in two parts—

(*a*) Part I: Adopted Persons; and
(*b*) Part II: Relatives.

(3) The Registrar General shall, on payment of such fee as may be prescribed, enter in Part I of the register the name and address of any adopted person who fulfils the conditions in subsection (4) and who gives notice that he wishes to contact any relative of his.

(4) The conditions are that—

(*a*) a record of the adopted person's birth is kept by the Registrar General; and
(*b*) the adopted person has attained the age of 18 years and—

(i) has been supplied by the Registrar General with information under section 51; or

(ii) has satisfied the Registrar General that he has such information as is necessary to enable him to obtain a certified copy of the record of his birth.

(5) The Registrar General shall, on payment of such fee as may be prescribed,

enter in Part II of the register the name and address of any person who fulfils the conditions in subsection (6) and who gives notice that he wishes to contact an adopted person.

(6) The conditions are that—

(*a*) a record of the adopted person's birth is kept by the Registrar General; and

(*b*) the person giving notice under subsection (5) has attained the age of 18 years and has satisfied the Registrar General that—

(i) he is a relative of the adopted person; and

(ii) he has such information as is necessary to enable him to obtain a certified copy of the record of the adopted person's birth.

(7) The Registrar General shall, on receiving notice from any person named in an entry in the register that he wishes the entry to be cancelled, cancel the entry.

(8) Any notice given under this section must be in such form as may be determined by the Registrar General.

(9) The Registrar General shall transmit to an adopted person whose name is entered in Part I of the register the name and address of any relative in respect of whom there is an entry in Part II of the register.

(10) Any entry cancelled under subsection (7) ceases from the time of cancellation to be an entry for the purposes of subsection (9).

(11) The register shall not be open to public inspection or search and the Registrar General shall not supply any person with information entered in the register (whether in an uncancelled or a cancelled entry) except in accordance with this section.

(12) The register may be kept by means of a computer.

(13) In this section—

(*a*) "relative" means any person (other than an adoptive relative) who is related to the adopted person by blood (including half-blood) or marriage;

(*b*) "address" includes any address at or through which the person concerned may be contacted; and

(*c*) "prescribed" means prescribed by the Secretary of State."

22.—(1) In section 55 (adoption of children abroad), in subsection (1) after the word "Scotland" there shall be inserted "or Northern Ireland" and for the words "vesting in him the parental rights and duties relating to the child" there shall be substituted "giving him parental responsibility for the child".

(2) In subsection (3) of that section for the words "word "(Scotland)"" there shall be substituted "words "(Scotland)" or "(Northern Ireland)"."

23.—(1) In section 56 (restriction on removal of children for adoption outside Great Britain),—

(*a*) in subsections (1) and (3) for the words "transferring the actual custody of a child to", in both places where they occur, there shall be substituted "placing a child with"; and

(*b*) in subsection (3)(*a*) for the words "in the actual custody of" there shall be substituted "with".

(2) In subsection (1) of that section—

(*a*) for the words from "or under" to "abroad)" there shall be substituted "section 49 of the Adoption (Scotland) Act 1978 or Article 57 of the Adoption (Northern Ireland) Order 1987"; and (*b*) for the words "British Islands" there shall be substituted "United Kingdom, the Channel Islands and the Isle of Man".

24.—(1) In section 57 (prohibited on certain payments) in subsection (1)(*c*), for the words "transfer by that person of the actual custody of a child" there shall be substituted "handing over of a child by that person".

(2) In subsection (3A)(*b*) of that section, for the words "in the actual custody of" there shall be substituted "with".

25. After section 57 there shall be inserted—

**"57A Permitted allowances**

(1) The Secretary of State may make regulations for the purpose of enabling adoption agencies to pay allowances to persons who have adopted, or intend to adopt, children in pursuance of arrangements made by the agencies.

(2) Section 57(1) shall not apply to any payment made by an adoption agency in accordance with the regulations.

(3) The regulations may, in particular, make provision as to—

(*a*) the procedure to be followed by any agency in determining whether a person should be paid an allowance;
(*b*) the circumstances in which an allowance may be paid;
(*c*) the factors to be taken into account in determining the amount of an allowance;
(*d*) the procedure for review, variation and termination of allowances; and
(*e*) the information about allowances to be supplied by any agency to any person who is intending to adopt a child.

(4) Any scheme approved under section 57(4) shall be revoked as from the coming into force of this section.

(5) Section 57(1) shall not apply in relation to any payment made—

(*a*) in accordance with a scheme revoked under subsection (4) or section 57(5)(*b*); and
(*b*) to a person to whom such payments were made before the revocation of the scheme.

(6) Subsection (5) shall not apply where any person to whom any payments may lawfully be made by virtue of subsection (5) agrees to receive (instead of such payments) payments complying with regulations made under this section."

26.—(1) In section 59 (effect of determination and orders made in Scotland and overseas in adoption proceedings), in subsection (1) for the words "Great Britain" there shall be substituted "the United Kingdom".

(2) For subsection (2) of that section there shall be substituted—

"(2) Subsections (2) to (4) of section 12 shall apply in relation to an order freeing a child for adoption (other than an order under section 18) as if it were an adoption order; and, on the revocation in Scotland or Northern Ireland of an order freeing a child for adoption, subsections (3) and (3A) of section 20 shall apply as if the order had been revoked under that section."

27. In section 60 (evidence of adoption in Scotland and Northern Ireland), in paragraph (*a*) for the words "section 22(2) of the Adoption Act 1958" there shall be substituted "section 45(2) of the Adoption (Scotland) Act 1978" and in paragraph (*b*) for the words from "section 23(4)" to "in force" there shall be substituted "Article 63(1) of the Adoption (Northern Ireland) Order 1987".

28. In section 62(5)(*b*) (courts), for the words from "section 8" to "child)" there shall be substituted—

"(i) section 12 or 18 of the Adoption (Scotland) Act 1978; or
(ii) Article 12, 17 or 18 of the Adoption (Northern Ireland) Order 1987".

29. After section 65 (guardians ad litem and reporting officers) there shall be inserted—

**"65A Panels for selection of guardians ad litem and reporting officers**

(1) The Secretary of State may by regulations provide for the establishment of panels of persons from whom guardians ad litem and reporting officers appointed under rules made under section 65 must be selected.

(2) The regulations may, in particular, make provision—

(*a*) as to the constitution, administration and procedures of panels;
(*b*) requiring two or more specified local authorities to make arrangements for the joint management of a panel;
(*c*) for the defrayment by local authorities of expenses incurred by members of panels;
(*d*) for the payment by local authorities of fees and allowances for members of panels;
(*e*) as to the qualifications for membership of a panel;
(*f*) as to the training to be given to members of panels;
(*g*) as to the co-operation required of specified local authorities in the provision of panels in specified areas; and
(*h*) for monitoring the work of guardians ad litem and reporting officers.

(3) Rules of court may make provision as to the assistance which any guardian ad litem or reporting officer may be required by the court to give to it."

30.—(1) Section 72(1) (interpretation) shall be amended as follows.

(2) In the definition of "adoption agency" for the words from "section 1" to the end there shall be substituted "—

(*a*) section 1 of the Adoption (Scotland) Act 1978; and
(*b*) Article 3 of the Adoption (Northern Ireland) Order 1987."

(3) For the definition of "adoption order" there shall be substituted—

" "adoption order"—

(*a*) means an order under section 12(1); and

(*b*) in sections 12(3) and (4), 18 to 20, 27, 28 and 30 to 32 and in the definition of 'British adoption order' in this subsection includes an order under section 12 of the Adoption (Scotland) Act 1978 and Article 12 of the Adoption (Northern Ireland) Order 1987 (adoption orders in Scotland and Northern Ireland respectively); and

(*c*) in sections 27, 28 and 30 to 32 includes an order under section 55, section 49 of the Adoption (Scotland) Act 1978 and Article 57 of the Adoption (Northern Ireland) Order 1987 (orders in relation to children being adopted abroad)."

(4) For the definition of "British adoption order" there shall be substituted—

" "British adoption order" means—

(*a*) an adoption order as defined in this subsection, and

(*b*) an order under any provision for the adoption of a child effected under the law of any British territory outside the United Kingdom."

(5) For the definition of "guardian" there shall be substituted—

" "guardian" has the same meaning as in the Children Act 1989."

(6) In the definition of "order freeing a child for adoption" for the words from "section 27(2)" to the end there shall be substituted "sections 27(2) and 59 includes an order under—

(*a*) section 18 of the Adoption (Scotland) Act 1978; and
(*b*) Article 17 or 18 of the Adoption (Northern Ireland) Order 1987".

(7) After the definition of "overseas adoption" there shall be inserted—

""parent" means, in relation to a child, any parent who has parental responsibility for the child under the Children Act 1989;

"parental responsibility" and "parental responsibility agreement" have the same meaning as in the Children Act 1989."

(8) After the definition of "United Kingdom national" there shall be inserted—

""upbringing" has the same meaning as in the Children Act 1989."

(9) For section 72(1A) there shall be substituted the following subsections—

"(1A) In this Act, in determining with what person, or where, a child has his home, any absence of the child at a hospital or boarding school and any other temporary absence shall be disregarded.

(1B) In this Act, references to a child who is in the care of or looked after by a local authority have the same meaning as in the Children Act 1989."

31. For section 74(3) and (4) (extent) there shall be substituted—

"(3) This Act extends to England and Wales only."

## Part II

### Amendments of Adoption (Scotland) Act 1978 (c 28)

32. In section 11 (restrictions on arranging of adoptions and placing of children) for subsection (2) there shall be substituted—

"(2) An adoption society which is—

(*a*) approved as respects England and Wales under section 3 of the Adoption Act 1976; or
(*b*) registered as respects Northern Ireland under Article 4 of the Adoption (Northern Ireland) Order 1987,

but which is not approved under section 3 of this Act, shall not act as an adoption society in Scotland except to the extent that the society considers it necessary to do so in the interests of a person mentioned in section 1 of that Act or, as the case may be, Article 3 of that Order."

33. For section 14(1) (adoption by married couple) there shall be substituted—

"(1) Subject to section 53(1) of the Children Act 1975 (which provides for the making of a custody order instead of an adoption order in certain cases), an adoption order shall not be made on the application of more than one person except in the circumstances specified in subsections (1A) and (1B).

(1A) An adoption order may be made on the application of a married couple where both the husband and the wife have attained the age of 21 years.

(1B) An adoption order may be made on the application of a married couple where—

(*a*) the husband or the wife—

(i) is the father or mother of the child; and
(ii) has attained the age of 18 years; and

(*b*) his or her spouse has attained the age of 21 years."

34. In section 16(1)(*a*) (parental agreement) for the words from "in England" to "revoked", in the second place where it occurs, there shall be substituted—

"(i) in Scotland under section 18.

(ii) in England and Wales under section 18 of the Adoption Act 1976; or

(iii) in Northern Ireland under Article 17(1) or 18(1) of the Adoption (Northern Ireland) Order 1987,

and not revoked".

35. In section 18(5) (effect of order freeing child for adoption) for the words "and (3)" there shall be substituted "to (4)".

36. In section 20(3)(*c*) (revocation of section 18 order) the words "section 12(3)(*b*) of the Adoption Act 1976 or of" shall cease to have effect.

37. For section 21 (transfer of parental rights and duties between adoption agencies) there shall be substituted—

**"21. Variation of section 18 order so as to substitute one adoption agency for another**

(1) On an application to which this section applies an authorised court may vary an order under section 18 so as to transfer the parental rights and duties relating to the child from the adoption agency in which they are vested under the order ('the existing agency') to another adoption agency ('the substitute agency').

(2) This section applies to any application made jointly by the existing agency and the would-be substitute agency.

(3) Where an order under section 18 is varied under this section, section 19 shall apply as if the parental rights and duties relating to the child had vested in the substitute agency on the making of the order."

38. In section 22(4) (notification to local authority of adoption application) for the word "receives" there shall be substituted "receive".

39. In section 29 (return of child taken away in breach of section 27 or 28) after the word "1976" in each place where it occurs there shall be inserted "or Article 28 or 29 of the Adoption (Northern Ireland) Order 1987".

40. In section 32 (meaning of "protected child"), at the end of subsection (2) there shall be added "or Article 33 of the Adoption (Northern Ireland) Order 1987".

41. In section 45 (adopted children register)—

(*a*) for the words from "or an approved" in subsection (5) to the end of subsection (6) there shall be substituted—

"Board or adoption society falling within subsection (6) which is providing counselling for that adopted person.

(6) Where the Registrar General for Scotland furnishes an adopted person with information under subsection (5), he shall advise that person that counselling services are available—

(*a*) if the person is in Scotland—

(i) from the local authority in whose area he is living;

(ii) where the adoption order relating to him was made in Scotland, from the local authority in whose area the court which made the order sat; or

(iii) from any other local authority in Scotland;

(*b*) if the person is in England and Wales—

(i) from the local authority in whose area he is living;

(ii) where the adoption order relating to him was made in England and Wales, from the local authority in whose area the court which made the order sat; or

(iii) from any other local authority in England and Wales;

(*c*) if the person is in Northern Ireland—

(i) from the Board in whose area he is living;

(ii) where the adoption order relating to him was made in Northern Ireland, from the Board in whose area the court which made the order sat; or

(iii) from any other Board;

(*d*) if the person is in the United Kingdom and his adoption was arranged by an adoption society—

(i) approved under section 3;

(ii) approved under section 3 of the Adoption Act 1976; or

(iii) registered under Article 4 of the Adoption (Northern Ireland) Order 1987,

from that society.

(6A) Where an adopted person who is in Scotland—

(*a*) is furnished with information under subsection (5); or

(*b*) applies for information under—

(i) section 51(1) of the Adoption Act 1976; or

(ii) Article 54 of the Adoption (Northern Ireland) Order 1987,

any body mentioned in subsection (6B) to which the adopted person applies for counselling shall have a duty to provide counselling for him.

(6B) The bodies referred to in subsection (6A) are—

(*a*) any local authority falling within subsection (6)(*a*); and

(*b*) any adoption society falling within subsection (6)(*d*) so far as it is acting as an adoption society in Scotland.";

(*b*) in subsection (7)—

(i) for the word "under" there shall be substituted "from a local authority, Board or adoption society falling within";

(ii) for the words "or adoption society which is providing that counselling" there shall be substituted ", Board or adoption society"; and

(iii) after the word "authority" where it second occurs there shall be inserted ", Board"; and

(*c*) after subsection (9) there shall be inserted the following subsection.

"(10) In this section—

"Board" means a Health and Social Services Board established under Article 16 of the Health and Personal Social Services (Northern Ireland) Order 1972; and

"local authority", in relation to England and Wales, means the council of a county (other than a metropolitan county), a metropolitan district, a London borough or the Common Council of the City of London.".

42. In section 49 (adoption of children abroad)—

(*a*) in subsection (1) after the word "Scotland" there shall be inserted "or Northern Ireland"; and

(*b*) in subsection (3) for the words "word "England"" there shall be substituted "words "(England)" or "(Northern Ireland)"".

43. In section 50(1) (restriction on removal of children for adoption outside Great Britain) after the word "1976" there shall be inserted "or Article 57 of the Adoption (Northern Ireland) Order 1987".

44. In section 53(1) (effect of determination and orders made in England and Wales and overseas in adoption proceedings)—

(*a*) in subsection (1) for the words "Great Britain" there shall be substituted "the United Kingdom"; and

(*b*) for subsection (2) there shall be substituted—

"(2) Subsections (2) to (4) of section 12 shall apply in relation to an order freeing a child for adoption (other than an order under section 18) as if it were an adoption order; and on the revocation in England and Wales or Northern Ireland of an order freeing a child for adoption subsection (3) of section 20 shall apply as if the order had been revoked under that section."

45. In section 54(*b*) (evidence of adoption in Northern Ireland) for the words from "section 23(4)" to "in force" there shall be substituted "Article 63(1) of the Adoption (Northern Ireland) Order 1987".

46. In section 65(1) (interpretation)—

(*a*) in the definition of "adoption agency", at the end there shall be added "and an adoption agency within the meaning of Article 3 of the Adoption (Northern Ireland) Order 1987 (adoption agencies in Northern Ireland)";

(*b*) for the definition of "adoption order" there shall be substituted—

""adoption order"—

(*a*) means an order under section 12(1); and

(*b*) in sections 12(3) and (4), 18 to 20, 27, 28 and 30 to 32 and in the definition of "British adoption order" in this subsection includes an order under section 12 of the Adoption Act 1976 and Article 12 of the Adoption (Northern Ireland) Order 1987 (adoption orders in England and Wales and Northern Ireland respectively); and

(*c*) in sections 27, 28 and 30 to 32 includes an order under section 49, section 55 of the Adoption Act 1976 and Article 57 of the Adoption (Northern Ireland) Order 1987 (orders in relation to children being adopted abroad);";

(*c*) for the definition of "British adoption order" there shall be substituted—

""British adoption order" means—

(*a*) an adoption order as defined in this subsection; and

(*b*) an order under any provision for the adoption of a child effected under the law of any British territory outside the United Kingdom;";

(*e*) in the definition of "order freeing a child for adoption" for the words from "section 27(2)" to the end there shall be substituted "sections 27(2) and 53 includes an order under—

(*a*) section 18 of the Adoption Act 1976; and

(*b*) Article 17 or 18 of the Adoption (Northern Ireland) Order 1987;".

---

**Reference** See generally para 11.1 ff.

---

## SCHEDULE 11

Section 92.

## JURISDICTION

### PART I

### GENERAL

*Commencement of proceedings*

1.—(1) The Lord Chancellor may by order specify proceedings under this Act or the Adoption Act 1976 which may only be commenced in—

(*a*) a specified level of court;
(*b*) a court which falls within a specified class of court; or
(*c*) a particular court determined in accordance with, or specified in, the order.

(2) The Lord Chancellor may by order specify circumstances in which specified proceedings under this Act or the Adoption Act 1976 (which might otherwise be commenced elsewhere) may only be commenced in—

(*a*) a specified level of court;
(*b*) a court which falls within a specified class of court; or
(*c*) a particular court determined in accordance with, or specified in, the order.

(3) The Lord Chancellor may by order make provision by virtue of which, where specified proceedings with respect to a child under—

(*a*) this Act;
(*b*) the Adoption Act 1976; or
(*c*) the High Court's inherent jurisdiction with respect to children,

have been commenced in or transferred to any court (whether or not by virtue of an order under this Schedule), any other specified family proceedings which may affect, or are otherwise connected with, the child may, in specified circumstances, only be commenced in that court.

(4) A class of court specified in an order under this Schedule may be described by reference to a description of proceedings and may include different levels of court.

*Transfer of proceedings*

2.—(1) The Lord Chancellor may by order provide that in specified circumstances the whole, or any specified part of, specified proceedings to which this paragraph applies shall be transferred to—

(*a*) a specified level of court;
(*b*) a court which falls within a specified class of court; or
(*c*) a particular court determined in accordance with, or specified in, the order.

(2) Any order under this paragraph may provide for the transfer to be made at any stage, or specified stage, of the proceedings and whether or not the proceedings, or any part of them, have already been transferred.

(3) The proceedings to which this paragraph applies are—

(*a*) any proceedings under this Act;
(*b*) any proceedings under the Adoption Act 1976;
(*c*) any other proceedings which—

(i) are family proceedings for the purposes of this Act, other than proceedings under the inherent jurisdiction of the High Court; and
(ii) may affect, or are otherwise connected with, the child concerned.

(4) Proceedings to which this paragraph applies by virtue of sub-paragraph (3)(*c*) may only be transferred in accordance with the provisions of an order made under this paragraph for the purpose of consolidating them with proceedings under—

(*a*) this Act;
(*b*) the Adoption Act 1976; or
(*c*) the High Court's inherent jurisdiction with respect to children.

(5) An order under this paragraph may make such provision as the Lord Chancellor thinks appropriate for excluding proceedings to which this paragraph applies from the operation of any enactment which would otherwise govern the transfer of those proceedings, or any part of them.

*Hearings by single justice*

3.—(1) In such circumstances as the Lord Chancellor may by order specify—

(*a*) the jurisdiction of a magistrates' court to make an emergency protection order;

(*b*) any specified question with respect to the transfer of specified proceedings to or from a magistrates' court in accordance with the provisions of an order under paragraph 2,

may be exercised by a single justice.

(2) Any provision made under this paragraph shall be without prejudice to any other enactment or rule of law relating to the functions which may be performed by a single justice of the peace.

*General*

4.—(1) For the purposes of this Schedule—

(*a*) the commencement of proceedings under this Act includes the making of any application under this Act in the course of proceedings (whether or not those proceedings are proceedings under this Act); and

(*b*) there are three levels of court, that is to say the High Court, any county court and any magistrates' court.

(2) In this Schedule "specified" means specified by an order made under this Schedule.

(3) Any order under paragraph 1 may make provision as to the effect of commencing proceedings in contravention of any of the provisions of the order.

(4) An order under paragraph 2 may make provision as to the effect of a failure to comply with any of the provisions of the order.

(5) An order under this Schedule may—

(*a*) make such consequential, incidental or transitional provision as the Lord Chancellor considers expedient, including provision amending any other enactment so far as it concerns the jurisdiction of any court or justice of the peace;

(*b*) make provision for treating proceedings which are—

(i) in part proceedings of a kind mentioned in paragraph (*a*) or (*b*) of paragraph 2(3); and

(ii) in part proceedings of a kind mentioned in paragraph (*c*) of paragraph 2(3),

as consisting entirely of proceedings of one or other of those kinds, for the purposes of the application of any order made under paragraph 2.

## Part II

## Consequential Amendments

*The Administration of Justice Act 1964 (c 42)*

5. In section 38 of the Administration of Justice Act 1964 (interpretation), the definition of "domestic court", which is spent, shall be omitted.

*The Domestic Proceedings and Magistrates' Courts Act 1978 (c 22)*

6. In the Domestic Proceedings and Magistrates' Courts Act 1978—

(*a*) for the words "domestic proceedings", wherever they occur in sections 16(5)(*c*) and 88(1), there shall be substituted "family proceedings";

(*b*) for the words "domestic court panel", wherever they occur in section 16(5)(*b*), there shall be substituted "family panel".

*The Justices of the Peace Act 1979 (c 55)*

7. In the Justices of the Peace Act 1979—

(*a*) for the words "domestic proceedings", wherever they occur in section 16(5), there shall be substituted "family proceedings";
(*b*) for the words "domestic court", wherever they occur in section 17(3), there shall be substituted "family proceedings court";
(*c*) for the words "domestic courts", wherever they occur in sections 38(2) and 58(1) and (5), there shall be substituted "family proceedings courts".

*The Magistrates' Courts Act 1980 (c 43)*

8. In the Magistrates' Courts Act 1980—

(*a*) in section 65(1) (meaning of family proceedings), the following paragraph shall be inserted after paragraph (*m*)—

"(*n*) the Children Act 1989";

(*b*) in section 65(2)(*a*) for the words "and (*m*)" there shall be substituted "(*m*) and (*n*)";
(*c*) for the words "domestic proceedings", wherever they occur in sections 65(1), (2) and (3), 66(1) and (2), 67(1), (2) and (7), 69(1), (2), (3) and (4), 70(2) and (3), 71(1) and (2), 72(1), 73, 74(1), 121(8) and 150(1), there shall be substituted "family proceedings";
(*d*) for the words "domestic court panel", wherever they occur in sections 66(2), 67(2), (4), (5), (7) and (8) and 68(1), (2) and (3), there shall be substituted "family panel";
(*e*) for the words "domestic court panels", wherever they occur in section 67(3) and (4), (5), and (6), there shall be substituted "family panels";
(*f*) for the words "domestic courts", wherever they occur in sections 67(1) and (3) and 68(1), there shall be substituted "family proceedings courts";
(*g*) for the words "domestic court", wherever they occur in section 67(2) and (5), there shall be substituted "family proceedings court".

*The Supreme Court Act 1981 (c 54)*

9. In paragraph 3 of Schedule 1 to the Supreme Court Act 1981 (distribution of business to the Family Division of the High Court), the following sub-paragraph shall be added at the end—

"(*e*) proceedings under the Children Act 1989".

*The Matrimonial and Family Proceedings Act 1984 (c 42)*

10. In section 44 of the Matrimonial and Family Proceedings Act 1984 (domestic proceedings in magistrates' courts to include applications to alter maintenance agreements) for the words "domestic proceedings", wherever they occur, there shall be substituted "family proceedings".

*Insolvency Act 1986 (c 45)*

11.—(1) In section 281(5)(*b*) of the Insolvency Act 1986 (discharge not to release bankrupt from bankruptcy debt arising under any order make in family proceedings or in domestic proceedings), the words "or in domestic proceedings" shall be omitted.

(2) In section 281(8) of that Act (interpretation), for the definitions of "domestic proceedings" and "family proceedings" there shall be substituted—

""family proceedings" means—

(*a*) family proceedings within the meaning of the Magistrates' Courts Act 1980 and any proceedings which would be such proceedings but for section 65(1)(ii) of that Act (proceedings for variation of order for periodical payments); and
(*b*) family proceedings within the meaning of Part V of the Matrimonial and Family Proceedings Act 1984.".

## SCHEDULE 12

Section 108(4)

### Minor Amendments

*The Custody of Children Act 1891 (c 3)*

1. The Custody of Children Act 1891 (which contains miscellaneous obsolete provisions with respect to the custody of children) shall cease to have effect.

*The Children and Young Persons Act 1933 (c 12)*

2. In section 1(2)(*a*) of the Children and Young Persons Act 1933 (cruelty to persons under sixteen), after the words "young person" there shall be inserted ", or the legal guardian of a child or young person,".

3. Section 40 of that Act shall cease to have effect.

*The Education Act 1944 (c 31)*

4. In section 40(1) of the Education Act 1944 (enforcement of school attendance), the words from "or to imprisonment" to the end shall cease to have effect.

*The Marriage Act 1949 (c 76)*

5.—(1) In section 3 of the Marriage Act 1949 (consent required to the marriage of a child by common licence or superintendent registrar's certificate), in subsection (1) for the words "the Second Schedule to this Act" there shall be substituted "subsection (1A) of this section".

(2) After that subsection there shall be inserted—

"(1A) The consents are—

(*a*) subject to paragraphs (*b*) to (*d*) of this subsection, the consent of—

(i) each parent (if any) of the child who has parental responsibility for him; and
(ii) each guardian (if any) of the child;

(*b*) where a residence order is in force with respect to the child, the consent of the person or persons with whom he lives, or is to live, as a result of the order (in substitution for the consents mentioned in paragraph (*a*) of this subsection);
(*c*) where a care order is in force with respect to the child, the consent of the local authority designated in the order (in addition to the consents mentioned in paragraph (*a*) of this subsection);
(*d*) where neither paragraph (*b*) nor (*c*) of this subsection applies but a residence order was in force with respect to the child immediately before he reached the age of sixteen, the consent of the person or persons with whom he lived, or was to live, as a result of the order (in substitution for the consents mentioned in paragraph (*a*) of this subsection).

(1B) In this section "guardian of a child", "parental responsibility", "residence order" and "care order" have the same meaning as in the Children Act 1989."

*The Births and Deaths Registration Act 1953 (c 20)*

6.—(1) Sections 10 and 10A of the Births and Deaths Registration Act 1953 (registration of father, and re-registration, where parents not married) shall be amended as follows.

(2) In sections 10(1) and 10A(1) for paragraph (*d*) there shall be substituted—

"(*d*) at the request of the mother or that person on production of—

(i) a copy of a parental responsibility agreement made between them in relation to the child; and

(ii) a declaration in the prescribed form by the person making the request stating that the agreement was made in compliance with section 4 of the Children Act 1989 and has not been brought to an end by an order of a court; or

(*e*) at the request of the mother or that person on production of—

(i) a certified copy of an order under section 4 of the Children Act 1989 giving that person parental responsibility for the child; and

(ii) a declaration in the prescribed form by the person making the request stating that the order has not been brought to an end by an order of a court; or

(*f*) at the request of the mother or that person on production of—

(i) a certified copy of an order under paragraph 1 of Schedule 1 to the Children Act 1989 which requires that person to make any financial provision for the child and which is not an order falling within paragraph 4(3) of that Schedule; and

(ii) a declaration in the prescribed form by the person making the request stating that the order has not been discharged by an order of a court; or

(*g*) at the request of the mother or that person on production of—

(i) a certified copy of any of the orders which are mentioned in subsection (1A) of this section which has been made in relation to the child; and

(ii) a declaration in the prescribed form by the person making the request stating that the order has not been brought to an end or discharged by an order of a court."

(3) After sections 10(1) and 10A(1) there shall be inserted—

"(1A) The orders are—

(*a*) an order under section 4 of the Family Law Reform Act 1987 that that person shall have all the parental rights and duties with respect to the child;

(*b*) an order that that person shall have custody or care and control or legal custody of the child made under section 9 of the Guardianship of Minors Act 1971 at a time when such an order could only be made in favour of a parent;

(*c*) an order under section 9 or 11B of that Act which requires that person to make any financial provision in relation to the child;

(*d*) an order under section 4 of the Affiliation Proceedings Act 1957 naming that person as putative father of the child."

(4) In section 10(2) for the words "or (*d*)" there shall be substituted "to (*g*)".

(5) In section 10(3) for the words from ""relevant order"" to the end there shall be substituted ""parental responsibility agreement" has the same meaning as in the Children Act 1989".

(6) In section 10A(2), in paragraphs (*b*) and (*c*) for the words "paragraph (*d*)" in both places where they occur there shall be substituted "any of paragraphs (*d*) to (*g*)".

*The Army Act 1955 (c 18)*

7. In section 151 of the Army Act 1955 (deductions from pay for maintenance of wife or child), in subsection (1A)(*a*) for the words "in the care of a local authority in England or Wales" there shall be substituted "being looked after by a local authority in England or Wales (within the meaning of the Children Act 1989)".

8.—(1) Schedule 5A to that Act (powers of court on trial of civilian) shall be ammended as follows.

(2) For paragraphs 7(3) and (4) there shall be substituted—

> "(3) While an authorisation under a reception order is in force the order shall (subject to sub-paragraph (4) below) be deemed to be a care order for the purposes of the Children Act 1989, and the authorised authority shall be deemed to be the authority designated in that deemed care order.
>
> (3A) In sub-paragraph (3) above "care order" means a care order which is not an interim care order under section 38 of the Children Act 1989.
>
> (4) The Children Act 1989 shall apply to a reception order which is deemed to be a care order by virtue of sub-paragraph (3) above as if sections 31(8) (designated local authority), 91 (duration of care order etc.) and 101 (effect of orders as between different jurisdictions) were omitted."

(3) In sub-paragraph (5)(*c*) for the words from "attains" to the end there shall be substituted "attains 18 years of age".

(4) In paragraph 8(1) for the words "Children and Young Persons Act 1969" there shall be substituted "Children Act 1989".

*The Air Force Act 1955 (c 19)*

9. Section 151 (1A) of the Air Force Act 1955 (deductions from pay for maintenance of wife or child) shall have effect subject to the amendment that is set out in paragraph 7 in relation to section 151(1A) of the Army Act 1955.

10. Schedule 5A to that Act (powers of court on trial of civilian) shall have effect subject to the amendments that are set out in paragraph 8(2) to (4) in relation to Schedule 5A to the Army Act 1955.

*The Sexual Offences Act 1956 (c 69)*

11. In section 19(3) of the Sexual Offences Act 1956 (abduction of unmarried girl under eighteen from parent or guardian) for the words "the lawful care or charge of" there shall be substituted "parental responsibility for or care of".

12. In section 20(2) of that Act (abduction of unmarried girl under sixteen from parent or guardian) for the words "the lawful care or charge of" there shall be substituted "parental responsibility for or care of".

13. In section 21(3) of that Act (abduction of defective from parent or guardian) for the words "the lawful care or charge of" there shall be substituted "parental responsibility for or care of".

14. In section 28 of that Act (causing or encouraging prostitution of, intercourse with, or indecent assault on, girl under sixteen) for subsections (3) and (4) there shall be substituted—

> "(3) The persons who are to be treated for the purposes of this section as responsible for a girl are (subject to subsection (4) of this section)—
>
> (*a*) her parents;
> (*b*) any person who is not a parent of hers but who has parental responsibility for her; and
> (*c*) any person who has care of her.

(4) An individual falling within subsection (3)(*a*) or (*b*) of this section is not to be treated as responsible for a girl if—

(*a*) a residence order under the Children Act 1989 is in force with respect to her and he is not named in the order as the person with whom she is to live; or

(*b*) a care order under that Act is in force with respect to her."

15. Section 38 of that Act (power of court to divest person of authority over girl or boy in case of incest) shall cease to have effect.

16.—(1) In section 43 of that Act (power to search for and recover woman detained for immoral purposes), in subsection (5) for the words "the lawful care or charge of" there shall be substituted "parental responsibility for or care of".

(2) In subsection (6) of that section, for the words "section forty of the Children and Young Persons Act 1933" there shall be substituted "Part V of the Children Act 1989".

17. After section 46 of that Act there shall be inserted—

**"46A Meaning of 'parental responsibility'**

In this Act "parental responsibility" has the same meaning as in the Children Act 1989."

*The Naval Discipline Act 1957 (c 53)*

18. Schedule 4A to the Naval Discipline Act 1957 (powers of court on trial of civilian) shall have effect subject to the amendments that are set out in paragraph 8(2) to (4) in relation to Schedule 5A to the Army Act 1955.

*The Children and Young Persons Act 1963 (c 37)*

19. Section 3 of the Children and Young Persons Act 1963 (children and young persons beyond control) shall cease to have effect.

*The Children and Young Persons Act 1969 (c 54)*

20. In section 5 of the Children and Young Persons Act 1969 (restrictions on criminal proceedings for offences by young persons), in subsection (2), for the words "section 1 of this Act" there shall be substituted "Part IV of the Children Act 1989".

21. After section 7(7) of that Act (alteration in treatment of young offenders, etc) there shall be inserted—

"(7B) An order under subsection (7)(*c*) of this section shall not require a person to enter into a recognisance—

(*a*) for an amount exceeding ;bp1,000; or

(*b*) for a period exceeding—

(i) three years; or

(ii) where the young person concerned will attain the age of eighteen in a period shorter than three years, that shorter period.

(7C) Section 120 of the Magistrates' Courts Act 1980 shall apply to a recognisance entered into in pursuance of an order under subsection (7)(*c*) of this section as it applies to a recognisance to keep the peace."

22. In section 12A of that Act (young offenders) for subsections (1) and (2) there shall be substituted—

"(1) This subsection applies to any supervision order made under section 7(7) of this Act unless it requires the supervised person to comply with directions given by the supervisor under section 12(2) of this Act."

23. After that section there shall be inserted—

**"12AA Requirement for young offender to live in local authority accommodation**

(1) Where the conditions mentioned in subsection (6) of this section are satisfied, a supervision order may impose a requirement ("a residence requirement") that a child or young person shall live for a specified period in local authority accommodation.

(2) A residence requirement shall designate the local authority who are to receive the child or young person and that authority shall be the authority in whose area the child or youn person resides.

(3) The court shall not impose a residence requirement without first consulting the designated authority.

(4) A residence requirement may stipulate that the child or young person shall not live with a named person.

(5) The maximum period which may be specified in a residence requirement is six months.

(6) The conditions are that—

(*a*) a supervision order has previously been made in respect of the child or young person;

(*b*) that order imposed—

(i) a requirement under section 12A(3) of this Act; or

(ii) a residence requirement;

(*c*) he is found guilty of an offence which—

(i) was committed while that order was in force;

(ii) if it had been committed by a person over the age of twenty-one, would have been punishable with imprisonment; and

(iii) in the opinion of the court is serious; and

(*d*) the court is satisfied that the behaviour which constituted the offence was due, to a significant extent, to the circumstances in which he was living,

except that the condition in paragraph (*d*) of this subsection does not apply where the condition in paragraph (*b*)(ii) is satisfied.

(7) For the purposes of satisfying itself as mentioned in subsection (6)(*d*) of this section, the court shall obtain a social inquiry report which makes particular reference to the circumstances in which the child or young person was living.

(8) Subsection (7) of this section does not apply if the court already has before it a social inquiry report which contains sufficient information about the circumstances in which the child or young person was living.

(9) A court shall not include a residence requirement in respect of a child or young person who is not legally represented at the relevant time in that court unless—

(*a*) he has applied for legal aid for the purposes of the proceedings and the application was refused on the ground that it did not appear that his resources were such that he required assistance; or

(*b*) he has been informed of his right to apply for legal aid for the purposes of the proceedings and has had the opportunity to do so, but nevertheless refused or failed to apply.

(10) In subsection (9) of this section—

(*a*) "the relevant time" means the time when the court is considering whether or not to impose the requirement; and
(*b*) "the proceedings" means—

(i) the whole proceedings; or
(ii) the part of the proceedings relating to the imposition of the requirement.

(11) A supervision order imposing a residence requirement may also impose any of the requirements mentioned in sections 12, 12A, 12B or 12C of this Act.

(12) In this section "social inquiry report" has the same meaning as in section 2 of the Criminal Justice Act 1982."

24.—(1) In section 15 of that Act (variation and discharge of supervision orders), in subsections (1)(*a*), (2A), (3)(*e*) and (4) after the word "12A", in each place where it occurs, there shall be inserted "12AA".

(2) In subsection (4) of that section for the words "(not being a juvenile court)" there shall be substituted "other than a juvenile court".

25.—(1) In section 16 of that Act (provisions supplementary to section 15), in subsection (3) for the words "either direct" to the end there shall be substituted—

"(i) direct that he be released forthwith; or
(ii) remand him."

(2) In subsection (4) of that section—

(*a*) in paragraph (*a*) for the words "an interim order made by virtue of" there shall be substituted "a remand under";
(*b*) in paragraph (*b*) for the words "makes an interim order in respect of" there shall be substituted "remands", and
(*c*) for the words "make an interim order in respect of" there shall be substituted "remand".

(3) In subsections (5)(*b*) and (*c*) and (6)(*a*) after the word "12A", in each place where it occurs, there shall be inserted "12AA".

26. For section 23 of that Act (remand to care of local authorities etc) there shall be substituted—

**"23 Remand to local authority accommodation, committal of young persons of unruly character, etc**

(1) Where a court—

(*a*) remands or commits for trial a child charged with homicide or remands a child convicted of homicide; or
(*b*) remands a young person charged with or convicted of one or more offences or commits him for trial or sentence,

and he is not released on bail, then, unless he is a young person who is certified by the court to be of unruly character, the court shall remand him to local authority accommodation.

(2) A court remanding a person to local authority accommodation shall designate the authority who are to receive him and that authority shall be the authority in whose area it appears to the court that—

(*a*) he resides; or
(*b*) the offence or one of the offences was committed.

(3) Where a person is remanded to local authority accommodation, it shall be lawful for any person acting on behalf of the designated authority to detain him.

(4) The court shall not certifiy a young person as being of unruly character unless—

(*a*) he cannot safely be remanded to local authority accommodation; and
(*b*) the conditions prescribed by order made by the Secretary of State under this subsection are satisfied in relation to him.

(5) Where the court certifies that a young person is of unruly character, it shall commit him—

(*a*) to a remand centre, if it has been notified that such a centre is available for the reception from the court of such persons; and
(*b*) to a prison, if it has not been so notified.

(6) Where a young person is remanded to local authority accommodation, a court may, on the application of the designated authority, certify him to be of unruly character in accordance with subsection (4) of this section (and on so doing he shall cease to be remanded to local authority accommodation and subsection (5) of this section shall apply).

(7) For the purposes of subsection (6) of this section, "a court" means—

(*a*) the court which remanded the young person; or
(*b*) any magistrates' court having jurisdiction in the place where that person is for the time being,

and in this section "court" and "magistrates' court" include a justice.

(8) This section has effect subject to—

(*a*) section 37 of the Magistrates' Courts Act 1980 (committal to the Crown Court with a view to a sentence of detention in a young offender institution); and
(*b*) section 128(7) of that Act (remands to the custody of a constable for periods of not more than three days),

but section 128(7) shall have effect in relation to a child or young person as if for the reference to three clear days there were substituted a reference to twenty-four hours."

27.—(1) In section 32 of that Act (detention of absentees), for subsection (1A) there shall be substituted the following subsections—

"(1A) If a child or young person is absent, without the consent of the responsible person—

(*a*) from a place of safety to which he has been taken under section 16(3) of this Act; or
(*b*) from local authority accommodation—

(i) in which he is required to live under section 12AA of this Act; or
(ii) to which he has been remanded under section 23(1) of this Act,

he may be arrested by a constable anywhere in the United Kingdom or Channel Islands without a warrant.

(1B) A person so arrested shall be conducted to—

(*a*) the place of safety;
(*b*) the local authority accommodation; or
(*c*) such other place as the responsible person may direct,

at the responsible person's expense.

(1C) In this section "the responsible person" means the person who made the arrangements under section 16(3) of this Act or, as the case may be, the authority designated under section 12AA or 23 of this Act."

(2) In subsection (2B) of that section for the words "person referred to in subsection (1A)(*a*) or (*b*) (as the case may be) of this section" there shall be substituted "responsible person".

28. In section 34(1) of that Act (transitional modifications of Part I for persons of specified ages)—

(*a*) in paragraph (*a*), for the words "13(2) or 28(4) or (5)" there shall be substituted "or 13(2)"; and

(*b*) in paragraph (*e*), for the words "section 23(2) or (3)" there shall be substituted "section 23(4) to (6)".

29. In section 70(1) of that Act (interpretation)—

(*a*) after the definition of "local authority" there shall be inserted—

""local authority accommodation" means accommodation provided by or on behalf of a local authority (within the meaning of the Children Act 1989)"; and

(*b*) in the definition of "reside" for "12(4) and (5)" there shall be substituted "12B(1) and (2)".

30. In section 73 of that Act (extent, etc)—

(*a*) in subsection (4)(*a*) for "32(1), (3) and (4)" there shall be substituted "32(1) to (1C) and (2A) to (4)"; and

(*b*) in subsection (6) for "32(1), (1A)" there shall be substituted "32(1) to (1C)".

*The Matrimonial Causes Act 1973 (c 18)*

31. For section 41 of the Matrimonial Causes Act 1973 (restrictions on decrees for dissolution, annulment or separation affecting children) there shall be substituted—

**"41 Restrictions on decrees for dissolution, annulment or separation affecting children**

(1) In any proceedings for a decree of divorce or nullity of marriage, or a decree of judicial separation, the court shall consider—

(*a*) whether there are any children of the family to whom this section applies; and

(*b*) where there are any such children, whether (in the light of the arrangements which have been, or are proposed to be, made for their upbringing and welfare) it should exercise any of its powers under the Children Act 1989 with respect to any of them.

(2) Where, in any case to which this section applies, it appears to the court that—

(*a*) the circumstances of the case require it, or are likely to require it, to exercise any of its powers under the Act of 1989 with respect to any such child;

(*b*) it is not in a position to exercise that power or (as the case may be) those powers without giving further consideration to the case; and

(*c*) there are exceptional circumstances which make it desirable in the interests of the child that the court should give a direction under this section,

it may direct that the decree of divorce or nullity is not to be made absolute, or that the decree of judicial separation is not to be granted, until the court orders otherwise.

(3) This section applies to—

(*a*) any child of the family who has not reached the age of sixteen at the date when the court considers the case in accordance with the requirements of this section; and

(*b*) any child of the family who has reached that age at that date and in relation to whom the court directs that this section shall apply."

32. In section 42 of that Act, subsection (3) (declaration by court that party to marriage unfit to have custody of children of family) shall cease to have effect.

33. In section 52(1) of that Act (interpretation), in the definition of "child of the family", for the words "has been boarded-out with those parties" there shall be substituted "is placed with those parties as foster parents".

*The National Health Service Act 1977 (c 49)*

34. In Schedule 8 to the National Health Service Act 1977 (functions of local social services authorities), the following sub-paragraph shall be added at the end of paragraph 2—

"(4A) This paragraph does not apply in relation to persons under the age of 18."

*The Child Care Act 1980 (c 5)*

35. Until the repeal of the Child Care Act 1980 by this Act takes effect, the definition of "parent" in section 87 of that Act shall have effect as if it applied only in relation to Part I and sections 13, 24, 64 and 65 of that Act (provisions excluded by section 2(1)(f) of the Family Law Reform Act 1987 from the application of the general rule in that Act governing the meaning of references to relationships between persons).

*The Education Act 1981 (c 60)*

36. The following section shall be inserted in the Education Act 1981, after section 3—

**"3A Provision outside England and Wales for certain children**

(1) A local authority may make such arrangements as they think fit to enable any child in respect of whom they maintain a statement under section 7 to attend an establishment outside England and Wales which specialises in providing for children with special needs.

(2) In subsection (1) above "children with special needs" means children who have particular needs which would be special educational needs if those children were in England and Wales.

(3) Where an authority make arrangements under this section with respect to a child, those arrangements may, in particular, include contributing to or paying—

(*a*) fees charged by the establishment;
(*b*) expenses reasonably incurred in maintaining him while he is at the establishment or travelling to or from it;
(*c*) those travelling expenses;
(*d*) expenses reasonably incurred by any person accompanying him while he is travelling or staying at the establishment.

(4) This section is not to be taken as in any way limiting any other powers of a local education authority.".

*The Child Abduction Act 1984 (c 37)*

37.—(1) Section 1 of the Child Abduction Act 1984 (offence of abduction by parent, etc.) shall be amended as follows.

(2) For subsections (2) to (4) there shall be substituted—

"(2) A person is connected with a child for the purposes of this section if—

(*a*) he is a parent of the child; or
(*b*) in the case of a child whose parents were not married to each

other at the time of his birth, there are reasonable grounds for believing that he is the father of the child; or

(*c*) he is a guardian of the child; or

(*d*) he is a person in whose favour a residence order is in force with respect to the child; or

(*e*) he has custody of the child.

(3) In this section 'the appropriate consent', in relation to a child, means—

(*a*) the conset of each of the following—

(i) the child's mother;

(ii) the child's father, if he has parental responsibility for him;

(iii) any guardian of the child;

(iv) any person in whose favour a residence order is in force with respect to the child;

(v) any person who has custody of the child; or

(*b*) the leave of the court granted under or by virtue of any provision of Part II of the Children Act 1989; or

(*c*) if any person has custody of the child, the leave of the court which awarded custody to him.

(4) A person does not commit an offence under this section by taking or sending a child out of the United Kingdom without obtaining the appropriate consent if—

(*a*) he is a person in whose favour there is a residence order in force with respect to the child, and

(*b*) he takes or sends him out of the United Kingdom for a period of less than one month.

(4A) Subsection (4) above does not apply if the person taking or sending the child out of the United Kingdom does so in breach of an order under Part II of the Children Act 1989."

(3) In subsection (5) for the words from "but" to the end there shall be substituted—

"(5A) Subsection (5)(*c*) above does not apply if—

(*a*) the person who refused to consent is a person—

(i) in whose favour there is a residence order in force with respect to the child; or

(ii) who has custody of the child; or

(*b*) the person taking or sending the child out of the United Kingdom is, by so acting, in breach of an order made by a court in the United Kingdom."

(4) For subsection (7) there shall be substituted—

"(7) for the purposes of this section—

(*a*) "guardian of a child", "residence order" and "parental responsibility" have the same meaning as in the Children Act 1989; and

(*b*) a person shall be treated as having custody of a child if there is in force an order of a court in the United Kingdom awarding him (whether solely or jointly with another person) custody, legal custody or care and control of the child."

(5) In subsection (8) for the words from "or voluntary organisation" to "custodianship proceedings or" there shall be substituted "detained in a place of safety, remanded to a local authority accommodation or the subject of".

38.—(1) In section 2 of that Act (offence of abduction of child by other persons), in subsection (1) for the words from "Subject" to "above" there shall be substituted

"Subject to subsection (3) below, a person, other than one mentioned in subsection (2) below".

(2) For subsection (2) of that section there shall be substituted—

"(2) The persons are—

(*a*) where the father and mother of the child in question were married to each other at the time of his birth, the child's father and mother;

(*b*) where the father and mother of the child in question were not married to each other at the time of his birth, the child's mother; and

(*c*) any other person mentioned in section 1(2)(*c*) to (*e*) above.

(3) In proceedings against any person for an offence under this section, it shall be a defence for that person to prove—

(*a*) where the father and mother of the child in question were not married to each other at the time of his birth—

(i) that he is the child's father; or

(ii) that, at the time of the alleged offence, he believed, on reasonable grounds, that he was the child's father; or

(*b*) that, at the time of the alleged offence, he believed that the child had attained the age of sixteen."

39. At the end of section 3 of that Act (construction of references to taking, sending and detaining) there shall be added "and

(*d*) references to a child's parents and to a child whose parents were (or were not) married to each other at the time of his birth shall be construed in accordance with section 1 of the Family Law Reform Act 1987 (which extends their meaning)."

40.—(1) The Schedule to that Act (modifications of section 1 for children in certain cases) shall be amended as follows.

(2) In paragraph 1(1) for the words "or voluntary organisation" there shall be substituted "within the meaning of the Children Act 1989".

(3) for paragraph 2(1) there shall be substituted—

"(1) This paragraph applies in the case of a child who is—

(*a*) detained in a place of safety under section 16(3) of the Children and Young Persons Act 1969; or

(*b*) remanded to a local authority accommodation under section 23 of that Act."

(4) In paragraph 3(1)—

(*a*) in paragraph (*a*) for the words "section 14 of the Children Act 1975" there shall be substituted "section 18 of the Adoption Act 1976"; and

(*b*) in paragraph (*d*) for the words "section 25 of the Children Act 1975 or section 53 of the Adoption Act 1958" there shall be substituted "section 55 of the Adoption Act 1976".

(5) In paragraph 3(2)(*a*)—

(*a*) in sub-paragraph (i), for the words from "order or", to "Children Act 1975" there shall be substituted "section 18 order or, if the section 18 order has been varied under section 21 of that Act so as to give parental responsibility to another agency", and

(*b*) in sub-paragraph (ii), for the words "(*c*) or (*e*)" there shall be substituted "or (*c*)".

(6) At the end of paragraph 3 there shall be added—

"(3) Sub-paragraph (2) above shall be construed as if the references to the court included, in any case where the court is a magistrates' court, a reference to any magistrates' court acting for the same area as that court".

(7) For paragraph 5 there shall be substituted—

"5. In this Schedule—

(*a*) "adoption agency" and "adoption order" have the same meaning as in the Adoption Act 1976; and

(*b*) "area", in relation to a magistrates' court, means the petty sessions area (within the meaning of the Justices of the Peace Act 1979) for which the court is appointed.".

*The Foster Children (Scotland) Act 1984 (c 56)*

41. In section 1 of the Foster Children (Scotland) Act 1984 (definition of foster child)—

(*a*) for the words "he is— (*a*)" there shall be substituted "(*a*) he is"; and

(*b*) the words "for a period of more than 6 days" and the words from "The period" to the end shall cease to have effect.

42. In section 2(2) of that Act (exceptions to section 1), for paragraph (f) there shall be substituted—

"(*f*) if he has been in that person's care for a period of less than 28 days and that person does not intend to undertake his care for any longer period."

43. In section 7(1) of that Act (persons disqualified from keeping foster children)—

(*a*) the word "or" at the end of paragraph (*e*) shall be omitted; and

(*b*) after paragraph (f) there shall be inserted "or

(*g*) he is disqualified from fostering a child privately (within the meaning of the Children Act 1989) by regulations made under section 68 of that Act,".

*The Disabled Persons (Services, Consultation and Representation) Act 1986 (c 33)*

44. In section 2(5) of the Disabled Persons (Services, Consultation and Representation) Act 1986 (circumstances in which authorised representative has right to visit etc. disabled person), after paragraph (*d*) there shall be inserted—

"(*dd*) in accommodation provided by any educational establishment".

*The Legal Aid Act 1988 (c 34)*

45. In paragraph 2 of Part I of Schedule 2 to the Legal Aid Act 1988 (proceedings in magistrates' courts to which the civil legal aid provisions of Part IV of the Act apply), the following sub-paragraph shall be added at the end—

"(*g*) proceedings under the Children Act 1989".

Date in force para 35 16 November 1989; para 36 16 January 1990.

## SCHEDULE 13

Section 108(5)

### Consequential Amendments

*The Wills Act 1837 (c. 26)*

1. In section 1 of the Wills Act 1837 (interpretation), in the definition of "will", for the words "and also to a disposition by will and testament or devise of the custody and tuition of any child" there shall be substituted "and also to an appointment by will of a guardian of a child".

*The Children and Young Persons Act 1933 (c 12)*

2. In section 1(1) of the Children and Young Persons Act 1933 (cruelty to persons under sixteen) for the words "has the custody, charge or care of" there shall be substituted "has responsibility for".

3. In the following sections of that Act—

(*a*) 3(1) (allowing persons under sixteen to be in brothels);
(*b*) 4(1) and (2) (causing or allowing persons under sixteen to be used for begging);
(*c*) 11 (exposing children under twelve to risk of burning); and
(*d*) 25(1) (restrictions on persons under eighteen going abroad for the purpose of performing for profit),

for the words "the custody, charge or care of" there shall, in each case, be substituted "responsibility for".

4. In section 10(1A) of that Act (vagrants preventing children from receiving education), for the words from "to bring the child" to the end there shall be substituted "to make an application in respect of the child or young person for an education supervision order under section 36 of the Children Act 1989".

5. For section 17 of that Act (interpretation of PartI) there shall be substituted the following section—

**"17 Interpretation of Part I**

(1) For the purposes of this Part of this Act, the following shall be presumed to have responsibility for a child or young person—

(*a*) any person who—

(i) has parental responsibility for him (within the meaning of the Children Act 1989); or
(ii) is otherwise legally liable to maintain him; and

(*b*) any person who has care of him.

(2) A person who is presumed to be responsible for a child or young person by virtue of subsection (1)(*a*) shall not be taken to have ceased to be responsible for him by reason only that he does not have care of him."

6.—(1) In section 34 of that Act (attendance at court of parent of child or young person charged with an offence etc.), in subsection (1) after the word "offence" there shall be inserted "is the subject of an application for a care or supervision order under Part IV of the Children Act 1989".

(2) In subsection (7) of that section after the words "Children and Young Persons Act 1969" there shall be inserted "or Part IV of the Children Act 1989".

(3) After subsection (7) of that section there shall be inserted—

"(7A) If it appears that at the time of his arrest the child or young person is being provided with accommodation by or on behalf of a local authority under section 20 of the Children Act 1989, the local authority shall also be informed as described in subsection (3) above as soon as it is reasonably practicable to do so."

7. In section 107(1) of that Act (interpretation)—

(*a*) in the definition of "guardian", for the words "charge of or control over" there shall be substituted "care of";
(*b*) for the definition of legal guardian there shall be substituted—

""legal guardian", in relation to a child or young person, means a guardian of a child as defined in the Children Act 1989".

*The Education Act 1944 (c 31)*

8.—(1) Section 40 of the Education Act 1944 (enforcement of school attendance) shall be amended as follows.

(2) For subsection (2) there shall be substituted—

"(2) Proceedings for such offences shall not be instituted except by a local education authority.

(2A) Before instituting such proceedings the local education authority shall consider whether it would be appropriate, instead of or as well as instituting the proceedings, to apply for an education supervision order with respect to the child."

(3) For subsections (3) and (4) there shall be substituted—

"(3) The court—

(*a*) by which a person is convicted of an offence against section 37 of this Act; or

(*b*) before which a person is charged with an offence under section 39 of this Act,

may direct the local education authority instituting the proceedings to apply for an education supervision order with respect to the child unless the authority, having consulted the appropriate local authority, decide that the child's welfare will be satisfactorily safeguarded even though no education supervision order is made.

(3A) Where, following such a direction, a local education authority decide not to apply for an education supervision order they shall inform the court of the reasons for their decision.

(3B) Unless the court has directed otherwise, the information required under subsection (3A) shall be given to the court before the end of the period of eight weeks beginning with the date on which the direction was given.

(4) Where—

(*a*) a local education authority apply for an education supervision order with respect to a child who is the subject of a school attendance order; and

(*b*) the court decides that section 36(3) of the Children Act 1989 prevents it from making the order;

the court may direct that the school attendance order shall cease to be in force."

(4) After subsection (4) there shall be inserted—

"(5) In this section—

"appropriate local authority" has the same meaning as in section 36(9) of the Children Act 1989; and

"education supervision order" means an education supervision order under that Act."

9. In section 71 of that Act (complaints with respect to independent schools), the following paragraph shall be added after paragraph (*d*), in subsection (1)—

"(*e*) there has been a failure, in relation to a child provided with accommodation by the school, to comply with the duty imposed by section 87 of the Children Act 1989 (welfare of children accommodated in independent schools);".

10. After section 114(1C) of that Act (interpretation) there shall be inserted the following subsections—

"(1D) In this Act, unless the context otherwise requires, "parent", in relation to a child or young person, includes any person—

(*a*) who is not a parent of his but who has parental responsibility for him, or

(*b*) who has care of him,

except for the purposes of the enactments mentioned in subsection (1E) of this section, where it only includes such a person if he is an individual.

(1E) The enactments are—

(*a*) sections 5(4), 15(2) and (6), 31 and 65(1) of, and paragraph 7(6) of Schedule 2 to, the Education (No 2) Act 1986; and

(*b*) sections 53(8), 54(2), 58(5)(*k*), 60 and 61 of the Education Reform Act 1988.

(1F) For the purposes of subsection (1D) of this section—

(*a*) "parental responsibility" has the same meaning as in the Children Act 1989; and

(*b*) in determining whether an individual has care of a child or young person any absence of the child or young person at a hospital or boarding school and any other temporary absence shall be disregarded."

*The National Assistance Act 1948 (c 29)*

11.—(1) In section 21(1)(*a*) of the National Assistance Act 1948 (persons for whom local authority is to provide residential accommodation) after the word "persons" there shall be inserted "aged eighteen or over".

(2) In section 29(1) of that Act (welfare arrangements for blind, deaf, dumb and crippled persons) after the words "that is to say persons" and after the words "and other persons" there shall, in each case, be inserted "aged eighteen or over".

*The Reserve and Auxiliary Forces (Protection of Civil Interests) Act 1951 (c 65)*

12. For section 2(1)(*d*) of the Reserve and Auxiliary Forces (Protection of Civil Interests) Act 1951 (cases in which leave of an appropriate court is required before enforcing certain orders for the payment of money), there shall be substituted—

"(*d*) an order for alimony, maintenance or other payment made under sections 21 to 33 of the Matrimonial Causes Act 1973 or made, or having effect as if made, under Schedule 1 to the Children Act 1989".

*The Mines and Quarries Act 1954 (c 70)*

13. In section 182(1) of the Mines and Quarries Act 1954 (interpretation), in the definition of "parent", for the words from "or guardian" to first "young person" there shall be substituted "of a young person or any person who is not a parent of his but who has parental responsibility for him (within the meaning of the Children Act 1989)".

*The Administration of Justice Act 1960 (c 65)*

14. In section 12 of the Administration of Justice Act 1960 (publication of information relating to proceedings in private), in subsection (1) for paragraph (*a*) there shall be substituted—

"(*a*) where the proceedings—

(i) relate to the exercise of the inherent jurisdiction of the High Court with respect to minors;

(ii) are brought under the Children Act 1989; or

(iii) otherwise relate wholly or mainly to the maintenance or upbringing of a minor;".

*The Factories Act 1961 (c 34)*

15. In section 176(1) of the Factories Act 1961 (interpretation), in the definition of "parent", for the words from "or guardian" to first "young person" there shall be substituted "of a child or young person or any person who is not a parent of his but who has parental responsibility for him (within the meaning of the Children Act 1989)".

*The Criminal Justice Act 1967 (c 80)*

16. In section 67(1A)(*c*) of the Criminal Justice Act 1967 (computation of sentences of imprisonment passed in England and Wales) for the words "in the care of a local authority" there shall be substituted "remanded to local authority accommodation".

*The Health Services and Public Health Act 1968 (c. 46)*

17.—(1) In section 64(3)(*a*) of the Health Services and Public Health Act 1968 (meaning of "relevant enactments" in relation to power of Minister of Health or Secretary of State to provide financial assistance), for sub-paragraph (xix) inserted by paragraph 19 of Schedule 5 to the Child Care Act 1980 there shall be substituted—

"(xx) the Children Act 1989."

(2) In section 65(3)(*b*) of that Act (meaning of "relevant enactments" in relation to power of local authority to provide financial and other assistance), for sub-paragraph (xx) inserted by paragraph 20 of Schedule 5 to the Child Care Act 1980 there shall be substituted—

"(xxi) the Children Act 1989."

*The Social Work (Scotland) Act 1968 (c 49)*

18. In section 2(2) of the Social Work (Scotland) Act 1968 (matters referred to social work committee) after paragraph (*j*) there shall be inserted—

"(*k*) section 19 and Part X of the Children Act 1989,".

19. In section 5(2)(*c*) of the Act (power of Secretary of State to make regulations) for the words "and (*j*)" there shall be substituted "to (*k*)".

20. In section 21(3) of that Act (mode of provision of accommodation and maintenance) for the words "section 21 of the Child Care Act 1980" there shall be substituted "section 23 of the Children Act 1989".

21. In section 74(6) of that Act (parent of child in residential establishment moving to England or Wales) for the words from "Children and Young Persons Act 1969" to the end there shall be substituted "Children Act 1989, but as if section 31(8) were omitted".

22. In section 75(2) of that Act (parent of child subject to care order etc moving to Scotland), for the words "Children and Young Persons Act 1969" there shall be substituted "Children Act 1989".

23. In section 86(3) of that Act (meaning of ordinary residence for purpose of adjustments between authrority providing accommodation and authority of area of residence), the words "the Child Care Act 1980 or" shall be omitted and after the words "education authority" there shall be inserted "or placed with local authority foster parents under the Children Act 1989".

*The Civil Evidence Act 1968 (c 64)*

24. In section 12(5)(*b*) of the Civil Evidence Act 1968 (findings of paternity etc as evidence in civil proceedings—meaning of "relevant proceedings") for sub-paragraph (iv) there shall be substituted—

"(iv) paragraph 23 of Schedule 2 to the Children Act 1989."

*The Administration of Justice Act 1970 (c 31)*

25. In Schedule 8 to the Administration of Justice Act 1970 (maintenance orders for purposes of Maintenance Orders Act 1958 and the 1970 Act), in paragraph 6 for the words "section 47 or 51 of the Child Care Act 1980" there shall be substituted "paragraph 23 of Schedule 2 to the Children Act 1989".

*The Local Authority Social Services Act 1970 (c 42)*

26.—(1) In Schedule 1 to the Local Authority Social Services Act 1970 (enactments conferring functions assigned to social service committee)—

(*a*) in the entry relating to the Mental Health Act 1959, for the words "sections 8 and 9" there shall be substituted "section 8"; and
(*b*) in the entry relating to the Children and Young Persons Act 1969, for the words "sections 1, 2 and 9" there shall be substituted "section 9".

(2) At the end of that Schedule there shall be added—

| | |
|---|---|
| "Children Act 1989<br>The whole Act, in so far as it confers functions on a local authority within the meaning of that Act. | Welfare reports.<br>Consent to application for residence order in respect of child in care.<br>Family assistance orders.<br>Functions under Part III of the Act (local authority support for children and families).<br>Care and supervision.<br>Protection of children.<br>Functions in relation to community homes, voluntary homes and voluntary organisations, registered children's homes, private arrangements for fostering children, child minding and day care for young children.<br>Inspection of children's homes on behalf of Secretary of State.<br>Research and returns of information.<br>Functions in relation to children accommodated by health authorities and local education authorities or in residential care, nursing or mental nursing homes or in independent schools." |

*The Chronically Sick and Disabled Persons Act 1970 (c 44)*

27. After section 28 of the Chronically Sick and Disabled Persons Act 1970 there shall be inserted—

**"28A Application of Act to authorities having functions under the Children Act 1989**

This Act applies with respect to disabled children in relation to whom a local authority have functions under Part III of the Children Act 1989 as it applies in relation to persons to whom section 29 of the National Assistance Act 1948 applies."

*The Courts Act 1971 (c 23)*

28. In Part I of Schedule 9 to the Courts Act Act 1971 (substitution of references to Crown Court), in the entry relating to the Children and Young Persons Act 1969, for the words "Sections 2(12), 3(8), 16(8), 21(4)(5)" there shall be substituted "Section 16(8).".

*The Attachment of Earnings Act 1971 (c 32)*

29. In Schedule 1 to the Attachment of Earnings Act 1971 (maintenance orders to which that Act applies), in paragraph 7, for the words "section 47 or 51 of the Child Care Act 1980" there shall be substituted "paragraph 23 of Schedule 2 to the Children Act 1989".

*The Tribunals and Inquiries Act 1971 (c 62)*

30. In Schedule 1 to the Tribunals and Inquiries Act 1971 (tribunals under direct supervision of the Council on Tribunals), for paragraph 4 there shall be substituted—

| | |
|---|---|
| "Registration of voluntary homes and children's homes under the Children Act 1989. | 4. Registered Homes Tribunals constituted under Part III of the Registered Homes Act 1984." |

*The Local Government Act 1972 (c 70)*

31.—(1) In section 102(1) of the Local Government Act 1972 (appointment of committees) for the words "section 31 of the Child Care Act 1980" there shall be substituted "section 53 of the Children Act 1989".

(2) In Schedule 12A to that Act (access to information: exempt information), in Part III (interpretation), in paragraph 1(1)(*b*) for the words "section 20 of the Children and Young Persons Act 1969" there shall be substituted "section 31 of the Children Act 1989".

*The Employment of Children Act 1973 (c 24)*

32.—(1) In section 2 of the Employment of Children Act 1973 (supervision by education authorities), in subsection (2)(*a*) for the words "guardian or a person who has actual custody of" there shall be substituted "any person responsible for".

(2) After that subsection there shall be inserted—

"(2A) For the purposes of subsection (2)(*a*) above a person is responsible for a child—

(*a*) in England and Wales, if he has parental responsibility for the child or care of him; and
(*b*) in Scotland, if he is his guardian or has actual custody of him.".

*The Domicile and Matrimonial Proceedings Act 1973 (c 45)*

33.—(1) In Schedule 1 to the Domicile and Matrimonial Proceedings Act 1973 (proceedings in divorce etc stayed by reference to proceedings in other jurisdiction), paragraph 11(1) shall be amended as follows—

(*a*) at the end of the definition of "lump sum" there shall be added "or an order made in equivalent circumstances under Schedule 1 to the Children Act 1989 and of a kind mentioned in paragraph 1(2)(*c*) of that Schedule";
(*b*) in the definition of "relevant order", at the end of paragraph (*b*), there shall be added "or an order made in equivalent circumstances under Schedule 1 to the Children Act 1989 and of a kind mentioned in paragraph 1(2)(*a*) or (*b*) of that Schedule";
(*c*) in paragraph (*c*) of that definition, after the word "children)" there shall be inserted "or a section 8 order under the Children Act 1989"; and

(*d*) in paragraph (*d*) of that definition for the words "the custody, care or control" there shall be substituted "care".

(2) In paragraph 11(3) of that Schedule—

(*a*) the word "four" shall be omitted; and
(*b*) for the words "the custody of a child and the education of a child" there shall be substituted "or any provision which could be made by a section 8 order under the Children Act 1989".

*The Powers of Criminal Courts Act 1973 (c 62)*

34. In Schedule 3 to the Powers of Criminal Courts Act 1973 (the probation and after-care service and its functions), in paragraph 3(2A) after paragraph (*b*) there shall be inserted—

"and

(*c*) directions given under paragraph 2 or 3 of Schedule 3 to the Children Act 1989".

*The Rehabilitation of Offenders Act 1974 (c 53)*

35.—(1) Section 7(2) of the Rehabilitation of Offenders Act 1974 (limitations on rehabilitation under the Act) shall be amended as follows.

(2) For paragraph (*c*) there shall be substituted—

"(*c*) in any proceedings relating to adoption, the marriage of any minor, the exercise of the inherent jurisdiction of the High Court with respect to minors or the provision by any person of accommodation, care or schooling for minors;

(*cc*) in any proceedings brought under the Children Act 1989;"

(3) For paragraph (*d*) there shall be substituted—

"(*d*) in any proceedings relating to the variation or discharge of a supervision order under the Children and Young Persons Act 1969, or on appeal from any such proceedings".

*The Domestic Proceedings and Magistrates' Courts Act 1978 (c 22)*

36. For section 8 of the Domestic Proceedings and Magistrates' Courts Act 1978 (orders for the custody of children) there shall be substituted—

**"8 Restrictions on making of orders under this Act: welfare of children**

Where an application is made by a party to a marriage for an order under section 2, 6 or 7 of this Act, then, if there is a child of the family who is under the age of eighteen, the court shall not dismiss or make a final order on the application until it has decided whether to exercise any of its powers under the Children Act 1989 with respect to the child."

37. In section 19(3A)(*b*) (interim orders) for the words "subsections (2) and" there shall be substituted "subsection".

38. For section 20(12) of that Act (variation and revocation of orders for periodical payments) there shall be substituted—

"(12) An application under this section may be made—

(*a*) where it is for the variation or revocation of an order under section 2, 6, 7 or 19 of this Act for periodical payments, by either party to the marriage in question; and
(*b*) where it is for the variation of an order under section 2(1)(*c*), 6, or 7 of this Act for periodical payments to or in respect of a child, also by the child himself, if he has attained the age of sixteen."

39.—(1) For section 20A of that Act (revival of orders for periodical payments) there shall be substituted—

"**20A Revivial of orders for periodical payments**

(1) Where an order made by a magistrates' court under this Part of this Act for the making of periodical payments to or in respect of a child (other than an interim maintenance order) ceases to have effect—

(*a*) on the date on which the child attains the age of sixteen, or

(*b*) at any time after that date but before or on the date on which he attains the age of eighteen,

the child may apply to the court which made the order for an order for its revival.

(2) If on such an application it appears to the court that—

(*a*) the child is, will be or (if an order were made under this subsection) would be receiving instruction at an educational establishment or undergoing training for a trade, profession or vocation, whether or not while in gainful employment, or

(*b*) there are special circumstances which justify the making of an order under this subsection,

the court shall have power by order to revive the order from such date as the court may specify, not being earlier than the date of the making of the application.

(3) Any order revived under this section may be varied or revoked under section 20 in the same way as it could have been varied or revoked had it continued in being."

40. In section 23(1) of that Act (supplementary provisions with respect to the variation and revocation of orders) for the words "14(3), 20 or 21" there shall be substituted "20" and for the words "section 20 of this Act" there shall be substituted "that section".

41.—(1) in section 25 of that Act (effect on certain orders of parties living together), in subsection (1)(*a*) for the words "6 or 11(2)" there shall be substituted "or 6".

(2) In subsection (2) of that section—

(*a*) in paragraph (*a*) for the words "6 or 11(2)" there shall be substituted "or 6"; and

(*b*) after paragraph (*a*) there shall be inserted "or".

42. In section 29(5) of that Act (appeals) for the words "sections 14(3), 20 and 21" there shall be substituted "section 20".

43. In section 88(1) of that Act (interpretation)—

(*a*) in the definition of "child", for the words from "an illegitimate" to the end there shall be substituted "a child whose father and mother were not married to each other at the time of his birth"; and

(*b*) in the definition of "child of the family", for the words "being boarded-out with those parties" there shall be substituted "placed with those parties as foster parents".

*The Magistrates' Courts Act 1980 (c 43)*

44.—(1) In section 59(2) of the Magistrates' Courts Act 1980 (periodical payments through justices' clerk) for the words "the Guardianship of Minors Acts 1971 and 1973" there shall be substituted "(or having effect as if made under) Schedule 1 to the Children Act 1989".

(2) For section 62(5) of that Act (payments to children) there shall be substituted—

"(5) In this section references to the person with whom a child has his home—

(*a*) in the case of any child who is being looked after by a local authority (within the meaning of section 22 of the Children Act 1989), are references to that local authority; and

(*b*) in any other case, are references to the person who, disregarding any absence of the child at a hospital or boarding school and any other temporary absence, has care of the child.".

*The Supreme Court Act 1981 (c 54)*

45.—(1) In section 18 of the Supreme Court Act 1981 (restrictions on appeals to Court of Appeal)—

(*a*) in subsection (1)(*h*)(i), for the word "custody" there shall be substituted "residence"; and

(*b*) in subsection (1)(*h*)(ii) for the words "access to", in both places, there shall be substituted "contact with".

(2) In section 41 of that Act (wards of court), the following subsection shall be inserted after subsection (2)—

"(2A) subsection (2) does not apply with respect to a child who is the subject of a care order (as defined by section 105 of the Children Act 1989)."

(3) In Schedule 1 to that Act (distribution of business in High Court), for paragraph 3(*b*)(ii) there shall be substituted—

"(ii) the exercise of the inherent jurisdiction of the High Court with respect to minors, the maintenance of minors and any proceedings under the Children Act 1989, except proceedings solely for the appointment of a guardian of a minor's estate;".

*The Armed Forces Act 1981 (c 55)*

46. In section 14 of the Armed Forces Act 1981 (temporary removal to, and detention in, place of safety abroad or in the United Kingdom of service children in need of care and control), in subsection (9A) for the words "the Children and Young Persons Act 1933, the Children and Young Persons Act 1969" there shall be substituted "the Children Act 1989".

*The Civil Jurisdiction and Judgments Act 1982 (c 27)*

47. In paragraph 5(*a*) of Schedule 5 to the Civil Jurisdiction and Judgments Act 1982 (maintenance and similar payments excluded from Schedule 4 to that Act) for the words "section 47 or 51 of the Child Care Act 1980" there shall be substituted "paragraph 23 of Schedule 2 to the Children Act 1989".

*The Mental Health Act 1983 (c 20)*

48.—(1) For section 27 of the Mental Health Act 1983 (children and young persons in care of local authority) there shall be substituted the following section—

**"27 Children and young persons in care**

Where—

(*a*) a patient who is a child or young person is in the care of a local authority by virtue of a care order within the meaning of the Children Act 1989; or

(*b*) the rights and powers of a parent of a patient who is a child or young person are vested in a local authority by virtue of section 16 of the Social Work (Scotland) Act 1968,

the authority shall be deemed to be the nearest relative of the patient in preference to any person except the patient's husband or wife (if any)."

(2) Section 28 of that Act (nearest relative of minor under guardianship, etc) is amended as mentioned in sub-paragraphs (3) and (4).

(3) For subsection (1) there shall be substituted—

"(1) Where—

(*a*) a guardian has been appointed for a person who has not attained the age of eighteen years; or

(*b*) a residence order (as defined by section 8 of the Children Act 1989) is in force with respect to such a person,

the guardian (or guardians, where there is more than one) or the person named in the residence order shall, to the exclusion of any other person, be deemed to be his nearest relative."

(4) For subsection (3) there shall be substituted—

"(3) In this section "guardian" does not include a guardian under this Part of this Act."

(5) In section 131(2) of that Act (informal admission of patients aged sixteen or over) for the words from "notwithstanding" to the end there shall be substituted "even though there are one or more persons who have parental responsibility for him (within the meaning of the Children Act 1989)".

*The Registered Homes Act 1984 (c 23)*

49.—(1) In section 1(5) of the Registered Homes Act 1984 (requirement of registration) for paragraphs (*d*) and (*e*) there shall be substituted—

"(*d*) any community home, voluntary home or children's home within the meaning of the Children Act 1989."

(2) In section 39 of that Act (preliminary) for paragraphs (*a*) and (*b*) there shall be substituted—

"(*a*) the Children Act 1989."

*The Mental Health (Scotland) Act 1984 (c 36)*

50. For section 54 of the Mental Health (Scotland) Act 1984 (children and young persons in care of local authority) there shall be substituted the following section—

**"54 Children and young persons in care of local authority**

Where—

(*a*) the rights and powers of a parent of a patient who is a child or young person are vested in a local authority by virtue of section 16 of the Social Work (Scotland) Act 1968; or

(*b*) a patient who is a child or young person is in the care of a local authority by virtue of a care order made under the Children Act 1989,

the authority shall be deemed to be the nearest relative of the patient in preference to any person except the patient's husband or wife (if any)."

*The Matrimonial and Family Proceedings Act 1984 (c 42)*

51. In section 38(2)(*b*) of the Matrimonial and Family Proceedings Act 1984 (transfer of family proceedings from High Court to county court) after the words "a ward of court" there shall be inserted "or any other proceedings which relate to the exercise of the inherent jurisdiction of the High Court with respect to minors".

*The Police and Ciminal Evidence Act 1984 (c 60)*

52. In section 37(14) of the Police and Criminal Evidence Act 1984 (duties of custody officer before charge) after the words "Children and Young Persons Act 1969" there shall be inserted "or in Part IV of the Children Act 1989".

53.—(1) In section 38 of that Act (duties of custody officer after charge), in subsection (6) for the words from "make arrangements" to the end there shall be substituted "secure that the arrested juvenile is moved to local authority accommodation".

(2) After that subsection there shall be inserted—

"(6A) In this section 'local authority accommodation' means accommodation provided by or on behalf of a local authority (within the meaning of the Children Act 1989).

(6B) Where an arrested juvenile is moved to local authority accommodation under subsection (6) above, it shall be lawful for any person acting on behalf of the authority to detain him.".

(3) In subsection (8) of that section for the words "Children and Young Persons Act 1969" there shall be substituted "Children Act 1989".

54. In section 39(4) of that Act (responsibilities in relation to persons detained) for the words "transferred to the care of a local authority in pursuance of arrangements made" there shall be substituted "moved to local authority accommodation".

55. In Schedule 2 to that Act (preserved powers of arrest) in the entry relating to the Children and Young Persons Act 1969 for the words "Sections 28(2) and" there shall be substituted "Section".

*The Surrogacy Arrangements Act 1985 (c 49)*

56. In section 1(2)(*b*) of the Surrogacy Arrangements Act 1985 (meaning of "surrogate mother", etc) for the words "the parental rights being exercised" there shall be substituted "parental responsibility being met".

*The Child Abduction and Custody Act 1985 (c 60)*

57.—(1) In sections 9(*a*) and 20(2)(*a*) of the Child Abduction and Custody Act 1985 (orders with respect to which court's powers suspended), for the words "any other order under section 1(2) of the Children and Young Persons Act 1969" there shall be substituted "a supervision order under section 31 of the Children Act 1989".

(2) At the end of section 27 of that Act (interpretation), there shall be added—

"(4) In this Act a decision relating to rights of access in England and Wales means a decision as to the contact which a child may, or may not, have with any person."

(3) In Part I of Schedule 3 to that Act (orders in England and Wales which are custody orders for the purposes of the Act), for paragraph 1 there shall be substituted—

"1. The following are the orders referred to in section 27(1) of this Act—

(*a*) a care order under the Children Act 1989 (as defined by section 31(11) of that Act, read with section 105(1) and Schedule 14);

(*b*) a residence order (as defined by section 8 of the Act of 1989); and

(*c*) any order made by a court in England and Wales under any of the following enactments—

(i) section 9(1), 10(1)(*a*) or 11(*a*) of the Guardianship of Minors Act 1971;

(ii) section 42(1) or (2) or 43(1) of the Matrimonial Causes Act 1973;

(iii) section 2(2)(*b*), (4)(*b*) or (5) of the Guardianship Act 1973 as applied by section 34(5) of the Children Act 1975;

(iv) section 8(2)(*a*), 10(1) or 19(1)(ii) of the Domestic Proceedings and Magistrates Courts Act 1978;

(v) section 26(1)(*b*) of the Adoption Act 1976."

*The Disabled Persons (Services, Consultation and Representation) Act 1986 (c 33)*

58. In section 1(3) of the Disabled Persons (Services, Consultation and Representation) Act 1986 (circumstances in which regulations may provide for the appointment of authorised representatives of disabled persons)—

(*a*) in paragraph (*a*), for the words "parent or guardian of a disabled person under the age of sixteen" there shall be substituted—

"(i) the parent of a disabled person under the age of sixteen, or
(ii) any other person who is not a parent of his but who has parental responsibility for him"; and

(*b*) in paragraph (*b*), for the words "in the care of" there shall be substituted "looked after by".

59.—(1) Section 2 of that Act (circumstances in which authorised representative has right to visit etc disabled person) shall be amended as follows.

(2) In subsection 3(*a*) for the words from second "the" to "by" there shall be substituted "for the words 'if so requested by the disabled person' there shall be substituted 'if so requested by any person mentioned in section 1(3)(*a*)(i) or (ii)'."

(3) In subsection (5) after paragraph (*b*) there shall be inserted—

"(*bb*) in accommodation provided by or on behalf of a local authority under Part III of the Children Act 1989, or".

(4) After paragraph (*c*) of subsection (5) there shall be inserted—

"(*cc*) in accommodation provided by a voluntary organisation in accordance with arrangements made by a local authority under section 17 of the Children Act 1989, or".

60. In section 5(7)(*b*) of that Act (disabled persons leaving special education) for the word "guardian" there shall be substituted "other person who is not a parent of his but who has parental responsibility for him".

61.—(1) In section 16 of that Act (interpretation) in the definition of "disabled person", in paragraph (*a*) for the words from "means" to "applies" there shall be substituted "means—

"(i) in the case of a person aged eighteen or over, a person to whom section 29 of the 1948 Act applies, and
(ii) in the case of a person under the age of eighteen, a person who is disabled within the meaning of Part III of the Children Act 1989".

(2) After the definition of "parent" in that section there shall be inserted—

"'parental responsibility' has the same meaning as in the Children Act 1989."

(3) In the definition of "the welfare enactments" in that section, in paragraph (*a*) after the words "the 1977 Act" there shall be inserted "and Part III of the Children Act 1989".

(4) At the end of that section there shall be added—

"(2) In this Act any reference to a child who is looked after by a local authority has the same meaning as in the Children Act 1989."

*The Family Law Act 1986 (c 55)*

62.—(1) The Family Law Act 1986 shall be amended as follows.

(2) Subject to paragraphs 63 to 71, in Part I—

(*a*) for the words "custody order", in each place where they occur, there shall be substituted "Part I order";

(*b*) for the words "proceedings with respect to the custody of", in each place where they occur, there shall be substituted "Part I proceedings with respect to"; and

(*c*) for the words "matters relating to the custody of", in each place where they occur, there shall be substituted "Part I matters relating to".

(3) For section 42(7) (general interpretation of Part I) there shall be substituted—

"(7) In this Part—

(*a*) references to Part I proceedings in respect of a child are references to any proceedings for a Part I order or an order corresponding to a Part I order and include, in relation to proceedings outside the United Kingdom, references to proceedings before a tribunal or other authority having power under the law having effect there to determine Part I matters; and

(*b*) references to Part I matters are references to matters that might be determined by a Part I order or an order corresponding to a Part I order."

63.—(1) In section 1 (orders to which Part I of the Act of 1986 applies), in subsection (1)—

(*a*) for paragraph (*a*) there shall be substituted—

"(*a*) a section 8 order made by a court in England and Wales under the Children Act 1989, other than an order varying or discharging such an order"; and

(*b*) for paragraph (*d*) there shall be substituted the following paragraphs—

"(*d*) an order made by a court in England and Wales in the exercise of the inherent jurisdiction of the High Court with respect to children—

(i) so far as it gives care of a child to any person or provides for contact with, or the education of, a child; but

(ii) excluding an order varying or revoking such an order;

(*e*) an order made by the High Court in Northern Ireland in the exercise of its jurisdiction relating to wardship—

(i) so far as it gives care and control of a child to any person or provides for the education of or access to a child; but

(ii) excluding an order relating to a child of whom care or care and control is (immediately after the making of the order) vested in the Department of Health and Social Services or a Health and Social Services Board."

(2) In subsection (2) of that section, in paragraph (*c*) for "(*d*)" there shall be substituted "(*e*)".

(3) For subsections (3) to (5) of that section there shall be substituted—

"(3) In this Part, "Part I order"—

(*a*) includes any order which would have been a custody order by virtue of this section in any form in which it was in force at any time before its amendment by the Children Act 1989; and

(*b*) (subject to sections 32 and 40 of this Act) excludes any order which would have been excluded from being a custody order by virtue of this section in any such form."

64. For section 2 there shall be substituted the following sections—

**"2 Jurisdiction: general**

(1) A court in England and Wales shall not have jurisdiction to make a section 1(1)(*a*) order with respect to a child in or in connection with matrimonial

proceedings in England and Wales unless the condition in section 2A of this Act is satisfied.

(2) A court in England and Wales shall not have jurisdiction to make a section 1(1)(*a*) order in a non-matrimonial case (that is to say, where the condition in section 2A of this Act is not satisfied) unless the condition in section 3 of this Act is satisfied.

(3) A court in England and Wales shall not have jurisdiction to make a section 1(1)(*d*) order unless—

(*a*) the condition in section 3 of this Act is satisfied, or

(*b*) the child concerned is present in England and Wales on the relevant date and the court considers that the immediate exercise of its powers is necessary for his protection.

**2A Jurisdiction in or in connection with matrimonial proceedings**

(1) The condition referred to in section 2(1) of this Act is that the matrimonial proceedings are proceedings in respect of the marriage of the parents of the child concerned and—

(*a*) the proceedings—

(i) are proceedings for divorce or nullity of marriage, and

(ii) are continuing;

(*b*) the proceedings—

(i) are proceedings for judicial separation,

(ii) are continuing,

and the jurisdiction of the court is not excluded by subsection (2) below; or

(*c*) the proceedings have been dismissed after the beginning of the trial but—

(i) the section 1(1)(*a*) order is being made forthwith, or

(ii) the application for the order was made on or before the dismissal.

(2) For the purposes of subsection (1)(*b*) above, the jurisdiction of the court is excluded if, after the grant of a decree of judicial separation, on the relevant date, proceedings for divorce or nullity in respect of the marriage are continuing in Scotland or Northern Ireland.

(3) Subsection (2) above shall not apply if the court in which the other proceedings there referred to are continuing has made—

(*a*) an order under section 13(6) or 21(5) of this Act (not being an order made by virtue of section 13(6)(*a*)(i)), or

(*b*) an order under section 14(2) or 22(2) of this Act which is recorded as being made for the purpose of enabling Part I proceedings to be taken in England and Wales with respect to the child concerned.

(4) Where a court—

(*a*) has jurisdiction to make a section 1(1)(*a*) order in or in connection with matrimonial proceedings, but

(*b*) considers that it would be more appropriate for Part I matters relating to the child to be determined outside England and Wales,

the court may by order direct that, while the order under this subsection is in force, no section 1(1)(*a*) order shall be made by any court in or in connection with those proceedings."

65.—(1) In section 3 (habitual residence or presence of child concerned) in subsection (1) for "section 2" there shall be substituted "section 2(2)".

(2) In subsection (2) of that section for the words "proceedings for divorce, nullity or judicial separation" there shall be substituted "matrimonial proceedings".

66.—(1) In section 6 (duration and variation of Part I orders), for subsection (3) there shall be substituted the following subsections—

"(3) A court in England and Wales shall not have jurisdiction to vary a Part I order if, on the relevant date, matrimonial proceedings are continuing in Scotland or Northern Ireland in respect of the marriage of the parents of the child concerned.

(3A) Subsection (3) above shall not apply if—

(*a*) the Part I order was made in or in connection with proceedings for divorce or nullity in England and Wales in respect of the marriage of the parents of the child concerned; and
(*b*) those proceedings are continuing.

(3B) Subsection (3) above shall not apply if—

(*a*) the Part I order was made in or in connection with proceedings for judicial separation in England and Wales;
(*b*) those proceedings are continuing; and
(*c*) the decree of judicial separation has not yet been granted."

(2) In subsection (5) of that section for the words from "variation of" to "if the ward" there shall be substituted "variation of a section 1(1)(*d*) order if the child concerned".

(3) For subsections (6) and (7) of that section there shall be substituted the following subsections—

"(6) Subsection (7) below applies where a Part I order which is—

(*a*) a residence order (within the meaning of the Children Act 1989) in favour of a person with respect to a child,
(*b*) an order made in the exercise of the High Court's inherent jurisdiction with respect to children by virtue of which a person has care of a child, or
(*c*) an order—

(i) of a kind mentioned in section 1(3)(*a*) of this Act,
(ii) under which a person is entitled to the actual possession of a child,

ceases to have effect in relation to that person by virtue of subsection (1) above.

(7) Where this subsection applies, any family assistance order made under section 16 of the Children Act 1989 with respect to the child shall also cease to have effect.

(8) For the purposes of subsection (7) above the reference to a family assistance order under section 16 of the Children Act 1989 shall be deemed to include a reference to an order for the supervision of a child made under—

(*a*) section 7(4) of the Family Law Reform Act 1969,
(*b*) section 44 of the Matrimonial Causes Act 1973,
(*c*) section 2(2)(*a*) of the Guardianship Act 1973,
(*d*) section 34(5) or 36(3)(*b*) of the Children Act 1975, or
(*e*) section 9 of the Domestic Proceedings and Magistrates' Courts Act 1978;

but this subsection shall cease to have effect once all such orders for the supervision of children have ceased to have effect in accordance with Schedule 14 to the Children Act 1989."

67. For section 7 (interpretation of Chapter II) there shall be substituted—

**"7 Interpretation of Chapter II**

In this Chapter—

(*a*) "child" means a person who has not attained the age of eighteen;

(*b*) "matrimonial proceedings" means proceedings for divorce, nullity of marriage or judicial separation;

(*c*) "the relevant date" means in relation to the making or variation of an order—

(i) where an application is made for an order to be made or varied, the date of the application (or first application, if two or more are determined together), and

(ii) where no such application is made, the date on which the court is considering whether to make or, as the case may be, vary the order; and

(*d*) "section 1(1)(*a*) order" and "section 1(1)(*d*) order" mean orders falling within section 1(1)(*a*) and (*d*) of this Act respectively."

68. In each of the following sections—

(*a*) section 11(2)(*a*) (provisions supplementary to sections 9 and 10),
(*b*) section 13(5)(*a*) (jurisdiction ancillary to matrimonial proceedings),
(*c*) section 20(3)(*a*) (habitual residence or presence of child),
(*d*) section 21(4)(*a*) (jurisdiction in divorce proceedings, etc), and
(*e*) section 23(4)(*a*) (duration and variation of custody orders),

for "4(5)" there shall be substituted "2A(4)".

69. In each of the following sections—

(*a*) section 19(2) (jurisdiction in cases other than divorce, etc),
(*b*) section 20(6) (habitual residence or presence of child), and
(*c*) section 23(5) (duration and variation of custody orders),

for "section 1(1)(*d*)" there shall be substituted "section 1(1)(*e*)".

70. In section 34(3) (power to order recovery of child) for paragraph (*a*) there shall be substituted—

"(*a*) section 14 of the Children Act 1989".

71.—(1) In section 42 (general interpretation of Part I), in subsection (4)(*a*) for the words "has been boarded out with those parties" there shall be substituted "is placed with those parties as foster parents".

(2) In subsection (6) of that section, in paragraph (*a*) after the word "person" there shall be inserted "to be allowed contact with or".

*The Local Government Act 1988 (c 9)*

72. In Schedule 1 to the Local Government Act 1988 (competition) at the end of paragraph 2(4) (cleaning of buildings: buildings to which competition provisions do not apply) for paragraph (*c*) there shall be substituted—

"(*c*) section 53 of the Children Act 1989."

*Amendments of local Acts*

73.—(1) Section 16 of the Greater London Council (General Powers) Act 1981 (exemption from provisions of Part IV of the Act of certain premises) shall be amended as follows.

(2) After paragraph (*g*) there shall be inserted—

"(*gg*) used as a children's home as defined in section 63 of the Children Act 1989".

(3) In paragraph (*h*)—

(*a*) for the words "section 56 of the Child Care Act 1980" there shall be substituted "section 60 of the Children Act 1989";
(*b*) for the words "section 57" there shall be substituted "section 60"; and
(*c*) for the words "section 32" there shall be substituted "section 53".

(4) In paragraph (*i*), for the words "section 8 of the Foster Children Act 1980" there shall be substituted "section 67 of the Children Act 1989".

74.—(1) Section 10(2) of the Greater London Council (General Powers) Act 1984 (exemption from provisions of Part IV of the Act of certain premises) shall be amended as follows.

(2) In paragraph (*d*)—

(*a*) for the words "section 56 of the Child Care Act 1980" there shall be substituted "section 60 of the Children Act 1989";
(*b*) for the words "section 57" there shall be substituted "section 60"; and
(*c*) for the words "section 31" there shall be substituted "section 53".

(3) In paragraph (*e*), for the words "section 8 of the Foster Children Act 1980" there shall be substituted "section 67 of the Children Act 1989".

(4) In paragraph (*l*) for the words "section 1 of the Children's Homes Act 1982" there shall be substituted "section 63 of the Children Act 1989".

## SCHEDULE 14

Section 108(6)

### Transitionals and Savings

#### *Pending Proceedings, etc*

1.—(1) Subject to sub-paragraph (4), nothing in any provision of this Act (other than the repeals mentioned in sub-paragraph (2)) shall affect any proceedings which are pending immediately before the commencement of that provision.

(2) The repeals are those of—

(*a*) section 42(3) of the Matrimonial Causes Act 1973 (declaration by court that party to marriage unfit to have custody of children of family); and
(*b*) section 38 of the Sexual Offences Act 1956 (power of court to divest person of authority over girl or boy in cases of incest).

(3) For the purposes of the following provisions of this Schedule, any reference to an order in force immediately before the commencement of a provision of this Act shall be construed as including a reference to an order made after that commencement in proceedings pending before that commencement.

(4) Sub-paragraph (3) is not to be read as making the order in question have effect from a date earlier than that on which it was made.

(5) An order under section 96(3) may make such provision with respect to the application of the order in relation to proceedings which are pending when the order comes into force as the Lord Chancellor considers appropriate.

2. Where, immediately before the date on which Part IV comes into force, there was in force an order under section 3(1) of the Children and Young Persons Act 1963 (order directing a local authority to bring a child or young person before a juvenile court under section 1 of the Children and Young Persons Act 1969), the order shall cease to have effect on that day.

CUSTODY ORDERS, ETC

*Cessation of declarations of unfitness, etc*

3. Where, immediately before the day on which Parts I and II come into force, there was in force—

(*a*) a declaration under section 42(3) of the Matrimonial Causes Act 1973 (declaration by court that party to marriage unfit to have custody of children of family); or
(*b*) an order under section 38(1) of the Sexual Offences Act 1956 divesting a person of authority over a girl or boy in a case of incest;

the declaration or, as the case may be, the order shall cease to have effect on that day.

*The Family Law Reform Act 1987 (c 42)*

*Conversion of orders under section 4*

4. Where, immediately before the day on which Parts I and II come into force, there was in force an order under section 4(1) of the Family Law Reform Act 1987 (order giving father parental rights and duties in relation to a child), then, on and after that day, the order shall be deemed to be an order under section 4 of this Act giving the father parental responsibility for the child.

*Orders to which paragraphs 6 to 11 apply*

5.—(1) In paragraphs 6 to 11 "an existing order" means any order which—

(*a*) as in force immediately before the commencement of Parts I and II;
(*b*) was made under any enactment mentioned in sub-paragraph (2);
(*c*) determines all or any of the following—
(i) who is to have custody of a child;
(ii) who is to have care and control of a child;
(iii) who is to have access to a child;
(iv) any matter with respect to a child's education or upbringing;
and
(*d*) is not an order of a kind mentioned in paragraph 15(1).

(2) The enactments are—

(*a*) the Domestic Proceedings and Magistrates' Courts Act 1978;
(*b*) the Children Act 1975;
(*c*) the Matrimonial Causes Act 1973;
(*d*) the Guardianship of Minors Acts 1971 and 1973;
(*e*) the Matrimonial Causes Act 1965;
(*f*) the Matrimonial Proceedings (Magistrates' Courts) Act 1960.

(3) For the purposes of this paragraph and paragraphs 6 to 11 "custody" includes legal custody and joint as well as sole custody but does not include access.

*Parental responsibility of parents*

6.—(1) Where—

(*a*) a child's father and mother were married to each other at the time of his birth; and
(*b*) there is an existing order with respect to the child,

each parent shall have parental responsibility for the child in accordance with section 2 as modified by sub-paragraph (3).

(2) Where—

(*a*) a child's father and mother were not married to each other at the time of his birth; and
(*b*) there is an existing order with respect to the child,

section 2 shall apply as modified by sub-paragraphs (3) and (4).

(3) The modification is that for section 2(8) there shall be substituted—

"(8) The fact that a person has parental responsibility for a child does not entitle him to act in a way which would be incompatible with any existing order or any order made under this Act with respect to the child".

(4) The modifications are that—

(*a*) for the purposes of section 2(2), where the father has custody or care and control of the child by virtue of any existing order, the court shall be deemed to have made (at the commencement of that section) an order under section 4(1) giving him parental responsibility for the child; and
(*b*) where by virtue of paragraph (*a*) a court is deemed to have made an order under section 4(1) in favour of a father who has care and control of a child by virtue of an existing order, the court shall not bring the order under section 4(1) to an end at any time while he has care and control of the child by virtue of the order.

*Persons who are not parents but who have custody or care and control*

7.—(1) Where a person who is not the parent or guardian of a child has custody or care and control of him by virtue of an existing order, that person shall have parental responsibility for him so long as he continues to have that custody or care and control by virtue of the order.

(2) Where sub-paragraph (1) applies, Parts I and II shall have effect as modified by this paragraph.

(3) The modifications are that—

(*a*) for section 2(8) there shall be substituted—

"(8) The fact that a person has parental responsibility for a child does not entitle him to act in a way which would be incompatible with any existing order or with any order made under this Act with respect to the child";

(*b*) at the end of section 10(4) there shall be inserted—

"(*c*) any person who has custody or care and control of a child by virtue of any existing order"; and

(*c*) at the end of section 34(1)(*c*) there shall be inserted—

"(*cc*) where immediately before the care order was made there was an existing order by virtue of which a person had custody or care and control of the child, that person."

*Persons who have care and control*

8.—(1) Sub-paragraphs (2) to (6) apply where a person has care and control of a child by virtue of an existing order, but they shall cease to apply when that order ceases to have effect.

(2) Section 5 shall have effect as if—

(*a*) for any reference to a residence order in favour of a parent or guardian there were substituted a reference to any existing order by virtue of which the parent or guardian has care and control of the child; and
(*b*) for subsection (9) there were substituted—

"(9) Subsections (1) and (7) do not apply if the existing order referred to in paragraph (*b*) of those subsections was one by virtue of which a surviving parent of the child also had care and control of him."

(3) Section 10 shall have effect as if for subsection (5)(*c*)(i) there were substituted—

"(i) in any case where by virtue of an existing order any person or persons has or have care and control of the child, has the consent of that person or each of those persons".

(4) Section 20 shall have effect as if for subsection (9)(*a*) there were substituted "who has care and control of the child by virtue of an existing order."

(5) Section 23 shall have effect as if for subsection (4)(*c*) there were substituted—

"(*c*) where the child is in care and immediately before the care order was made there was an existing order by virtue of which a person had care and control of the child, that person."

(6) In Schedule 1, paragraphs 1(1) and 14(1) shall have effect as if for the words "in whose favour a residence order is in force with respect to the child" there were substituted "who has been given care and control of the child by virtue of an existing order".

*Persons who have access*

9.—(1) Sub-paragraphs (2) to (4) apply where a person has access by virtue of an existing order.

(2) Section 10 shall have effect as if after subsection (5) there were inserted—

"(5A) Any person who has access to a child by virtue of an existing order is entitled to apply for a contact order."

(3) Section 16(2) shall have effect as if after paragraph (*b*) there were inserted—

"(*bb*) any person who has access to the child by virtue of an existing order."

(4) Sections 43(11), 44(13) and 46(10), shall have effect as if in each case after paragraph (*d*) there were inserted—

"(*dd*) any person who has been given access to him by virtue of an existing order."

*Enforcement of certain existing orders*

10.—(1) Sub-paragraph (2) applies in relation to any existing order which, but for the repeal by this Act of—

(*a*) section 13(1) of the Guardianship of Minors Act 1971;
(*b*) section 43(1) of the Children Act 1975; or
(*c*) section 33 of the Domestic Proceedings and Magistrates' Courts Act 1978,

(provisions concerning the enforcement of custody orders) might have been enforced as if it were an order requiring a person to give up a child to another person.

(2) Where this sub-paragraph applies, the existing order may, after the repeal of the enactments mentioned in sub-paragraph (1)(*a*) to (*c*), be enforced under section 14 as if—

(*a*) any reference to a residence order were a reference to the existing order; and
(*b*) any reference to a person in whose favour the residence order is in force were a reference to a person to whom actual custody of the child is given by an existing order which is in force.

(3) In sub-paragraph (2) "actual custody", in relation to a child, means the actual possession of his person.

*Discharge of existing orders*

11.—(1) The making of a residence order or a care order with respect to a child who is the subject of an existing order discharges the existing order.

(2) Where the court makes any section 8 order (other than a residence order) with respect to a child with respect to whom any existing order is in force, the existing order shall have effect subject to the section 8 order.

(3) The court may discharge an existing order which is in force with respect to a child—

(*a*) in any family proceedings relating to the child or in which any question arises with respect to the child's welfare; or
(*b*) on the application of—

(i) any parent or guardian of the child;
(ii) the child himself; or
(iii) any person named in the order.

(4) A child may not apply for the discharge of an existing order except with the leave of the court.

(5) The power in sub-paragraph (3) to discharge an existing order includes the power to discharge any part of the order.

(6) In considering whether to discharge an order under the power conferred by sub-paragraph (3) the court shall, if the discharge of the order is opposed by any party to the proceedings, have regard in particular to the matters mentioned in section 1(3).

## GUARDIANS

*Existing guardians to be guardians under this Act*

12.—(1) Any appointment of a person as guardian of a child which—

(*a*) was made—

(i) under sections 3 to 5 of the Guardianship of Minors Act 1971;
(ii) under section 38(3) of the Sexual Offences Act 1956; or
(iii) under the High Court's inherent jurisdiction with respect to children; and

(*b*) has taken effect before the commencement of section 5,

shall (subject to sub-paragraph (2)) be deemed, on and after the commencement of section 5, to be an appointment made and having effect under that section.

(2) Where an appointment of a person as guardian of a child has effect under section 5 by virtue of sub-paragraph (1)(*a*)(ii), the appointment shall not have effect for a period which is longer than any period specified in the order.

*Appointment of guardian not yet in effect*

13. Any appointment of a person to be a guardian of a child—

(*a*) which was made as mentioned in paragraph 12(1)(*a*)(i); but
(*b*) which, immediately before the commencement of section 5, had not taken effect,

shall take effect in accordance with section 5 (as modified, where it applies, by paragraph 8(2)).

*Persons deemed to be appointed as guardians under existing wills*

14. For the purposes of the Wills Act 1837 and of this Act any disposition by will and testament or devise of the custody and tuition of any child, made before the commencement of section 5 and paragraph 1 of Schedule 13, shall be deemed to be an appointment by will of a guardian of the child.

## Children in care

*Children in compulsory care*

15.—(1) Sub-paragraph (2) applies where, immediately before the day on which Part IV comes into force, a person was—

(*a*) in care by virtue of—

(i) a care order under section 1 of the Children and Young Persons Act 1969;

(ii) a care order under section 15 of that Act, on discharging a supervision order made under section 1 of that Act; or

(iii) an order or authorisation under section 25 or 26 of that Act;

(*b*) deemed, by virtue of—

(i) paragraph 7(3) of Schedule 5A to the Army Act 1955;

(ii) paragraph 7(3) of Schedule 5A to the Air Force Act 1955; or

(iii) paragraph 7(3) of Schedule 4A to the Naval Discipline Act 1957,

to be the subject of a care order under the Children and Young Persons Act 1969;

(*c*) in care—

(i) under section 2 of the Child Care Act 1980; or

(ii) by virtue of paragraph 1 of Schedule 4 to that Act (which extends the meaning of a child in care under section 2 to include children in care under section 1 of the Children Act 1948),

and a child in respect of whom a resolution under section 3 of the Act of 1980 or section 2 of the Act of 1948 was in force;

(*d*) a child in respect of whom a resolution had been passed under section 65 of the Child Care Act 1980;

(*e*) in care by virtue of an order under—

(i) section 2(1)(*e*) of the Matrimonial Proceedings (Magistrates' Courts) Act 1960;

(ii) section 7(2) of the Family Law Reform Act 1969;

(iii) section 43(1) of the Matrimonial Causes Act 1973; or

(iv) section 2(2)(*b*) of the Guardianship Act 1973;

(v) section 10 of the Domestic Proceedings and Magistrates' Courts Act 1978,

(orders having effect for certain purposes as if the child had been received into care under section 2 of the Child Care Act 1980);

(*f*) in care by virtue of an order made, on the revocation of a custodianship order, under section 36 of the Children Act 1975;

(*g*) in care by virtue of an order made, on the refusal of an adoption order, under section 26 of the Adoption Act 1976 or any order having effect (by virtue of paragraph 1 of Schedule 2 to that Act) as if made under that section.

(2) Where this sub-paragraph applies, then, on and after the day on which Part IV commences—

(*a*) the order or resolution in question shall be deemed to be a care order;

(*b*) the authority in whose care the person was immediately before that commencement shall be deemed to be the authority designated in that deemed care order; and

(*c*) any reference to a child in the care of a local authority shall include a reference to a person who is the subject of such a deemed care order,

and the provisions of this Act shall apply accordingly, subject to paragraph 16.

*Modifications*

16.—(1) Sub-paragraph (2) only applies where a person who is the subject of a care order by virtue of paragraph 15(2) is a person falling within sub-paragraph (1)(*a*) or (*b*) of that paragraph.

(2) Where the person would otherwise have remained in care until reaching the age of nineteen, by virtue of—

(*a*) section 20(3)(*a*) or 21(1) of the Children and Young Persons Act 1969; or

(*b*) paragraph 7(5)(*c*)(i) of—

(i) Schedule 5A to the Army Act 1955;

(ii) Schedule 5A to the Air Force Act 1955; or

(iii) Schedule 4A to he Naval Discipline Act 1957,

this Act applies as if in section 91(12) for the word "eighteen" there were substituted "nineteen".

(3) Where a person who is the subject of a care order by virtue of paragraph 15(2) is a person falling within sub-paragraph (1)(*b*) of that paragraph, this Act applies as if section 101 were omitted.

(4) Sub-paragraph (5) only applies where a child who is the subject of a care order by virtue of paragraph 15(2) is a person falling within sub-paragraph (1)(*e*) to (*g*) of that paragraph.

(5) Where a court, on making the order, or at any time thereafter, gave directions under—

(*a*) section 4(4)(*a*) of the Guardianship Act 1973; or

(*b*) section 43(5)(*a*) of the Matrimonial Causes Act 1973,

as to the exercise by the authority of any powers, those directions shall continue to have effect (regardless of any conflicting provision in this Act) until varied or discharged by a court under this sub-paragraph.

*Children placed with parent etc while in compulsory care*

17.—(1) This paragraph applies where a child is deemed by paragraph 15 to be in the care of a local authority under an order or resolution which is deemed by that paragraph to be a care order.

(2) If, immediately before the day on which Part III comes into force, the child was allowed to be under the charge and control of—

(*a*) a parent or guardian under section 21(2) of the Child Care Act 1980; or

(*b*) a person who, before the child was in the authority's care, had care and control of the child by virtue of an order falling within paragraph 5,

on and after that day the provision made by and under section 23(5) shall apply as if the child had been placed with the person in question in accordance with that provision.

*Orders for access to children in compulsory care*

18.—(1) This paragraph applies to any access order—

(*a*) made under section 12C of the Child Care Act 1980 (access orders with respect to children in care of local authorities); and
(*b*) in force immediately before the commencement of Part IV.

(2) On and after the commencement of Part IV, the access order shall have effect as an order made under section 34 in favour of the person named in the order.

19.—(1) This paragraph applies where, immediately before the commencement of Part IV, an access order made under section 12C of the Act of 1980 was suspended by virtue of an order made under section 12E of that Act (suspension of access orders in emergencies).

(2) The suspending order shall continue to have effect as if this Act had not been passed.

(3) If—

(*a*) before the commencement of Part IV; and
(*b*) during the period for which the operation of the access order is suspended,

the local authority concerned made an application for its variation or discharge to an appropriate juvenile court, its operation shall be suspended until the date on which the application to vary or discharge it is determined or abandoned.

### *Children in voluntary care*

20.—(1) This paragraph applies where, immediately before the day on which Part III comes into force—

(*a*) a child was in the care of a local authority—

(i) under section 2(1) of the Child Care Act 1980; or
(ii) by virtue of paragraph 1 of Schedule 4 to that Act (which extends the meaning of references to children in care under section 2 to include references to children in care under section 1 of the Children Act 1948); and

(*b*) he was not a person in respect of whom a resolution under section 3 of the Act of 1980 or section 2 of the Act of 1948 was in force.

(2) Where this paragraph applies, the child shall, on and after the day mentioned in sub-paragraph (1), be treated for the purposes of this Act as a child who is provided with accommodation by the local authority under Part III, but he shall cease to be so treated once he ceases to be so accommodated in accordance with the provisions of Part III.

(3) Where—

(*a*) this paragraph applies; and
(*b*) the child, immediately before the day mentioned in sub-paragraph (1), was (by virtue of section 21(2) of the Act of 1980) under the charge and control of a person falling within paragraph 17(2)(*a*) or (*b*),

the child shall not be treated for the purposes of this Act as if he were being looked after by the authority concerned.

### *Boarded out children*

21.—(1) Where, immediately before the day on which Part III comes into force, a child in the care of a local authority—

(*a*) was—

(i) boarded out with a person under section 21(1)(*a*) of the Child Care Act 1980; or

(ii) placed under the charge and control of a person, under section 21(2) of that Act; and

(*b*) the person with whom he was boarded out, or (as the case may be) placed, was not a person falling within paragraph 17(2)(*a*) or (*b*),

on and after that day, he shall be treated (subject to sub-paragraph (2)) as having been placed with a local authority foster parent and shall cease to be so treated when he ceases to be placed with that person in accordance with the provisions of this Act.

(2) Regulations made under section 23(2)(*a*) shall not apply in relation to a person who is a local authority foster parent by virtue of sub-paragraph (1) before the end of the period of twelve months beginning with the day on which Part III comes into force and accordingly that person shall for that period be subject—

(*a*) in a case falling within sub-paragraph (1)(*a*)(i), to terms and regulations mentioned in section 21(1)(*a*) of the Act of 1980; and

(*b*) in a case falling within sub-paragraph (1)(*a*)(ii), to terms fixed under section 21(2) of that Act and regulations made under section 22A of that Act,

as if that Act had not been repealed by this Act.

*Children in care to qualify for advice and assistance*

22. Any reference in Part III to a person qualifying for advice and assistance shall be construed as including a reference to a person within the area of the local authority in question who is under twenty-one and who was, at any time after reaching the age of sixteen but while still a child—

(*a*) a person falling within—

(i) any of paragraphs (*a*) to (*g*) of paragraph 15(1); or

(ii) paragraph 20(1); or

(*b*) the subject of a criminal care order (within the meaning of paragraph 34).

*Emigration of children in care*

23. Where—

(*a*) the Secretary of State has received a request in writing from a local authority that he give his consent under section 24 of the Child Care Act 1980 to the emigration of a child in their care; but

(*b*) immediately before the repeal of the Act of 1980 by this Act, he has not determined whether or not to give his consent,

section 24 of the Act of 1980 shall continue to apply (regardless of that repeal) until the Secretary of State has determined whether or not to give his consent to the request.

*Contributions for maintenance of children in care*

24.—(1) Where, immediately before the day on which Part III of Schedule 2 comes into force, there was in force an order made (or having effect as if made) under any of the enactments mentioned in sub-paragraph (2), then, on and after that day—

(*a*) the order shall have effect as if made under paragraph 23(2) of Schedule 2 against a person liable to contribute; and

(*b*) Part III of Schedule 2 shall apply to the order, subject to the modifications in sub-
paragraph (3).

(2) The enactments are—

(*a*) section 11(4) of the Domestic Proceedings and Magistrates' Courts Act 1978;
(*b*) section 26(2) of the Adoption Act 1976;
(*c*) section 36(5) of the Children Act 1975;
(*d*) section 2(3) of the Guardianship Act 1973;
(*e*) section 2(1)(*h*) of the Matrimonial Proceedings (Magistrates' Courts) Act 1960,

(provisions empowering the court to make an order requiring a person to make periodical payments to a local authority in respect of a child in care).

(3) The modifications are that, in paragraph 23 of Schedule 2—

(*a*) in sub-paragraph (4), paragraph (*a*) shall be omitted;
(*b*) for sub-paragraph (6) there shall be substituted—

"(6) Where—

(*a*) a contribution order is in force;
(*b*) the authority serve a contribution notice under paragraph 22; and
(*c*) the contributor and the authority reach an agreement under paragraph 22(7) in respect of the contribution notice,

the effect of the agreement shall be to discharge the order from the date on which it is agreed that the agreement shall take effect"; and

(*c*) at the end of sub-paragraph (10) there shall be inserted—

"and

(*c*) where the order is against a person who is not a parent of the child, shall be made with due regard to—

(i) whether that person had assumed responsibility for the maintenance of the child, and, if so, the extent to which and basis on which he assumed that responsibility and the length of the period during which he met that responsibility;
(ii) whether he did so knowing that the child was not his child;
(iii) the liability of any other person to maintain the child."

## Supervision orders

### *Orders under section 1(3)(b) or 21(2) of the 1969 Act*

25.—(1) This paragraph applies to any supervision order—

(*a*) made—

(i) under section 1(3)(*b*) of the Children and Young Persons Act 1969; or
(ii) under section 21(2) of that Act on the discharge of a care order made under section 1(3)(*c*) of that Act; and

(*b*) in force immediately before the commencement of Part IV.

(2) On and after the commencement of Part IV, the order shall be deemed to be a supervision order made under section 31 and—

(*a*) any requirement of the order that the child reside with a named individual shall continue to have effect while the order remains in force, unless the court otherwise directs;
(*b*) any other requirement imposed by the court, or directions given by the supervisor, shall be deemed to have been imposed or given under the appropriate provisions of Schedule 3.

(3) Where, immediately before the commencement of Part IV, the order had been in force for a period of more than six months, it shall cease to have effect at the end of the period of six months beginning with the day on which Part IV comes into force unless—

(*a*) the court directs that it shall cease to have effect at the end of a different period (which shall not exceed three years);
(*b*) it ceases to have effect earlier in accordance with section 91; or
(*c*) it would have ceased to have had effect earlier had this Act not been passed.

(4) Where sub-paragraph (3) applies, paragraph 6 of Schedule 3 shall not apply.

(5) Where, immediately before the commencement of Part IV, the order had been in force for less than six months it shall cease to have effect in accordance with section 91 and paragraph 6 of Schedule 3 unless—

(*a*) the court directs that it shall cease to have effect at the end of a different period (which shall not exceed three years); or
(*b*) it would have ceased to have had effect earlier had this Act not been passed.

*Other supervision orders*

26.—(1) This paragraph applies to any order for the supervision of a child which was in force immediately before the commencement of Part IV and was made under—

(*a*) section 2(1)(*f*) of the Matrimonial Proceedings (Magistrates' Courts) Act 1960;
(*b*) section 7(4) of the Family Law Reform Act 1969;
(*c*) section 44 of the Matrimonial Causes Act 1973;
(*d*) section 2(2)(*a*) of the Guardianship Act 1973;
(*e*) section 34(5) or 36(3)(*b*) of the Children Act 1975;
(*f*) section 26(1)(*a*) of the Adoption Act 1976; or
(*g*) section 9 of the Domestic Proceedings and Magistrates' Courts Act 1978.

(2) The order shall not be deemed to be a supervision order made under any provision of this Act but shall nevertheless continue in force for a period of one year beginning with the day on which Part IV comes into force unless—

(*a*) the court directs that it shall cease to have effect at the end of a lesser period; or
(*b*) it would have ceased to have had effect earlier had this Act not been passed.

PLACES OF SAFETY ORDERS

27.—(1) This paragraph applies to—

(*a*) any order or warrant authorising the removal of a child to a place of safety which—

(i) was made, or issued, under any of the enactments mentioned in sub-paragraph (2); and
(ii) was in force immediately before the commencement of Part IV; and

(*b*) any interim order made under section 23(5) of the Children and Young Persons Act 1963 or section 28(6) of the Children and Young Persons Act 1969.

(2) The enactments are—

(*a*) section 40 of the Children and Young Persons Act 1933 (warrant to search for or remove child);
(*b*) section 28(1) of the Children and Young Persons Act 1969 (detention of child in place of safety);
(*c*) section 34(1) of the Adoption Act 1976 (removal of protected children from unsuitable surroundings);
(*d*) section 12(1) of the Foster Children Act 1980 (removal of foster children kept in unsuitable surroundings).

(3) The order or warrant shall continue to have effect as if this Act had not been passed.

(4) Any enactment repealed by this Act shall continue to have effect in relation

to the order or warrant so far as is necessary for the purposes of securing that the effect of the order is what it would have been had this Act not been passed.

(5) Sub-paragraph (4) does not apply to the power to make an interim order or further interim order given by section 23(5) of the Children and Young Persons Act 1963 or section 28(6) of the Children and Young Persons Act 1969.

(6) Where, immediately before section 28 of the Children and Young Persons Act 1969 is repealed by this Act, a child is being detained under the powers granted by that section, he may continue to be detained in accordance with that section but subsection (6) shall not apply.

### Recovery of children

28. The repeal by this Act of subsection (1) of section 16 of the Child Care Act 1980 (arrest of child absent from compulsory care) shall not affect the operation of that section in relation to any child arrested before the coming into force of the repeal.

29.—(1) This paragraph applies where—

(*a*) a summons has been issued under section 15 or 16 of the Child Care Act 1980 (recovery of children in voluntary or compulsory care); and

(*b*) the child concerned is not produced in accordance with the summons before the repeal of that section by this Act comes into force.

(2) The summons, any warrant issued in connection with it and section 15 or (as the case may be) section 16, shall continue to have effect as if this Act had not been passed.

30. The amendment by paragraph 27 of Schedule 12 of section 32 of the Children and Young Persons Act 1969 (detention of absentees) shall not affect the operation of that section in relation to—

(*a*) any child arrested; or

(*b*) any summons or warrant issued,

under that section before the coming into force of that paragraph.

### Voluntary organisations: Parental rights resolutions

31.—(1) This paragraph applies to a resolution—

(*a*) made under section 64 of the Child Care Act 1980 (transfer of parental rights and duties to voluntary organisations); and

(*b*) in force immediately before the commencement of Part IV.

(2) The resolution shall continue to have effect until the end of the period of six months beginning with the day on which Part IV comes into force unless it is brought to an end earlier in accordance with the provisions of the Act of 1980 preserved by this paragraph.

(3) While the resolution remains in force, any relevant provisions of, or made under, the Act of 1980 shall continue to have effect with respect to it.

(4) Sub-paragraph (3) does not apply to—

(*a*) section 62 of the Act of 1980 and any regulations made under that section (arrangements by voluntary organisations for emigration of children); or

(*b*) section 65 of the Act of 1980 (duty of local authority to assume parental rights and duties).

(5) Section 5(2) of the Act of 1980 (which is applied to resolutions under Part VI of that Act by section 64(7) of that Act) shall have effect with respect to the resolution as if the reference in paragraph (*c*) to an appointment of a guardian under section 5 of the Guardianship of Minors Act 1971 were a reference to an appointment of a guardian under section 5 of this Act.

### Foster children

32.—(1) This paragraph applies where—

(*a*) immediately before the commencement of Part VIII, a child was a foster child within the meaning of the Foster Children Act 1980; and

(*b*) the circumstances of the case are such that, had Parts VIII and IX then been in force, he would have been treated for the purposes of this Act as a child who was being provided with accommodation in a children's home and not as a child who was being privately fostered.

(2) If the child continues to be cared for and provided with accommodation as before, section 63(1) and (10) shall not apply in relation to him if—

(*a*) an application for registration of the home in question is made under section 63 before the end of the period of three months beginning with the day on which Part VIII comes into force; and

(*b*) the application has not been refused or, if it has been refused—

(i) the period for an appeal against the decision has not expired; or

(ii) an appeal against the refusal has been made but has not been determined or abandoned.

(3) While section 63(1) and (10) does not apply, the child shall be treated as a privately fostered child for the purposes of Part IX.

### Nurseries and child minding

33.—(1) Sub-paragraph (2) applies where, immediately before the commencement of Part X, any premises are registered under section 1(1)(*a*) of the Nurseries and Child-Minders Regulation Act 1948 (registration of premises, other than premises wholly or mainly used as private dwellings, where children are received to be looked after).

(2) During the transitional period, the provisions of the Act of 1948 shall continue to have effect with respect to those premises to the exclusion of Part X.

(3) Nothing in sub-paragraph (2) shall prevent the local authority concerned from registering any person under section 71(1)(*b*) with respect to the premises.

(4) In this paragraph "the transitional period" means the period ending with—

(*a*) the first anniversary of the commencement of Part X; or

(*b*) if earlier, the date on which the local authority concerned registers any person under section 71(1)(*b*) with respect to the premises.

34.—(1) Sub-paragraph (2) applies where, immediately before the commencement of Part X—

(*a*) a person is registered under section 1(1)(*b*) of the Act of 1948 (registration of persons who for reward receive into their homes children under the age of five to be looked after); and

(*b*) all the children looked after by him as mentioned in section 1(1)(*b*) of that Act are under the age of five.

(2) During the transitional period, the provisions of the Act of 1948 shall continue to have effect with respect to that person to the exclusion of Part X.

(3) Nothing in sub-paragraph (2) shall prevent the local authority concerned from registering that person under section 71(1)(*a*).

(4) In this paragraph "the transitional period" means the period ending with—

(*a*) the first anniversary of the commencement of Part X; or

(*b*) if earlier, the date on which the local authority concerned registers that person under section 71(1)(*a*).

### Children accommodated in certain establishments

35. In calculating, for the purposes of section 85(1)(*a*) or 86(1)(*a*), the period of time for which a child has been accommodated any part of that period which fell before the day on which that section came into force shall be disregarded.

### Criminal care orders

36.—(1) This paragraph applies where, immediately before the commencement of section 90(2) there was in force an order ("a criminal care order") made—

(*a*) under section 7(7)(*a*) of the Children and Young Persons Act 1969 (alteration in treatment of young offenders etc); or
(*b*) under section 15(1) of that Act, on discharging a supervision order made under section 7(7)(*b*) of that Act.

(2) The criminal care order shall continue to have effect until the end of the period of six months beginning with the day on which section 90(2) comes into force unless it is brought to an end earlier in accordance with—

(*a*) the provisions of the Act of 1969 preserved by sub-paragraph (3)(*a*); or
(*b*) this paragraph.

(3) While the criminal care order remains in force, any relevant provisions—

(*a*) of the Act of 1969; and
(*b*) of the Child Care Act 1980,

shall continue to have effect with respect to it.

(4) While the criminal care order remains in force, a court may, on the application of the appropriate person, make—

(*a*) a residence order;
(*b*) a care order or a supervision order under section 31;
(*c*) an education supervision order under section 36 (regardless of subsection (6) of that section); or
(*d*) an order falling within sub-paragraph (5),

and shall, on making any of those orders, discharge the criminal care order.

(5) The order mentioned in sub-paragraph (4)(*d*) is an order having effect as if it were a supervision order of a kind mentioned in section 12AA of the Act of 1969 (as inserted by paragraph 23 of Schedule 12), that is to say, a supervision order—

(*a*) imposing a requirement that the child shall live for a specified period in local authority accommodation; but
(*b*) in relation to which the conditions mentioned in subsection (4) of section 12AA are not required to be satisfied.

(6) The maximum period which may be specified in an order made under sub-paragraph (4)(*d*) is six months and such an order may stipulate that the child shall not live with a named person.

(7) Where this paragraph applies, section 5 of the Rehabilitation of Offenders Act 1974 (rehabilitation periods for particular sentences) shall have effect regardless of the repeals in it made by this Act.

(8) In sub-paragraph (4) "appropriate person" means—

(*a*) in the case of an application for a residence order, any person (other than a local authority) who has the leave of the court;
(*b*) in the case of an application for an education supervision order, a local education authority; and
(*c*) in any other case, the local authority to whose care the child was committed by the order.

## MISCELLANEOUS

### *Consents under the Marriage Act 1949 (c 76)*

37.—(1) In the circumstances mentioned in sub-paragraph (2), section 3 of and Schedule 2 to the Marriage Act 1949 (consents to marry) shall continue to have effect regardless of the amendment of that Act by paragraph 5 of Schedule 12.

(2) The circumstances are that—

(*a*) immediately before the day on which paragraph 5 of Schedule 12 comes into force, there is in force—

(i) an existing order, as defined in paragraph 5(1); or

(ii) an order of a kind mentioned in paragraph 16(1); and

(*b*) section 3 of and Schedule 2 to the Act of 1949 would, but for this Act, have applied to the marriage of the child who is the subject of the order.

### *The Children Act 1975 (c 72)*

38. The amendments of other enactments made by the following provisions of the Children Act 1975 shall continue to have effect regardless of the repeal of the Act of 1975 by this Act—

(*a*) section 68(4), (5) and (7) (amendments of section 32 of the Children and Young Persons Act 1969); and

(*b*) in Schedule 3—

(i) paragraph 13 (amendments of Births and Deaths Registration Act 1953);

(ii) paragraph 43 (amendment of Perpetuities and Accumulations Act 1964);

(iii) paragraphs 46 and 47 (amendments of Health Services and Public Health Act 1968); and

(iv) paragraph 77 (amendment of Parliamentary and Other Pensions Act 1972).

### *The Child Care Act 1980 (c 5)*

39. The amendment made to section 106(2)(*a*) of the Children and Young Persons Act 1963 by paragraph 26 of Schedule 5 to the Child Care Act 1980 shall continue to have effect regardless of the repeal of the Act of 1980 by this Act.

### *Legal aid*

40. The Lord Chancellor may by order make such transitional and saving provisions as appear to him to be necessary or expedient, in consequence of any provision made by or under this Act, in connection with the operation of any provisions of the Legal Aid Act 1988 (including any provision of that Act which is amended or repealed by this Act).

## SCHEDULE 15

Section 108(7)

### Repeals

| Chapter | Short title | Extent of repeal |
|---|---|---|
| 1891 c 3 | The Custody of Children Act 1891 | The whole Act. |
| 1933 c 12 | The Children and Young Persons Act 1933 | In section 14(2), the words from "may also" to "together, and".<br>In section 34(8), "*(a)*" and the words from "and *(b)*" to the end.<br>Section 40.<br>In section 107(1), the definitions of "care order" and "interim order". |
| 1944 c 31 | The Education Act 1944 | In section 40(1), the words from "or to imprisonment" to the end.<br>In section 114(1), the definition of parent. |
| 1948 c 53 | The Nurseries and Child-Minders Regulation Act 1948 | The whole Act. |
| 1949 c 76 | The Marriage Act 1949 | In section 3(1), the words "unless the child is subject to a custodianship order, when the consent of the custodian and, where the custodian is the husband or wife of a parent of the child of that parent shall be required".<br>Section 78(1A).<br>Schedule 2. |
| 1956 c 69 | The Sexual Offences Act 1956 | Section 38. |
| 1959 c 72 | The Mental Health Act 1959 | Section 9. |
| 1963 c 37 | The Children and Young Persons Act 1963 | Section 3.<br>Section 23.<br>In section 29(1), the words "under section 1 of the Children and Young Persons Act 1969 or".<br>Section 53(3).<br>In Schedule 3, paragraph 11. |
| 1964 c 42 | The Administration of Justice Act 1964 | In section 38, the definition of "domestic court". |
| 1968 c 46 | The Health Services and Public Health Act 1968 | Section 60.<br>In section 64(3)*(a)*, sub-paragraphs (vi), (vii), (ix) and (xv).<br>In section 65(3)*(b)*, paragraphs (vii), (viii) and (x). |
| 1968 c 49 | The Social Work (Scotland) Act 1968 | Section 1(4)*(a)*.<br>Section 5(2)*(d)*.<br>In section 86(3), the words "the Child Care Act 1980 or".<br>In Schedule 8, paragraph 20. |
| 1969 c 46 | The Family Law Reform Act 1969 | Section 7. |
| 1969 c 54 | The Children and Young Persons Act 1969 | Sections 1 to 3.<br>In section 7, in subsection (7) the words "to subsection (7A) of this section and", paragraph *(a)* and the words from "and subsection (13) of section 2 of this Act" to the end; and subsection (7A).<br>Section 7A. |

| Chapter | Short title | Extent of repeal |
|---|---|---|
| | | In section 8(3), the words from "and as if the reference to acquittal" to the end.<br>In section 9(1), the words "proceedings under section 1 of this Act or".<br>Section 11A.<br>Section 14A.<br>In section 15, in subsection (1) the words "and may on discharging the supervision order make a care order (other than an interim order) in respect of the supervised person"; in subsection (2) the words "and the supervision order was not made by virtue of section 1 of this Act or on the occasion of the discharge of a care order"; in subsection (2A), the words "or made by a court on discharging a care order made under that subsection"; and in subsection (4), the words "or made by a court on discharging a care order made under that section".<br>In section 16, in subsection (6)(*a*), the words "a care order or"; and in subsection (8) the words "or, in a case where a parent or guardian of his was a party to the proceedings on an application under the preceding section by virtue of an order under section 32A of this Act, the parent or guardian".<br>In section 17, paragraphs (*b*) and (*c*).<br>Sections 20 to 22.<br>Section 27(4).<br>Section 28.<br>Sections 32A to 32C.<br>In section 34(2) the words "under section 1 of this Act or", the words "2(3) or" and the words "and accordingly in the case of such a person the reference in section 1(1) of this Act to the said section 2(3) shall be construed as including a reference to this subsection".<br>In section 70, in subsection (1), the definitions of "care order" and "interim order"; and in subsection (2) the words "21(2), 22(4) or (6) or 28(5)" and the words "care order or warrant".<br>In Schedule 5, paragraphs 12(1), 37, 47 and 48. |
| 1970 c 34 | The Marriage (Registrar General's Licence) Act 1970 | In section 3(*b*), the words from "as amended" to "1969". |

| Chapter | Short title | Extent of repeal |
|---|---|---|
| 1970 c 42 | The Local Authority Social Services Act 1970 | In Schedule 1, in the entry relating to the Children and Young Persons Act 1969, the words "welfare, etc of foster children"; the entries relating to the Matrimonial Causes Act 1973, section 44, the Domestic Proceedings and Magistrates' Courts Act 1978, section 9, the Child Care Act 1980 and the Foster Children Act 1980. |
| 1971 c 3 | The Guardianship of Minors Act 1971 | The whole Act. |
| 1971 c 23 | The Courts Act 1971 | In Schedule 8, paragraph 59(1). |
| 1972 c 18 | The Maintenance Orders (Reciprocal Enforcement) Act 1972 | Section 41. |
| 1972 c 70 | The Local Government Act 1972 | In Schedule 23, paragraphs 4 and 9(3). |
| 1972 c 71 | The Criminal Justice Act 1972 | Section 51(1). |
| 1973 c 18 | The Matrimonial Causes Act 1973 | Sections 42 to 44.<br>In section 52(1), the definition of "custody".<br>In Schedule 2, paragraph 11. |
| 1973 c 29 | The Guardianship Act 1973 | The whole Act. |
| 1973 c 45 | The Domicile and Matrimonial Proceedings Act 1973 | In Schedule 1, in paragraph 11(1) the definitions of "custody" and "education" and in paragraph 11(3) the word "four". |
| 1973 c 62 | The Powers of Criminal Courts Act 1973 | In section 13(1), the words "and the purposes of section 1(2)(*bb*) of the Children and Young Persons Act 1969".<br>In Schedule 3, in paragraph 3(2A), the word "and" immediately preceding paragraph (*b*). |
| 1974 c 53 | The Rehabilitation of Offenders Act 1974 | In section 1(4)(*b*) the words "or in care proceedings under section 1 of the Children and Young Persons Act 1969".<br>In section 5, in subsection 5(*e*), the words "a care order or"; and in subsection (10) the words "care order or". |
| 1975 c 72 | The Children Act 1975 | The whole Act. |
| 1976 c 36 | The Adoption Act 1976 | Section 11(5).<br>Section 14(3).<br>In section 15, in subsection (1), the words from "subject" to "cases)" and subsection (4).<br>Section 26.<br>In section 28(5), the words "or the organisation".<br>Section 34.<br>Section 36(1)(*c*).<br>Section 37(1), (3) and (4).<br>Section 55(4).<br>In section 57, in subsection (2), the words from "and the court" to the end and subsections (4) to (10). |

| Chapter | Short title | Extent of repeal |
|---|---|---|
| | | In section 72(1), the definition of "place of safety", in the definition of "local authority" the words from "and" to the end and, in the definition of "specified order", the words "Northern Ireland or".<br>In Schedule 3, paragraphs 8, 11, 19, 21 and 22. |
| 1977 c 45 | The Criminal Law Act 1977 | Section 58(3). |
| 1977 c 49 | The National Health Service Act 1977 | In section 21, in subsection (1)(*a*) the words "and young children".<br>In Schedule 8, in paragraph 1(1), the words from "and of children" to the end; in paragraph 2(2) the words from "or (*b*) to persons who" to "arrangements"; and in paragraph 3(1) "(*a*)" and the words from "or (*b*) a child" to "school age".<br>In Schedule 15, paragraphs 10 and 25. |
| 1978 c 22 | The Domestic Proceedings and Magistrates' Courts Act 1978 | Sections 9 to 15.<br>In section 19, in subsection (1) the words "following powers, that is to say" and sub-<br>paragraph (ii), subsections (2) and (4), in subsection (7) the words "and one interim custody order" and in subsection (9) the words "or 21".<br>In section 20, subsection (4) and in subsection (9) the words "subject to the provisions of section 11(8) of this Act".<br>Section 21.<br>In section 24, the words "or 21" in both places where they occur.<br>In section 25, in subsection (1) paragraph (*b*) and the word "or" immediately preceding it and in subsection (2) paragraphs (*c*) and (*d*).<br>Section 29(4).<br>Sections 33 and 34.<br>Sections 36 to 53.<br>Sections 64 to 72.<br>Sections 73(1) and 74(1) and (3).<br>In section 88(1), the definition of "actual custody".<br>In Schedule 2, paragraphs 22, 23, 27, 29, 31, 36, 41 to 43, 46 to 50. |
| 1978 c 28 | The Adoption (Scotland) Act 1978. | In section 20(3)(*c*), the words "section 12(3)(*b*) of the Adoption Act 1976 or of".<br>In section 45(5), the word "approved".<br>Section 49(4).<br>In section 65(1), in the definition of "local authority", the words |

| Chapter | Short title | Extent of repeal |
|---|---|---|
| | | from "and" to the end and, in the definition of "specified order", the words "Northern Ireland or". |
| 1978 c 30 | The Interpretation Act 1978 | In Schedule 1, the entry with respect to the construction of certain expressions relating to children. |
| 1980 c 5 | The Child Care Act 1980 | The whole Act. |
| 1980 c 6 | The Foster Children Act 1980 | The whole Act. |
| 1980 c 43 | The Magistrates' Courts Act 1980 | In section 65(1), paragraphs (*e*) and (*g*) and the paragraph (*m*) inserted in section 65 by paragraph 82 of Schedule 2 to the Family Law Reform Act 1987.<br>In section 81(8), in the definition of "guardian" the words "by deed or will" and in the definition of "sums adjudged to be paid by a conviction" the words from "as applied" to the end.<br>In section 143(2), paragraph (i).<br>In Schedule 7, paragraphs 78, 83, 91, 92, 110, 116, 117, 138, 157, 158, 165, 166 and 199 to 201. |
| 1981 c 60 | The Education Act 1981 | In Schedule 3, paragraph 9. |
| 1982 c 20 | The Children's Homes Act 1982 | The whole Act. |
| 1982 c 48 | The Criminal Justice Act 1982 | Sections 22 to 25.<br>Section 27.<br>In Schedule 14, paragraphs 45 and 46. |
| 1983 c 20 | The Mental Health Act 1983 | In section 26(5), paragraph (*d*) and the word "or" immediately preceding it.<br>In section 28(1), the words "(including an order under section 38 of the Sexual Offences Act 1956)".<br>In Schedule 4, paragraphs 12, 26(*a*), (*b*) and (*c*), 35, 44, 50 and 51. |
| 1983 c 41 | The Health and Social Services and Social Security Adjudications Act 1983 | Section 4(1).<br>Sections 5 and 6.<br>In section 11, in subsection (2) the words "the Child Care Act 1980 and the Children's Homes Act 1982".<br>In section 19, subsections (1) to (5).<br>Schedule 1.<br>In Schedule 2, paragraphs 3, 9 to 14, 20 to 24, 27, 28, 34, 37 and 46 to 62.<br>In Schedule 4, paragraphs 38 to 48.<br>In Schedule 9, paragraphs 5, 16 and 17. |
| 1984 c 23 | The Registered Homes Act 1984 | In Schedule 1, in paragraph 5, sub-paragraph (*a*) and paragraphs 6, 7 and 8. |
| 1984 c 28 | The County Courts Act 1984 | In Schedule 2, paragraph 56. |
| 1984 c 37 | The Child Abduction Act 1984 | In section 3, the word "and" immediately preceding paragraph (*c*). |

| Chapter | Short title | Extent of repeal |
|---|---|---|
| | | In the Schedule, in paragraph 1(2) the words "or voluntary organisation" and paragraph 3(1)(*e*). |
| 1984 c 42 | The Matrimonial and Family Proceedings Act 1984 | In Schedule 1, paragraphs 19 and 23. |
| 1984 c 56 | The Foster Children (Scotland) Act 1984 | In section 1, the words "for a period of more than 6 days" and the words from "The period" to the end.<br>In section 7(1), the word "or" at the end of paragraph (*e*).<br>In Schedule 2, paragraphs 1 to 3 and 8. |
| 1984 c 60 | The Police and Criminal Evidence Act 1984 | In section 37(15), the words "and is not excluded from this Part of this Act by section 52 below".<br>Section 39(5).<br>Section 52.<br>In section 118(1), in the definition of parent or guardian, paragraph (*b*) and the word "and" immediately preceding it.<br>In Schedule 2, the entry relating to section 16 of the Child Care Act 1980.<br>In Schedule 6, paragraphs 19(*a*) and 22. |
| 1985 c 23 | The Prosecution of Offences Act 1985 | Section 27. |
| 1985 c 60 | The Child Abduction and Custody Act 1985 | Section 9(*c*).<br>Section 20(2)(*b*) and (*c*).<br>Section 25(3) and (5).In Schedule 3, paragraph 1(2). |
| 1986 c 28 | The Children and Young Persons (Amendment) Act 1986 | The whole Act. |
| 1986 c 33 | The Disabled Persons (Services, Consultation and Representation) Act 1986 | In section 16, in the definition of "guardian", paragraph (*a*). |
| 1986 c 45 | The Insolvency Act 1986 | In section 281(5)(*b*), the words "in domestic proceedings". |
| 1986 c 50 | The Social Security Act 1986 | In Schedule 10, paragraph 51. |
| 1986 c 55 | The Family Law Act 1986 | In section 1(2), in paragraph (*a*) the words "(*a*) or" and paragraph (*b*).<br>Section 3(4) to (6).<br>Section 4.<br>Section 35(1).<br>In section 42(6), in paragraph (*b*) the words "section 42(6) of the Matrimonial Causes Act 1973 or", in paragraph (*c*) the words "section 42(7) of that Act or" and in paragraph (*d*) the words "section 19(6) of the Domestic Proceedings and Magistrates' Courts Act 1978 or".<br>In Schedule 1, paragraphs 10, 11, 13, 16, 17, 20 and 23. |
| 1987 c 42 | The Family Law Reform Act 1987 | Section 3.<br>Sections 4 to 7.<br>Sections 9 to 16. |

| Chapter | Short title | Extent of repeal |
|---|---|---|
| | | In Schedule 2, paragraphs 11, 14, 51, 67, 68, 94 and 95. |
| | | In Schedule 3, paragraphs 11 and 12. |
| 1988 c 34 | The Legal Aid Act 1988 | Section 3(4)(*c*). |
| | | Section 27. |
| | | Section 28. |
| | | In section 30, subsections (1) and (2). |
| | | In Part I of Schedule 2, paragraph 2(*a*) and (*e*). |

# Index